UNPOPULAR SOVEREIGNTY

Unpopular Sovereignty

Mormons and the Federal Management of Early Utah Territory

BRENT M. ROGERS

UNIVERSITY OF NEBRASKA PRESS
Lincoln and London

© 2017 by the Board of Regents of the University of Nebraska

Portions of chapter 1 originally appeared as "'Armed men are coming from the state of Missouri': Federalism, Interstate Affairs, and Joseph Smith's Final Attempt to Secure Federal Intervention in Nauvoo," in *Journal of the Illinois State Historical Society* 109, no. 2 (Summer 2016): 148–79.

Portions of chapters 3, 4, and 5 originally appeared as "A 'distinction between Mormons and Americans': Mormon Indian Missionaries, Federal Indian Policy, and the Utah War," in *Utah Historical Quarterly* 82, no. 4 (Fall 2014): 250–71. This article won the 2015 Arrington-Prucha Prize from the Western History Association.

All rights reserved
Manufactured in the United States of America

∞

Library of Congress Cataloging-in-Publication Data
Names: Rogers, Brent M., author.
Title: Unpopular sovereignty: Mormons and the federal management of early Utah Territory / Brent M. Rogers.
Description: Lincoln; London: University of Nebraska Press, [2017] | Includes bibliographical references and index.
Identifiers: LCCN 2016012916 (print) | LCCN 2016013989 (ebook) | ISBN 9780803276772 (cloth: alk. paper) | ISBN 9780803295858 (pbk.: alk. paper) | ISBN 9780803296442 (epub) | ISBN 9780803296459 (mobi) | ISBN 9780803296466 (pdf)
Subjects: LCSH: Representative government and representation—Utah—History—19th century. | Utah—History—19th century. | United States—Territories and possessions—Politics and government. | Religion and politics—Utah—History—19th century. | Mormon Church—History—19th century. | Church of Jesus Christ of Latter-day Saints—History—19th century.
Classification: LCC JK8490.R64 2017 (print) | LCC JK8490 (ebook) | DDC 979.2/02—dc23
LC record available at http://lccn.loc.gov/2016012916

Set in Minion Pro by Westchester Publishing Services.

For Ashley, Keagan, Makinsey, and Braxton
and
In loving memory of Eugene Ahlstrom and Elmerae Rogers, my grandfathers

CONTENTS

List of Illustrations   ix

Acknowledgments   xi

Introduction   1

1. *Imperium in Imperio*: Sovereignty and the American Territorial System   20

2. Intimate Contact: Gender, Plural Marriage, and the U.S. Army in Utah Territory, 1854–1856   65

3. Missionaries to the Indians: Mormon and Federal Indian Policies   97

4. Confronting the "Twin Relics of Barbarism": The Mormon Question, the Buchanan Administration, and the Limits of Popular Sovereignty   135

5. The Utah War and the Westward March of Federal Sovereignty, 1857–1858   182

6. The U.S. Army and the Symbolic Conquering of Mormon Sovereignty   230

7. To 1862: The Codification of Federal Authority and the End of Popular Sovereignty in the Western Territories   270

Conclusion   292

Notes 299

Bibliography 343

Index 373

ILLUSTRATIONS

Map

1. Overview map of the West, 1849–1861   2

Figures

1. Map of the United States, 1857   7

2. Stephen A. Douglas   36

3. Brigham Young   40

4. Eliza R. Snow   47

5. Indian farm in Utah   127

6. James Buchanan   141

7. View of Salt Lake City   144

8. The Buchanan administration   155

9. *Frank Leslie's* cartoon   159

10. Military map of the West   184

11. Proclamation by Brigham Young   189

12. Washakie and Shoshones   198

13. *Yankee Notions* cartoon   204

14. Army marching through Salt Lake City   239

15. *Harper's Weekly* cartoon   249

16. Utes at Camp Floyd   252

17. Camp Douglas   276

ACKNOWLEDGMENTS

I have long been fascinated by reading the "Acknowledgments" section of historical monographs. I am always amazed at the number of people that help shape an individual scholar's thinking in bringing a book to fruition. Now having gone through the process of researching, writing, and editing a historical monograph, I see just how many people truly shaped the course of this book. Though my name graces the cover and any success or pitfalls of the work ultimately fall to me, I wish to express my gratitude to those individuals and institutions that supported and influenced me in the process.

This book was once a dissertation, but before I could reach that stage I received some great advice in my pursuit of knowledge. While working on a Master's degree in public history, Lee M. A. Simpson and Joseph Pitti at California State University, Sacramento, strongly encouraged me to pursue a PhD. For their instruction and push to continue my education, I will always be grateful. The faculty in the Department of History at the University of Nebraska–Lincoln provided me numerous opportunities to engage in the work and practice of history while I pursued a doctoral degree. Many thanks go to the committee who steered me through the dissertation process. William G. Thomas, Jeannette E. Jones, Timothy R. Mahoney, and Kenneth Price were all incredibly generous with their insights, incisive comments, and careful readings of my work. Douglas Seefeldt guided my doctoral education before he moved on to Ball State University and continues to be my advocate. It is always enjoyable and enlightening to talk with Doug, but especially fun to discuss the latest Buffalo Bill work. Thanks, Doug, for everything! Though not on my dissertation committee, Peter Maslowski, James Le Sueur, Andrew R. Graybill, and Margaret D. Jacobs taught me much about history, writing, and life. John R. Wunder deserves a special recognition. He was a phenomenal mentor to me since I arrived in Lincoln, and he continues to be a source of wisdom and friendship.

Many individuals read this book at various stages. The following deserve special recognition and my appreciation for their thoughtful attention to my work: Nicole Etcheson, W. Paul Reeve, Brian Q. Cannon, Christopher Childers, Matthew C. Godfrey, Matthew J. Grow, Spencer W. McBride, Jenny Reeder, David Grua, Holly George, Mark Ellis, Andrea Radke-Moss, Thomas G. Alexander, Todd M. Kerstetter, Margaret D. Jacobs, and Barbara Berglund. I deeply respect all of these scholars and cannot thank them enough for the time and effort they gave in offering astute suggestions to strengthen this book. Other scholars including Will Bagley, William P. MacKinnon, Richard E. Turley Jr., Reid L. Neilson, Lisa Olsen Tait, Ardis Parshall, Ronald W. Walker, and Tonia M. Compton generously shared sources and were influential in both encouraging and challenging me as I researched and wrote this book. Brandon Plewe and his students, especially DJ Herr, Austen McCleary, Parker Summers, and Allison Erickson, performed excellent cartographic work and produced the fine overview map found herein. Bridget Barry and the staff at the University of Nebraska Press also deserve many thanks and much praise. Bridget supported this work at its earliest stages and shepherded it in a marvelous way. I am deeply grateful for her always timely edits and counsel, and for our mutual fanaticism of Nebraska football, even in these down times.

Several other entities and individuals helped make this book possible. Since joining the Joseph Smith Papers Project, I have received generous support from the project's management and Editorial Board to pursue my research and writing interests. I could not have completed the writing and editing without the gift of time given to me by them, and for that I express deep gratitude. Generous research and publication grants from the Charles Redd Center for Western Studies at Brigham Young University, the Center for Great Plains Studies at the University of Nebraska–Lincoln, and the LDS Church History Department provided essential funds to research and to complete this work. In addition, a Warren F. and Edith R. Day Dissertation Fellowship from the University of Nebraska–Lincoln's Office of Graduate Studies allowed me to travel to Washington DC to research in federal repositories so crucial for this study.

I am also extremely thankful to the many helpful librarians and archivists who assisted my research, particularly those at the University of Nebraska's Love Library, Brigham Young University's L. Tom Perry Special Collections, the California State Library, Duke University's Rare Book, Manuscript, and Special Collections Library, the Kansas Historical Society, the LDS Church History Library (especially Jeffrey G. Cannon, who helped track down photographs for this book), the Library of Congress, the National Archives and Records Administration (especially Rod Ross at the Center for Legislative Archives), the Nebraska State Historical Society, Stanford University's Special Collections, the University of Chicago's Special Collections, the University of Michigan's William L. Clements Library, the University of Utah's J. Willard Marriott Library Special Collections, and the Utah State Historical Society.

I have made numerous acquaintances and a few good friends along the way, and I wish to thank a few of them. From my days at San Diego State when my passion for engaging in the historian's craft emerged, and even before that, Tyler Rhodes and his family, Bryan Healea and his family, Derek Dahlkamp and his family, David Gassaway and his family, and Dustin Hale supported me in numerous ways. You all are deeply embedded in my history and I will forever cherish our common past. In graduate school and beyond I have had the good fortune of developing new friendships with Brenden Rensink,

Jason Heppler, Andrew Hedges, Gerrit Dirkmaat, Christian Heimburger, Elizabeth Kuehn, Nathan Waite, and Leslie Sherman. Thank you for some good conversations and some even better adventures. I would also be remiss if I did not offer an acknowledgment of thanks to the McDonalds in Centerville, Utah, for providing work space, copious amounts of Coca-Cola, and the world's best fries, all of which sustained many hours of work on this book. For any I have neglected to mention, I am truly sorry.

I am certain that I can never express enough gratitude to my family. Steven Rogers, Pamela Ahlstrom, Brad and Alyce Rogers, Brandice and Jasen Herr, Ellen Ahlstrom-Reichoff, Becky Rogers, and Tim, Shelley, Ashley, and Austin Heesacker have loved and supported me throughout my life. I love you all. Tim and Denise Tiner, Dustin and Kerri Tiner, Cassidy and Michael Lundberg, Karlie and Neza Prieto, Travis and MacKenzie Tiner, Jim and Kay Tiner, and Dale and Julee Hunter have offered constant encouragement and a variety of other supports. Thank you all.

I am humbled by the privilege that I have had to research and write this history and hope that my research and interpretations can help others better understand the events and ideas presented in this book. But in the end, this book would never have been possible without four very special people. Words cannot express how much I love and how much I owe to the remarkable Ashley Rogers. Ashley has been an unwavering source of inspiration and strength and always the voice of reassurance and praise when she knew I needed it. I am privileged to be her companion and am eternally grateful to her. Ash, I know I will never be able to make up for the time spent on this book, but maybe now I will take you on that vacation you've always wanted. Maybe. The greatest joys in my life are my children, Keagan, Makinsey, and Braxton. I thank them for their unending and unfailing love, energy, and smiles. You three enrich my life more than you will know. For your many sacrifices I dedicate this book and my life to you, my beloved family.

UNPOPULAR SOVEREIGNTY

Introduction

At its creation in 1850, and for the remainder of that antebellum decade, Utah Territory was a contested place. A cohesive settler group—members of the Church of Jesus Christ of Latter-day Saints (LDS), better known as Mormons—sought to establish and maintain their own sovereign space in the Great Basin.[1] The Mormons simultaneously attempted to subsume indigenous peoples' sovereignty under their control and competed with U.S. federal officials who were responsible for expanding American national sovereignty to new territories. The ways in which those contests played out had ramifications on the national political stage. In particular, Latter-day Saint leaders and the U.S. federal government implemented policies, often in reciprocal relationship to one another, to manage sovereignty, especially the 1850s version of "popular sovereignty."

Popular sovereignty emerged as a concept in the American Revolution. It was the idea that the entire body of people, not just a single ruler, could exercise the sovereign will of the nation through a written constitution that granted and guided the legitimate exercise of government authority. Once the people created the government, it could and would enforce the people's will.[2] The interpretation of popular sovereignty transformed following the acquisition of Mexican lands in 1848. As the nation expanded even farther west, so too did sectional tensions over slavery's expansion into new lands. Northern Democrats, particularly Lewis Cass of Michigan and Stephen A. Douglas of Illinois, offered

1

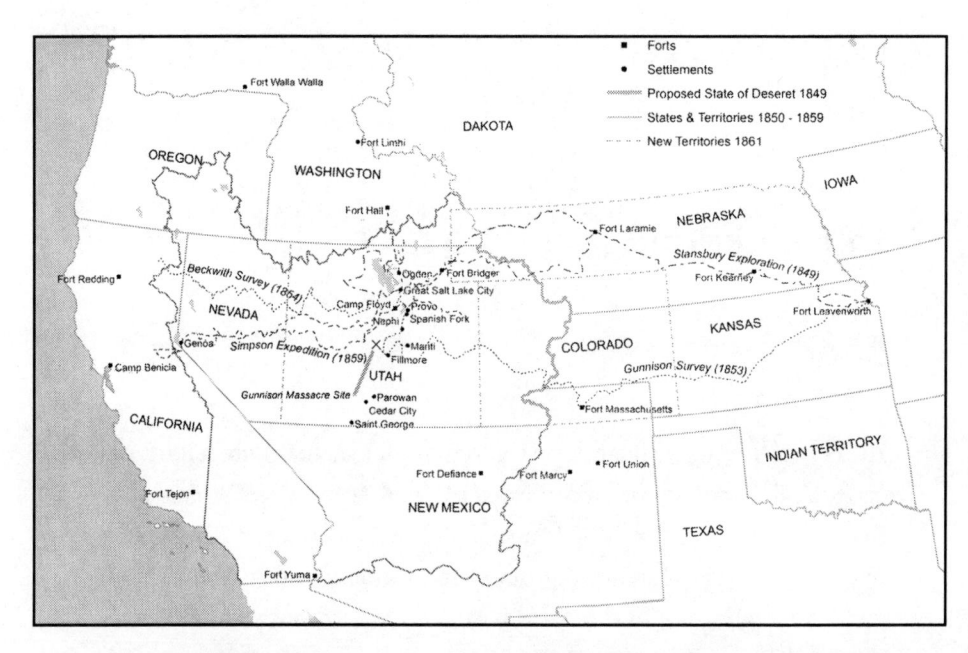

MAP 1. Map of the West, 1849–1861, with the proposed Mormon state of Deseret and federal surveying and exploration routes to and through Utah. Produced by DJ Herr, Austen McCleary, and Parker Summers, Think Spatial, Brigham Young University Geography Department.

a middle-of-the-road approach to quell the potentially incendiary problems brought by slavery's growth in the West. They proposed popular sovereignty, called squatter sovereignty by its detractors, as the solution. This new Democratic adaptation allowed the people of newly created territories the opportunity to decide their local domestic institutions for themselves, outside of congressional or presidential influence. The political philosophy of territorial self-government was thus meant as a singular answer to the question of slavery extension, but the language and rhetoric surrounding it and the people impacted by it invited unintended multiplicity.

By removing the slavery question from the deliberations of the federal government, the entity constitutionally responsible for deciding the fate of domestic institutions in the territories, the proponents of popular sovereignty sought to remove the slavery question from national political discourse and make it a local decision. Much to the contrary of this expectation, the political doctrine ultimately put the territorial issue at the center of national politics and public discourse. Utah Territory, though historically overlooked, emerged as a key battleground and hotbed of antebellum debate over popular sovereignty.[3] Utah presented a different problem for popular sovereignty as Mormons in that territory employed the concept to protect and govern themselves. Local governance generally and another domestic institution—plural marriage—drew Utah into the national political discourse, especially in the aftermath of the passage of the Kansas-Nebraska Act in 1854.

The Kansas-Nebraska Act applied the same formula of popular sovereignty to Kansas and Nebraska Territories that the Compromise of 1850 introduced into the organic acts of Utah and New Mexico Territories. The 1854 act opened up two new expansive territories to white settlement and the potential creation of new slave states by allowing the people to choose for themselves whether to permit slavery. It had nearly unanimous support in the South and tepid support from northern Democrats. However, Missouri senator Thomas Hart Benton, like Alexander Stephens and many others of the era, did not think that popular sovereignty applied to territories, which were properly minors or wards of the federal government because they had not proven their readiness for republican self-government.[4] Problems with popular sovereignty and slavery extension arose in Kansas as the mechanisms of voting and enacting popular will failed to peacefully materialize.[5] The Kansas experience turned violent and revealed major flaws in the philosophy of local self-determination on slavery. In the end, the Kansas-Nebraska Act did not bring to the South additional slaveholding territory. Instead, the violent physical troubles and political liabilities created by "Bleeding Kansas" and the federal government's role in that territory left southerners feeling even more embittered and distrustful that northern politicians would block slavery's growth.[6] Furthermore, the fallout from the Kansas-Nebraska Act helped spur the creation of a new, major political party—the Republican Party—that opposed the extension of slavery and the allowance of plural marriage in the territories, and advocated greater federal control over territorial decision-making.

"Bleeding Kansas" became a symbol of sectional controversy, but it was not the sole locus of national debate over popular sovereignty. Utah Territory and the Mormon question also symbolized growing disillusionment with popular sovereignty and the fear of stimulating further sectional agitation. The fighting over slavery in Kansas and the 1857 Utah War individually and collectively signaled the failure of popular sovereignty to bring to the nation a guiding principle of territorial governance that its proponents had hoped would maintain national unity on the slavery question. While this book does not seek to offer a comparative analysis of Kansas and Utah, it does endeavor to demonstrate the complexities of sovereignty in the antebellum American territorial system using Utah as a case study while pointing to Kansas and the comparable histories of other territories when appropriate as signposts of the broader national context. The Utah and Kansas examples in particular demonstrate the interplay and reverberations of western events on politics in the nation's capital. The federal government behaved differently in each territory, thus demonstrating its dynamism and variability, though its responses to its western territories proved the volatility of the popular sovereignty philosophy and its own authority in the West. These western histories also reveal the imperfect nature of territorial government and the exercise of power in the American federal system of divided, or shared, sovereignty. Western events, including those west of Kansas, played a significant role in the political debates that ended popular sovereignty and that drove the nation farther down the road to disunion.

Though its originators wanted it to be, popular sovereignty was not a singular political philosophy. It was multifaceted in its meanings and implications; it meant different things to different people. This variety is showcased in the federal government's relationship with Utah

Territory, proving that there was at least one domestic institution beyond slavery that popular sovereignty had to address. There were, in effect, multiple popular sovereignties. The Democratic Party's doctrine could not be the all-encompassing answer for all territorial matters when it was designed to answer the singular, though seemingly ubiquitous, question of slavery expansion. Debate over and federal action in Utah eliminated popular sovereignty as a middle ground for political maneuvering around territorial debates and accelerated political polarization on the topic, thereby demonstrating that the political concept could not accommodate multiple and competing sovereignties. Ultimately, popular sovereignty in Utah illustrated the contingent, contested, and unstable nature of local sovereignty at the conjunction of state formation and territorial management and reminded the nation of the doctrine's fatal flaw: that territories were not states, but were wards of the federal government, and local decisions in those geopolitical entities were subject to federal oversight.

The question of sovereignty—or determining who possessed and could exercise governing, legal, social, and even cultural power—is at the crux of Utah Territory's early history. At its core, it is a history of establishing, asserting, and maintaining such powers. This book will investigate the complex relationship between sovereignty and territory along three main currents in Utah: the implementation of a republican form of government; the administration of Indian policy that managed interactions between Native peoples and non-Natives; and the performance of gender and familial relations pertaining to marriage. Though these three currents could be looked at separately, they were, in many ways, interrelated. Each of them informed national discourse and public perception that led to federal decision-making while simultaneously influencing events that played out on the ground in Utah. In this way, this book will demonstrate the interplay between the sovereignty battle that occurred on the ground and its impact on national political discourse to provide a deeper understanding of popular sovereignty and territorial governance from the late 1840s to 1862.

As early as 1780, Thomas Jefferson encouraged the growth of the United States as an "empire for liberty," founded on liberalism, free men, private property, and republican government.[7] In 1809, he restated this belief to James Madison when he wrote, "No constitution was ever before so well calculated as ours for extensive empire."[8] Jefferson envisioned American empire in the form of an expansive polity of affiliated self-governing states, unified through the federal government. He recognized settlers as having foundational entitlement to autonomous sovereignty as long as those settler populations could operate within constitutional boundaries. Through popular sovereignty, or local, settler political independence, Jefferson imagined the growth of the United States as an "empire for liberty."[9] The key here, however, was for local populations in conquered lands or settlers moving to those places of acquisition to extend, and not compete with, federal order. Indeed, the concept and understanding of sovereignty were fluid for antebellum Americans.

In the dual sovereignty established in the U.S. Constitution, sovereign states shared supremacy with the federal government. From this shared supremacy developed the idea and practice of local self-determination. This guaranteed to the people of each state the right to determine laws and domestic institutions that served the constituents' best interests outside of congressional interference. However, complications emerged with the acquisition of new territory and the introduction of greater numbers of immigrants and minority peoples into the Union. New territories were designed to be extensions of American national sovereignty and jurisdiction, and not necessarily the sovereign political space of the local population. The Constitution authorized the acquisition of new territory and out of the new lands permitted the development and addition of new states, as long as the people in those geopolitical entities operated a republican form of government.[10]

In the mid-nineteenth century, the United States acquired land in the West as a result of the Louisiana Purchase, the U.S.-Mexico War, and other land acquisitions, making the United States a transconti-

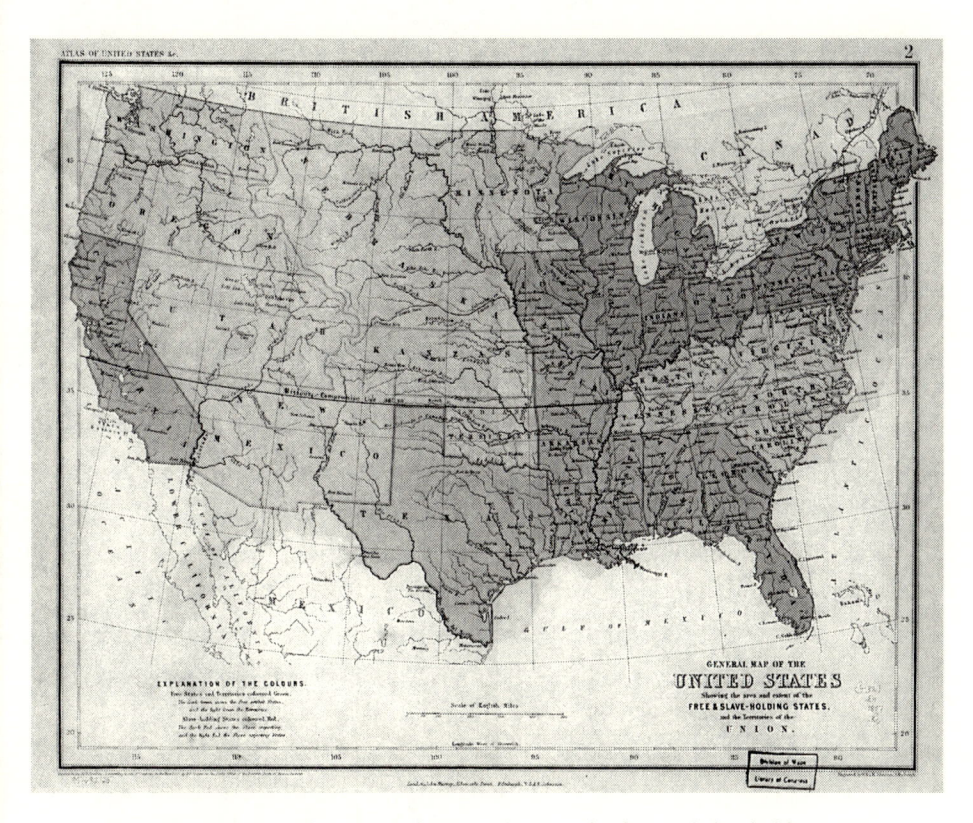

FIG. 1. General map of the United States, showing the free and slaveholding states and the territories of the Union, by Henry D. Rogers, 1857. Courtesy of the Library of Congress, Geography and Map Division.

nental nation. By 1854, the trans-Missouri West consisted of the state of California and seven territories: Indian, Kansas, Nebraska, New Mexico, Oregon, Utah, and Washington. In 1857, Secretary of War John B. Floyd described the vast region. Floyd wrote, "From our western frontier of settlements to those of northern Oregon the distance is about 1,800 miles; from the same frontier to the settlements of California, *via* Salt Lake, is 1,800 miles; from the frontier of Arkansas, at Fort Smith, by Albuquerque or Santa Fé, to Fort Tejon, is about 1,700 miles; and from San Antonio, by El Paso, to San Diego, near the borders of the white settlements, is 1,400 miles; constituting an aggregate line of 6,700 miles which ought to be occupied."[11] In essence, Floyd's description highlighted a major problem for the federal government: the entity responsible for exercising sovereign control over this immense space had almost no presence. The 1850s marked the first time that the square mileage of territories exceeded that of the states. In other words, the proportion of territory in the United States shifted, outweighing the land mass of states. Under the Constitution, then, the management of these lands and the people therein fell to the federal government, which was responsible to fully incorporate the western lands and peoples into the growing "empire for liberty," making the Mormon presence in Utah and the protean concept of sovereignty in the territorial system all the more significant.

In order to follow Jefferson's dream of expansion, the federal government needed to fill these lands with loyal white settlers. Loyal settlers and federal appointees, ideally, introduced American republican governance as well as legal and cultural institutions for the diverse groups of peoples residing in those territories to emulate as a condition for the transference of sovereign capacity.[12] Federal officials would instruct the people of the territories and transform them in the American image of good, republican citizens. Territories held a different legal status from the sovereign states in that they were directly subject to congressional and presidential power and decision-making. Territories were subsidiary units of power that emanated from and remained subordinate to the national sovereignty. The perceptions of those in the federal government and in the eastern United States often determined the loyalty of the new western population. Language, religion, race relations, government form, and the structure of the family and marriage had all influenced perceptions in Congress and the eastern states about conquered peoples in new territories and whether they would owe allegiance to the Union.[13] Expansion was testing the permanence of the nation and the loyalty of western inhabitants to the federal union.

In 1846, the Mormons left the boundaries of the United States in search of a place where they could exercise their own religiously directed sovereignty. Having previously contemplated going to the contested Oregon country or attaching themselves to Texas, by 1847 they settled near the southeastern shore of the Great Salt Lake, a place they expected to make *their* country, *their* own cradle of liberty.[14] The Mormon community claimed sovereignty over that land, to exercise power to make laws, and to manage their own affairs free from outside interference. From that time and for the next decade, Mormons jealously guarded their autonomy while their inclinations toward and ties to the United States were ambiguous at best.

When the United States conquered the Mexican territory in which the Mormons then resided, the Mormons maintained their belief in their sovereign right to the land. Though they had come to understand the realities of the American political system and made various efforts to work within it, the Mormons nevertheless remained determined to exercise sovereignty to protect themselves and their rights. Professing their sovereign rights because of their status as the first whites to settle the Great Basin, Latter-day Saints held that the local lawmaking capacity of their church was "the real seat of government."[15] The Mormon view of proper government maintained dependence on religious authority and divine direction in civil affairs, which opposed and competed with the nation's secular vesting of sovereign authority to a pluralistic people.

Regarding the Mormons' move and their self-governing capacity, John Taylor, then an elder of the LDS church, stated, "The first thing we did when we came to this land was to organize a government for our protection, which was according to the pattern set us by our neighbors—Oregon.... We came out here because we were disenfranchised, exiled, robbed of our rights as American citizens, and forced to wander in the wilderness to seek among the savages of the forest that freedom denied us by Christianity."[16] For the Mormons, according to Taylor, it was the "Kingdom of God or Nothing."[17] Taylor explained what that meant. The male priesthood hierarchy of the LDS church governed the people. Taylor verified that the Kingdom of God was "both Church and State, to rule both temporally and spiritually.... Because the Kingdom of God is higher and its laws are so much more exalted than those of any other nation, that it is the easiest thing in life for a servant of God to keep any of their laws." That is why, he claimed, the Latter-day Saints could faithfully adhere to both the Kingdom of God and to the Constitution of the United States.[18] The Mormons were something of a contradiction in that way as they established the independent state of Deseret in the Great Basin. They believed themselves commissioned to prepare the world for a millennial reign when the heavenly and earthly kingdoms of God would be joined. Until then, they sought to make those two kingdoms work in concert in a theocratic government, according to their understanding of the laws of heaven and earth. In addition, Mormon leader Brigham Young organized a colonization effort to establish towns and outposts at various locations from San Bernardino, California, to Oregon Territory. These locations were to establish a Mormon sphere of influence in the region. All the while, the Mormons, under the auspices of religious proselytizing, attempted to subsume Native American sovereignty under their own governing system. The Latter-day Saints had established arguably the strongest government in the West to date and had a vision different for its sovereign space than did the rest of America. Mormon sovereignty thus was tangible and preceded the United States in the Great Basin.

Having heard the many public denunciations of theocracy as antirepublican for several years, Brigham Young—Utah Territory's civil governor, superintendent of Indian affairs, and the religious leader of the Church of Jesus Christ of Latter-day Saints—gave a public speech in September 1857 that described his understanding of republican government. "A Republican Government consists in letting the people rule by their united voice," Young declared, "without a dissension; in learning what is for the best and unitedly doing it. This is true Republicanism."[19] In this speech, Young described why he believed theocracy was the ideal form of republican government. To know God's will, he explained, meant to do and choose right. The people, then, would choose to exercise God's will. This 1857 view mirrored what Young and other Mormon leaders discussed in the Nauvoo, Illinois, Council of Fifty some thirteen years earlier. At a 5 April 1844 meeting of that entity, Young asserted, "Revelations must govern. The voice of God shall be the voice of the people.... Republicanism is, to enjoy every thing there is in heaven, earth or hell to be enjoyed, and not infringe upon the rights of another."[20] In 1844, as in 1857, the Mormon leader sought to govern his people according to religious dictates in order to protect their rights and any others who were not receiving the full blessings of American liberty. In this way, Young and by extension the Mormon people saw no apparent contradiction between republicanism and theocracy. Young even suggested that a theocratic government was in every sense of the word "a republican government, and differs but little in form from our National, State, and Territorial Governments." Young also used the idea of theocracy as an example of shared sovereignty between God and the people; he spoke against the growing American democratic sense that the vox populi was the vox Dei.[21] Republicanism was the common ideology of the American people; individualism the hallmark of American character. Mormonism in Utah Territory was neither republican nor individual. It was characterized by a centralized authority, a hierarchy leading a highly unified people that extended religious and familial ideologies into temporal and governmental affairs.

What was seen as true republicanism to Mormons was seen as tyrannical by other Americans suffused in the political culture of democracy. The Mormons' combining of church and state, which was inherent in its operation of a theocratic form of government, made it nearly impossible for the federal government to trust their loyalty.[22] The fear of the LDS church's power over the civil government came from a similar nativist strain in antebellum America that voiced ardent opposition to immigrants and Catholics, whose perceived social practices placed loyalty to the church and Pope above allegiance to republican notions of civic governance. Americans, including the Know-Nothings and Republicans, believed Catholics were a threat to and subverters of American republicanism.[23] When Americans differed with each other politically, it was often over their perceptions of what most threatened the survival of republicanism, and Americans almost universally viewed Mormons as a dire threat to republicanism in the West.[24]

At the same time Americans balked at Mormon political organization, federal officials recoiled at reports that the Mormons controlled the local Native population and that they violated federal Indian policies. The rapid expansion of the Mormons in the Great Basin precipitated a dramatic shift in power relations among the region's Indian nations and for the federal government.[25] LDS church leaders set up their own complex Indian policy that was ultimately meant to facilitate the expansion of Mormon influence in the region but that also wrought sovereign dispossession to Native communities. As it pertained to Indian affairs, the Mormons waged their sovereignty battle on two fronts. One was local. They had invaded indigenous homelands, and though they tried to develop mutually beneficial relationships with the inhabitants based in their proselytizing program, Mormons ultimately sought to subsume Native sovereignty in their own efforts to be a self-governing people. The other front was national. Indian affairs was a primary site of struggle in the federal government's efforts to exercise sovereign authority over new territories. Non-Mormon federal officials and the press perceived the Mormons' Indian policy as an attempted Mormon-Indian alliance against the United States and the rest of white America. Mormons battled that perception. Still, the perceived threat of the Mormons' Indian policy raised new questions about sovereignty and governmental control in Utah.

From the federal side, the most egregious Mormon policy toward the Native population was the practice of sending missionaries to work with them and educate them in the LDS religion. "We know but little," Commissioner of Indian Affairs Luke Lea reported in November 1850, "of the Indians in Utah, beyond the fact that they are generally peaceable in their disposition and easily controlled."[26] However, in a critical development, one that encouraged conflict in Utah, it was the Mormons, not the federal government, that were perceived to "easily control" the Great Basin Indians. Federal Indian agents, U.S. Army officers, and eventually the president believed that the Mormons in Utah wielded too much power over Indian affairs. In 1855, Army officer Sylvester Mowry echoed the sentiments of Colonel Edward J. Steptoe, who was his superior, and federal Indian agent Garland Hurt, when he reported, "Utah Indians... had been taught that the Mormons were a superior people to the Americans, and that the Americans were the natural enemies of the Indians, while the Mormons were their friends and allies."[27] The Mormons, in fact, did not and could not control the region's Native peoples. Still, the many indigenous groups of the Great Basin added to the multiplicity of contested sovereignties in Utah as they navigated the changing situation according to their own best interests and in their efforts to maintain autonomy and self-determination. Native peoples, in the triangular relationships they formed and the information they passed to both Mormons and federal authorities, emerge as essential agents in the history of sovereignty in Utah Territory in the 1850s. The administration of federal Indian policy in the territory loomed large in the discussion over whether Mormons were fit to govern and figured prominently in the ultimate decision to send the army to Utah to enforce Indian policy and diminish Mormon sovereignty in this key arena.

In addition to the contest over Indian affairs, the male struggle over marriage and female sexuality is equally important to understanding the contest over sovereignty in Utah. The Mormon plural marriage system, and the nonrepublican form of government that protected it, became national news in the context of the Kansas-Nebraska Act with its focus on popular sovereignty and even more so in the presidential election of 1856 when the Republican Party introduced the territorial issue of the "Twin Relics of Barbarism" that equated the evils of the existence of slavery and polygamy in the western territories. In Utah in the 1850s, plural marriage, or the marriage of one man to more than one woman, was the preferred marriage system over monogamy, which existed as the national norm. The Mormons had an alternative familial model according to American standards, though their polygamist practices were not yet illegal in the territories. Americans generally abhorred plural marriage and considered it a disgusting practice that blighted the established monogamous family model, which undergirded American society and government. Middle-class moralists preached the doctrine of sexual restraint and the majority public opinion of the era seemed to hold this view, particularly in condemning the Mormon practice of plural marriage as indulgent, unrestrained, and generally full of inordinate lust. Plural marriage in the West made Mormons public enemies.

The non-Mormon outsider viewed Mormon women as white slaves and Mormon men as vicious patriarchs, while the insider Mormon perspective held up plural marriage as a religious principle protected by the Free Exercise clause of the Constitution. Mormons, like Catholics, considered marriage a religious rite rather than a civil one, and they governed the institution through ecclesiastical rules first established in 1843. Conflicts over plural marriage with non-Mormons presented another challenge to Mormon sovereignty and further encouraged federal interference in the territory.[28]

What made these issues of republicanism, Indian affairs, and marriage in Utah especially important was the growing and increasingly polarizing question of popular sovereignty. When it came to supporting the antebellum political doctrine of popular sovereignty, particularly when it provided hope for protecting plural marriage, Mormons resembled southerners in their opportunistic support of the Democratic political doctrine. Mormons viewed popular sovereignty as a useful tool and adopted its principles because it served their needs and desires concerning their marriage and political practice, just as southern slaveholders viewed it as a way to promote the protection and ultimate expansion of slavery. After 1856 and the issuance of the Republican Party platform that tied the Mormon familial model together with concerns of the expansion of slavery in the territories, the Utah case becomes all the more important, as it offers a fresh look at how Americans and the federal government dealt with the other "twin relic of barbarism."

Plural marriage became the key sticking point for Mormon self-determination efforts, especially during and following the Civil War and the passage of federal legislation prohibiting the practice. The 1862 Morrill Anti-Bigamy Act codified federal control over marriage in the territories but simultaneously shifted the focus almost entirely to the contest between the federal government and Mormons over marital structure. Congress required Utah's state constitution to prohibit polygamy for the transference of sovereignty and admission to the Union, which did not come until 1896.

Federal interventions in the nineteenth-century West—within the borders of the United States—focused on extending dominion over racial and exotic "others," or those groups whose identity appeared to be the antithesis of the mainstream group's identity.[29] The Mormons in the Great Basin were among the "new and different peoples," who were constructed as "others."[30] In the 1840s and especially in the 1850s, Mormons were seen as subversive, antirepublican, hostile, and lascivious people. While the Mormons projected an image of themselves as self-governing arbiters of true republicanism, non-Mormons viewed with suspicion the Mormon theocratic form of governance, their policies toward Native Americans, and their plural marriage family structure, which appeared more characteristic of "oriental despots" than of Americans. The construction of this identity for Mormons made them too different to be able to govern themselves as proper Americans. In other words, Americans viewed Mormons as unpopular candidates for popular sovereignty. While American public rhetoric remained relatively constant in its perception of Mormons, the Latter-day Saints' portrayal of Americans shifted. They aligned themselves with the image of good, republican ideals when it best suited their needs and as a persecuted people in search of independent sovereignty contingent upon political changes, proximity of federal officers, and army movements. Each group's discursive constructions of difference were meant to create cultural and political distance.

Sovereign capacity in the American federal system was based in perception, and there were social, cultural, political, and familial differences that informed the American perception of Mormons. In the antebellum United States, as in continental Europe, technological advances created a publication explosion that brought with it one of the highest literacy rates in the world. Americans experienced and engaged political and cultural trends by reading books, newspapers, pamphlets, or government reports. Such texts highlight the contemporary ideas about the extremes and norms of political expression; sovereignty emerged as a keyword in the nation's vocabulary.[31] By examining public discourse in newspapers, government reports, congressional debates, and other textual documents on Utah affairs and then placing the findings in a broader context of debates over popular sovereignty and expansion, it is possible to understand the contested and unstable nature of sovereignty in Utah and in nineteenth-century American political thought. Private discourse in the form of personal papers, letters, and journals also provides understanding of how events on the ground influenced broader perceptions and how the context of antebellum politics and territorial policies influenced individuals and their actions.

In the mid-nineteenth century, the genuine public fear of Mormons and the possibility of their establishing a new sovereign order in the West demanded action by the federal government. Rhetorical modes emerged that convinced the public that Mormons were not fit to exercise sovereignty in an American territory. The press's perception of the

Mormons fed national fears of usurpation of sovereignty, tyranny, foreign invasion, societal disorder, and violence in the Great Basin, leading many to conclude that Mormons deserved army surveillance and restructuring of their government and society. Anti-Mormon diatribes rationalized and even validated political and martial action against the Mormons and the dismantling of their local sovereignty. Such rhetoric was part of the many processes that coincided to cause the federal government to take action to control the Mormons in the West.

Approximately four months before Brigham Young's September 1857 speech and declaration of martial law that proved Mormon resolve to maintain local sovereignty, President James Buchanan, a Democrat, and his cabinet had already concluded that the civil authorities in Utah did not operate a republican government or uphold federal law and had tampered with the local indigenous population against the interest of the federal government. In a move to shift sovereign control to the federal government and better manage the vast western territory, the Buchanan administration sent a large contingent of the U.S. Army to Utah in May 1857. This move initiated a lengthy and inexact process of establishing and maintaining American sovereignty over the Great Basin West.

Buchanan chose to willingly use the legal power given to him by federal law to initiate what was officially called the Utah Expedition but popularly referred to as the Utah War.[32] The Utah War involved two opposing systems, each of which attempted to outmaneuver the other. It was an organized armed intervention with the stated goal of restoring and maintaining "the sovereignty of the Constitution and laws over the Territory of Utah."[33] The Buchanan administration moved to mitigate Mormon sovereignty and ensure that republicanism, not theocracy, would reign in the West. The federal government made a powerful effort to subsume Mormon sovereignty, just as the Mormons had attempted to do to the indigenous peoples upon their arrival in the Great Basin. The establishment of two military forts and other important federal infrastructure in Utah occurred with the arrival of the army. These forts helped consolidate the United States' sovereignty in the West as the federal government contested, with some temporary success, Mormon control over local and territorial institutions. During the Utah War, Congress debated popular sovereignty and the raising of more troops to send to Utah, and in those debates, new questions emerged about the actual power of the federal government in the territories.

The relationship that the federal government had with the territories of the West first began to take shape in the 1850s. The Utah episode offers a look at the struggle to extend federal power over a strong and independent people. The alternative sovereignty espoused by the Mormons forced President Buchanan to exercise federal control over the political, cultural, and bureaucratic affairs of a strong, cohesive settler community in a move that clarified the relationship of the federal government to its territories.

Buchanan's move had important consequences for national political discourse as it further tainted his party's policy of territorial popular sovereignty. Buchanan's government, though supportive of states' rights and local popular sovereignty, used powers enumerated in federal laws, including Indian policies, to demonstrate the supremacy of federal authority at the expense of the political realities of popular sovereignty to secure its hold on the Great Basin lands and to demonstrate that a territory was indeed an extension of American national sovereignty.[34]

By legislating against and advancing control over a Mormon sovereignty that protected plural marriage in Utah Territory, the federal government signaled to the rest of the country that it, especially with the ascendancy of the Republican Party, could wreak havoc on southern interests for slavery's expansion as well. The prospect of federal or congressional proscription of slavery expansion had long been a fear of southerners and often split Americans along sectional lines, and the growing specter of the Republican Party's control of the federal government brought that fear closer to reality. In other words, the federal government's relationship with Utah revealed a major flaw in the popular sovereignty doctrine. Democrats could not have it both ways. They could not advocate for federal noninterference in local territorial decision-making when it came to slavery expansion and then pursue strong federal action against a local population's domestic institution of marriage without creating a backlash and the possibility of future federal action against the other peculiar institution of slavery.

Democrats eventually squirmed internally at what was seen as a gross reversal of their central political principle when questioned by the press and their political foes. Republicans, including Abraham Lincoln, employed the Utah War as a foil for the Democratic doctrine of popular sovereignty, using it to expose and imperil the political concept as a situation-based, ad hoc sham. The doctrine of popular sovereignty had stood as a middle ground against northern demands for congressional exclusion of slavery, and southerners' insistence on federal noninterference in the territories. However, direct federal actions in the western territories, like the Utah War, shattered the illusion of popular sovereignty and gave rise to greater federal power in the West.

Utah was testing the durability and limits of American sovereignty as much as any other geopolitical entity of the 1850s, and it took the threat of force to negotiate the parameters of that territory's relationship with the United States. Managing sovereignty in Utah proved to be explosive and far reaching in its consequences, as debates over the propriety of governmental efforts to police the Mormons both undermined the singularity of popular sovereignty and helped to lay a foundation for the government's use of force to rein in and reconstruct the South during and after the Civil War and in the later Indian wars in the West.

1   *Imperium in Imperio*
Sovereignty and the American Territorial System

From the passage of the 1787 Northwest Ordinance onward, territories were the official unit of American expansion and, as such, were designed to pass through a process of political tutelage under the federal government's regulatory supervision. The Lockean idea of consent of the governed, coupled with the idea that governments should offer a balance of authority and liberty, provided American revolutionists with rhetorical fodder to rebel against the British system of colonial control. The colonists in America, propagandists insisted, had come of age and had reached a level of political maturity sufficient to be self-governing and independent from England.[1] Following their attaining independence, Americans began to implement their own system of expansion that they hoped would be unlike the British colonial model. The difference between England and the model of the new United States was the antipatriarchal ideology of the republican territorial system, which was to provide governmental education to a territory's inhabitants and establish a path to political maturity and self-government for them. The system of federal management over the territories required the participation of the local population in practicing republican government as federally appointed officials transmitted approved political ideas and practices from east to west.[2] According to the U.S. Constitution, the transference of national sovereignty to state sovereignty could not occur without the assurance that the people of a territory could and would operate a republican form of government.

In other words, the Constitution would not allow the admittance of new states formed from federal territory if the people residing within those geopolitical boundaries were deemed incapable of republican self-governance. The establishment of Utah Territory in 1850 formally brought Great Basin Mormons and American Indians under the direct supervision of the federal government and created a scenario wherein competing visions of sovereignty and government emerged and informed an increasing tension between the federal government and the settler community over self-governing capacity.

Territories in the American federalist system were viewed as eventual candidates for statehood and self-government through a preparatory process that included electing a legislature, establishing laws, and operating a republican government as the foundations for admittance to the Union. For the founding generation and Americans that followed, republicanism meant a promise that a collection of self-governing communities would exercise their sovereignty to inhibit consolidated power and the threat of control by the few.[3] Territorial governments on the path to statehood required governors, prosecutors, judges, Indian agents, surveyors, and other officials to enforce and execute the laws of the United States in the territory. The president appointed these officials—subject to Senate confirmation—and gave orders for any U.S. troops stationed in the territories.[4] The president and Congress also had discretionary power to deprive a territory of representative government and change local government when necessary, thereby making the territorial system a colonial arm of the state. Looked at another way, the federal government had the responsibility to raise and educate the territories to be good, loyal states in the Union in the same way that parents have the societal responsibility to raise their children to be good, loyal citizens of the nation. Once a territory's inhabitants proved they could responsibly and loyally operate a republican government, federal authority would give way to state sovereignty.

As the nation expanded, the Northwest Ordinance enabled the national government to exercise its authority and protect its interests in new territories while promising settlers in those lands the opportunity to attain their full rights of self-government when new states were created and admitted to the Union. That ordinance represents foundational American thinking about the nature of a colonial system for a republican empire as the federal government assumed and maintained the ultimate authority in the territories but provided the route toward sovereign equality in the Union.[5] The Northwest Ordinance established the governor as the executive authority in a territory, who served through federal appointment and was restricted to a term limit; however, federal authority could remove the governor at any time.[6] What is more, the Northwest Ordinance first codified federal control over territorial boundaries while it set the terms for territorial governance and power, all of which was later solidified by the Constitution.

The Constitution established a dual or divided sovereignty between the states and the federal government, each of which was sovereign in its assigned sphere, thereby providing a new definition of *imperium in imperio*, or sovereignty within sovereignty, that was coordinate and not subversive. Though the vision to create a self-governing republic was indeed noble, some entity had to decide what measure of self-government to provide to what people and when to preserve union among many interests, peoples, and states. The Constitution made clear, when it gave Congress power "to dispose of and make all needful Rules and Regulations respecting the Territory or other Property belonging to the United States," that the federal government controlled new territories legislatively as part of a process of integrating new parts into the national whole.[7] The Constitution was the instrument the federal government used to create a particular system of expansion to cast a republican superstructure across the North American continent. These two foundational documents, the Constitution and the Northwest Ordinance, provided a blueprint for continental expansion through the territorial system. For the founding generation, the territorial system signaled that the United States would become a flourishing and expanding republican nation.[8]

As the nation added new lands and peoples through the territorial process, the idea of local self-government was increasingly debated. Self-government could occur in new lands only after the parent institution properly instructed the peoples therein to be loyal, self-governing sovereign citizens of the Union. In antebellum-era politics, Americans grappled with reconciling liberty and regulation in the territories, particularly concerning vital issues of the day, and no issue was more important than slavery. Some citizens considered the colonial relationship of the territorial system inconsistent with the principles of republican government because the federal government could withhold the right of elective franchise and prevent the people from having a say in the choosing of their government officers. Still, the ultimate sovereignty for the territories remained in the hands of the federal government and would remain therewith through antebellum discussions of popular sovereignty.

The contest over sovereignty in Utah had its origins in the fifteen years that preceded the Mormons' arrival in the intermountain West. The Latter-day Saints' struggle to find a place within the American system of divided sovereignty in those years informed their actions, their responses, and the realities of the 1850s Utah territorial experience.

The Mormon faith was born during the Second Great Awakening, a time of religious division and conflict over biblical interpretation. During that chaotic time, however, the culture of evangelical Protestantism swept over the United States, making it "the most thoroughly Christian nation in the world."[9] Amid the religious fervor of western New York, Joseph Smith claimed to have found, with angelic assistance, an ancient record written on a set of gold plates that he then translated "by the gift and power of God." In Palmyra, New York, in 1830, Smith published the translation as the Book of Mormon, which he proclaimed was a new book of scripture to add to the Holy Bible.[10] That same year, he established a church founded on this new record and himself as a latter-day prophet. The church and its new scripture gave to believers a sense of divine authority in that it claimed to faithfully restore the church established by Jesus Christ during his earthly ministry. This unique faith evolved from those beginnings adding, among other things, religious rituals, a priesthood with apostles and keys of divine power, and continuing revelations in the first-person voice of Jesus Christ through Smith.[11]

The Mormons, as the followers of Smith and adherents to the new religious scripture came to be called, believed the Constitution to be an inspired document and continental America to literally be God's country.[12] However much that was the case, the Book of Mormon presented a combination of theocracy and monarchy as the ideal form of government. In an American culture saturated with republican ideas, the political principles embodied in the Book of Mormon were not republican and featured governments run by prophet-kings. Outsiders as well as early church members accused Joseph Smith of being an autocratic despot who sought "after monarchal power and authority."[13] Furthermore, and hardly inconsequential for the Mormons' first thirty years of existence, the Book of Mormon proclaimed that the American continent was the chosen land for American Indians and encouraged the religious group to cultivate relationships and to bring Native peoples into the new religious fold. From 1830 onward, Protestant Christian denominations viewed the new faith as aberrant in its theology. Most observers understood the Mormons to be a culturally, economically, and politically cohesive group.[14] The scripture and the ideology that it fostered among Mormons put members of the sect on the wrong side of justice and liberty in Missouri in the 1830s and in Illinois in the 1840s.

The first fifteen years of Mormon history can perhaps best be summarized by periodic disputes and physical confrontations between Mormons and their neighbors. In the early 1830s, a large body of Mormons settled in Jackson County, Missouri, a location that a Joseph Smith revelation claimed to be the central gathering place for their faith. After a significant increase in the Mormon population had the potential to change the political landscape there, non-Mormon residents felt threatened by the amount of land Mormons had acquired, as well as the religionists' stance against slavery and their unusual relationships with Native Americans.[15] Tensions soon boiled over, and mob actions against the Mormons resulted in their eviction from Jackson County in the fall of 1833.[16] The Latter-day Saints moved north into Clay County, Missouri, but in their violent ejection had lost their land and property without compensation from their attackers. Starting in early 1834, the Mormons fastidiously sought redress for the violence committed against them and for the restoration of their stolen property. They fought through the Missouri state justice system and took their case to all levels of Missouri government but to no avail. They were denied by the state several times. They never received compensation for their losses.

Over the decade that followed, Mormons also petitioned federal authorities to receive redress but heard from those authorities that the federal government could do nothing to aid them in their plight.[17] They told the Mormon petitioners to take their case back to Missouri authorities. Church leaders had also petitioned U.S. president Andrew Jackson in April 1834 with a recitation of the Missouri violence in hopes that he would "send a force of men" to protect the Mormons in their rights and allow them to return to their lands. The church leaders also hoped that federal troops would establish and maintain peace between Mormons and other Jackson County residents.[18] The Mormons' appeal for federal action arose in the aftermath of Jackson's deployment of uncompromising presidential power in a state during the South Carolina Nullification Crisis and at roughly the same time that he sent federal troops to quell a labor riot in Maryland.[19] While Jackson demonstrated the potential power the president held, shows of federal strength were few and far between in antebellum America. The Mormon plea for federal assistance reached the desk of Secretary of War Lewis Cass. In his response Cass stated that the president did not have the constitutional right or authority to send federal troops into

Missouri to aid in the enforcement of state laws. Despite Jackson's earlier displays of power, the secretary of war was technically correct. The constitutional foundation of the Mormon petition in fact required that a state authority, whether the legislature or the chief executive, request federal intervention.[20] Therefore, Cass noted that Mormon complaints revealed violations of state law, to be taken up by state courts, and not of federal law. In no uncertain terms, Cass stated that the religionists' petition fell outside of the president's and the national government's jurisdiction.[21]

Law enforcers in the state of Missouri did not protect the rights of the religious group. Another five years of difficulties for the Mormons in Missouri reached a head in the fall of 1838. Following the forcible removal from Jackson County, tensions forced Mormons to vacate their temporary Clay County residences even before the Missouri state legislature created Caldwell County as a "Mormon county" in December 1836.[22] Less than two years later the clash in Missouri grew extreme when the state governor, Lilburn W. Boggs, issued an extermination order that called for the removal of all Mormons from the state or death for members of that faith who remained.[23] The Mormons were to either leave the state or be killed. In other words, the state sanctioned and sponsored the wholesale expulsion or extermination of American citizens. At a time when local mob activity and rioting were on the rise in the United States, particularly to enforce the local majority's power and interests, Missourians, too, used violence effectively to rid their geopolitical boundaries of the hated minority sect.[24] The cohesive religious group ultimately left the state in accordance with the extermination order. They traveled east, finding refuge in Quincy, Illinois, before heading north, where they established a community named Nauvoo on the east shore of the Mississippi River.

That church members received no redress or justice from these events at any level of government left them dismayed at the American system of divided authority and republican governance in practice. While they maintained their stance that the Constitution was inspired by God, Latter-day Saint leaders largely believed that the men running the government were corrupt and not living up to the Constitution's principles. In a supposed land of liberty, Mormons stated, minority rights were not protected and the prevalent idea of states' rights left the federal government impotent in its ability to ensure the constitutional rights of all citizens.[25]

In antebellum America, most Democrats believed in a strict system of states' rights in which the federal government did not interfere in the affairs of an individual state. Particularly following Jackson's threats to use the military to ensure that states adhered to federal law, politicians proceeded with caution when it came to the use of federal power. Fearing that use or abuse of power would upset the precarious balance in the Union, especially as it related to the slavery issue, political figures leaned more and more toward majority rule and local or states' rights as the ultimate source of authority in a democratic society.[26] Democrats even refused to support national internal improvement projects for fear that they might establish a precedent for the federal exercise of interstate commerce powers over the interstate slave trade.[27]

Among the proponents of this localist philosophy was Martin Van Buren. While serving as president of the United States in the winter of 1839–1840, Van Buren told Mormon petitioners, including Joseph Smith, that the federal government could provide no redress for their expulsion from the state of Missouri because the persecution incidents were a matter to be handled at the state level.[28] Van Buren waxed political when he told Smith that his cause was just but that he could do nothing for fear that he would "come in contact with the whole State of Missouri."[29] Van Buren's sentiment rankled Joseph Smith. The Mormon leader felt betrayed that the president would yield to the power, and votes, of a state when American citizens' First Amendment rights to religious liberty were being violated. The president and the federal government, Smith thought, had the power to protect citizens, but in the Mormons' case chose not to act. The church's many appeals to

Congress met with almost identical replies, and the Mormons found themselves in a difficult position. They had approached the federal government only after their appeals to municipal and state governments were ignored or denied. Federal authorities consistently displayed an unwillingness to assist the Mormons. The federal government's denial of the Latter-day Saints' appeals on the basis of the states' rights philosophy signaled to members and leaders of the sect that no level of government would ensure their constitutional rights. Though states had certain powers, the federal government was responsible for maintaining the "inalienable rights" of all Americans. That was the position of Latter-day Saint leaders. The Mormons believed that American federalism in action was failing them.

Frustrated but determined, the Mormons continued to seek after federal redress while they devised new means to protect themselves. The Illinois legislature granted the Mormon community a charter to legally organize Nauvoo as a city with a litany of local, municipal powers. The Nauvoo charter allowed the Mormons to form a city council, a municipal court with jurisdiction over local cases and the power to issue writs of habeas corpus that shielded Joseph Smith and others from legal issues, and a local militia unit.[30] The combination of powers in the charter and the exercise of those powers in Nauvoo effectively made the Mormon community a self-governing and self-protecting entity.[31] But that growing power also resurrected accusations of Mormon despotism. Critics called Joseph Smith the "Mormon King," and non-Mormons generally viewed the Mormon community as a growing threat to become a mighty and independent empire governed by an ecclesiastical dictator.[32] Mormons again clashed with their neighbors. As Illinois governor Thomas Ford later wrote of the Mormons, "their residence among us led to a mobocratic spirit, which resulted in their expulsion."[33]

In late 1843, Joseph Smith wrote to five potential presidential candidates for the 1844 election "to enquire what their feelings were or what their course would be towards the saints if they were elected."[34] Three of the prospective presidential candidates eventually answered the Mormon leaders' inquiry.[35] One of the respondents was none other than Lewis Cass, who was the governor of Michigan Territory before serving as Jackson's secretary of war. Similar to his response to the Mormons nine years earlier, Cass wrote that "if your application for the redress to which you consider yourselves entitled has been, as you say rejected by the constituted authorities of the state of Missouri, and by Congress, I do not see what power, the President of the United States can have over the matter or how he can interfere in it."[36] John C. Calhoun, a former vice president and U.S. senator who had met with Smith and a Mormon delegation to Washington DC in 1840, responded that if elected president, he would strive "to administer the government according to the Constitution and the laws of the union; and that as they make no distinction between citizens of different religious creeds," neither would he. Calhoun added, however, that where Mormon accusations against Missouri were concerned, "candor compels me to repeat, what I said to you at Washington; that according to my views the case does not come within the jurisdiction of the federal government, which is one of limited and specific powers."[37] Calhoun, like Cass, Van Buren, and other staunch states' rights proponents, believed that communities often looked to the federal government for too much when, in that era's political climate, it chose not to exercise its power to intervene in intrastate matters.[38]

Joseph Smith rebutted Calhoun's letter and laid out his own perspective on the constitutional division of governmental power and local rights.[39] Smith protested the logical extension of Calhoun's position—that a state could expel citizens with impunity. He further denied that the federal government had no jurisdiction in the Mormon-Missouri case. Rather, in a system of divided sovereignty, one entity had to have more authority than the other, to right wrongs to American citizens as they occurred. He could not comprehend how a sovereign state was "so much more powerful than the United States, the parent Government, that it can exile you at pleasure, mob you with impunity; confiscate your lands and property, have the Legislature sanction it; yea, even murder you as an edict of an Emperor, *and it does no wrong*, for the noble Senator of South Carolina, says, the power of the Federal Government, is *so limited and specific, that it has no jurisdiction of the case!* What think ye of *Imperium in imperio*[?]"[40] Smith thus displayed his intense disillusionment that none of the prospective presidential candidates were willing to openly assist the Mormons.

The Mormons attempted to explore another option in their quest to obtain federal recognition and assistance as they petitioned the national government to grant the city of Nauvoo territorial status. Since the federal government had not helped them with the Missouri issues, the church and its leaders believed that the nation's highest governing body would live up to its constitutional design to protect the people if they were under its direct supervision and jurisdiction in a territorial form.[41] Though the Nauvoo city charter provided significant power to the municipality's people and leaders, the city government was still ultimately subject to the state.[42] Territories were subject to federal organization and oversight. Joseph Smith believed that if his people could come under federal jurisdiction the federal government would use its power to protect them. After so many failed appeals, this appeared to be the best remaining option for obtaining federal protection for the citizenship rights of the church and its members while maintaining a semblance of the self-governance that they craved and that they enjoyed under the Nauvoo charter. On 21 December 1843, Joseph Smith and other civic leaders in Nauvoo drafted the petition, which contained a provision that Nauvoo officials could call upon federal troops to assist the Nauvoo legion "repel the invasion of mobs," but it was not presented to Congress until 5 April 1844.[43] On that day, James Semple, senator from Illinois, presented the "memorial from the mayor and aldermen of the city of Nauvoo, in Hancock county, Illinois, praying that the powers and privileges of a territorial government may be extended to that city." The Senate sent the petition to its Committee on Judiciary, which took no further action.[44] Territorial status failed to materialize for the Mormons at that time. The Mormons clearly understood the political climate in which they lived and attempted to work within it, but inasmuch as they had exhausted all of their options for so doing, Smith and other Mormon leaders created a committee they called the Council of Fifty, which had among its goals supporting Smith's candidacy for president of the United States. By helping Smith obtain the country's highest office, the Council of Fifty sought to establish a leader and government that would protect and extend constitutional rights to minority groups, Mormon or otherwise.[45]

When Joseph Smith campaigned for the nation's executive office, he offered up a theodemocratic model, or a blend of American republicanism and divine authority, as the ideal form of republican government to guarantee and protect all individual liberties and rights.[46] Smith respected the idea of American government as expressed in the Constitution, but he did not believe that the men running the government lived up to their duties because of the many violent experiences the Mormons had faced during the preceding ten years. By 1844, Joseph Smith and many of his close associates sought to protect the rights and privileges belonging to all citizens of the American Republic, regardless of their race or religious minority status. The Mormon leader complained, "Party spirit cuts the cords of the Union; patronage veils the face of justice, and bribery closes the lips of honor, and when the wicked rule, the people mourn."[47]

In his presidential platform, Smith reenvisioned the divided sovereignty of the U.S. federal system. He advocated a nationalist approach to empower the president and the federal government to protect people whose constitutional rights were being violated regardless of states' rights issues and rhetoric. Smith interpreted the Constitution more broadly than most of his era and believed that it provided the nation's executive and federal government with the means and power to act to preserve freedoms and guarantee the enumerated and implicit rights to all Americans, even in a state.[48] For most antebellum Americans, local democracy and sovereignty were sacrosanct in the relationship between citizens and the state, which made Smith's nationalist approach unpopular. Smith's 1844 presidential campaign argued that the U.S. president should have "full power to send an army to suppress mobs." Referring to earlier responses to the Mormon pleas for federal intervention in Missouri, the Latter-day Saint leader also proposed legislative action to repeal the constitutional clause that "makes it necessary for the Governor of a State to make the demand of the President for troops, in case of invasion or rebellion."[49] As Smith's campaign got underway, a maelstrom developed in the Saints' city of Nauvoo.

Tension hit a fever pitch after 8 June when the Nauvoo City Council, led by the mayor, Joseph Smith, declared the *Nauvoo Expositor* a nuisance and issued orders for its destruction. The *Expositor* opposed Joseph Smith and his power; the paper led by former Mormons and non-Mormons called for the repeal of the Nauvoo charter. In its first and only issue printed on 7 June 1844, the *Expositor* printed its prospectus and several resolutions, some of which condemned Joseph Smith's assumption of power in the name of religion and his undue influence over local affairs.[50] John P. Greene, the Nauvoo city marshal, accompanied by hundreds of Mormons carried out Smith's order to destroy the opposition press on 10 June.[51] Shortly thereafter, Francis Higbee, the publisher of the *Expositor*, charged Smith and others for inciting a riot. Nauvoo courts discharged Smith and the others from arrest, though Illinois governor Thomas Ford quickly insisted that they come to Carthage for a hearing on the riot charge.

Mob activity increased, and the growing plot to kill Smith penetrated nearly every aspect of city life in Nauvoo following the *Expositor* destruction. Mobbing, rioting, and vigilante actions were not uncommon in Illinois at this time.[52] Governor Ford explained that two main reasons existed for mob activity. "First," Ford stated, "the laws fail to provide remedies for great evils."[53] "The second cause of mobs," according to Ford, "is that men engaged in unpopular projects expect more protection from the laws than the laws are able to furnish in the face of a popular excitement. They read in the Constitution the guaranty of their rights, and they insist upon the enjoyment of these rights to the fullest extent, no matter what may be the extent of popular opposition against them.... The men engaged in projects which may be odious to the people, call upon government for that protection which it cannot give."[54] Ford's statement placed the Mormons' case in the latter category, but it could likewise be argued that the non-Mormons in the vicinity of Nauvoo believed that the laws of the state or nation were not preventing the "great evils" of Mormon control over the Nauvoo city government and its legal system. The people would then have to enact popular will against the centralized authority of Joseph Smith.

Joseph Smith's stronghold on local power was about to come under literal fire. The Mormon leader began making contingencies. He planned to communicate the reports of the interstate mob to Thomas Ford, governor of Illinois, and to U.S. president John Tyler in hopes of gaining state and federal protection, which would prevent the pending shift in local power that vigilantes were instigating.[55] In another move to stem the tide of mob movements and protect his religious followers, on 18 June 1844, Smith put the city of Nauvoo under martial law. With good reason to fear the arrival of an organized interstate mob in the city to murder, plunder, and destroy property, Smith as city mayor authorized the Nauvoo Legion to hold itself in readiness, equipped in the best possible manner for defense. Officers continued parade ground routines and reviews as they planned for defense.[56]

Smith was in the Carthage jail when a mob gathered and descended on the small two-story structure. Smith was first charged for inciting the *Nauvoo Expositor* riot and then imprisoned for treason for declaring martial law in Nauvoo. On 27 June 1844, some of the more than two hundred armed men barged into the jail and opened fire on Smith and the other Mormon prisoners. Smith and his brother Hyrum were shot and Smith fell out of the jail's second story window. The mob had killed the powerful Mormon leader.[57]

Joseph Smith strongly believed in the power of the federal government and of the president to protect the rights of all people, but antebellum American society stressed local autonomy and control. Smith and the Mormons had gained local control in Nauvoo, but when their non-Mormon neighbors on both sides of the Mississippi River threatened that control by violent means, Smith was undoubtedly naïve to think that the president or any federal authorities would use their power to act for an unpopular religious minority, particularly one that had so enraged the local majority. In western Illinois, vigilantes took back local power from the Mormons by violent means, a frequent reality in antebellum America. The only chance Smith and other Mormons seemed to have for protection of constitutional rights came through municipal city actions. However, non-Mormons believed that those actions demonstrated an overextension of power and authority and that only "democratic" violence against them could rebalance sovereignty. In an ironic turn of events, the Illinois executive officer invoked the authority of the federal government to force the Mormons out of the state. Approximately eighteen months after Joseph Smith's death, Governor Ford threatened the Mormons with the possibility that he would ask the president to send the federal army to intervene against the Mormons, to arrest members of their leadership, and to cause general chaos for the religious body.[58] Ford's threat had the desired effect. The religious group soon left Illinois and the boundaries of U.S. sovereignty where the federal system had once again failed to protect their religious and civil liberties and constitutional rights.

Having experienced a series of violent encounters that they cast as religious persecution and receiving no governmental or legal protection or redress against that violence, the Mormons decided to physically leave the United States in 1846. Prior to their departure from the United States, the Latter-day Saints were acutely aware of the nation's westward movement and in some ways advocated for American continental expansion.[59] In early December 1843, President John Tyler delivered his third annual message to Congress, in which he called for American expansion through the establishment of military posts along the line of travel to the Pacific coast so that American law would follow them and enable the "free system of government" to develop the republican model in the West. Joseph Smith read this message in the *Nauvoo Neighbor*, a local Mormon newspaper.[60] Reacting to the contemporary jingoism related to possible war with Britain over the Pacific Northwest, Smith requested authorization from Congress to gather a 100,000-man army to march to, settle, and govern the Oregon country to strengthen the United States' northern border and prevent foreign intrusion from Britain.[61] Congress denied Smith's request. The Mormon prophet also closely followed the challenges and victories of the Texas Republic and eyed the possibility of removing his people there.[62] The Mormons, like Sam Houston and the Texans, were willing to go to great lengths to achieve the twin goals of security and self-rule for their people.[63] In Joseph Smith's 1844 presidential platform, the religious leader employed expansionist rhetoric that supported bringing Oregon, Texas, Canada, and Mexico into the American union.[64] In Smith's view, the Mormons not only identified with America but also sought to expand the power, territory, and institutions of the nation they believed was created by divine intervention.

The Mormons had long been told that the federal government could not assist or protect them in their rights because of states' powers in the federal system of divided sovereignty. They came to understand this very well. On 11 June 1844, Orson Hyde, a Mormon then visiting Washington DC on political business for the church, visited with President John Tyler. When Hyde asked the president about Smith's proposal to settle the Oregon country and the rights and authority of the government to protect the Mormons, Tyler frankly remarked that "the general government cannot interfere with the laws and regulations of the states but, says he, the moment you get beyond the States into the United States territories, then you come under the immediate protection of the general government. . . . I wish, he says, you to distinctly understand this difference."[65] Hyde communicated this information to Joseph Smith and the Mormon leaders back in Nauvoo,

FIG. 2. Stephen A. Douglas, ca. 1860. Courtesy of the Library of Congress, Prints and Photographs Division.

immediately writing a letter the same day. The president's response encapsulated the Mormons' past experiences and clarified their understanding of the exercise of sovereignty in the United States. It emphasized the strength of local power and the perceived limits of federal power.

During his time in Washington, Hyde had also met with congressmen, including then-representative from Illinois Stephen A. Douglas. The Illinois representative had established a positive relationship with the Mormons in Illinois. He even visited Nauvoo in 1841 and 1843 and presided over an 1841 legal case involving Joseph Smith, which Douglas dismissed on procedural grounds.[66] Douglas had praised the Mormons for their improvements in Nauvoo and in return Smith celebrated the politician. In 1841, Smith wrote of Douglas, "No man stands more deservedly high in the public estimation, as an able and profound jurist, politician, and statesman."[67] Douglas's once friendly relationship with the Latter-day Saints drew the ire of his political opponents in the 1840s and would prove costly for his political future.[68] Nevertheless, when Douglas visited with Hyde in 1844 he presented the Mormon visitor with a copy of John C. Frémont's report of his expedition through the Rocky Mountains to Oregon and California.[69] Douglas also gave Hyde valuable advice about settling in the West. Douglas strongly suggested that the Mormons move to the West—he was specifically talking about Oregon, but the concept is more widely applicable—before too many other settlers got there in advance of the religious group. Retelling his conversation with Douglas, Hyde wrote that the senator furthermore said "he would equally as soon go to that country without an act of congress as with; and that in 5 years a noble State might be formed, and then if they would not receive us into the Union, we would have a government of our own."[70] Again, Hyde reported this information to church leaders. The path to Mormon sovereignty in the West appeared open and possible.

After Smith's death, Mormon leaders looked carefully at their options. Rather than migrate to another state in the Union where they would continue to have no power to govern themselves or combat anti-Mormon violence, the Mormons initially bypassed state power entirely. They decided to go to the Rocky Mountains, then under Mexico's rule. But the Mormons had not secured permission from Mexican authorities to settle in their country. They left the nation's borders in search of a new place to make *their* country where they could govern themselves without interference, perhaps hoping that they could more easily negotiate with Mexico for their sovereign space. Groups often emigrated from their homelands in order to govern themselves and establish new sovereign orders. The Mormons left the United States for precisely that purpose.[71]

Still, the Mormons were a complex and conflicted people when it came to their affection for the United States. They simultaneously disavowed a nation that would not protect them and wanted to be a self-governing part of that nation, to be a part of the divided sovereignty. As the religious group prepared to leave the United States, many speculated that they would become a subversive threat to the nation. The *Times and Seasons* reprinted a *New York Sun* article claiming the threat of a mighty and independent "Mormon empire" on the Pacific coast where the Latter-day Saints would establish their own government and live according to their own religiously dictated laws.[72] Even while en route out of national boundaries to the Great Basin in 1846, however, the new Mormon leader, Brigham Young, accepted President James K. Polk's call to create a Mormon Battalion to serve in the U.S.-Mexico War then taking place. Polk wanted to create a Mormon military group for two purposes: to determine Mormon loyalty and to keep an eye on them during the war.[73] Polk specifically wanted to conciliate the Mormons after their tumultuous first fifteen years and "prevent them from assuming a hostile attitude towards the United States" after their arrival in the West. Polk feared that disgruntled Latter-day Saints would side with Mexicans or the British against the United States in the war to proclaim a protectorate in upper California, thwarting the president's expansionist designs.[74] Young wrote to Polk to prove the Mormons' loyalty to the United States and state his desire to have a territorial government created for the Mormons upon their arrival in the Great Basin. The one caveat that Young requested, though, was that he did not want Washington to appoint men over his people who might "promote the misery of their fellows, for their own aggrandizement or lustful gratification."[75] In essence, the Mormon leader expressed his hope that Washington would appoint civic leaders from among the religious body. He wanted a measure of self-government. Young sought to prove the loyalty of his people and link the fortunes of his religion with those of the United States. Young, following in the footsteps of his predecessor, even proposed to build a series of forts to protect American expansion along the developing Oregon Trail.[76]

Brigham Young understood the likelihood that the entire North American continent would eventually come under the governing jurisdiction of the United States. When that happened, he wanted his people to be the first settlers in the newly acquired lands.[77] The Mormons could then set the tone in government and culture. The idea of arriving first, or early, in a newly created territory to have a stake in the direction and control of territorial governance, or economic opportunities, was not unique. Settlers in Oregon, California, and Texas likewise established provisional governments to serve their local needs, while settlers in Kansas and Nebraska were heavily influenced by the formation of vigilante groups in the territorial period to protect land claims and other economic interests.[78] By establishing a government in a newly conquered land, they hoped to protect themselves and their interests and avoid the conflict they faced in Missouri, Ohio, and Illinois where they came to an established community and were viewed as attempting to fundamentally change or manipulate that community. During one of their episodes of turmoil in Missouri, the Mormons learned that a Clay County citizens' committee recommended that they investigate and remove to the then–Territory of Wisconsin because "it is almost entirely unsettled; they [church members] can there procure large bodies of land together, where there are no settlements, and none to interfere with them. . . . We therefore, in a spirit of frank and friendly kindness, do advise them to seek a home where they may obtain large and separate bodies of land, and have a community of their own."[79] The Mormons had learned from painful experience after being run out of Missouri and Illinois that they needed to go to a new place with few to no white settlers so that they could establish their own self-governing community.

FIG. 3. Brigham Young, "The Mormon President," 1854. Courtesy of the Library of Congress, Prints and Photographs Division.

In 1847, in the midst of the U.S.-Mexico War, the Mormons found refuge in the Great Basin. Without consulting either the Mexican or U.S. government, leaders of the LDS church founded a colony, like Texas, and formed a civil government they called the state of Deseret filled with its ecclesiastical dignitaries, a hierarchy with the prophet Brigham Young at the head. The Latter-day Saints believed these men of God were capable of running Christ's church. Therefore, they also considered them capable to run the civil government. There was no separation between the LDS church and the formation of their state in the Great Basin. The Mormons' goal with their state of Deseret government was to establish and exercise political, legal, and cultural power for the fullest measure of self-rule in the place they chose to settle.[80]

Upon hearing of the Treaty of Guadalupe Hidalgo in 1848, which ended the United States' war with Mexico, the Mormons debated whether to request a territorial or state government. They did not make this decision uninformed. Five years earlier, on 21 December 1843, Joseph Smith proposed a memorial to Congress that the federal government grant to Nauvoo all the powers, rights, and immunities belonging to territories of the United States. That memorial asked that the mayor of Nauvoo be authorized to call upon federal troops, when necessary, to help the Nauvoo Legion "repel the invasion of mobs, keep the public peace, and protect the innocent from the unhallowed ravages of lawless banditti that escape justice on the Western frontier." The Mormons believed then that the federal government would protect them if under its purview. In 1849, they were not so sure.[81] Latter-day Saints had not received federal protection when they had previously sought it and now desired full self-governing status.

In February 1849, Latter-day Saint leaders ultimately proposed that their community and government be admitted to the Union as a state named Deseret. They drew up a grand proposal that sought a large, sprawling geographic space for the Mormon community ranging from present-day San Diego, California, to Denver, Colorado. Rather than wait for Congress to act, the Mormon leaders moved forward with their self-governing provisional state of Deseret to suit their "present necessities" to develop laws for the benefit of security, peace, and prosperity in hopes of demonstrating that they were fit to bring a "sovereign and Independent state into the Union upon an equal footing with the original states."[82] A memorial to Congress described how the provisional government satisfied local needs. It stated:

> Immediately consequent upon the settlement of this colony, a large and heterogeneous emigration followed upon our heels, remaining

here a shorter or longer time, imperatively requiring the establishment of an efficient government for the speedy protection of life, peace, virtue, and property. In addition to a transient and ungovernable emigration, almost constant Indian depredations have pleaded, like the irresistible maw of death, for the institution of some formidable order and power of government among us. A provisional government was accordingly formed, which has met the exigencies of the people, and secured general tranquility, order, and satisfaction.[83]

It was unclear at the time, however, whether the Mormons intended their provisional government to be an interim or permanent entity. On 3 December 1849, at a meeting of the Senate and House of Representatives of the state of Deseret, Brigham Young recommended that they reject a territorial relationship with the federal government and "act as a State" regardless of the congressional decision of geopolitical status.[84] Another legislative member at that meeting, Ezra T. Benson, suggested that the Mormons "remain independent, from this time forth, & forever." Young then stated that he had "dreamed" that the federal government would "let the Mormons alone for ten years" that they might govern themselves. The Latter-day Saints had formed a strong government, and the tangibility of their sovereignty was real. They had recognized this and believed they were in a position of strength to negotiate the parameters of their sovereignty with the United States. Perhaps if the Mormons demonstrated they could act like a state the federal government would extend to them state sovereignty. The available state of Deseret minutes indicate nothing else on the matter of the provisional government, but this discussion indicates that the Mormon logic was to establish and maintain its own sovereign order to operate autonomously outside of the federal territorial system.[85]

The establishment of a provisional government in a U.S. territory was not unprecedented. The people of Oregon Territory made a strong movement for local autonomy by establishing their own government and system of law. For at least six years prior to receiving territorial status in 1848, Oregonians lived under a government of their own making. While Oregonians had established a provisional government that provided freedom and the responsibility of self-rule, the arrival of the territorial government formed by Congress meant the extension of U.S. law over Oregon. Some in the territory soon became convinced that the territorial government also meant "a loss of political rights and a reduction to a 'colonial' status."[86] For Oregon Territory, Congress allowed laws passed by the provisional government to remain in force so long as they were not incompatible with the Constitution, but it removed from the people the right to choose their own officers.

Oregonians felt increasingly discontented with the administration of territorial government that took autonomy from settlers in the early 1850s and inspired a movement for a greater degree of self-government through a revision of the American territorial system. In the course of this movement, Oregonians demanded sovereignty on par with the several states to protect their local interests. They denounced the territorial system. It was "diametrically opposed to the fundamental principles of American liberty" because the men of the territory, they claimed, were capable of governing themselves.[87] That Oregonians were capable of self-government had been amply demonstrated by the efficient operation of the provisional government.

The Mormons too wanted local autonomy. They understood the separation of sovereign powers in the American federal system because they had been rebuffed by the federal government for aid against state-sanctioned violence. They had learned that as a state, they would be free to elect their own officers, to be ruled by those of their own choosing, and to regulate their own marital practices, which were subject to state law under the system of divided sovereignty. Having experienced the great power of governmental authority in the sovereign states of Missouri and Illinois, the Mormon leadership yearned for that same status. They reasoned that state sovereignty would have afforded church members the protection and the right to govern themselves free from outside influence. Territorial status would not have the same guarantees, and Latter-day Saint leaders did not want "starved office seekers" appointed from Washington to rule over them.[88] Though Brigham Young first initiated a petition for the establishment of a territory, after California and New Mexico petitioned for statehood, Young changed course and pushed to bypass the territorial stage and move directly to statehood. On the advice of Thomas L. Kane, a trusted political ally and a sympathetic non-Mormon from Pennsylvania, Young and his cohort tried to abandon the application for territorial status because they understood that they would not be able to select their own governing officials and would lose much of their autonomy. The Mormons wanted affirmation of their sovereignty as a state, and therefore, largely outside of federal interference in local matters.

The provisional state of Deseret's constitution outlined a republican form of government where all political power came from the people with a design to protect the people and offer them security and benefits.[89] This proposal was rejected during the intense debate over how to organize the Mexican War cession into geopolitical entities. Congress finally agreed to a compromise in 1850 that brought California into the Union as a free state and, thanks in large part to the tireless efforts of Illinois senator Stephen A. Douglas, organized New Mexico and Utah into territories fashioned out of the remainder of the newly acquired land. Those territories were organized on the basis of popular sovereignty that allowed the inhabitants to determine whether they would permit slavery and certain domestic institutions. Utah Territory, named after the Utes, one of the larger Native American groups of the Great Basin, replaced the proposed state of Deseret. The federal government did not recognize Utah's settler population as capable or loyal enough to bestow the autonomy they craved. The Mormons were denied statehood. Instead they became subject to federal purview in the territorial system. However, Mormon expressions and aspirations for state sovereignty did not end with that defeat.

The Utah Organic Act demonstrated the supremacy of national sovereignty over the territory. Despite popular sovereignty rhetoric and in line with the apparatus of territorial administration, the Constitution and laws were to be extended over and declared in force in the territory, while the president, with the approval of the Senate, retained authority for the appointment of governor, chief justice and associate justices, Indian agents, and other officials as in all other territories. The nature of territorial governance gave the federal government ultimate control to supervise and shape new lands according to republican values.[90]

The creation of Utah Territory forever altered relations between the U.S. federal government and the Mormons. The Mormons feared that territorial government would result in federal control exercised by non-Mormons, which would reverse the autonomy they were trying to build with their colony in the Great Basin. Great Basin Mormons called on the federal government to fill territorial government vacancies with people of their faith in order to enjoy the "full administration of every department of government speedily, as the prosperity of the Territory shall require."[91] They did not want their society governed by strangers who might oppose popular will. Though the idea that the Mormons would move government speedily may have suggested an undemocratic process to outsiders, the Mormons, based on the treatment they received from Missouri, Illinois, and the federal government in the 1840s, worried that non-Mormons running the territorial government would prevent them from meeting their local needs. Even worse, non-Mormon territorial officials might interrupt the harmony of the Mormon government, foster an atmosphere of lawlessness, and impose iniquitous authority. These were the ingredients of a common Mormon argument against territorial officers from outside their own community.

Brigham Young lobbied and argued that "all Republican Government emanates from the people," indicating, as Douglas did with his popular sovereignty rhetoric, that the people of the territory had the right to legislate for themselves. Dr. John M. Bernhisel, the Mormon political representative in Washington DC, urged President Millard Fillmore to appoint all Mormons to official territorial positions. Bernhisel invoked the rhetoric of imperial crisis and popular sovereignty in his discussions with Fillmore. He asserted that Latter-day Saints, as American citizens, deserved and considered it their right to choose those who governed them. Mirroring the complaints of American revolutionaries who decried the authority of the British crown to appoint all colonial governors and the imperial control of the other aspects of colonial government, Bernhisel, along with Thomas Kane, attempted to procure a measure of self-government for the Mormons within the territorial system. Fillmore initially offered the position of governor to Kane, but Kane turned down the offer and requested that the president select a Mormon to the post and to the other federal territorial positions. Kane and Bernhisel eventually convinced Fillmore of the good character of Brigham Young. Kane, in particular, vouched for Young and quelled Fillmore's fears of the "principle of monarchy and centralism" that might accompany Young's appointment as the territorial governor.[92] Fillmore ultimately appointed Brigham Young as governor and superintendent of Indian affairs in Utah Territory. The president's choice of governor, however, proved to embolden Young and the Mormons' resolve.

The president did not choose Mormons to fill every federal post. Two supreme court judges, one Indian affairs subagent, and the secretary of the territory were all positions filled by outsiders.[93] These federally appointed officers concerned the territory's inhabitants about the promise of self-government, while Judge Perry Brocchus, Judge Lemuel Brandebury, and Secretary Broughton D. Harris arrived in Utah in July 1851 and soon found Mormon power overwhelming.[94] Speeches by Mormons on 24 July 1851, the church's celebration of its arrival in the Salt Lake Valley, offended the outsider officers and demonstrated to them the religionists' theocratic government and overall disloyalty to the

FIG. 4. Eliza R. Snow, Mormon observer and poet, ca. 1860s. Courtesy of the Church History Library, Salt Lake City, UT.

Union.[95] According to Judge Brocchus's report of that day's speeches, the Mormons claimed "the U.S. was going to hell as fast as it could" and that the federal government was odious.[96] The non-Mormon officers generally believed that the church's members and particularly its leaders were a malicious and seditious people that sought "to alienate the affections of the people from the Government of the United States."[97] Brocchus gave a speech at a general conference shortly thereafter that chastised the Mormons for their disloyal conduct unbecoming American citizens.

Eliza R. Snow and other Mormons viewed these events differently. They saw Brocchus as attacking Mormons generally and Mormon womanhood specifically. In a poem written about the adversarial federal officials, Snow encapsulated Mormon thought, not only about the officials, but also about Mormon political views. According to Snow's poem and contrary to Brocchus's statements, Mormons were advocates for liberty, the champions of America's cause, and firm supporters of the law. She wrote, "This Territory shall not rate Inferior to our sister States," perhaps indicating the Mormon feeling that they wanted to be a part of the sisterhood of states and could and should be trusted to govern themselves on the same footing as the rest of the states in the federal union.[98]

Almost as quickly as the federal officers arrived in Utah, they left their posts. By 26 September 1851, just two months after they reached Utah, following a rhetorical war with the territory's inhabitants and fearing for their lives, the federal appointees absconded from the territory. No federal officials filled their posts for at least two years. Shortly after the territorial officials left their posts, they arrived in Washington DC, where they made public reports of an incendiary nature concerning Mormon society and governmental administration. In particular they spoke against Mormon disloyalty to the United States and resistance to federal sovereignty as embodied in the non-Mormon appointees. More generally, they submitted that the authority of the federal government was in danger in Utah.[99] A primary concern of these officials, whom the Mormons would later dub the "runaway officials," was the great power that Brigham Young, in his triplicate role as governor, superintendent of Indian affairs, and leader of the LDS church, wielded in the territory. Young's positions allowed him to appoint district-level judges and Indian subagents; he could issue pardons; and his veto power could play a considerable role in legislation. With his authority as superintendent of Indian affairs, Young soon established a program of licensing Mormon missionaries to preach to the region's Native population and convert to control them. With such power in one individual and with motives not necessarily in line with American thinking, the departed appointees argued that Utah could not be properly educated by the federal government. Furthermore, a transference of sovereignty could not occur, in this case because federal sovereignty had not yet been established in the territory. With no non-Mormon federal officials to run the government, Mormon power and tenacity increased.

Washington politicians sought after answers and more information concerning Utah affairs. On 15 December 1851, the U.S. House of Representatives requested from the president any information in his possession "calculated to show the actual condition of things in the Territory of Utah, and especially to enable the House to ascertain whether the due execution of the laws of the United States has been resisted or obstructed; whether there has been any misapplication of the public funds; and whether the personal rights of our citizens have been interfered with in any manner."[100] In mid-January 1852, President Fillmore issued a message on Utah. He included with it a letter written to him from territorial secretary Broughton Harris, who claimed that Brigham Young sought to persuade him to make illegal disbursements of federal money.[101] Harris was the steward over the money and, according to some accounts, refused to pay out a single dime to Utah residents who badly needed the funds because he feared that Brigham Young would use the federal money to benefit the church.

In another financial matter from this period, Congress advanced a sum of twenty thousand dollars to Utah on 7 March 1851 to construct suitable public buildings at the seat of government for the operation of the territorial government. Governor Young later rendered an account setting forth the expenditure of $10,373.48 for an expedition to locate a site for the seat of government and for labor and materials for a legislative hall. Jacob H. Holeman, the federal Indian agent assigned to Utah, accused Young of misappropriating funds for his own or the church's usage. Money earmarked for the construction of public buildings in the territory, Holeman charged, was used to build a church council-house in Salt Lake City, some 150 miles from the seat of government in Fillmore. Mormons had begun to build a council-house in 1849 as the home of government for the state of Deseret; they may have seen the continuation of construction as using the funds for a civic building even though structures to accommodate the territorial government were to be built in remote Fillmore. Holeman, nevertheless, stated that this misappropriation of federal money showed "conclusively that base deception and fraud have been practiced on the general government" by Brigham Young. Finally, the Indian agent claimed that Young used part of the federal money to pay down church debts including ten thousand dollars to the merchant firm of Livingston and Kinkaid. Based on the report of Holeman and the earlier missives from Brocchus, Brandebury, and Harris, Congress declared that it would not grant further appropriations to Utah "until it shall be shown that the $20,000 already appropriated has been applied to the object intended."[102] The federal government displayed its power over the local population as it withheld precious funds from the territory in this episode. This early investigation into Utah affairs demonstrated a real concern, at the national level, that the cohesive Mormon group could not be trusted and was not acting in the best interest of the United States. The struggle over the disbursement of public funds was one facet of this early sovereignty question of national versus local authority.[103] In the end, the federal government did not approve of the officials' departure from the territory, and President Millard Fillmore eventually determined that these "runaway officials" were derelict in their duties.[104] As much as that was the case, the president did nothing to fix the problems in Utah.

While the former territorial officers' reports were being made available, other important documents on Utah and the Mormons were coming into the public consciousness. In the fall of 1849, U.S. Army Corps of Topographical Engineers captain John W. Gunnison served as second-in-command to Captain Howard Stansbury, a veteran civil engineer of more than twenty years in the federal government's topographical bureau, in an expedition to explore and survey the Great Salt Lake.[105] Additional orders for the Stansbury expedition directed the surveyors to examine travel routes from Fort Leavenworth to the Great

Salt Lake, observe conditions in Mormon settlements, assess their abilities to produce provisions including foodstuffs and iron, and determine their loyalty to the United States, something in question in Washington since at least the Polk administration. In addition, this first expedition to the Salt Lake was to identify the number, character, and condition of the Native peoples in the vicinity and select the best position for a military post "in comparison with Fort Hall, and in reference to the land route to Oregon."[106]

Their reconnoitering venture lasted approximately one year. It provided valuable intelligence for federal plans in the region. Published reports of the expedition offered the federal government—then trying to expand its influence westward—unique insights and new knowledge about the Great Basin and its peoples, including Mormons and their vision of sovereignty. The contemporary observations from Captain Stansbury, published in March 1851, and Gunnison, who published *The Mormons* in early 1852, raised warning flags about Mormon ideas of self-governance but did not indict Mormons as disloyal to the federal government with the same vitriol as the runaway officers.[107] Still, the two surveyors depicted the Mormons' displeasure with the territorial system that limited their autonomy.

Stansbury's report totaled 487 pages and concentrated on travel, trail exploration, tables of distances, and flora and fauna. Stansbury devoted minimal space to observations of the Mormon community. He further indicated that the domestic relations of the Mormons had been misunderstood. Whereas many believed Mormon plural marriage was "nothing more nor less than unbridled license of indiscriminate intercourse between the sexes," Stansbury explained that nothing "can be further from the real state of the case. The tie that binds a Mormon to his second, third, or fourth wife is just as strong, sacred, and indissoluble, as that which unites him to his first."[108] Though his report was generally positive about the Mormons, Stansbury's affirmation of plural marriage among the Mormons surely did little to ease the federal government's concerns about the large religious body in the Great Basin.

Gunnison's book provided far more detail about the Mormon people and their customs than did Stansbury's report. Gunnison commended Mormon dedication and achievement in a hostile environment and recognized their potential benefits to the nation as a supply center for westward emigration. Gunnison also described the character of the region's Native Americans and the substantial influence of Mormons on the tribes among whom they settled. In and around Salt Lake City there were Utes. There were Shoshones to the north, Crows to northeast, Sioux to the east, Cheyennes south and east, Paiutes and Goshutes to the west and southwest. According to Gunnison, "The different tribes of the Utahs are frequently at war with each other, and they have an eternal national war with the Shoshones. The Mormon settlements partially interpose between the two great tribes, exerting an influence upon both, and ensuring them a controlling power ultimately." He proposed that either the army or another federal entity gain a commanding influence over the Native groups by establishing a defensive fortification in the Green River basin, on Black's Fork, near Fort Bridger. A fort and Indian agency, Gunnison suggested, "on this neutral war-ground of all these tribes," would enable an agent to communicate with each, learn their plans, and play them off "against each other, and advantage taken of their animosities. If a humane policy is the proper one, then here is the place for a pacificator." A federal establishment at this strategic point, Gunnison added, would "control and aid the emigrant travel to Oregon and California, as the routes must fork in that section."[109] However, the current situation in Utah left the Mormons able to control this crossroads and the Indians in the region, Gunnison observed.

The Mormons also took on the subject of government in the Great Basin, or as Gunnison labeled it, "the controlling government of Deseret." According to Gunnison, the Mormons believed that the federal government owed them the privilege of self-government because of its failure to protect them in Missouri and Illinois in the preceding decades. The Mormons sought to exercise just laws over their own people, and of their faith, by persons of their own choice or recommendation. Non-Mormon governors and authority figures had historically treated them unjustly. Therefore, according to Gunnison, "to enjoy their own laws of a republican character, permitted and sanctioned by the Constitution, they are determined upon doing, and have the administration of them in their own way."[110] The surveyor described the governmental structure in Utah as formed on the model of a republican state and compared their demand for self-government to that of the American revolutionary generation's plight. The Mormons, he noted, thought it an imperial injustice to have the law enforced upon them "by *foreigners*," or people from outside their own community. He stated that the Mormons would "abide their time, in accession of strength by numbers, when they may be deemed fit to take a sovereign position."[111]

Gunnison warned that to enforce law over them by the power of arms would entail perpetual war or necessitate raising a standing armed force in the territory to assert national sovereignty, which would mean a large expenditure of national funds annually. Lastly, Gunnison cautioned that the Mormons would dread the "contaminating influence of an idle soldiery" among them and particularly upon their peculiar institution of plural marriage.[112] Ultimately, Gunnison advised government officers to allow the Mormons to govern themselves with representatives of their own choosing as the best method of pacifying the religious group and preventing a civil war with them.

While Gunnison's book indicated that Salt Lake City would serve overland travelers well, some overlanders left evidence of friction with Mormons during their brief layovers, conflicts and misunderstanding that revolved primarily around the Mormons' plural marriage societal structure. Even prior to the LDS church's public announcement of plural marriage in 1852, overland travelers through Utah on their way to California and Oregon observed the practice. Overlander Henry Sterling Bloom wrote in 1850, "I have no doubt but they practice polygamy here and perhaps some other evils equally as great."[113] Bloom, observing the third anniversary celebrations of the Mormon arrival in Utah, composed a letter to his wife, expressing his opinion that this place "would be great if not for this type of familial system and the repression of women."[114] At a church meeting on 11 August 1850, Henry Atkinson Stine, a traveler en route to California, listened as Mormon elder Orson Pratt gave a sermon in which he "cautioned the emigrants not to run off with the feminines."[115]

Though Stine thought the Mormon sermon strange, he remarked that the people were largely very friendly to and sociable with the emigrants. He observed that the Mormon women were quite beautiful and could "make a stranger almost forget that he is only at a resting place in the midst of a Desert country."[116] The halfway point to California, Salt Lake City attracted many non-Mormons and brought them into contact with Mormon society. LDS leaders made efforts to keep Mormon–non-Mormon encounters at a minimum for fear that the overlanders would either harm or lure away Mormon women.[117] This anxiety felt by male Mormon leaders was not unfounded, as Mormon women were violently and sexually assaulted in Missouri and were the lifeblood of the Mormon religious and social system.[118] Such panic about Mormon women would lead to future conflicts as the growing, and more permanent, presence of non-Mormon men in the territory became reality in 1854 and beyond.

From the runaway officials to overland passers-through in Utah, non-Mormons accused Mormons of setting up an un-American theocratic empire within the United States. Since at least the early 1840s, American public rhetoric feared the potential existence and growth of a Mormon empire. An 1842 *New York Herald* article described the Mormons in Illinois as actively "organizing their military and scientific, social and religious institutions, so as to form the centre of a great western empire."[119] Another 1844 article accused then–Mormon prophet Joseph Smith of "becoming more and more dictatorial and threatening towards the worldly powers."[120] In the 1850s cries against *imperium in imperio* focused on the Mormons' concentration of power in its ecclesiastical superiors and accused them of abusing popular sovereignty to protect plural marriage in Utah Territory. The Latin phrase *imperium in imperio*, meaning sovereignty within sovereignty, was frequently invoked to rhetorically cast the Mormons as a subversive group who owed utmost fealty to their leader subordinate to the interests of the nation.[121] The question confronting Americans was not whether sovereignty could be divided but by what means that divided sovereignty could be found legitimate and sustained in Utah. In the dual sovereignty of the American federal system, local governments were supposed to coordinate with the federal government. The states were not meant to be subversive entities within a supreme authority, but part of a federal system in which both governments were assigned sovereignty and authority in separate spheres as outlined by the Constitution. LDS church leaders organized a theocratic form of government and combined ecclesiastical with civil authority. Although its leaders were primarily Americans by birth and citizenship, outsider rhetoric and perceptions labeled them as "foreign" and their antecedents as "of the worst character" because they governed in a way that opposed the American system of republican governance.[122] In other words, Mormons were seen as a sovereign government independent of the authorized federal government. The internal sovereignty, that of the LDS church, was powerful and externally respected as strong enough to be dangerous to the sovereignty and constituents of the United States, particularly because it was growing in the very heart of the recently acquired U.S. public domain.

The federal government faced difficulties in imposing American republican government and culture over much of the populated areas of the Mexican cession. Both New Mexico and Utah territories, created in the Compromise of 1850, had significant ethnic and religious populations already residing within the boundaries at the time of their creation. New Mexico's struggle for statehood was lengthy because of a strong Hispanic population with heavy influence in politics, and because of its ethnic and linguistic divergence from the American mainstream. Difficulties attended the initiation of a republican government in New Mexico, as federal officials could not persuade the peoples therein to retire certain traditional political habits, particularly the concentrating of legal and political power in the hands of Catholic priests who were often the seat of power in a given community. The church and state had virtually been the joint rulers of New Mexico in the past.[123] Nineteenth-century writers used similar arguments about Utah Territory. Mormons and Catholics were not perceived as fit for republican governance. Newspapers and public officials often explicitly compared the two religions and associated them with other unpopular groups including blacks, Chinese, and American Indians. Mormons and Catholics were depicted as dangerous to American values of republicanism and morality, subversive groups with unscrupulous leaders and deceived members who unquestioningly obeyed the evil commands of their superiors.[124] In general, these "others" and their alien tenets impeded the transference of full sovereign capacity from the federal government in the nineteenth century.

Soon after the creation of Utah Territory and for the first half of the 1850s, eastern newspapers teemed with accounts about governmental and social affairs in Utah. The national press, based on the runaway officials' charges, the Gunnison and Stansbury reports, and stories from overland travelers, perpetuated an image of the LDS church embracing separation from the United States and attempting to take the West Coast by conquest for their new and independent empire.[125] For example, in November 1853, a Philadelphia *North American and United States Gazette* article labeled the Mormon "quasi-independent" government as an "*imperium in imperio* in the heart of the confederacy" that held the power to restrain non-Mormon emigration to the West. The author of this article feared the power that Brigham Young had as president of the LDS church and governor and superintendent of Indian affairs was contradictory to a republican form of government. The *Gazette*'s article also suggested it farcical to consider "any thing republican in a Mormon government wielded by Mormons themselves; or that citizens of other portions of the Union, not Mormons, can ever enjoy rest, peace, or equal rights among them."[126] The only method to diminish Mormon power was the immediate removal of the current governing system in Utah to better "govern the Territory in conformity with the Constitution of the United States."[127] Finally, the article provided an idea for controlling the territory. It was the same blueprint earlier suggested by Captain Gunnison and the same track that the president would follow four years later. It suggested the need to move a large military force to Utah where they "would be exceedingly useful," especially "in facilitating a transference of the Territorial power from the unsafe hands to which it has been so long, so imprudently, and so unworthily committed."[128]

Another newspaper, the *Raleigh Register*, carried a similar message that no alternative existed "but to establish military rule at a great expense to the nation at large, attended perhaps by bloodshed, or to continue the Government in the hands of the fanatical knaves themselves."[129] Having constructed the Mormons as antirepublican despots, newspaper editors and other public opinion makers recommended that the federal government control, as a *Raleigh Register* article suggested, "that *imperium in imperio*, the kingdom of the Mormons," because "their whole politico-religious system of the Mosaic and Mormon combinations is utterly at war with the constitution and institutions of the United States, with the moralities of civilized society, and is an enigma and stigma upon our 'model republic.'"[130]

The rhetoric of *imperium in imperio* was employed to depict a threat to the United States' expanding empire for liberty. Public discourse claimed that the Mormons sought to establish an independent or supreme authority within the jurisdiction of the United States, thereby constructing them as subversive and not as coordinate. Those rhetorical devices, coupled with federal officials' reports on Utah, trickled into public consciousness about Utah, while Congress and the nation debated popular sovereignty and the creation of Nebraska and Kansas territories. The political discussion of popular sovereignty would complicate the perceived defenselessness of national sovereignty in competition with Mormon control in Utah.

Talk of popular sovereignty permeated antebellum political discourse following the acquisition of land in the aftermath of the U.S.-Mexico War. As sectional concerns grew over the prospect of congressional prohibition of slavery from western territories and politicians discussed and debated the extension of slavery in new acquisitions, beginning with the well-known Wilmot Proviso, the specter of southern secession was prominently raised if Congress or the federal government should ever fully prohibit slavery's growth west. Congress eventually agreed to the Compromise of 1850 when popular sovereignty emerged as a guiding principle of balance on the slavery question. Many Americans, primarily those affiliated with the Democratic Party, believed that the territories were entitled to local self-government, similar to the position of the states in the United States' system of dual sovereignty. That prominent political party advocated the limitation of federal powers and the extension of local autonomy, particularly the power to decide territorial institutions outside of congressional interference, as a means to resolve the tension surrounding slavery extension and U.S. geographic expansion. However, expansion brought severe problems to the states' rights or local autonomy ideology. As a by-product of expansion, the federal government, vested with sovereignty over the territories by the Constitution and other foundational national laws, sought to extend its power to control new territories in the West and ensure that the peoples in those lands conformed to American political and social traditions.[131]

Popular sovereignty became the Democratic Party's doctrine for the right of local self-government to attempt to maintain balance in the nation over the potential of slavery expansion in new territories. Illinois senator Stephen A. Douglas influenced federal dealings with the trans-Missouri West until the outbreak of the Civil War. Introduced by Douglas, the Democratic railroad expansion and western settlement advocate, in January 1854 and passed on 30 May 1854, the Kansas-

Nebraska Act created the territories of Kansas and Nebraska, opened new lands for settlement, repealed the 1820 Missouri Compromise, and allowed settlers in the territories to determine their own domestic institutions on the basis of popular sovereignty. Douglas and the Democratic Party defined popular sovereignty as the right of the people of an organized territory, under the Constitution and laws of the United States, to govern themselves with respect to their own internal policy and domestic affairs and helped codify the doctrine in the Compromise of 1850 and the Kansas-Nebraska Act of 1854. Popular sovereignty seemed to exemplify the highest ideals of the founding of the American republic by providing the people of the territories the power to legislate and determine the local social institutions that best served their needs and interests, as long as those needs did not violate federal law and met with expanding the national ideal of republican governance. The doctrine also removed the assumption of territorial residents' political immaturity, contrary to the idea of need for political tutelage.[132] Connecting back with the original idea of popular sovereignty, this political maneuver indicated that the people in the territories, as the people in states, were the sovereigns of their particular geopolitical space and could determine their own domestic institutions in their own way. Even dedicated nationalists conceded that domestic institutions—which included, among other things, property, family affairs, education, morality, public health, and slavery—were the exclusive domain of the individual states. For the proponents of popular sovereignty it therefore made sense to allow territorial citizens the same privilege of deciding their local domestic institutions.[133]

Still, it must be remembered that popular sovereignty was a doctrine introduced to solve a particular political problem. Douglas wanted to get southern votes to organize Nebraska and Kansas territories. The intent of popular sovereignty was to lessen sectional tensions by removing the question of slavery extension to the West from a federal government that was responsible for deciding the fate of domestic institutions in the territories and provide an opportunity for the people to decide whether they would legalize slavery in newly organized lands. The idea of local decision-making on this omnipresent question, many politicians believed, would satiate the American public's divisions and keep slavery out of the halls of Congress. But the Kansas-Nebraska Act repealed the thirty-four-year-old Missouri Compromise line that protected slavery's expansion into the West. Slavery could now exist in any new western territory. Territorial citizens could also vote to forbid the institution in any new western territory. In other words, balance on slavery was no longer mandated.

Although territories were subject to federal organization as political entities, the doctrine of popular sovereignty opened the door for many questions that concerned federalism and the spread of certain peculiar domestic institutions in the new West. Stephen Douglas and his fellow Democrats pushed popular sovereignty to strengthen and maintain balance in the nation regarding slavery in the new territories, but other factors, such as self-governing capacity and plural marriage, soon found their way into the discussion on local autonomy.[134] In Utah Territory, for instance, the principles of decentralization, liberty, power, and republicanism were called into question largely because of the "foreign" marital structure that politicians and pundits believed spawned a government in favor of centralization, authority, and tyranny led by the leader of the LDS church. For example, during debates on the Kansas-Nebraska Act, John Clayton, a senator from Delaware and former U.S. secretary of state, questioned the judiciousness of the Compromise of 1850 that erected a territorial government for Utah and wondered if that bill and the Kansas-Nebraska Act which promoted popular sovereignty legally established and condoned slavery in all new territories and "a Mormon theocracy" that protected plural marriage in Utah.[135] Similarly, Massachusetts senator Charles Sumner tied Mormon Utah with the slave south when he suggested that the Mormon with his harem and the southern slaveholder were equally incapable or unworthy of having the right to local self-government.[136]

The Mormon settlers in Utah sought to fulfill their self-governing dreams. Settlers in other territories such as Oregon, Kansas, Nebraska, and New Mexico acted likewise. People in each territory demanded complete self-government, the popular election of all territorial officers, and the removal of the congressional veto from territorial legislation according to the dictates of the act. Despite the prevalent popular sovereignty rhetoric being espoused, and in accordance with its constitutional and legal mandates, the federal government did not take itself out of the territorial system. Rather, it placed itself in the thick of territorial matters and attempted to exercise control over the expansive federal territory. Political speeches, such as one by Iowa Democrat Augustus Hall, highlighted the problems that surfaced following the passage of the Kansas-Nebraska Act relating to sovereignty and power. Hall stated "that the people of the territories ought not to be permitted to form their domestic institutions in their own way," but that Congress retained the power to fashion and control their domestic institutions and dictate their fundamental law. The common confusion concerning popular sovereignty arose when legislators suggested, according to Hall, that Congress had "no more authority in this respect over the territories than we have over the states."[137] While the Mormons, like other territorial inhabitants, wanted to govern their local affairs according to popular sovereignty rhetoric, territorial governance remained firmly under the federal government's purview. That many lost sight of the latter fact—in their singular thinking to settle the explosive slavery question—caused problems for territorial management.

The territorial population of the far west in particular criticized and attacked the absolute control they perceived to be levied on them by the national government and saw in the Democratic Party's doctrine of popular sovereignty a long-overdue revision to broaden territorial self-government. Territorial self-government, the people thought, remained necessary to the cause of freedom and republicanism because it provided the power to elect from the community to serve their immediate needs and answer all domestic questions vested in the people.

Under the American territorial system, they believed themselves subject to colonial rule where the president could send people at his discretion to govern them.[138] Federal territorial administration, the Mormons and others in the West soon understood, meant that popular sovereignty offered less local control than it purported.

The Mormons wanted local autonomy to control every aspect of their settler colonial experiment. From Salt Lake City, the church leadership directed colonizing efforts within the Great Basin. They sent church members and families to found new towns, such as Carson Valley; to begin economic and business ventures, such as the mission to extract iron ore in southern Utah; or to convert and control regional Native Americans, as they attempted with the Southern Indian Mission. Church leaders, chiefly Brigham Young, designed these directives to extend the Mormon sphere of influence and protect their sovereignty. Their sovereignty resembled an authoritarian theocratic alternative to American republicanism. Brigham Young, for instance, stated that God allowed his people to establish a free and independent government in the Great Basin to correct the disorder and corruption they believed rampant in American politics.[139] According to this thought, God led the Mormon people to Utah to establish a new sovereign order and to control the local population, which to them superseded Native American claims to land and resources and led to campaigns of conquest under the guise of religious imperatives.

Despite ideals of popular sovereignty, the political situation merely served to bring into sharper focus the iniquities of the territorial system. Douglas based most of his arguments in favor of the Kansas-Nebraska Act on the achievement of self-government for the territories because he disagreed with the decades-old assumption by the national government that those who settled the western territories were incapable of governing themselves but must pass through a period of pupilage. The Kansas-Nebraska Act passage soon intensified public examination of the federal government's relationship with the territories and the nation. In the mid-1850s, many believed the act a democratic step forward toward enlarging the rights of American citizens in the territories, admitting them competent and equal to the duties of self-government. The characteristics of the Kansas-Nebraska Act were western and not southern, as it recognized the importance of the West and recognized that the people therein had certain rights.[140] Some regarded the bill as a great innovation in territorial government, but it did not circumvent the stipulations of authority set forth in the Northwest Ordinance and the Constitution. The ultimate sovereignty over the territories remained in the hands of the federal government.

During the congressional debates on the Kansas-Nebraska Act, Douglas received numerous letters from Latter-day Saints asking for assistance in their plight and in their efforts for total local self-government. Brigham Young reminded him of "our *strictly constitutional* domestic regulations" in the territories when commenting that perhaps conversation wandered from "the legitimate channel of the debate into episodical comments" upon Mormonism and domestic institutions in congressional debates surrounding the Kansas-Nebraska Act.[141] Young further elaborated that the Mormons should not be exempt from popular sovereignty and the enjoyment of self-government. In this regard, Mormons resembled other Americans who wanted to exercise local decision-making. They wanted to be sovereign in their assigned sphere and decide their domestic institutions for themselves. Similar to the Jeffersonian ideal of self-governing autonomy, the Mormons viewed popular sovereignty as an inherent right of the people to govern themselves. However, reports from territorial officials on the ground in Utah and the press viewed Mormon self-government not only as unpopular but also as an unacceptable and subversive *imperium in imperio*.

While Mormons vacillated, they ultimately wanted to be a part of the divided sovereignty in the American system, albeit under their own governance. They had come to understand and agree with the Democratic Party's ideal of popular sovereignty and sought to apply it in their own area. They understood the separation of powers because they had appealed to the national government for assistance against the Missouri government and had been rebuffed. They had learned that as a state, they would be free to elect their own officers and to regulate their own marriage practices because these were aspects of state sovereignty under the system of divided sovereignty. If they could not be a state, they wanted to exercise territorial popular sovereignty because of its promise of autonomy. Unfortunately for them, the national system of territorial government—with outsider officials appointed by Washington—virtually guaranteed that the Mormons would remain a part of the national agenda and that disputes between the Latter-day Saints and the appointed officials would remain national business as debates over popular sovereignty became more heated in the mid- to late 1850s.

Even while espousing local self-government and decision-making, the Kansas-Nebraska Act indicated that the federal government maintained ultimate authority in territorial matters.[142] Therein lay the ambiguity of antebellum popular sovereignty. The federal government controlled the appointing of territorial government officers including the governor, and it held superseding authority over territorial legislation, which meant that it legally could veto or inhibit local decisions made at the ballot concerning domestic institutions. The Democratic policy of local self-government purportedly removed the federal government from local choice and interest. However, national territorial law left the door open for the federal government to meddle with local popular will, often at the discretion of the nation's executive. Said more succinctly, federal jurisdiction over the territories remained and ultimately undermined the political philosophy of popular sovereignty. A series of encounters in Utah during the 1850s would demonstrate the role and strength of federal influence and power over the territories. Utah's history also revealed that balance in territorial affairs was difficult to maintain and largely dependent on the nation's executive.

2   Intimate Contact

Gender, Plural Marriage, and the U.S. Army in Utah Territory, 1854–1856

In the fall of 1853, Captain John W. Gunnison returned to the Great Basin. This time he brought a federal surveying crew to explore a proposed route for the Pacific railroad near the thirty-eighth and thirty-ninth parallels of latitude. Gunnison's survey represented part of the federal government's plan to connect the nation and integrate the West into the American empire for liberty by promoting white settler expansion to the Pacific coast. During this fateful exploration, Gunnison and several of his crew were murdered in Utah Territory. The murders prompted Secretary of War Jefferson Davis to send a small detachment of the U.S. Army to Utah as enforcers to assist in bringing the murderers to justice. At the same time, officers and troops sent missives and reports east that influenced national perceptions of Mormons' capacity for self-government. The presence of the army in Salt Lake City also challenged Mormon ideas and church policies regarding the "protection," or regulation, of female sexuality. Sexual relationships between soldiers and Mormon women occurred, and some female Latter-day Saints, one as young as thirteen, threatened to leave with the army in the spring of 1855. The army's temporary residence in the city struck at and revealed some fissures in the group's cohesion. Thus, for many Mormons, the army's very presence in their capital represented a major, albeit temporary, intrusion into local sovereignty.

In the 1850s, the United States experienced a burst of railroad growth as northerners and southerners alike poured energy and resources into railroad construction and expansion. While regional railroad growth exploded, the United States still needed a direct transcontinental link between its coasts and "a plan to network the nation." Networking the nation, according to transcontinental railroad promoter Asa Whitney, included the Americanization processes of settling new immigrants and other peoples in new lands in accordance with the Jeffersonian ideal. With distances between the Missouri River and the Pacific coast extending more than 1,800 miles in many places, politicians agreed that constructing a transcontinental railroad would accelerate settlement and expansion westward. Not only would the railroad bring American institutions to outlying regions of the country, but it would also supply provisions for army forts and strengthen the internal security of the nation. The strategic development of the railroad would create an efficient system of communication and transportation to bind together a transcontinental republic. Rail, which California senator William Gwin viewed as the primary tool of national unification, coupled with expansive overland roads and water transportation would link the interior of the nation to coastal metropolises and benefit the new west coast state.[1] The lack of internal transportation connections threatened to slow growth in California's trade, commerce, and material wealth. Separated from the rest of the states by thousands of miles of plains, deserts, and intimidating mountains, Californians felt isolated economically and from the protective power of the federal government.

By 1853 almost no one questioned the necessity of such a national project. That year Congress debated and approved measures to fund exploratory transcontinental railroad surveys. Much of the debate centered on sectional interests, which had long caused disagreements among politicians as to where to locate the transcontinental route. For example, Senator John Bell of Tennessee stated, "Every city and State in the Union has an interest in the location of this road; for it is destined by its more or less favorable point of connections with their respective railroads and other channels of communication, to affect all their commercial and social interests." Mormons too made efforts to coax the federal government into constructing a railroad through the territory in order to promote growth in the Great Basin Mormon population, to prevent the dangers adherents experienced in overland travel, and to expand their ecclesiastical mission. The people of Utah wrote petitions to Congress as early as 1852 in hopes that the federal government would build the national central railroad through the territory. In April 1854, Brigham Young continued to press for the railroad in Utah. He wrote to Stephen A. Douglas to inquire about his efforts to secure congressional support for a railroad to the Pacific. Young hoped that Douglas would support a route by the "Box Elder pass in the Black Hills, Bridger's pass in the Rocky Mountains, Timpanogos or Provo Cañon, &c, as the best line for the first Railway to be built from the Missouri to the Pacific." Whatever route that railroad would take, Young eagerly declared, "will be the very best one for the interests of Utah." As Senator John Bell predicted, everyone had a great interest in the location of the railroad.[2]

Planning for the transcontinental railroad initiated a new phase in federal-territorial relations. In May 1853, Secretary of War Jefferson Davis commissioned five surveys to explore possible routes for the proposed transcontinental railroad. In the years between 1853 and 1856, the army corps of topographical engineers undertook the monumental task of exploring, mapping, and describing the potential railway routes east and west from the Mississippi River to the Pacific Ocean and north and south from San Diego to Puget Sound. Davis chose Captain John W. Gunnison, a veteran of the 1850–51 Stansbury Expedition to the Great Basin, and a surveying crew to explore the thirty-eighth parallel through central Utah Territory. The Gunnison exploration was to provide a faithful description of the nation's interior country and convey to the federal government "a true picture of the country explored" for the practicality of a Pacific railway route.

Gunnison's party started from St. Louis in June 1853, proceeding west across Missouri before heading southwest through Kansas along the Arkansas River. In present-day Colorado, the party proceeded northwest through Cochetopa Pass and eventually reached Sevier Lake in west central Utah in October 1853.[3]

It was here that Gunnison felt "an unusual feeling of security." Upon his arrival in Utah, Gunnison had learned of a recent quarrel between Pahvant Utes, led by their chief Moshoquop, and some white emigrants passing through the area that had resulted in several deaths, including the chief's father. Based on intelligence he received at the territorial capital of Fillmore, Gunnison believed that all difficulties with the band had been resolved. Under the impression that the area was safe, Gunnison decided to set up camp on the north shore of Sevier Lake. The captain then took several men from his crew to explore and survey the lake and its surrounding landscape.[4]

On the frosty dawn of 26 October 1853, a group of Pahvant Utes murdered Gunnison and seven of the men in his command at their campsite northeast of the lake along the Sevier River. According to the official report of the incident, a volley of rifle bullets and a shower of arrows engulfed the camp, disrupting the morning silence. Captain Gunnison stepped out of his tent, calling to the Pahvants that his crew meant no harm. Still, the Pahvants rushed into the camp. Some of the surveying crew escaped on horseback, but the band killed eight, including Gunnison, whom they "pierced with fifteen arrows." Gunnison's second in command, Lieutenant Edward G. Beckwith, stated that the Pahvant band attacked the camp to avenge the deaths of their fallen brothers, particularly Chief Moshoquop's father.[5] The murder of Captain Gunnison would prove to have continuing ramifications on Great Basin Native peoples, Mormons, and the federal government's management of Utah Territory.

Beckwith assumed command of the crew after Gunnison's death and directed the second phase of the survey in the spring of 1854. The second phase was a survey of the Stansbury-Bridger Pass along the forty-first parallel route from Fort Bridger to California. After exploring the Wasatch Mountains, Beckwith turned west to locate a route across the Great Basin and into California. It proved to be an enormously successful operation. Beckwith located two suitable passes through the mountains and into the Sacramento River valley. Beckwith's exploration surveyed the route eventually taken by the first transcontinental railroad, which Beckwith recommended the government pursue. Unfortunately, he neglected to include cost estimates for the railroad over that route, and his report was virtually ignored in the evaluation of these initial surveys. In addition, the Gunnison-Beckwith expedition explored and mapped Utah Territory to the greatest extent to date. The reports of the Gunnison-Beckwith survey provided the federal government and army with more detailed knowledge of the Great Basin's topography, as well as its peoples and settlements, complete with information on mileage figures, watercourses, and structures within settlements.[6]

It did not escape the federal government's attention that the heart of the Mormon community existed on the main transcontinental traffic-ways of the nation. Two of the proposed transcontinental railroad routes bisected Utah Territory proper, which ranged from the forty-second to the thirty-seventh parallel. Even the southern route favored by Jefferson Davis and others passed through the Mormon "state" of Deseret, which claimed a religious, cultural, and political sphere of influence that included a colony at San Bernardino and a visible presence at San Diego. Mormons had become a major concern for the U.S. government. Salt Lake City's position in the Great Basin lay nearly directly in the middle of the most central line across the continent at the veritable crossroads of the West. Salt Lake City, since its founding, linked important overland trails where overlanders could purchase new animals and refit their wagon trains, but it remained largely isolated from federal infrastructure, particularly army forts. Additionally, it lay not far distant from Fort Bridger, a private supply fort and the main diversion point for nearly all routes to California,

Oregon, and Utah for emigrants traveling from east to west. The principal Mormon city also served as an oasis on the north-to-south route from New Mexico. While the nation's eyes turned west, the accelerated growth of railroads in the north and south and the opening of new territories to settlement created an uncertain future for both sections with the future of slavery a central issue. In such a divisive climate, the project to build the transcontinental railroad stalled amid sectional disagreement in the 1850s. Even still, the Mormon capital's geographic importance grew exponentially as the federal government moved to secure its political and cultural claims to the American West in the years to come.[7]

In the end, the most immediate result of the Gunnison-Beckwith survey was the government's determination to investigate and prosecute Gunnison's murder in Utah Territory, which would influence the course of federal-territorial relations for the next four years. Though locating the route of the great transcontinental railroad held the attention of the nation, Secretary of War Jefferson Davis and others in the federal government wanted answers and justice for the murder of Captain Gunnison and members of his crew in Utah. In the spring of 1854, Davis ordered Brevet Lieutenant Colonel Edward J. Steptoe to lead 175 soldiers, accompanied by roughly 150 civilians—a much larger contingent than any other federal body that had previously visited Utah—to California via Salt Lake City. Steptoe's detachment was to assist the federal investigation into the murders. Davis also tasked Steptoe's command with examining the possibility of constructing military roads from Salt Lake City to California.

Since the formation of Utah Territory, federal officials desired an army presence for protection, not just for themselves but also for travelers and to aid in exercising federal authority. In his official letter of declination of office, Samuel Stokely, a lawyer and former congressman from Steubenville, Ohio, elected not to accept an appointment as a supreme court judge in Utah because of the lack of federal troops in the vicinity. His letter of 14 July 1852 argued for support for a platoon of federal troops to escort the federal officers to and remain in the territory. He had received information that the territorial officials for Utah Territory, appointed to replace Brocchus, Brandebury, and Harris, were expected to go out with some troops from Fort Leavenworth. However, when no army escort was provided, Stokely declined his appointment in Utah. Based on the previous officials' reports, Stokely did not seem to think he could execute his duties as a federal judicial officer in the territory without the backing of the army.[8] As Stokely's case suggests, the federal government found it difficult making and replacing federal appointees for Utah. The gaps in non-Mormon federal representation left the Mormons relatively free to govern themselves. The next wave of federal appointees came in 1854 as did a contingent of the U.S. Army, both of which shook the foundations of Mormon sovereignty. While the Steptoe military detachment was not meant to remain in Utah as the permanent presence Stokely and others desired, it was a new federal presence to aid in enforcing the law. But it also brought Mormons and federal officers into intimate contact to a level not yet experienced by the religionists in Utah.

The military expedition reached Salt Lake City by the end of August and quartered in the city until the spring of 1855. During this brief sojourn, Steptoe, Second Lieutenant Sylvester Mowry, and others sent reports to Washington and points east that detailed the problems they observed in Mormon society and local government and law enforcement, which lent credence to popular ideas of Mormon sovereign incapacity.[9] At face value, the Steptoe expedition was simply a military patrol to deliver horses and mules to a military outpost in Benicia, California, and ensure that the murderers of Gunnison and his crew would face federal trial. However, the presence of authoritative non-Mormon men and migrants in Salt Lake City soon left the Mormon hierarchy and many Latter-day Saint congregants unsettled.

When the army arrived in Salt Lake City, Mormon fears intensified. They believed that the presence of outsiders would disrupt their familial system and that they would be unable to prevent or manage sexual encounters that might lead to the removal of Mormon women from Utah. Mormon women were vital and their removal would have weakened Mormon manhood and patriarchal authority. The Mormon familial structure was built on plural marriage, or the marriage of one man to more than one woman. In the 1840s and 1850s Mormon leaders believed that God commanded some of His servants, whom their prophet and other male leaders believed themselves to be, to marry additional wives. As a part of their developing theology, Mormons instituted "a latter-day recapitulation of the ancient Patriarchal age," with a new family pattern that restored biblical patriarchies as demonstrated in the histories of Abraham, Isaac, Jacob, and Moses.[10] The Bible and the Latter-day Saint canon argued that while God had chastised humans for adultery, fornication, and divorce, He had, at certain times, inspired man and allowed and blessed His servants for engaging in plural marriages.[11] The plural marriage doctrine encouraged Latter-day Saint obedience to God's commands while it fostered increased commitment within families as it taught the church's principles of eternal life and exaltation. In other words, marriage and family relationships were necessary for salvation. They were crucial for an individual's opportunity to achieve an exalted state; plural marriage cemented the belief that those willing to live the principle in faith and obedience would receive heavenly blessings in their mortal lives and in the hereafter.

Plural marriage was a Mormon doctrinal matter, but it had a social impetus and social implications in that it engendered a closed and hierarchal society. As the historian Kathryn Daynes has argued, "The act of accepting plural marriage was itself a dramatic sign of loyalty to the community's leader because entering plural marriage caused considerable anguish.... In Nauvoo, those taught about plural marriage were asked to accept the belief that this type of marriage was necessary to achieve the highest glory in heaven."[12] In its very essence, the doctrine of plural marriage placed loyalty to the church and its prophet above all else.

While some sources suggested that Joseph Smith knew about the principle of polygamy as early as 1831 and may have married a plural wife in the mid- or late 1830s, the practice was not generally adopted until 1841 and not made public until 1852.[13] During the 1850s, plural marriages reached their peak; approximately half of the entire Utah population lived in a polygamous family.[14] Despite the common belief of non-Mormon Americans that Joseph Smith instituted and Brigham Young continued the practice because of lustful and licentious desires, Mormons considered the doctrine a divine revelation and not a personal proclivity.[15] Mormons held up plural marriage as a religious principle protected by the Free Exercise clause of the Constitution. Mormons, like Catholics, considered marriage a religious rite rather than a civil one, and they governed the institution through ecclesiastical rules. As an article on plural marriage in the Latter-day Saint periodical *The Seer* stated, "Have any of the States or Territories a constitutional right to pass laws 'prohibiting the free exercise of the religion' which the Church of the Saints conscientiously and sincerely believe to be essential to their salvation? No: they have no such right."[16] In fact, plural marriage in Utah Territory did not legally conflict with national marriage laws of the day.

The moral aspect of marriage in the western territories, however, was contested and would lead to a clamoring for a national law against plural marriage. Mormons openly acknowledged their sexual relationships and multiple marital unions, whereas the open secret among the rest of American men was the widespread existence of adultery or fornication, especially in eastern cities. American men, however, tried to keep up appearances and keep their extramarital relations out of sight. Mormons did not, and non-Mormons considered plural marriage a form of "notorious adultery" and an "outrage upon decency and morality."[17] Mormon plural marriages and the social structure spawned by them differed from the society based in the nineteenth-century American ideal of companionate marriage, which was founded in more of a mutual dependence between spouses versus the unchallenged superiority and power of male authority in the home.[18]

For a people trying to build their sovereignty on a theocratic structure that was supported by a social order tied to plural marriage, women were crucial and the literal and spiritual life force of Mormon religion. LDS theology entreated members of the faith to "protect" their families, especially women because they contributed a great deal to further the church, its goals, and men's spiritual progression. Contrary to the image that would emerge of plural marriage as a haven for the unrestrained lust of men, Mormons strictly regulated sexuality both in and outside of marriage. For Mormons, marriage was not a civil union sanctioned by the state, but rather a religious covenant inextricably linked to Latter-day Saint belief in post–earth life exaltation. Thus, sexual relations had to take place within the confines of marriage.[19]

Female sexuality at this time, in Utah and in American society, was largely about male power and identity. Mormon men constructed their masculinity and manhood first around the priesthood, which intimately tied men to women through marriage. The priesthood, believed by Mormons as the power for men to act in God's name, was endowed on all worthy, righteous, and upright male members of the LDS church and was the central pillar of Mormon masculinity. The man who could marry multiple women in 1850s Utah, because of religious piety, financial well-being, or other prerequisites often held a higher status within the Mormon community. Although all "worthy" men could hold the priesthood and could approach church leaders requesting permission for additional wives, only certain men were appointed to marry multiple women. A man's marriage to multiple women became a marker of power, representing a higher status, higher authority, and stronger masculinity within Mormon society. Plural marriage and its priesthood ties outwardly demonstrated the Mormon belief that their alternative marital system facilitated the highest degrees of heavenly exaltation for both men and women. Ultimately, Mormon masculinity and patriarchal power derived much from marital relationships with women.[20] While priesthood served as a marker of Mormon manliness, women also held the priesthood in conjunction with their husbands through marriage, which made plural marriage a crucial extension of access to priesthood authority for women. Men and women were seen as having complementary roles in the Mormon belief of marriage, as each shared in the highest blessings of the priesthood through marriage covenants.[21] Threats to those marital relationships threatened Mormon male power as well as religious blessings for both men and women.

The LDS church held that women were indispensable to propagating the religion and growing the white population of Utah Territory. The church argued that without the contributions of Mormon "sisters," much of the building up of the church would have faltered during the move west from Illinois, as well as during the migrants' first decades in Utah. Many Latter-day Saint women had to assume positions as heads of households while their husbands were away proselytizing. They had to support themselves and their children, and it fell to them to teach their sons and daughters the "principles of righteousness." In their prescribed roles, Mormon mothers bore little difference from "republican" mothers charged with educating their children to be worthy, loyal citizens of the United States.[22]

In innumerable ways, women proved crucial to Mormon group cohesion and strength. Mormon women participated in community work through the Relief Society. The church and women themselves encouraged faith-based benevolent activities, such as feeding the hungry, clothing the poor, and tending to the sick, activities that were perfectly acceptable for women to pursue outside the home in antebellum America. From early in the settlement of Utah, Mormon women reestablished the Relief Society in several wards in the Salt Lake valley. Although all the Saints were relatively poor, the women helped those in greater need. In particular, one group of women organized to make clothing for Indian women and children, while others coordinated to feed, clothe, and provide other materials to Native peoples.[23]

With this background, it can be understood why Mormon men feared the presence of and competition from outsider men. The Mormons' inability to successfully police intimate encounters would deal a heavy blow to their power. In Utah, soldiers' sexual encounters with Latter-day Saint women became a key battleground to diminish Mormon sovereignty in the territory. Potential sexual encounters also incited Mormon men to police future relationships with outsiders as part of their efforts to control their familial, cultural, and governing system. From the pulpit, church leaders cautioned women to stay away from army men. Furthermore, they admonished men to protect the chastity of women and fight the "defilers of the innocent," who were considered the "worst of felons." These efforts to police women's movements and sexuality led to a political encounter between Mormon men and the army that influenced national discussions of popular sovereignty in Utah Territory.[24]

Roughly four years before the Steptoe expedition, Howard Stansbury's expeditionary crew made Salt Lake City its home base for a year. Stansbury's outfit was much smaller, consisting of just eighteen men. Steptoe's command, on the other hand, with its civilian camp followers consisted of approximately three hundred men. Whereas LDS church leaders could monitor the movements of Stansbury's small crew, regulating any intimate contact between Mormon women and Steptoe's men proved much more difficult. At the outset, the Mormons and army men had good relations. However, when intimate encounters between army men and Mormon women occurred, that relationship deteriorated.[25]

One army officer, First Lieutenant Sylvester Mowry, left detailed documentation of his intimate encounters with the Mormons. In a series of letters to his friend Edward J. "Ned" Bicknall in Providence, Rhode Island, Mowry boasted about his relations with the Latter-day Saints and his endeavors to seduce Mormon women. Once Mowry arrived in Salt Lake City, he wrote to Bicknall. "All you have heard about polygamy is true," Mowry explained, "and a damned sight more Brigham Young has a great number of wives or whores as you please." Mowry estimated that Young had fifty wives and other church leaders and members held wives in proportion to their rank in the society's hierarchy. Regarding the political structure in the territory, Mowry commented that Young was "an absolute Dictator here." At an unidentified meeting, Young apparently told Mowry and his compatriots that they would receive the best treatment as long as they kept their hands off the women. According to Mowry's letter, at a church meeting held shortly after the army contingent arrived in the Salt Lake Valley, Young exhorted his female followers to keep themselves pure by avoiding interactions with the new men. Mowry stated that Young and the Mormon leadership quickly grew troubled by the troops and were afraid the soldiers "were going to f–k [their] way through the town." "Perhaps we shall," Mowry exclaimed. On the one hand, Mowry's letter reveals the Mormon leadership's attempt to assert its manhood to shame Mormon women and by intimating that any sexual relationship between Mowry's crew and the women would debase their womanhood. On the other, Mowry demonstrated his disdain for both Mormon men and women by referring to Mormon wives as "whores" and insinuating that his men would have sex with Mormon women indiscriminately—and, one could argue, without the women's consent. Mowry's ideas and writings raise the specter of him and his fellow soldiers engaging in seduction or rape of Mormon women as a tool of warfare against a social system that he, and Americans generally, despised. In any case, competing ideas about manhood were at stake—one rooted in patriarchal control over women, the other in a Lothario-like "conquest" of women.[26]

Mowry's lengthy first letter to Bicknall expressed his affections for one of Brigham Young's daughters-in-law, Mary J. Ayers Young, whom he described as "the prettiest woman I have seen yet."[27] He commented that her husband, Joseph A. Young, had gone on a mission to England and Mowry made known his intent to seduce and sleep with Mary. He also suggested that many women, including Mary, dissented against the plural marriage structure and that there were "a great many disaffected persons" in the territory, women in particular. Mary Young apparently told Mowry that "Salt Lake City needs only to be *roofed* in to be the biggest whore house in the world."[28] Some Latter-day Saint women and visiting soldiers apparently saw the Latter-day Saint society the same way. Second Lieutenant LaRhett Livingston likewise perceived the city as a veritable whorehouse.[29] Mowry complained that to "see one man openly parading half a dozen or more women to church with as many more 'confined' at home is the devil according to my ideas of morality, virtue and decency. It is just that any man who can afford it can attach a whore house to his own for private use and they do it." Mowry further lamented that the "big men of the Church are all rich and getting richer. The lower classes poor and doing no better fast. They pay one tenth of all property owned or made into the Church. If any man becomes troublesome he is ordered off on a mission—and he has to go. Brigham's son, husband of the pretty woman I mentioned, raised hell so he was sent off to arrest the scandal of his debaucheries and so presently he is a missionary." Mowry's letter detailed his earliest observation of the power of church leaders and Mormon missionary character. His words confirmed his belief in the need to rescue Mormon women from the "whoring" practice of plural marriage. Ironically, Mowry sought to "rescue" the purity of these women by sleeping with them. Mowry's moral sensibilities did not preclude what many Americans considered adultery and fornication (sexual intercourse with women he deemed whores). Ultimately, Mowry's claim to moral superiority designated women as sexual objects of men.[30]

In a later letter to Bicknall dated 31 December 1854, Mowry reflected on his efforts at sexual intimacy with the governor's daughter-in-law over the three months since his last letter. He affirmed that his affair with Mary "went on quietly but swimmingly for several weeks." According to the lieutenant, the two met privately, until a "damned infamous report was circulated in the city that I had been 'caught in the act' by several persons." Mowry lamented that he had not achieved his salacious ends when the governor learned of the tryst. "Here was hell," he told Bicknall.[31] Mowry's reputation was "ruined among the females or rather among those who have the care of the females. They think me *dangerous* and I can't get a woman to look at me scarcely except in the ballroom." Mowry was being watched, by whom he did not exactly know, but he knew that he could never again be alone with Mary. Nevertheless, his letter continued with more intrigue. "With the greatest difficulty," Mowry boasted, "I persuaded a pretty girl and a great favorite with us to let me take her home from Judge Kinneys party and when I got her into the carriage she laid down in my arms let me feel her bust &c. &c.—showing that the difficulty is not with the women but with their keepers."[32] After discussing his cavorting in poker and gambling, Mowry further lamented the Mormon male control over women. He closed his letter to Bicknall by stating, "We have every reason to believe that the authorities and the well judging part of the community are favorably disposed towards us and have done and will do every thing in their power to make our stay pleasant—except in the case of admitting us quickly to the society of their women. In this they are inflexible and perhaps wisely so for gallantry and polygamy are congenial associates."[33] Mowry indicated that Mormon men intended to maintain their patriarchal gender order by policing Mormon women and preventing non-Mormon male access to the women.

The situation of Mowry and Mary Young created a stir and an atmosphere of distrust developed between Mormon men and army men. Brigham Young became "raving mad about it," so much so that Colonel Steptoe considered the territory unsafe for his lieutenant. Mowry indicated that Governor Young sent him word that if he took Mary, the Governor "would have me killed before I could get out of the Territory."[34] The lieutenant believed Young a man of his word in those matters and he feared for his life. Young felt beleaguered by this encounter with federal troops, and set out to use Mowry as an example of the supposed threat of troops "carrying off" Mormon women.[35]

In an effort to both protect and display his own manliness, Young aggressively struck back at Mowry's attempt to seduce a woman of Young's own family.

By the time Mowry departed Utah in April 1855, on orders from Colonel Steptoe to record and calculate distances from Salt Lake City to Los Angeles via San Bernardino and the Old Spanish Trail, he had found a new Mormon woman to "enjoy" in intimate company. The lieutenant again wrote to his friend in Rhode Island, focusing his thoughts on a young girl named Amanda Matilda Tanner. Mowry described Tanner, whom he called "Tilly" and his sexual replacement for Mary Young, as a "rather tall prettily formed" girl of fourteen years old. He told Bicknall:

> "Tilly" wanted to go to California. One fine afternoon a certain pair of horses and buggy conveyed her out of Salt Lake City to my camp. I followed in a day or two—and one night we went to bed together—and have slept together ever since.... Tilly's father raised hell at first of course. Swore he would blow somebody's brains out, &c &c. I hear he is pacified now and is going to send me her wardrobe.[36]

That a Mormon woman, or girl in this case, wanted to go to California was not new. For example, Martha Monks, a plural wife of Parley P. Pratt, became disillusioned with Mormonism's plural marriage system, particularly after her first child died, and left with a group of men headed to California in July 1849. While men lauded the plural marriage system and most women supported it, others found the opportunity to leave both exciting and desirable; California offered an enticing alternative to Utah.[37] "More than half of the women want to leave with us," Sylvester Mowry claimed as the army was about to depart Utah for California. Mowry's braggadocio was overblown but did represent a segment of Mormon society that was not satisfied with life in Utah and looked for an escape.

Mowry was not the only soldier to test his sexual prowess on Mormon women. According to the first lieutenant, every one of the army men excepting Colonel Steptoe and Major Reynolds had at least one Mormon woman with whom they had relations, and Assistant Surgeon Horace R. Wirtz, had three: a mother and her two daughters. Mowry wrote, "The mother cooks for him and the daughters sleep with him."[38] At this same time, Quartermaster Rufus Ingalls was accused of abducting thirteen-year-old Rachel Nowell from a Latter-day Saint family. When she returned to her family in Salt Lake City, Ingalls wrote a letter of apology to Nancy Butterfield, Rachel's mother. In that letter, Ingalls stated that he did not have sexual relations with Rachel, though the Mormons who accused him believed he had. Ingalls wrote, "Your daughter returns to you as pure in every respect as when she left the City."[39] While the truthfulness of Mowry's claims is difficult to assess, his letters and the other recorded attempts of seduction by army men demonstrate the sexual objectification of Mormon women and the repercussion of sexual relationships that resulted in some women leaving the Mormon community. This sexualization and use of sex to lure away women struck at the heart of Mormon masculinity and group cohesion. Mormon men could not control or protect the Mormon women in this episode and therefore viewed the Steptoe detachment's stay in Salt Lake City as a federal injustice and an attack on local sovereignty.[40]

Mormon men battled to prevent the soldiers from gaining sexual access to women—a struggle that they believed informed the way the army visitors perceived their self-governing capacity. Lieutenant Mowry represented the type of man that Mormon male leaders dreaded in their society. As a result of intimate relations between soldiers and Mormon women, Heber C. Kimball and other church leaders spoke about the perils of fraternization that would supposedly bring destruction to the peaceful city. Mormon leaders vigorously defended their marital and sexual system through efforts at policing women, arguing that such actions would retain community strength and preserve local autonomy. A member of the U.S. Army, LaRhett Livingston, observed on 7 February 1855 that the soldiers formed "a part of the subject of their discourse, nearly every Sunday & they have gone so far as to tell all their females, that if they went with us, they should be cut off from the Church & eternally d—d."[41] That same day, Sylvester Mowry wrote again to his friend Ned Bicknall. In that letter, Mowry stated that Heber C. Kimball and other church leaders "gave the women hell—for associating with those not of the Church." Mowry also reported that Kimball encouraged the women to keep their *"things"* sacred and warned that if a Mormon "married a Gentile she committed adultery."[42]

In a mid-February 1855 sermon, Brigham Young publicly addressed relations between Mormons and the army. Like Heber C. Kimball and other male church leaders, the church president used rhetoric that characterized potential sexual encounters between Mormon women and army men as a strategic policy or tool of the federal government to exert continued power and control over Mormon local institutions. He warned women about keeping company with non-Mormon men. He vociferously stated his opposition to "a man's coming here as an officer, with a bit of sheep's skin in his pocket having some great man's name to it, and beginning to set up his rules of discipline for the people, and saying, 'I am a gentleman, I am a high-minded gentleman; can you tell me where I can find a woman to sleep with me to-night?'" Young painted the soldiers as self-important seducers of women. He further deplored the establishment of gambling shops and the heavy drinking and carousing done by the visitors. He claimed that these men stirred up strife by engaging in these pursuits and "then lecturing the people on morality, wishing them to become like other communities," while simultaneously trying to seduce Mormon women. The Latter-day Saint prophet admonished men to be prudent fathers and husbands to watch over their daughters, wives, and sisters to remind them that they should have "no business with strangers." Young declared that he would "use up" any man who intruded upon the chastity of his family and all "the congregation said Amen."[43]

Young believed that because of the church leadership's stance to "protect" women and family, the non-Mormons said "God damn the Mormons, they are opposed to the Federal Government, because they will not let us sleep with their wives and daughters." The Mormon leader opposed "such men" declaring that he was "after them with the barbed arrows of the Almighty.... Such characters may cry, 'Aliens, aliens; the Mormons are all hostile to the government,' and they may cry it until they are in hell." Young requested that his people be able to choose their own leaders, as a republican government allowed. He also declared the Mormon intent to live their religion despite what he viewed as "odious colonial oppression" coming from Washington. He further affirmed his love of country and of the Constitution and claimed that he would not permit corrupt men to "walk these streets with impunity, and if that is alienism to the Government, amen to it. The Constitution of the United States we sustain all the day long, and it will sustain and shield us, while the men who say we are aliens and cry out 'Mormons disturbance' will go to hell." The Mormon leader simultaneously employed victimization rhetoric with defiance.[44] Young's aggressive response to the territorial system that he perceived to be colonial and meant to enforce control over people that were capable of governing themselves demonstrated his conviction in Mormon self-government and sovereignty.

The words emanating from the church's leadership revealed a settler complaint of imperial interference in local affairs. Young's rhetoric tapped into the language of imperialism and described the Mormons as a settler society attempting to resist its colonial overlords. At the same time, their rhetoric defied American imperialism by espousing autonomous sovereignty outside of the prescribed forms of governance. It demonstrated to the non-Mormons who heard it a competing sovereignty that would not be subordinate to the federal government or its officers.

The Steptoe expedition represented the first major intrusion into Mormon sovereignty. As the army left the territory in April 1855, as many as one hundred Mormon women, some of whom were as young as thirteen years old, joined them.[45] This appears to have been a male contest over the female body lost by Mormon men during the army's temporary intrusion in Utah. It appears that way primarily because of available source material. Mormon women's voices are silent on this encounter. Accounts from Mary Young, Amanda Tanner, or any other Mormon females who departed the territory are scant, do not survive, or have not been located. Mormon women's records from the early 1850s are scarce and most of those that are available are reminiscences given decades later.

When the army arrived at Fort Benicia, California, news of the troops' sojourn in Utah reached the east coast. The *Brooklyn Daily Eagle* wrote, "Brigham Young, complains very bitterly of the troops who were quartered at Utah last winter. It appears that they created quite a rebellion among the women, and when they left for California, carried off a number with them. Brigham vows vengeance and death to all who shall in future make any such demonstration towards his female flock. The President had better send a regiment out there with instructions to court the women. It would very soon break up the nest. Get the women away and the men would not stay long."[46] If the army could infiltrate Mormon society through sexual conquest of the women, as had Steptoe's command, federal authorities could ultimately reduce "those Turks of the desert" to "the Christian standard of one wife apiece." Steptoe's troops, according to this newspaper, had discovered the best method to divide and conquer the Mormons. Indeed, the months-long encounter in Utah underscored the importance of women to Mormon society. Conversely and colored by their experiences with an army quartered among them, the Mormon community stiffened its resolve to protect its social traditions, to guard its way of life, and to preserve its adopted homeland.[47]

Americans in the antebellum era paid close attention to sex, marriage, and the family, particularly as they constructed ideals of manhood.

American men defined their masculinity not as much in relation to women, but in relation to other men. Masculinity was largely a homosocial enactment with parallel and competing visions of masculinity that coexisted in American society. American men tried to control their sexual urges, and they displaced their fears about gender norms and sexuality onto others. While much of the historical discussion on American manhood and sites of sexual anxiety concern blacks, Indians, immigrants, and women, Americans equally perceived Mormons as threats to the sexual order. Mormon men and plural marriage were considered an affront to American masculinity.[48]

Political, legal, and cultural authorities in the United States endorsed and aimed to perpetuate nationally a singular and particular marriage model that in no way embraced plural marriage. In the Great Basin, anxiety over marriage emerged because the region was undergoing rapid colonization, expansion, and settlement. Since 1852, when the Church of Jesus Christ of Latter-day Saints publicly announced its practice of plural marriage as a central tenet to its religion, the nation at large felt its new territorial lands were in danger of usurpation at worst, or at best, unfit to produce the seedbeds of republican governance to which the monogamous marriage and family were fundamental. Public authorities—in the case of the territories, the federal government—set the terms for marriage. Public affirmation becomes the key here because neither the public writ large nor the federal government condoned alternative models to monogamous marriage primarily due to the understanding that good republican government emanated from the monogamous family structure. Though the majority of Mormon men did not engage in plural marriage, American popular opinion stigmatized the people of Utah as polygamists.[49]

In practicing plural marriage, Mormon men lived in open defiance of Victorian morality by not embracing the era's ideal of sexual self-control. In that way, non-Mormons portrayed Mormon men as bestial and hypermasculine, in the negative sense, and even women as indulging their sensual propensities without restraint. Medical experts, reformers, and lay counselors of the time advocated that sturdy manhood might bend or break under too-frequent expenditure of semen. The carnal desires required control to harness energy toward productive activity. Kimmel writes that advice books such as George Peck's *The Formation of Manly Character* (1853) and Timothy Arthur's *Advice to Young Men* (1855) addressed men's need for self-control over passion, temptation, and masturbation, which would sap their vital energies, make them more prone to disease, and leave men's bodies effeminate, making them unfit for the larger tasks of, among other things, administering government. Since men constituted the electorate and ran government at all levels, they needed the energy and mental capacity to undertake such great responsibility. In other words, according to this logic, overindulgence in sex or the expenditure of male energies through masturbation was not only deviant but also destructive to American politics and society. Mormons were assumed to be sexual libertines that were savage or barbarous men when compared to the ideal form of the self-controlled American man.[50] Contemporary observers cited the destructive tendencies of a plural marriage familial system as leading to overindulgence in sexual activity (men having coitus with multiple women), which in turn hampered the Mormon capacity to self-govern.[51]

While Americans advocated self-control over sexual desire, Mormons believed that adding more wives checked the male sex drive. Plural marriages permitted men to exude their sexual passions within marital relationships. Under Mormon priesthood structure a man could not commit adultery because religious law allowed him to have multiple wives, or sexual partners. Mormons compared their "sanctified" marital structures and views on sexuality to that of the broader American society, and found the latter problematic. Men were supposed to control their sexuality, but often found outlets in the form of prostitutes or extramarital affairs. Mormons challenged this restrained manhood that reified a monogamous model that seemed to permit men to engage in extramarital relations. They argued that promoting plural marriage as a system allowed every woman the chance to marry and produce children, while it forced men to keep their sexual relations within marriage. A simplistic reading of this formulation reduces women's desires to becoming wives and mothers, and men's to engaging in coitus with multiple females. However, Latter-day Saints argued that such desires were in keeping with their religious values and largely for procreative purposes.[52]

Americans did not accept the Mormon arguments in favor of plural marriage. Public concern focused on the supposedly unrestrained sexuality of Mormon men and the moral and physical degradation of Mormon women in the "strange system" of plural marriage. The 1851 book *Fruits of Mormonism* summed up these sentiments. It stated:

> The system of polygamy makes many of the females very unhappy—makes them wretched in the extreme. . . . The secret miseries many of them endure are untold. Sometimes they are shamefully neglected by their husbands. Especially is this the case with first wives, after other wives, younger and more beautiful are taken into the household. Those wives who can make themselves most attractive and agreeable to their common husband, usually receive the greatest share of his attentions. He cares so little about them, and feels so little respect for them, that they are obliged to resort to various stratagems, to secure any share of that esteem to which wives are entitled from their husband. In short, the Mormon women are degraded and subjected by the system to a state of mental and physical slavery more abject and perfect than attaches to the inmates of a Turkish harem.[53]

This account identified and expressed the otherness, the supposed "Oriental" nature of the Mormon familial system. An imagined carnal ravenousness made Mormons into non-American "others." Such views depicted sister wives as concubines and the Mormon plural household as a harem. Writers, journalists, and politicians constructed similar images of black men as beastlike in their sexuality and bent on ravishing innocent white women.[54]

Popular rhetoric that imagined the Mormons as exotic others more closely aligned with "barbarous" Muslims than with Christian Americans. Arabs and "Arabo-Islamic figures" featured prominently in the racialist imaginations of midcentury writers and the intellectual elite, and so drawing analogies between Mormonism and Islam, especially their plural marriage family structure and deceptive and despotic traits, proved convenient to attempts to depict Mormons as oddities and anti-American villains.[55] For example, an article in the *New York Times* commenting on the growth of Mormonism in Utah stated that the United States owed its Christian civilization, stability, and refinement "to the institution of marriage," though it decried the Mormon experiment of plural marriage as "one of the most offensive of the barbarisms of Asiatic life." Print culture imagined Mormon men imprisoning women as sex slaves during a time rife with debate over racial slavery. The image of Mormon men as human traffickers of white women highlighted their lust and sexual insatiability. The Mormon promotion of a society based on multiple marriage partners provided outsiders a rationale for believing that the men enslaved the women, and proved to the nation their unchecked sexual desire, which was often tied directly to the notion that Mormons were incapable of governing themselves. Some periodicals began advocating for Congress to pass legislation prohibiting plural marriage in Utah and preventing the Mormons from exercising government at all.[56] Congressman Caleb Lyon of New York similarly railed against territorial legislation regarding the rights of polygamists and strongly argued that Mormonism was more suitable to the Orient than to the United States. A people that practiced plural marriage displayed a tendency toward barbarism. "Point me to a nation where polygamy is practiced," Lyon orated, "and I will point you to heathens and barbarians." The Mormon plural marriage structure, Lyon declared, "seriously affects the prosperity of States, it retards civilization, it uproots Christianity." Ultimately, Lyon argued that Mormons were not properly Christian Americans and could not be entrusted with sovereignty because of plural marriage.[57]

Based on unspecified U.S. Army intelligence, the editor of the *Christian Advocate and Journal* also questioned the Mormons' ability to exercise sovereignty by portraying Utah's inhabitants as inhuman, savage, and barbarous. That publication condemned the Mormon system as one that "trampled" on women "to the utmost depth of degradation." The commentary continued:

> The United States are nursing on their territories a brood of serpents, which will soon be too formidable to be crushed. We say nursing, for we have not only permitted them to occupy our land, but have countenanced them by actually appointing the chief of the tribe governor of the territory, and thus investing his denomination with the authority of our sovereignty, and one of their dirty clan has been permitted to sit in Congress. We have been entirely patient under their insults. We have permitted them to drive away our officers, and at this day they reign in undisputed sovereignty over a large and fertile territory of this Union, and are impudently inviting the vagabonds of all countries to make their home there. . . . It is impossible that they can have any loyalty to the American Union, and it is shameful that they should have ever been recognized as a lawful community.

This article made explicit connections between Mormons maintaining their current level of sovereignty and possibly gaining more rights as an equal state in the Union, something that evoked in that writer a profound horror and trepidation. The imagery in the article also spoke to the ways in which eastern newspapers depicted Mormons as "savages," "serpents," or "barbarians." Specifically, attempts to analogize Mormons to "tribes" and "dirty" clans allowed the press to depict the Latter-day Saints as dangerous and unfit for assimilation or incorporation into the American body politic. That Mormons engaged in plural marriage and supposedly "trampled" on women made them even more dubious as future republicans in a period when public discourse emphasized restraint in all matters sexual.[58] For the *Christian Advocate* writer and many contemporaries, Utah presented more than a religious and social aberration. It existed as a political threat to the integrity and growth of the United States because of the plural marriage structure that bolstered its theocratic organization of government.[59]

In March 1855 *Putnam's Monthly* published an article written by political theorist Francis Lieber that asked the interminable question: should the United States admit Utah into the Union? Lieber argued that monogamy was fundamental to American civilization and morality, and was not just a question of localism. Lieber believed that the Constitution did set moral limits on localism.[60] He theorized that plural marriage led to "the patriarchal principle, and which, when applied to large communities, fetters the people in stationary despotism, while that principle cannot exist long in monogamy."[61] Lieber highlighted the local versus national issues at hand in this territorial matter, which, in the era's political climate and discussions of popular sovereignty, had an "inescapable connection to slavery."[62] The *Putnam's* article presented a fictitious scene where the Mormons knocked at the gate of the nation's capital asking admittance. Leaders of a Mormon delegation discussed the issue through a "key-hole" with congressmen when the Speaker of the House asked about the Mormons' republicanism. The Mormon response acknowledged the constitutional guarantee that each state would have a republican form of government, and suggested that the church-run theocracy was republican because "every year, Brigham, appointed by the Lord, asks the Mormons whether that appointment suits them" to which they all replied yes. Lieber indicated a preference to "vote for the admiration of a piratical State into our Union, than allow such a crew to call itself a sister State." Perhaps as a veiled reference to Barbary pirates such as Turks, Moors, and Arabs and captivity narratives popular in the federal era, Lieber appears to have been trying to pose a stark dichotomy regarding the limits of American democratic inclusion. To demonstrate that the Mormons were so opposite to American national identity the writer suggested that a body of Turkish or Moorish pirates would fit into the Union better than would a body of Mormons.[63]

The fictitious scene continued as the Speaker queried about the Mormon marital structure and its connection to government. The Mormons responded: "You call marriage an element of civilization, do you? Why, sir, we swim in this element. You call the family the basis of all political society? We make families as plenty as chicken-coops." The fictional Mormon likened the women to animals, or creatures, which brought men greater power and glory, while simultaneously calling their society progressive and expansive because it did not limit marriage, family, or society to establishing wedlock between one man and one woman. This made for a mixed government, which the Mormon character called the best form of government over republicanism. The scene ended with the Speaker suggesting to the Mormons that Congress would take their request under consideration.[64]

Lieber then described what he thought Congress would consider in a statehood campaign. Since Latter-day Saints did not promote a republican form of government, Utah, as then constituted, could never become an equal state. The *Putnam's Monthly* article emphasized that the Mormon polity was not a republic, as it had no division of power and that one man held all of the power. The Mormons could not govern themselves as a republic because their society was a hierarchy. Furthermore, the structure of Mormon families under plural marriage was condemned as enslaving women and instituting a hierarchy among males, all factors which placed it in direct opposition to monogamy and political liberty. Should that society in Utah be admitted to the status of an equal state in the Union? It absolutely should not, Lieber declared.[65] Many more publications and politicians would ask and answer this same question in the same way in the years that followed. What emerged was a consensus. Mormon Utah certainly did not deserve to be recognized as a state in the Union, and it could hardly be privileged with local autonomy in the territorial system according to the dictates of popular sovereignty. Instead, greater federal supervision over the Great Basin population was advocated.

Also unfolding in Utah in the middle of the decade was a growing colonization effort directed by the Mormon leadership that had ramifications for federal understanding of territorial affairs. In Carson Valley, an area approximately 575 miles away from Salt Lake City at the far western boundaries of Utah Territory that bordered California near present-day Carson City, Nevada, animosity between Mormons and non-Mormons occurred. The friction focused on plural marriage as the non-Mormon whites in the valley called for assistance from federal congressional committees to combat Mormon influence. In January 1854, the Utah Territorial Legislature created Carson County. This act established the county as Utah's Third U.S. Judicial District and gave it one vote in the Utah Territorial Legislature for the territory's far western region. Many non-Mormons had settled there to take advantage of the trade opportunities and provide lodging and accommodations to overland travelers to California. Since their arrival in Carson Valley, non-Mormons had clamored for separation from the Mormon-dominated Utah territorial government because the seat of government was some five hundred miles to the east and was not sensitive to the local needs of the settlers. With no established government, the non-Mormon settlers drafted a petition to Congress asking for a distinct territorial government for western Utah. They also drafted a petition to the California legislature asking the Golden State to annex the region to its east for judicial and governmental purposes. Congress or California's legislative body did not act upon these petitions, but they raised the ire of Utah governor Brigham Young.[66]

After the territorial legislature established Carson County in 1854, Young appointed Orson Hyde, a member of the church's Twelve Apostles; George P. Stiles; and some thirty-eight other Mormons to a colonizing mission to Carson Valley. The legislature made Stiles the presiding judge, and Hyde was appointed the county probate judge. In September of

1855, they held county elections; all but one officer elected was Mormon. The *Daily National Intelligencer*, a Washington DC–based newspaper, reported on these activities and intimated that the political authorities at Salt Lake City established a colony in Carson Valley "obviously with a view to throwing enough Mormons into it to control the county." The *Intelligencer*'s report further described the "gold placers" on the Carson River and its tributaries and the influx of mining interests that the area would draw. However, the report revealed, "all this is in Utah, and these miners are subject to the laws and decrees of Brigham Young and his coadjutors. Can these people get along with the Mormons? They want a separate territory organized for them, and we think it will have to be done sooner or later." The non-Mormon residents in Carson Valley fumed at the realization of Mormon domination in the county and began drafting new petitions to Congress to encourage annexation to California or the creation of a new geopolitical entity.[67]

The annexation attempts by non-Mormons in Utah presented another challenge to Mormon sovereignty. In the winter of 1855–56, they again called for the congressional committees on territorial affairs to give expedient attention to the propriety of annexing the valley, or a larger western portion of Utah Territory, to the state of California. One of the petitions declared that the non-Mormon citizens of Carson Valley were already closely allied to or identified with the interests of California and further explained that they remained in a detached situation from the seat of government of Utah Territory, "being some eight hundred miles" through a "barren desert and Indian country thereby rendering it quite impracticable for the citizens of these vallies to receive the benefits of Legislative operations necessary to the prosperity of any portion of country." The laws of the territory did not meet the Carson Valley citizens' approval either. The laws that supported a plural marriage family system and discounted those not of the Mormon faith struck them as wholly inequitable. The operations of the territorial government and system of justice, they said, lay in the hands of Mormon leaders and gave them opportunities "to severely injure the party who may chance to fall with their power." In many ways, they were correct in asserting that Mormons and their rule of law dominated the territory. However, it is not clear what injuries might have befallen non-Mormons at the hands of the church.[68]

Men and women in Carson Valley, like those in most other places outside Utah, saw marriage as a sacred arena where man and woman practiced the Christian virtues of love and self-denial in establishing monogamous families as the fundamental unit of American society and governance. The non-Mormon women of Carson Valley sent their own petition to Washington. The female petitioners focused on plural marriage. They declared that there were few Mormon families in the valley "and yet Orson Hyde, one of their leading Elders, and the present Probate Judge of this County has had the audacity to have one of his '*Spirituals*' brought here, and introduced to us, as his wife, expecting, of course, our intercourse and sociality with the same." The women found the idea deplorable. They further announced "the avowed intention, both of the Mormons here, and at Salt Lake, to have families from Salt Lake, emigrate here, the ensuing season, sufficient to manage the *Political* and *Religious* interests of the Valley; and then we, the '*Gentile*' minority may submit to reside, and rear up our daughters, in a place where the female society is composed mostly of '*Spiritual Wives.*'" The women feared that they would be forced to leave their pleasant homes in the valley or be forced to live in an atmosphere defiled by the "despotic" Mormon system. The Carson Valley women earnestly prayed that Congress prevent these alternatives and attach the adjoining valleys to California, where, they stated, "the Mormons very well know, their *peculiar* laws and tenets will not be tolerated." In a later debate on antipolygamy legislation, Representative Thomas Nelson of Tennessee stated, "The existence of such an institution as prevails in Utah, under the protection of the laws of the United States, is an outrage upon the moral feelings of our whole population. It is, as I conceive, an insult to our own wives and our own daughters, and the wives and daughters of our constituents." Using the same logic that free-labor advocates used against the institution of slavery—that slavery debased and affronted the paid laborer—it is telling that Representative Nelson, like the Carson Valley citizens and others, believed that plural marriage was an affront to American men and women. Many arguments against plural marriage used similar rhetoric that plural marriage debased the monogamous couple, American institutions of domesticity in particular and politics more generally. It was a central tenet to arguments against Mormon self-government.[69]

Carson Valley citizens in general did not approve of the laws of the territory. They considered them unconstitutional and beneficial only to Mormons. What the Carson Valley constituents described was a subversive *imperium in imperio*, or sovereignty within sovereignty. The internal sovereignty of the church was seen as powerful and strong enough to be dangerous to the non-Mormon residents. The territory being the sovereign possession of the nation had within it a group of people owing the utmost fealty to their church leaders and subordinating the interests of the national group to the authority of the internal group's leader. Non-Mormon settlers continued to agitate for federal intervention and a separate territory with a separate government for the remainder of the decade. Carson Valley citizen William M. Ormsby wrote to Stephen A. Douglas, then serving as chair of the Senate's committee on the territories, declaring the immediate urgency for organizing separate territorial governments. Suggesting that about six thousand inhabitants with families have "no protection of either life or property" with no possible means of communication with California and residing to their east, Ormsby noted, "We have for neighbors a people that are not only declared enemies, but also open enemies of the General Government." Ormsby, like his predecessors, feared Mormon sovereignty.[70]

These sentiments were similar to eastern newspaper accounts about Utah's "quasi-independent" government and the threat of "*imperium in imperio* in the heart of the confederacy" that would prevent any non-Mormon from enjoying "rest, peace, or equal rights among them."[71] These petitions to Congress coupled with reports to officials on territorial governance and public rhetoric all pointed to the question of Mormon sovereignty in Utah, particularly as it pertained to plural marriage. The Mormons' alternative familial structure and religious monarchy threatened national interests because their presence jeopardized the expansion of monogamy and American sovereignty at a critical geographic crossroads in the West.

3 Missionaries to the Indians
Mormon and Federal Indian Policies

Indian policy shaped both outside perceptions of Utah and the realities of life within the territory itself. During the 1840s and 1850s, two groups of people—Mormons and agents of the U.S. federal government—invaded Great Basin indigenous homelands and employed competing philosophies of Indian affairs. Both groups sought to control the Native peoples: the federal government to protect emigrant routes and encourage the expansion of white settlement in the West and the Mormons to fulfill religious imperatives and foster peace between the growing settler and indigenous populations. Indian affairs in Utah brought jurisdictional conflict between the local population and the federal government over federal Indian laws, particularly the Trade and Intercourse Act. Non-Mormon observers of Utah's Indian affairs also informed national perception about Mormon-Indian relations. The Mormons governed Indian affairs in a way that asserted and demonstrated their local sovereign capacity; they forged their own Indian policy in order to benefit them in their relationships with Great Basin Native peoples. However, this autonomy where Indian policy was concerned often came at the expense of federal officials and directives. Federal authorities in Washington received numerous reports that Mormons had gained influence over the territory's indigenous population at an unacceptable cost: the violation of federal Indian policy and the gross dismissal of federal sovereignty. The enforcement of federal Indian laws necessitated and provided a legal justification for a permanent military presence in Utah. These facets are essential in understanding the federal-territorial relationship and the realities of exercising sovereignty in Utah. They also foreshadow and illuminate the complex origins, execution, and impact of the Utah War.[1]

Upon their arrival in the Great Basin in 1847, the Mormons settled on Ute, Paiute, Goshute, and Shoshone lands and disrupted an already precarious natural environment by adding new competition for fish, game, water, timber, and other resources.[2] Mormons continued to pour into the area and to displace the Indians from their lands, to diminish the natural fish and game populations, and to replace the natural vegetation with non-native crops. At the same time, the Ute chief Wákara sat atop a lucrative trading and raiding economy that specialized in human trafficking as far west as California, as far east as the Great Plains, and south into Mexico.[3] Leaders and members of the LDS church initially accepted as settlers in the Great Basin by Utes and Southern Paiutes altered Native American economies by curtailing and legislating against the trade in horses, child slaves, and tribute between Utes and Mexicans. Nevertheless, at the outset, many Native peoples chose to affiliate or engage with Mormons and develop friendly relations with them. Utes viewed Mormons as stable and permanent trade partners, while the Paiutes saw their new neighbors as potential protectors against raiding bands of Utes and Shoshones.[4] In the 1850s, however, Mormons legislated against the Indian slave trade, even as the white population grew and tensions between the settlers and the indigenous population, particularly the Utes, increased.[5]

In the midst of intermittent, occasionally intense conflict between indigenous groups and Mormon settlers, LDS church leaders set up their own Indian policy outside of and competing with federal administration. In 1850, Congress agreed to the legislative package that created Utah Territory and placed the Mormons in the Great Basin under a territorial government. However, the first wave of federal officials—who had been assigned to establish vital components of that territorial government—left quickly after their arrival in 1851 because of growing conflict with the Latter-day Saints. The federal government did not approve of their departure from the territory, and President Millard Fillmore determined that these "runaway officials" were derelict in their duties.[6] Still, the reports these early officials sent to Washington became the basis for federal knowledge about Mormon Indian policy.

"We know but little," commissioner of Indian affairs Luke Lea reported in November 1850, "of the Indians in Utah, beyond the fact that they are generally peaceable in their disposition and easily controlled."[7] Upon his arrival in Salt Lake City in 1851, the federal Indian agent Jacob Holeman wrote to Lea that he found Brigham Young and his fellow Mormon Indian agent Stephen B. Rose on an expedition to the Indians. According to Holeman, Young and Rose had taken with them "several hundred dollars' worth of Indian goods as presents, for the purpose, no doubt, of conciliating the Indians and getting their permission to extend his settlements, thus making use of his office as superintendent, and the money of the government to promote the interest of his church." Holeman observed that while the Native peoples of Utah were generally friendly towards whites, he recommended that some arrangement be made with them by which their rights as well as those of the federal government should be distinctly understood.[8] The federal agent suggested that "no Mormon should, officially, have anything to do with the Indians" because, as he stated, "every effort will be made by the Mormons to prevent the government from peaceably extending her laws over the Territory." Holeman believed that early on Mormon Indian policies in Utah stood in stark contrast to the interest and expectations of the federal government. Young and the Mormons, according to these early outside observers, were not properly teaching the Great Basin's indigenous peoples about federal authority and law. Rather the Mormons were expending federal funds to ingratiate themselves with the Native population at the literal and figurative expense of the federal government. Other federal officials would make similar allegations. Despite the many Mormon-Indian conflicts that represented the reality on the ground and the agency of the region's Native peoples, it was the Mormons, according to Holeman, who "easily controlled" the Great Basin's Indians.[9]

Young was the federally appointed territorial governor and superintendent of Indian affairs. With this authority, he could license trade and intercourse between whites and Indians. In other words, Young was responsible for governing white-Indian relations. On 20 October 1851, Young wrote to President Millard Fillmore to inform him "that upon Indian affairs I have never received any instructions." According to Young, Holeman—the territorial Indian agent subordinate to Young—left immediately after arriving in Utah for business in Wyoming and had not yet returned. Meanwhile, Henry R. Day, the Indian subagent, had come to Utah with other federal officers, but, as Young presumed, referencing the runaway officials, "upon meeting with Mr. Holeman they all returned to the States together."[10]

Brigham Young thus represented the only federal presence in the territory, though he was seen as privileging Mormons and not as an agent of the federal government. With unclear instructions about how to execute federal Indian policy and mounting conflict between his people and regional Native bands, he implemented an Indian policy that would benefit the white population of the territory, who belonged almost entirely to the church that he led. Though the federal government had purview over Indian affairs, especially in its territories, Young made decisions to respond to the immediate needs of the people on the ground, primarily those of his coreligionists. In so doing, he pitted his local authority against the federal government.

Mormons were connected with Native peoples both by their religious mandates and in the American popular imagination as early as 1830 and the introduction of the Book of Mormon. That book portrayed the Native Americans, also known as Lamanites to the Mormons, as people destined to join with the Mormons and be instruments in God's hands to prepare for the second coming of Jesus Christ.[11] Early members of the LDS church identified American Indians as descendants of the Lamanites, a people described in the Book of Mormon as the descendants of the biblical Joseph of Egypt and members of scattered Israel.[12] Indeed, the title page of the Book of Mormon stated that the book was written particularly "to the Lamanites." The historian Richard Lyman Bushman characterized the general awareness of the religious doctrine shortly after its publication: "Almost as frequently as the book was called a 'gold bible' it was called a history of the Indians."[13] The Book of Mormon "is not just sympathetic to Indians; it grants them dominance—in history, in God's esteem, and in future ownership of the American continent."[14] Interpreting Indians as the rightful possessors of North American lands was anathema to the way Americans viewed their historical trajectory and future progress.

The concept of Indians as worthy and capable of salvation equal to white Latter-day Saints existed in early Mormon thought as those church members worked to teach Native peoples Mormon doctrine in hopes of "redeeming" them and ushering in the Millennium. Mormons were deeply concerned with Native salvation and had, since the church's inception, made efforts to reform, convert, and bring American Indians into their religious fold.[15] In fact, the church's first formal proselytizing mission was to the American Indians in present-day Kansas in 1830–31.[16] Such missionary efforts were seen as subversive in Missouri during the 1830s, where active Mormon proselytizing among Indians created anxieties among non-Mormons about their intentions.[17]

In February 1831, Indian affairs agent Richard W. Cummins wrote to William Clark, the famous explorer of the Louisiana Purchase territory who had by then become superintendent of Indian affairs over the St. Louis agency, that two Mormon men went among the Shawnee and Delaware to instruct them in religious matters. Cummins opposed the Mormon efforts to preach to the indigenous groups. "The men act very strange," he wrote of the Mormon missionaries; "they say they are sent by God and must preach, they have a new revelation with them, as their guide in teaching the Indians, which they say was shown to one of their sect in a miraculous way." But this was a different type of religion than Cummins had known. It was not the mainstream Protestant Christianity that was more familiar and comfortable to him, and it was the Mormons' overall vision for the Indians—based on what he called a strange new revelation—that frightened Cummins. The Indian agent may have also learned of the Mormon missionaries teaching doctrine relating to Native redemption and their potential succession of power in America that could have been viewed as advocating a potential Mormon-Indian alliance. Cummins found the Mormons so problematic that he "refused to let them stay or go among the Indians until they obtain permission from you or some of the officers of the Gen'l Government who I am bound to obey. I am informed that they intend to apply to you for permission to go among the Indians, if you refuse, then they will go to the Rocky Mountains, but what they will be with the Indians."[18] The Mormon missionaries did not obtain a license from Cummins or from Clark to legally preach to the Shawnee and Delaware. That they had delivered unlicensed messages to Native peoples foreshadowed a major issue between federal authorities and the Mormons.

Isaac McCoy, a Baptist missionary who preached among the American Indians in the areas around Independence, Missouri, and present-day eastern Kansas during the early 1830s, provided a statement in late 1833 after the Mormons had been physically forced from their lands in Jackson County in November of that year. McCoy stated, "The Mormons, as I suppose from information, came here so ignorant of laws, regulating intercourse with the Indian tribes, that they expected to pass on into the Indian Territory, procure lands of the Indians, aid them in adopting habits of civilization, and attach them to their party. At the western line of Missouri, they were arrested by the proper authorities of government. Frustrated in this design, they located in this [Jackson] county." McCoy pointed to the Latter-day Saint violation of federal Indian law, in particular the Trade and Intercourse Act. The missionary further explained that he and his white neighbors "strongly suspected [the Mormons] of secretly tampering with the neighboring Indians, to induce them to aid in the event of open hostility; for myself, I could not resist the belief that they had sought aid from the Indians though I have not ascertained that legal evidence of the fact could be obtained."[19] McCoy accused the Mormons of seeking aid from the Indians west of the Missouri River during the Jackson County struggles and revealed his belief that the Mormons sought to establish a martial alliance with Indians against non-Mormon whites. McCoy's statement and Cummins's 1831 letter provide early examples of the white and federal fear of the potential nefariousness of a Mormon-Indian association.

Americans, including Missourians, considered strange the notion that the United States was the Promised Land for American Indians who had been enlightened by Mormon theology when they largely insisted that the federal government remove Native peoples from their homelands and onto reservations of the worst land.[20] From the early 1830s through the 1850s there developed a formulaic response among federal officials and other white Americans to Mormon-Indian relations: the Mormons were strange with a religious message to the Indians different from that of "mainstream" Protestantism. That strangeness engendered fears of a grand conspiracy and a nefarious plot that the Mormons interfered with federal efforts to control and "civilize" Indians and that the two groups were allying with one another against white America. Indeed, some Mormons came to believe that American Indians would become the "Battleaxe of the Lord" in wreaking vengeance upon Mormon enemies.[21] The Mormon expulsions from various Missouri counties and eventually the entire state, and their exodus from Nauvoo, Illinois, and the later Utah War were all events notably marked by claims that Mormons were combining with Indians to wage war against the government and Protestant white America. The prophesied and providential destiny of the Indians to Latter-day

Saints "helped to shape the next several decades of the Latter-day Saint experience."[22] To be sure, Indian relations informed Latter-day Saints' efforts in Utah and shaped non-Mormon perceptions of them.

Mormon Indian policy in Utah Territory remained concerned with Native redemption and salvation. Brigham Young, however, simultaneously had to deal with political and economic realities that conflicted with the spiritual obligations to convert Native peoples.[23] The relationship between Mormons and Great Basin Indians vacillated between the Mormons' religious motivations to redeem them and armed confrontations that emerged from the clash of cultures, the disruption of Native trade networks, and competition over the area's limited natural resources. Hostility and bloodshed as much as benevolence and conciliation characterized Mormon-Indian relations in Utah, due primarily to the Mormon paternalistic notion of white superiority.[24] A *Deseret News* article perhaps summed up the relationship best: "The events that have transpired, since the settlement of 1847, have brought the settlers and Natives of Utah into frequent and extended intercourse under very diverse circumstances; sometimes pleasant, and mutually beneficial—at others quite the reverse."[25]

Above all, Young attempted to secure the safety of his religious followers and pursued the best methods to obtain that end. These particularly included peaceful overtures such as giving gifts of food, clothing, and other supplies to regional Native Americans. This policy was eventually encapsulated in the idea that "it was cheaper to feed the Indians than fight them."[26] As part of their efforts to secure peace and promote their own safety, LDS church leaders sought to implement a regulatory governing program to make the region's Native peoples dependent upon them.

Though couched in peaceful and co-beneficial terms, Brigham Young unilaterally conducted a twofold Utah Indian policy to make the region's indigenous population one with or dependent upon the Mormons. Young and his followers insisted on their autonomous capacity to control indigenous policy and moved for local internal control to manage the population—Mormon and Indian—without federal interference. Young, as Utah Territory's superintendent of Indian affairs, articulated a broad-based program to bring about Native dependence on and acculturation to Mormon lifeways through proselytizing efforts.

In December 1850, Brigham Young called on approximately 120 people to establish an iron manufacturing enterprise in southern Utah. This venture, known as the Iron County Mission, brought Mormons and Indians into close proximity and provides a microcosm of the precariousness of Mormon-Indian relations. Led by Mormon elder George A. Smith, this group eventually settled in Parowan in January 1851 and went to work building roads and mills. Smith left a journal of his experiences detailing the business of colonization and his encounters with Indians. He observed the industriousness and agricultural capabilities of the area's natives.[27] On 15 January 1851, Smith recorded a meeting with Ute chief Peteetneet and seven others of his tribe. He described them as "quite friendly," informative on the movements of Wákara, and "glad that we were settling in Little Salt Lake Valley." A Mormon gave the Utes some tobacco and together they smoked, which pleased them both.

Over the next several weeks, the Mormons received many Native visitors and traded with them.[28] Smith met with the great Ute chief Wákara in early February for the first time and then again in early March. At the second meeting, the two embraced each other with hugs and handshakes, smoked together and "conversed freely in a very friendly manner," though Smith acknowledged the conversation was "carried on by signs and guess work." The two dined together, and Smith took away from their interaction the belief that Wákara desired to build his house among the Mormons and teach his children to work. Smith described the Ute leader as "very much a gentleman in manners and one of the most intelligent Indians I ever saw. No doubt the master spirit of the Utah Nation."[29] Smith gave Wákara and Peteetneet foodstuffs and clothing in a harsh winter. In return, the Ute chiefs taught Smith and other Mormon elders about the land and brokered positive relations with Tauguant, the chief of the Paiutes, after another Mormon, Isaac Brown, was killed by members of that tribe. According to Smith's journal, Wákara told Smith "that he had visited all the bands of Indians in this country. He told them that the Mormons were good people and that if they settled on any of their lands, they must not molest them or disturb even a brute of theirs."[30] Wákara and Peteetneet made expressions of friendship, and Smith reported that Wákara preached "a Mormon sermon to the Pihede Captain, told him he must be honest, must not steal anything, must not disturb a brute belonging to us. He must go and get buckskins and bring them here and trade for knives, shirts, etc., but not for powder. When the weather got warmer he must be baptized and he would be good all the time, and that he must tell all the Pihede far and near that they must be honest and not steal anything from us."[31] Mormons assisted the Utes to develop friendships first and then entice them to become members of the church. Wákara, the powerful leader of the Ute tribe, considered Mormon assistance during the harsh winter of 1850–51 a major service and tangible proof of their friendship.[32] Shortly thereafter, the Ute leader and 126 Ute men and women formally became Mormon converts by baptism, an act that they probably viewed as an expression of friendship and alliance.

Nevertheless, peace and positive relations did not last. Misunderstandings about Mormon military drills and disputes over trading and the disappearance of different horses and cattle soon poisoned Mormon-Indian relations in Parowan. Mormons complained that Indians killed their draught animals and hampered their business enterprise. By August 1851, the Mormon leadership in southern Utah passed a resolution prohibiting the Indians from working in their agricultural fields, even though George Smith indicated that such a resolution interfered with the council of Brigham Young to employ the Indians that were willing to work. Iron County mission leaders altered the resolution, but many Mormons tried to distance themselves from Native peoples regardless of Young's decrees.[33]

Missionary efforts among the Indians by Mormons were successful to a degree, but conflict was inevitable.[34] Gaining and maintaining influence over Native peoples was a task easier said than done: the 1853–54 Walker War and other conflicts and skirmishes attest to the inability of the Mormons to establish unfettered control over indigenous groups who were trying a variety of methods to navigate a new and changing situation that left them in a dire competition for resources and something of a reliance on the settler population for life's necessities. Mormons and Native Americans clashed over Indian slave trading and the region's natural resources. Conflict erupted in a regional power struggle known as the Walker War. Surely informed by his dual role as governor and superintendent of Indian affairs, on 19 August 1853 Brigham Young issued a proclamation regarding the state of warfare. He declared that the Ute Indians were in a state of open war that wreaked havoc on the Mormon settlers of the territory "at every opportunity, killing them, driving off their stock and burning their mills and dwellings." In order to promote public safety, and preserve the "*property* and *lives* of the people from hostile Indians," Young called on the territorial militia, the Nauvoo Legion, to stand in a state of readiness to march to any point at a moment's notice.[35] He alerted Utah citizens to remain prepared to defend themselves, their families, and others when necessary. The proclamation demanded that no one "whether resident, or non resident," traffic arms, ammunition, or lead, or render "to any Utah Indian, any aid, shelter, food, or comfort either directly or indirectly." As the territory's superintendent of Indian affairs, Young revoked all licenses to trade with Indians and ordered rigid compliance with this prohibition.[36] With resources scarce in Utah, Young's order to withhold foodstuffs and other goods forced the Utes and other groups to turn away from diplomatic relations and toward raiding for their survival.

In the early fall of 1853, Utes killed settlers; raided the towns of Fillmore, Manti, and Spring City; and stole herds of cattle. Mormons and Utes committed brutal murders against one another in and around the town of Nephi.[37] That same fall, a non-Mormon wagon train passing along the southern route killed several members of the Pahvant band of Ute Indians. Captain John Gunnison's surveying crew reached its camp on the Sevier River in south-central Utah in the midst of this warring and was tragically killed by the Pahvant band in retaliation for the earlier act.

During this spike in violence, the Latter-day Saints renewed their convictions to preach, convert, and control the local Indian groups. On 6 October 1853, Brigham Young called more than twenty men as he sanctioned the creation of the Southern Indian Mission to teach Native peoples in the territory about the Mormon faith and about farming. The Southern Indian Mission promised to increase resources to the management of territorial Indian affairs. As designed, the mission covered much of the south-central part of the territory, ranging geographically from St. George in the south to Spanish Fork in the north, but concentrated in Parowan, Cedar City, and Harmony. Missionary work connected with the new mission did not commence until 10 April 1854 with instructions to "civilize and instruct the Indians in this region that they might come up to inherit the blessings pertaining to them because of the works and promises of their Fathers."[38]

In the spring and summer of 1854, the Southern Indian Mission began in earnest. Missionaries in the field and Mormon leaders in Salt Lake City concurred that the best way to achieve their desired aims of conversion, dependence, and control came by teaching indigenous peoples the gospel in their own language, giving them food, and setting a good example. On a visit to the Southern Indian missionaries in mid-May 1854, just after he had negotiated a peace with Wákara to temporarily end the violence, Brigham Young counseled the men to "learn their language, and you can do this more effectually by living among them, as well as writing down a list of words, go with them where they go, live with them & when they rest let them live with you, feed them, clothe them and teach them as you can, & thus being with you all the time, you will soon be able to teach them in their own language, they are our brethren, we must seek after them."[39] To better serve and potentially attract a greater number of Native converts, missionaries engaged in intensive language study. Near Provo, some Utes lived in and around Mormon settlements, giving church members an opportunity to learn their language.[40] Within a short time, the LDS church had published pamphlets containing vocabularies and translations of Ute, Paiute, and Shoshone dialects.[41] While these vocabularies were produced to benefit whites in their proselytizing and diplomatic efforts to better understand and develop peaceful relations with their Great Basin neighbors, that they were created attests to the willingness of some Utes, Paiutes, and Shoshones to share their language, culture, and heritage with both Latter-day Saints and other white Americans and their desire to form and cultivate mutually beneficial relationships with these people that brought great change to their homelands. Misunderstandings and complications inevitably arose between the peoples, but these vocabularies are by-products of Native-white affiliations and represent important sources for analyzing and understanding communication and diplomacy in the Great Basin in the nineteenth century.

On Sunday, May 21, 1854, the Mormon apostle Parley P. Pratt spoke to the Southern Indian missionaries. His message concerned the instruction of Native Americans and the example of the Mormon people as a powerful teaching method. Pratt had received word that some of the LDS members living within the boundaries of the Southern Indian Mission spent their time in idleness, wrestling, and gambling. Pratt expounded that all living in the area were to serve as missionaries, women not excepted, through model behavior. The Mormon apostle stated that all should take up the duty to feed, clothe, and instruct their Native neighbors. He suggested that even though the two peoples may not understand each other verbally, "there is one language that all can understand and feel—kindness, sympathy, this they can feel." Pratt instructed missionaries to focus their efforts on the younger generation of Indians, which, he thought, would be the most effective way to bring Native peoples into the Mormon fold.[42]

In the summer of 1854, the *Deseret News* provided further instruction for all church members in their interactions with indigenous peoples. An article entitled "The Best Course" stated "that the most absolute *peaceable* subjection of one person to another, arises when an individual is clothed, fed, and sustained at another's expense, without compensation" and, if the Mormons could accomplish that subjection, then the Indians would have nowhere else to turn for their support system.[43] A 26 July 1854 letter from Brigham Young to the leaders of the Southern Indian Mission demonstrated the overarching idea in Mormon policy: to control the region's Indian peoples. In this, his first letter to the Southern Indian missionaries, Young was encouraged that his people had created a good influence among the Indians. He thought this the best time to "become more and more identified" with the tribes, "until they can be brought to an understanding of our principles." The Indians, he paternalistically wrote, required constant attention to improve them and to improve Mormon intercourse with them. Young promoted increased assistance to Indians in their work and further instruction to them in their farming operation. By providing for necessities, setting a good example, and gaining the confidence of the region's tribes, Young stated, "we shall be able ultimately to control and govern them, as it is now, whenever an excitement arises among them against the whites, they immediately become unapproachable and we find it difficult to get access to them at all." The Mormon leader wanted his followers to be "so well established in their confidence and friendship as to control and influence them & more or less, be with them all the time." "Do you not see," Young rhetorically asked, "that all such excitements should be kept down & we should be able through this agency to have peace & control the natives if this policy could be carried into general effect."[44] Governing the region's indigenous population was, ostensibly, a means of self-preservation for the Mormons and the mode for peacemaking in the territory.

In his dual role as superintendent of Indian affairs and leader of the LDS church, Young said, "If we can secure the good will of the Indians by conferring favors upon them we not only secure peace for the time being but gradually bring them to depend upon us until they eventually will not be able to perceive how they can get along without us."[45] Young assumed that Mormon policies could bring about Indian dependence on permanent settlers, who were invested in establishing and maintaining peaceful relationships in the territory. On the other hand, the Mormon leader could not believe that transient white overland travelers or federal officials were devoted to creating such a harmonious atmosphere. Young implored his followers to trade material goods to the Natives for fur, hides, and horses to maintain good relations. He likewise used church and government funds to provide food, clothing, and other material goods and sent missionaries to preach to and live among them to reorder their lives in accordance with the church so that the Indians would become dependent upon the Mormon people and to prevent fighting with them.

From 1853 forward, Brigham Young directed missionary efforts among the Indians to preach the Mormon gospel to them, to educate them in Mormon ways, and to gain influence over them. In the wake of the perceived success of the Southern Indian Mission, Mormon Indian missionary work increased in 1855 after some 160 missionaries were called to seek out their Native neighbors. For example, Mormon missionaries settled among the Nez Percé, Shoshone, Bannock, and Flathead groups in Oregon Territory. Missionaries at Fort Limhi in the Salmon River country of present-day western Idaho found fifty-five Shoshone amenable to their faith; those Shoshone were converted to Mormonism in late October 1855.[46] Mormon missionary work with indigenous groups in the Great Basin and adjacent regions was indefatigable, but it irritated non-Mormons and provoked fears of a subversive alliance forming as a result of a lack of federal surveillance and implementation of federal Indian policy. Subversion was feared because of the extreme departure of Mormon-Indian relations from other Americans and territorial officials, who sought to extinguish Indian land claims and move them onto reservations. Instead, Mormons established settlements among the Indians and attempted to live peacefully with them at places such as Las Vegas, Carson Valley, Fort Supply near Fort Bridger in present-day Wyoming, and Fort Limhi. Many of these locations sat on main avenues of overland travel at a time of substantial white westward migration.

As part of the effort to cajole Native peoples and ingratiate themselves in Native communities, Mormons distinguished themselves from other whites. As Mormon missionaries began to labor with the Great Basin's American Indians, they found many opportunities to demonstrate the differences between Mormons and other whites, particularly federal Indian agents. In July 1855, Thomas D. Brown, a Mormon missionary, wrote in his journal about an exchange of goods and ideas between Mormons and Indians. Brown and other missionaries gave the Indians a few blankets and other presents which, according to Brown, "caused them to say 'The Americans sometimes very good, give us clothes.'" Brown initially thought that it "would have been a difficult task to explain to them why U.S. nincompoops had frequently more in their power to do them good than we had." He delighted, however, in his ability to exhibit the benefits and confirm the friendship of the Mormons, who, he told his new Native associates, did everything in their power to provide assistance. Through "united & unfeigned attention and kindness to them," Brown wrote, "we gained upon their affections."[47]

This exchange provided the Mormon missionary with an opportunity to expound "upon the oft repeated cruelties, shootings and killings" perpetrated on the Indians by the "American" emigrants, crossing Utah en route to California. Brown explained that these crimes far outweighed the paltry presents the Indians received from Americans, which caused his new friends to exclaim, "The American no good, they won't allow us to come into their camps as the Mormons do, they are not our friends, but you are; we are Mormons and no longer Pahutes."[48] According to Brown's record, these Paiutes chose, within the context of two competing entities, to improve their relationships with the Mormons, among whom they lived. In addition, these types of statements from Paiutes might have helped maintain peace between the two groups, even as they encouraged the Mormons to continue to offer protection against opposing Native bands and passing white travelers.

Mormon missionaries and other church members discussed and debated their relationships with Native peoples and questioned whether the U.S. government had benefited the Indians at all. For instance, the Indian missionary George W. Bean argued that the federal government had done nothing, particularly in comparison with Mormon efforts. Bean depicted the "lasting friendship" he and his compatriots had developed with a group of Indians.[49] At a meeting in Cedar City in late April 1856, Rachel Woolsey Lee recorded a discourse given by a Mormon elder named Nathaniel V. Jones that similarly depicted the competing policies of Mormons and federal officials toward Native peoples. Lee wrote that Jones "showed plainly that our policy would eventually result in the greatest good and finally prove the Salvation and exhaltation of these Lamanites in fulfillment of the Prophcys of their forefathers as recorded in the Book of Mormon."[50] While these accounts indicate a Mormon disregard for Native sovereignty and only discuss the differences in whether Mormons or federal officials should govern the indigenous peoples, that Mormons openly compared and contrasted their efforts to those of the federal government suggests that they might have used such comparisons in their communications to curry favor and encourage peace in the minds of the Native peoples they encountered. Conversely, non-Mormon onlookers certainly could have understood these messages as evidence that Mormons were disturbing the peace and attempting to alienate Great Basin Indians from other Americans and from the federal government.

Although little known to the American public at the time, in early February 1854, sixteen women in Salt Lake City responded to Young's exhortation to befriend and aid the Indians by organizing "a society of females for the purpose of making clothing for Indian women and children." This charitable Indian Relief Society elected its own officers and met weekly until June 1854, when Young explicitly encouraged women to "form themselves into societies" and meet in their own wards to make clothing for the Lamanites, the Book of Mormon term for American Indians. Members of the initial group later disbanded to join their respective ward organizations. During 1854, some twenty-two Indian Relief Societies were organized in Salt Lake City and outlying LDS settlements, and their members contributed enough bedding and clothing to meet the demand for such goods. Patty Bartlett Sessions, a Mormon midwife and a respected woman in the community, recorded in her diary on 10 June 1854 that she went "to the ward meeting of the sisters" who "organized a benevolent society to clothe the Indians & squas," as part of the broader missionary work among the area's Native peoples.[51] During 1854, Mormon women organized at least twenty-two Indian Relief Societies in Salt Lake City and outlying settlements. Their members contributed substantial amounts of food, bedding, and clothing to help maintain positive relations between the settlers and the local indigenous population.[52] For much of the middle years of the 1850s, these efforts helped maintain relatively peaceful relations between the Saints and the local indigenous population. This women-led effort furthered Mormon Indian policy of attempting to establish a relationship of dependence on Mormons and away from federal officials.[53]

As part of their effort to establish and enhance their sovereign authority in the Great Basin, the Mormons sought to replace traditional Native independent lifeways with Native dependence. They sought internal control to make the region's indigenous peoples one with them or dependent upon them. While Mormonism tempered how the Latter-day Saints approached their relations with Natives, in the end, the story of displacement and replacement by the new settler majority was nearly identical to that in other parts of the West. The Indian mission served as a tool of Mormon colonialism as these settlers invaded the Native lands, brought change to their lifeways, and made efforts to instruct and make the indigenous dependent on the Mormons.[54] The Mormons continued in their Indian policy of promoting sovereign dependence even as the federal presence in Utah grew with the arrival of Steptoe's detachment and new federal Indian agents in 1854. They insisted on their autonomous capacity to control indigenous policy despite the fact that it was under the direct purview of the federal government.

Great Basin Indians, including Shoshones, Paiutes, and Utes, often looked to the Mormons, who were using and consuming the majority of the available game and other natural resources, for provisioning and compensation. This imbalance of dependency meant that federal authority would become hamstrung. With no federal presence, Brigham Young said, "If we drive [indigenous peoples] to take care of themselves it begets an independent and self-reliance among them which would prove detrimental to the Mormons."[55] Instead, Young wanted Mormons to confer favors and gain Native dependency. This philosophy, in the absence of government-sponsored Indian reservations, guided Brigham Young's relations with the Indians and influenced even his less direct associations with the Indians during Mormon conflicts with the Indian agents on the ground, government officials for Indian affairs in Washington, non-Mormon immigrants passing through the Great Basin, and the army.[56] Passers through the territory, territorial officials, and others believed Young's policy influential in creating alliances with local Natives and further generated fears that he held too much power. Such a fear was manifest in the prosecution of the trial for the murderers of the Gunnison party.

In February 1855, Mormons and army officers negotiated with Pahvant Ute chief Kanosh, who eventually agreed to deliver six men and one woman for trial for the Gunnison expedition murders.[57] That same month, and before the Gunnison trial commenced, however, the judicial system in Utah Territory became another arena of federal-territorial conflict. Localized enactment of judicial practices had constituted a crucial component to settler possession for the Mormons because local juries could enforce settler power against external interference.[58] The Mormons wanted to administer their own justice in civil courts in their own way to punish immorality according to religious dictates. As such they typically settled matters internally or in lower-level probate courts and had invalidated the use of national common law in the territory.

Perhaps the most significant component of the conflict in Utah's judicial affairs concentrated on the use of common law.[59] An act of the Utah territorial legislature, passed in 14 January 1854, created provisions in the territorial laws. Section 1 of this act stated that "no laws nor parts of laws shall be read, argued, cited, or adopted in any court, during any trial, except those enacted by the Governor and Legislative Assembly of this Territory, and those passed by Congress of the United States when applicable; and no report, decision, or doings of any court shall be read, argued, cited, or adopted as precedent in any other trial."[60] In essence, this act prohibited courts at all levels in the territory from citing common law and decisions rendered by judges in other jurisdictions. Common law citation could be used to invalidate territorial sovereignty related to marriage, grand jury selection, and probate court decisions. Common law was an extremely sensitive subject to the Mormon presidency, which maintained an aversion to outside interference in legal matters, largely based in the church's earlier legal entanglements in Missouri and Illinois.[61]

In a February 1855 supreme court session, Utah territorial chief justice John F. Kinney took on the question of common law applicability. In November 1854, in a case of aggravated assault with the intent to kill, *People v. Moroni Green*, Green's defense team moved to have the case dismissed on the grounds that the grand jurors who produced the original bill of indictment for assault were from the First Judicial District and not from the body of the Great Salt Lake county jurors, in which county the crime was committed. The case involved questions about the powers of a grand jury in district courts and the regulation of judicial procedure in criminal cases. The law in question, and the law the grand jurors had cited was in force, was section 17 of the Organic Act, which extended common law to Utah Territory.

In the February 1855 Supreme Court trial, Kinney ruled to not dismiss the case, stating that district courts could inquire into violations of criminal law, while Associate Justice William W. Drummond opined that federal grand juries could be constituted as provided for under common law. Drummond further pronounced that no territorial legislature could take away the power of Congress as put forth in the Territorial Organic Act.[62] A Mormon man and attorney named Hosea Stout recorded his observations of the court in his journal. He stated that question before the court was "whether the Common Law was in force in this Territory or not, a law of the Legislature to the contrary. The Court ruled that it was, which settles a point which has been a vexed question in our Courts since the organization of the Territory."[63] In Kinney's judgment the territorial legislature's 14 January 1854 act could not overrule the Organic Act and therefore could not forbid the implementation of common law in the territory. The *Moroni Green* decision, then, vindicated the Organic Act and pointed to the supremacy of national law over the territorial legal system. Although Kinney maintained friendly relations with LDS leaders prior to his decision in *Moroni Green*, after it, he faced mounting criticism and alienation in Utah.[64] Mormons considered this decision an egregious usurpation of their local self-government. They believed it opened up more opportunities for federal interference in local legal and social relations.[65]

The trial for Gunnison's murderers the next month, in March 1855, also brought conflict within the territory, and the reporting of it encouraged greater speculation and fear about the Mormon capacity for local self-government and control over Indian policy in Utah. On Friday, 23 March, the prosecution opened with arguments against the Pahvant defendants. The U.S. attorney closed the arguments the same day, followed by Chief Justice Kinney, who provided the jury with instructions. Kinney explicitly directed the jurors to find the prisoners guilty of murder in the first degree or acquit them entirely.[66] According to Mormon Indian missionary Andrew Love, the jury "returned to their room" and deliberated until eight p.m. that evening before handing over a verdict of "Murder in the Second degree." The jury deliberately ignored Kinney's instructions and recommended that "Whitetree, Anklejoint & Sandyhair," three of the seven Pahvant Utes arrested for the Gunnison crime, "be sentenced to three years hard labor & five hundred dollars fine Each."[67] The outcome incensed Colonel Edward Steptoe. "The trial was abortive," he wrote to the national commissioner of Indian affairs. It was appalling, he thought, that the local jury ignored the federal judge's order. But he hoped that it would have two good outcomes. Steptoe suggested to the commissioner that this outcome would have beneficial effects "upon the savages," and "upon the general government, which will now understand the undue sympathy felt by the Mormons for the Indians." The colonel's experience in Utah and with the trial led him to believe that Indian affairs in Utah required the "immediate attention of the Indian Bureau" to neutralize the pernicious influence of the Mormons over the Indians.[68]

The jury's decision in the Gunnison trial demonstrated Mormon resolve to exercise local sovereignty and control over the federal judiciary by manipulating the outcome and sentences of the accused. That seven Pahvant Utes were arrested and brought up on charges for the Gunnison murders and that the local all-Mormon jury dismissed the judge's explicit instructions, although convicting three of the suspects on a lesser charge, created a public outcry. Some reports suggested that Mormons, under Brigham Young's instructions, had directed the murders and gave that as the reason why the jury failed to convict any Natives for murder in the first degree with an appropriate sentence. The convicts were brought to the penitentiary near Salt Lake City on 26 March and escaped custody five days later.[69] Following the trial, the *National Era* reprinted a *New York Times* article that opined that the convicted Utes were "accordingly handed over to the authorities of

Utah, (Mormons,) and committed to prison to serve out their terms. But, within less than a week, they were *permitted to escape*, and are again at large. We learn from our private correspondence that no doubt whatever is entertained by Col. Steptoe and the authorities, that the whole thing has been brought about by the Mormons, for the express purpose of conciliating the Indians, and exasperating them against the Federal authority."[70] One newspaper decried the sham of a trial, stating that the murderers had gone free due "entirely to the *interference of the Mormons*, who seem to be in league with the Indians in resisting the authority of the United States."[71] Mormon missionaries were believed to be conciliating the Indians and creating a system of tampering with the Indians by turning their loyalty away from Americans and toward the Mormons.[72] Fear emerged in public discourse that the Mormons might enlist the Indians, "the head of thousands of savage warriors, armed with deadly rifles," protected in the Rocky Mountains to cut off American expansion at a critical geographic crossroads.[73] Articles such as these seemed to confirm the growing idea of a subversive Mormon-Indian alliance.

Young later wrote to Jefferson Davis, refuting what he referred to as malicious claims against his people. Young told of the recapture of the Indians. His letter claimed, "After waiting a few days, to see if any one would take interest enough in the matter, to re-capture them, and finding there was not, I sent for, and obtained them, and they are now, and have been since their re-capture in the prison of the Territory according to the sentence of the Court."[74] Captain Gunnison's second-in-command had already made a similar assessment. In his official report, Beckwith maintained that the Pahvants acted on their own, killing to avenge an earlier murder of Indians by whites.[75] According to Chief Justice Kinney, the evidence showed conclusively that the Indians committed the crime of their own volition. The private and official intercourse of Captain Gunnison with Governor Young was of the friendliest character, and all needful aid in the prosecution of his work was cheerfully extended to the captain by the governor. In spite of this, however, Judge Kinney's associate, Judge William W. Drummond, infuriated by the outcome at court, asserted that Captain Gunnison and his party were murdered by Indians, under orders, advice, and direction of the Mormons.[76] Rumors continued to circulate in papers nationwide that militant Mormons orchestrated the murder and allowed the arrested Indians to escape any punishment. The murderers of Gunnison and his party, then, were virtually left unpunished. Resulting from the published reports in the press, it was widely assumed that the Mormons controlled Indian affairs contrary to federal Indian policy and federal officers were not safe in that territory.

In the early 1850s, newspaper accounts of Indians attacking Mormons and battles full of pandemonium between the two peoples were a constant.[77] By the mid-1850s, following the Gunnison murder and trial and based on reports from the army, the coverage shifted. Typical headlines read, "The Mormons Exciting the Indians against Americans." Newspapers emphasized not only the hostility of the Mormons toward the general United States but also the perceived control the Mormons had over the Great Basin's Native peoples.[78] Another aspect of Mormon-Indian relations that occasionally appeared in public and press reports concerned Mormon intermarriage with regional Native Americans. A correspondent of the *New York Times* reported that "for some time past, Mormon missionaries have been maintained among the Indians, and Brigham Young has proposed that *intermarriage* between the Indians and the Mormons be introduced and encouraged, as rapidly as possible. These occurrences indicate a commencement of a system of tampering with the Indians on the part of the Mormon leaders, from which the worst results may be apprehended."[79] While intermarriage between Indians and Mormons was not widespread in the 1850s, these ideas about interracial marriage demonstrate a public fear of the two groups combining against the United States.[80] Intermarriage constituted one facet of a supposed sinister plot of a Mormon-Indian alliance against the United States. The image of Mormons and Indians uniting politically, socially, and sexually against the United States provided further justification that the system in Utah Territory required greater federal oversight. The LDS church's geographic presence emerged as a major factor in shaping the public's perception following the murders because the discourse viewed Mormons and their Native allies as impediments to the agents of imperial expansion and progress.

Popular discourse in the United States maligned Native Americans and other racial groups that stood in the path of supposedly progressive and superior peoples. The doctrine of progress and biological racism contributed to continental expansion that enlarged the boundaries of the nation.[81] The American public conceived such groups in terms of their deficiencies measured against the ideals of individualism, republicanism, and liberty. In order for Americans to claim the legitimacy of the right to conquer and control the continent and prevent outsider groups from establishing nonrepublican governments in the land they believed theirs, they employed rhetoric to label threats as "Indian," foreign, or alien to highlight a cultural or political deficit in a particular group of people.[82] Newspaper articles often conveyed to the public the stark differences between Mormon and federal Indian policy, and cemented the idea that the Mormons were fundamentally incapable of governing Native peoples, let alone themselves. The American popular imagination at this time and into the future often correlated Mormons, despite the whiteness of their skin, with Indians.

Suspicion of Mormon complicity with Indians in subverting American sovereignty grew in Washington. Brevet Lieutenant Colonel Edward J. Steptoe, Lieutenant Sylvester Mowry, and Garland Hurt, the newly appointed federal Indian agent for Utah, each sent reports to Washington that brought into stark relief the role of Mormon Indian policy in Utah Territory. Their concerns echoed the warning Captain Gunnison had articulated in his 1852 book. He had mentioned, and these federal officers emphasized, the problems with Mormon missionary work among regional American Indians.[83] Based on his observations and from his interactions with Great Basin Indians during his time in Utah, Steptoe stated that the Indians in the territory had learned "*for the first time*, what relation they hold to the government, and that to *it alone* they must look for encouragement in well doing, or chastisement for misconduct."[84] Steptoe earnestly asked for the full support of the government to establish federal control over Indian administration in the territory. Steptoe's report triggered a fear that Young had plotted to usurp the "authority of our sovereignty," and that his "tribe" reigned with undisputed sovereignty over a large territory of the American Union.[85] Steptoe's report noted and foreshadowed a growing belief that Latter-day Saint missionaries and their teachings had uniformly created a distinction between members of their church and government agents, in order to create an alliance against the United States.

Despite the reality of habitual conflict and often tenuous relations between Native Americans and Mormons in the Great Basin, the American press and Congress perceived a growing threat from the two groups' close proximity and believed that through missionary efforts the two groups were allying. Reports from Utah emerged that Indians were turning to Mormons for food, clothing, and instruction. The distant federal government had little influence with this region's Native groups. Mountain men in the Great Basin area also reported that Mormons provoked the Indians to "attack emigrants, plunder and commit murder whenever they find a party weak enough to enable them to do so."[86] Many outside of Utah did not see or hear about the violent confrontations that resembled typical Euro-American-Native relations. People reading about Utah in the press saw and heard about Natives converting to Mormonism, serving in Mormon houses, and residing within and near Mormon settlements. Such close associations and proximities caused the American public to regard the Mormon-Native behavior as suspicious and threatening as a result of intimate contact between Mormons and Indians.

Garland Hurt, a St. Louis physician, arrived in Utah Territory in February 1855 to serve as an Indian agent, an organizational subordinate of Young in the office of Indian affairs. His letters and reports to his superiors in Washington helped confirm the image of a subversive Mormon-Indian relationship. Hurt primarily criticized the Mormon missionaries because they taught the Indians their theology and gave gifts in the form of food and clothing, paid for by the U.S. government but attributed to LDS largesse.

The Indian agent was so disgusted with Mormon missionary practices that he went over Young's head to communicate to his superiors in Washington. The Indian agent explained his distress, stating that every tribe on the continent would receive a visit from the Mormons and that their missionaries would teach the "wretched savages that they are the rightful owners of the American soil, and that it has been wrongfully taken from them" by the United States.[87] In a May 1855 letter to Manypenny, Hurt categorized Mormon Indian missionaries as "a class of rude and lawless young men, such as might be regarded as a curse to any civilized community," and offered a legal means to remedy the problems he saw in Mormon Indian policy. Hurt thought it expedient that the federal government should observe the violations of that law to regulate trade and intercourse with the Indian tribes, and to preserve peace on the frontier with a policy to watch with an eye of vigilance the movements of the Mormons; and in case their efforts, under the guise of missionary labors, should tend to create a spirit of insubordination among the Indians averse to the interests of the government.[88] Much like Isaac McCoy in 1833, Hurt's observations of Mormon-Indian interactions led to accusations that the missionaries had violated the long-standing federal Trade and Intercourse Act by sending messages to the Indians meant to encourage their alliance with the Mormons against federal agents, the government, and American citizens.[89]

The Mormons were no strangers to the Trade and Intercourse Act. In late 1851 and early 1852, Mormon officials used the act to arrest and convict Don Pedro León Luján, a New Mexican who traded with Utes for Indian captives without a proper license in Utah. At that time, Mormons attempted to combat the Mexican-Indian slave trade and employed the Trade and Intercourse Act as the legal means to do so.[90] Just as the Mormons utilized the Intercourse Act as a legal means to thwart the Indian slave trade, Hurt and others accused the Mormons of violating the act as the means to curb the Mormon influence over the region's indigenous peoples and to promote federal authority.

Acting commissioner of Indian affairs Charles E. Mix received Hurt's letter in July 1855.[91] Within a month, Mix wrote to the secretary of the interior, Robert McClelland, regarding the Mormons' Indian policy. Mix stated that the Mormon missionaries had "either accidentally or purposely created a distinction in the minds of the Indian tribes of the Territory between the Mormons and the citizens of the United States which must prove prejudicial to the interests of the latter."[92] Mix pled with McClelland to send a permanent body of U.S. troops to Utah to scrutinize and regulate Mormon actions and teachings. Mix warned that the federal government needed to intervene "as a precautionary step to preserve the harmony of our relations with the Indian tribes" and prohibit potential Mormon designs to interrupt the peace and turn the Indians against American travelers and the government in general.[93] McClelland apparently took no action at this time, but Hurt's many letters were kept on file and were eventually included in the official report on the factors "which gave rise to the military expeditions ordered to Utah Territory."[94]

Other federal officers made similar reports. On his way out of Utah, Lieutenant Sylvester Mowry, who had been involved in scandalous situations with Mormon women prior to his departure, led an army detachment to Los Angeles via the southern route following the Gunnison trial. In his final report to the U.S. Army adjutant general in July 1855, he took up the subject of Indians separately and in heavy detail because of its great importance in the territory. He began by citing Steptoe's belief "that the Utah Indians inhabiting the Valleys of Salt Lake, Juab and Fillmore had been taught that the Mormons were a superior people to the Americans, and that the Americans were the natural enemies of the Indians, while the Mormons were their friends and allies." Mowry confirmed that during his march along the Santa Clara, Virgin, Muddy, and Vegas Rivers he encountered "several hundred Warriors who had undergone the same tutelage." "In each tribe," he reported, "two or more Mormon Missionaries were found, whose object was to impress upon the Indians the belief in the inferiority and hostility of the Americans and the superiority and friendship of the Mormons." He stated that many of the Natives he encountered had been heavily supplied with good rifles, other arms, and ammunition by Mormons. "To counteract as far as lay in my power the mischievous impression made upon them by the Mormons," Mowry added that he "'talked' with all the Chiefs [and] explained to them the true relation existing between Americans and Mormons issued rations to the tribes as far as I could afford to do so, and made the Chiefs some trifling presents of old uniforms, tobacco and shirts."[95]

Lieutenant Mowry commented further on his observations of Mormon and Indian relations resulting from LDS missionary efforts. "The enmity of the Mormons went so far in one instance," Mowry detailed, "to induce the Chief of the Pah-Utes of the Muddy River to believe that my Command was on its way to attack his tribe. The Squaws and children were hurried into the Canons, and when I arrived on the Muddy the whole tribe was in 'War paint' to receive me. By kindness I so completely changed the opinion of this Chief that he followed the train some miles to 'renew the assurances' of his friendship towards all Americans." Mowry then suggested that troops "be sent over this route every year, with instructions to the Commanding Officer to seek for opportunities to meet the Indians and assure them by kindness and by presents of the real strength and good intentions of the Government towards them. If some such precaution is not taken I am satisfied they will become formidable allies of the Mormons." Mowry reiterated that the Mormons gained influence over some of the most powerful Indians of the region, mentioning Wákara, Arrapeen, and Kanosh by name as chiefs who became members of the LDS church. Mowry continued by warning his superior in Washington of the dangers in the Mormon counsel to intermarry with the Natives. He referred to "the 'counsel' of Brigham and the 'Apostles' to the 'Brethren' to inter-marry with the Indians. I have heard several members of high standing in the Church express their willingness to take in addition to their already numerous household a few Squaws *because Brigham said it was right.*" Mowry praised the able efforts of Indian agent Garland Hurt and felt confident that Hurt would make every effort to destroy this dangerous influence. The lieutenant closed his report with observances of defensible and indefensible places along the southern route out of Utah. He suggested the need to maintain friendship or at least neutrality with the region's Native Americans because they were "necessary to a successful march to or from Salt Lake. As enemies they cannot be too much dreaded armed and directed by an intelligence superior to their own. I have no desire to predict an intestine war, but it is in the minds of all intelligent men who have lived among this God forsaken people of Utah only a question of time."[96] Mowry, like Steptoe and Gunnison before him, concluded that to have a beneficial effect on Indian relations, the federal government must station a permanent armed presence in Utah to control the routes of travel and to diminish the Mormon-Indian alliance.

It is not clear if Mowry or anyone in his detachment spoke any Indian dialect, let alone Paiute. Native Americans in the "Valleys of Salt Lake, Juab and Fillmore" likely had a limited command of the English language. Therefore, it is difficult to discern how much of the conversation and corrective offered by Mowry in his report actually occurred. Nevertheless, the Indians decided to share information with Mowry and other federal agents they encountered, which became vital to the agents' understanding of Indian relations in Utah and added to the tensions between the Mormons and the federal government. The information they chose to share prompted federal agents to consider that the messages Mormons delivered among the region's indigenous groups would hinder larger federal efforts in the territory. According to the reports they sent to Washington—based partly on

FIG. 5. Indian agent Garland Hurt working with Native peoples at a federal Indian farm in Utah, ca. 1856. Used by permission, Utah State Historical Society.

the information received from the Native peoples—Mowry, like Hurt and Steptoe, argued that the teachings of the Mormons contradicted the aims of the federal government and its agents.

In an August 1856 letter, Utah deputy surveyor Columbus L. Craig similarly observed Mormon Indian policy. Prejudicial to surveying operations in Utah, Craig stated, "Arapeen, a noted chief of the Ute nation, who has been baptised in the church, said to me, afterwards that he 'had been told by Mormons, in Salt Lake City, that we intended, after surveying the lands, to put the Indians in chains, and drive off the Mormons.' These facts, given to us by the Indians themselves, confirm a suspicion which I have had respecting the policy which the Mormons have been pursuing in regard to the Indians, which is, that they have been endeavoring in every possible way to establish a difference between *Mormons* and *Americans*, to prejudice them against the latter."[97] These federal officials nearly universally requested a larger and more permanent armed federal presence in Utah to establish and validate national sovereignty and authority in the territory. While Mormons and federal agents competed over how best to manage the Indians, Native actions and reactions to the competing entities often informed white decision-making.

Indian agent Garland Hurt piled on. He wrote still more letters on Mormon-Indian relations to John M. Elliott, a congressional representative from Kentucky. In one letter, Utah's Indian agent labeled Mormon missionaries as "unprincipled men" who sought to prejudice the minds of the indigenous population against the federal government and himself as its accredited agent through their "debasing and corrupting doctrines." He further implied that the Mormons must be made to respect the laws and institutions of the government "or reap the penalties."[98] Hurt asked that Elliott use his influence to advise the president, the secretary of the interior, and the commissioner of Indian affairs on his report, which Elliott forwarded to the commissioner in December 1856.[99] Hurt's reports and observations suggested the importance of maintaining federal laws in Utah Territory and of combating the messages delivered by missionaries that could potentially form divisions between Mormons and Americans in the minds of the region's indigenous population.

In late October 1856, Hurt sent a letter to Brigham Young. In it, Hurt stated, "Soon after commencing my labors among the Indians of this Territory, I learned that they made a distinction between Mormons and Americans, which I thought was not altogether compatible with correct policy, believing that it would ultimately operate to the prejudice of one or the other party." According to his letter, Hurt had expressed his views "on all suitable occasions" and had endeavored to teach the Indians that "no distinction" existed between "the two classes, but that we were all the Great Father's people." Hurt noted his disappointment with Mormon men who would "so far forget themselves, and the relations they sustain, both to Indians and to government, as to be guilty of gross misrepresentations so fatal to their own peace and prosperity."[100] When federal officials observed the ways in which Mormons represented themselves as different from other Americans, they perceived the Mormons as disloyal citizens. Finally, Hurt, in a separate letter, condemned what he viewed as the introduction of improper conduct toward and education to the area's indigenous groups.[101]

The education of Native groups during the Jacksonian era was merely one device to gain influence over them.[102] The idea behind removal, advocated by William Clark and others, was to move Indians beyond contact with whites where they could be taught farming by federal agents, live in houses on private property, and learn to improve their condition.[103] Among the federally approved agents who interacted with Indians were a federal field representative (often an Indian agent or subagent who was appointed by the president with congressional consent) and other whites employed by the Office of Indian Affairs, including religious missionaries, farmers, teachers, and blacksmiths. Groups like the American Board of Commissioners for Foreign Missions or the Missionary Society for the Methodist Episcopal Church typically recommended potential employees to the federal Indian office.[104] With the federal government's consent, small groups of Protestant men and women carried out the missions to the Indians in the antebellum West. The largest—and primary—difference between those missionaries and Mormon missionaries was that in the former, small groups of men and women from different religions went west and created missions to Indians with federal sanction. Mormons, on the other hand, had a unique religion, were sanctioned by the government only inasmuch as Brigham Young was the de facto superintendent of Indian affairs, and belonged to a large, cohesive, and semiautonomous group that lived among the Indians. Through their missions, the Mormons became the primary white contacts for Indians in the Great Basin, which created a fear of a large Mormon-Indian alliance against the United States.[105] Federal officers in Utah, much like Indian agent Richard Cummins in 1831, grew concerned about the nefariousness of Mormon-Indian relations.

Though the federal government entrusted other religious groups with communicating and interacting with Indians, officials in that body—particularly those in the Office of Indian Affairs—apparently became uncomfortable with the Mormons' proselytizing program.[106] The federal government certainly did not want Mormons responsible for educating Great Basin Indians. A Washington DC paper, the *Daily National Intelligencer*, perhaps gave the best summary of the vexatious feelings of those in the nation's capital when it ran an article stating that Mormon missionaries "will be sent among all the Indian tribes, to teach them agriculture, the mechanic arts, and *military tactics!*"[107] Whites outside Utah maintained a callous attitude of cultural and racial superiority and were suspicious that Mormons desired the Indians' friendship only for sinister motives.[108]

Mormons cooperating with, providing food and arms and ammunition to, and possibly having violent influence over area Native peoples created a new wrinkle in western expansion and the continued colonization of the indigenous in the United States. Typically, whites had desired to remove Indians and fight against them, never to join with them against the federal government or its agents. Reports to Washington indicated that Indians in Utah were well supplied with guns and horses, with which they constantly raided overland emigrants.[109]

Annual reports from the commissioner of Indian affairs, George W. Manypenny, reveal the necessity of procuring more assistance from the federal government in Utah. As early as 1854, the commissioner wrote in his annual report, "Our citizens ought to have proper protection from Indian depredations; but in the present State of things" in Utah, Manypenny lamented, it "is impossible."[110] The Mormon-controlled government offered little assistance, the Indian agents believed, as they preferred gift giving in the form of arms, food, and clothing rather than offering protection to overland emigrants.

On 10 April 1854, in order to make provisions for negotiating treaties with the Indian tribes of Utah, commissioner of Indian affairs

Manypenny recommended that Robert McClelland propose legislation for the separation of the offices of superintendent of Indian affairs and governor in Utah. Manypenny did not deem it good policy to provide Young with more power to negotiate treaties with Utah Indians on behalf of the federal government. He referred to precedents in legislation made by Congress respecting Indian affairs in Oregon. The Territorial Organic Act for Oregon provided that the territorial governor would also serve as the ex officio superintendent of Indian affairs, as in Utah. However, Congress made a provision for the negotiation of treaties with the Indian tribes of Oregon repealing the joint duties and separating the governorship for the office of superintendent of Indian affairs.[111] Manypenny suggested that the time had come to separate the two offices in Utah and have the Department of the Interior take more control over Indian affairs in Utah. Congress, however, would not act on this suggestion for over two years.[112] More immediately actionable was the Mormon violation of the federal Trade and Intercourse Act. Federal officials demanded the full power and support of the government be used to establish federal law and sovereign authority over Indian administration in Utah Territory.[113]

The Trade and Intercourse Act, passed 30 June 1834, was the final codification of similar acts regulating commerce between Natives and non-Natives designed to preserve peace as the nation expanded west. A complex document composed of thirty sections, it was passed alongside a bill that organized the Department of Indian Affairs to eliminate confusion and ambiguity in the federal Indian service and to regulate interactions with Native peoples.[114] A 27 February 1851 congressional act that authorized Indian agents for the territories of New Mexico and Utah also extended the provisions of the aforementioned trade and intercourse acts over those territories.[115]

One vital aspect to the Trade and Intercourse Act is found in section 2 and relates to the power of the superintendent of Indian affairs for a given territory. It states,

That no persons shall be permitted to trade with any of the Indians (in the Indian country) without a license therefore from a superintendent of Indian affairs, or Indian agent, or sub-agent, which license shall be issued for a term not exceeding two years.... And no trade with the said tribes shall be carried on within their boundary, except at certain suitable and convenient places, to be designated from time to time by the superintendents, agents, and sub-agents, and to be inserted in the license. And it shall be the duty of the persons granting or revoking such licenses, forthwith to report the same to the commissioner of Indian affairs, for his approval or disapproval.[116]

Section 3 states, "That any superintendent or agent may refuse an application for a license to trade, if he is satisfied that the applicant is a person of bad character, or that it would be improper to permit him to reside in the Indian country."[117] With Brigham Young as the primary grantor of licenses to trade, or interact with area Indians, the federal government could do little about the perceived character issues of Mormon missionaries, unless it divided Young's power and appointed a new superintendent of Indian affairs to oversee the granting of licenses for the territory.

Reports to the commissioner of Indian affairs from Utah's Indian agent, missives from army officers who had previously served in Utah, other federal reports, and press accounts all expressed misgivings about Mormon missionaries exciting prejudices among the region's tribes contrary to the interests and policy of the federal government and in direct violation of the Trade and Intercourse Act of 1834. Section 13 of that act declared illegal "any citizen or other person residing within the United States or the territory thereof, [to] send any talk, speech, message, or letter to any Indian nation, tribe, chief, or individual, with an intent to produce a contravention or infraction of any treaty or other law of the United States, or to disturb the peace and tranquility of the United States." Section 14 further held that anyone who knowingly transmitted such a communication "to or from any Indian nation, tribe, chief, or individual" faced a large fine. Finally, section 15 punished anyone who "shall alienate, or attempt to alienate, the confidence" of Native peoples from the government.[118] According to federal representatives, the Mormons had indeed alienated Great Basin Indians from other American citizens and especially the U.S. government through their teachings and gift-giving practices.

Two sections of the Trade and Intercourse Act also empowered the U.S. president with the legal authority to send forth the army to apprehend anyone breaking this law.[119] Though reports and letters from federal representatives in Utah may have been flawed or somewhat exaggerated, they provided evidence of Mormons violating that act and they were the primary pieces of intelligence that key members of the federal government in Washington read and understood. Mormon missionary diaries and the church's newspaper, the *Deseret News*, likewise suggested that the Mormons were attempting to ally with the Indians both to influence them and to prove themselves friendlier than U.S. government officials.[120] The 1834 act authorized the president to use military force against all persons in a given territory acting contrary to that law; officials in Washington, knowing only what they read in the reports from their agents in Utah and perhaps what they read in the newspapers, believed that the Mormons and their missionaries had violated federal law.[121]

The Trade and Intercourse Act further endowed the president with the legal power to send forth the army to apprehend any person or persons breaking this law. The act's twenty-third section states, "It shall be lawful for the military force of the United States to be employed in such manner and under such regulations as the President may direct, in the apprehension of every person who shall or may be found in the Indian country in violation of any of the provisions of this act."[122] Reports to the commissioner of Indian affairs from the Utah Indian agents, reports from army officers who previously served in Utah, and press reports of Mormon-Indian complicity expressed suspicion toward Mormon missionaries among indigenous peoples. They further demonstrated the potential unlawful actions of the missionaries who they believed were sending and giving messages of subversion to the Indians. The federal government, thus, had evidence of violations of the act. Even Mormon missionary diaries suggest that Mormons were intending to alienate the Indians to whom they preached from the U.S. government.[123] While it appears that both Mormons and American Indian groups were each trying to navigate the political, legal, and cultural world of antebellum America that best suited their own local needs, the three-decades-long perception that Mormons broke federal laws by tampering with Indians to oppose white American or federal government interests proved that the Mormons were incapable of republican self-governance, especially over a vital aspect of western expansion. The Indian population in close proximity and in perceived alliance with the Mormons allowed the press and government to enter into a discourse that conflated the two militarily as an essential justification to move with federal force into Utah.[124]

As the United States looked to become a truly transcontinental nation, the Mormon-Indian activity in a federal territory positioned along the principal overland routes to the Pacific coast was not acceptable and was a major problem that the president of the United States would have to confront. With the Trade and Intercourse Act in effect and the violation of that law by Mormon missionaries, the president had the legal power to send the army to reestablish that authority. An overt demonstration of federal authority, however, would eventually prove harmful to the Democratic strategy of popular sovereignty and the precarious balance in national politics. Indian policy emerged as a crucial factor in the federal government's effort to assert national power and authority in Utah Territory in the 1850s and was one central element of the tension that led to the Utah War.

4 Confronting the "Twin Relics of Barbarism"

The Mormon Question, the Buchanan Administration, and the Limits of Popular Sovereignty

The mid-1850s reports from federal appointees and army officers during their sojourns in Utah prompted more discussion about the Mormon capacity for local self-government and control over Indian policy. The 1856 presidential election and its aftermath, however, did more than anything else to foster debate on and eventually encourage a permanent invasion of local Mormon sovereignty. Democratic Party leaders continued to promote the politically contingent doctrine of popular sovereignty, first introduced in the Compromise of 1850 and solidified in the 1854 Kansas-Nebraska Act. The 1856 election also introduced the Republican Party to the presidential political arena. One of the Republican platform's core tenets was the federal prohibition of the "twin relics of barbarism" in the territories. The Republicans struck at and criticized the idea of popular sovereignty, which emerged as a key rhetorical battleground during and after the 1856 election.[1] The Democratic Party's philosophy suffered a greater blow in 1857 when an executive action followed by a publicized speech by Stephen Douglas created ideological uncertainty about the role of the federal government in enforcing a republican form of government and national sovereignty in a territory.

The year 1856 was a restless one in Utah. Utah legislators again assembled a constitutional convention in Salt Lake City on 17 March

1856 and ten days later adopted a state constitution. This was their second attempt to gain statehood in the American union. George A. Smith and John Taylor traveled to Washington to present the constitution to Congress, but after meeting with John M. Bernhisel, Stephen A. Douglas, and others, the Mormon representatives found the political climate intemperate and saw the futility in submitting the petition for statehood. At about the same time in the Tintic and Cedar valleys in Utah, Mormons and Utes engaged in a series of armed skirmishes over resources in what is now called the Tintic War. Finally, in the latter part of 1856 Mormons in Utah underwent a religious reformation wherein church members recommitted to the doctrines of their faith and which led to an increase in plural marriages and group cohesion.[2]

The year 1856 was likewise critical for the United States. In a year that would culminate in a presidential election, sectional relations were strained and territories were at the heart of the political unrest. In Kansas free-soil and proslavery settlers established competing governments in Topeka and Lecompton, respectively. The struggle for control was bitter, vicious, and passionate. Violence in Kansas erupted in 1855 over voting fraud and the efforts to pass a free-state constitution. Physical confrontations increased in 1856 as Missourians invaded the territory to aid the proslavery element in attacking the town of Lawrence. Passions and emotions ran hot in Congress over the Kansas situation, leading to the brutal beating of Republican senator Charles Sumner by South Carolina representative Preston Brooks in May. Popular sovereignty was failing in practice as bloodshed marked the Kansas territorial experience both on the ground in the plains and in the halls of Congress. "Bleeding Kansas," as it was known, became a weapon for the Republicans during the 1856 presidential campaign using it to attack the Democratic administration and its popular sovereignty doctrine that sided with the proslavery forces in Kansas.[3] The emergence of the Republican Party to national prominence in 1856 exacerbated concern over popular sovereignty in the western territories and made the Mormon question a particularly important one for the national political scene. The 1856 Republican platform coupled polygamy with slavery as the "twin relics of barbarism" and further argued that it was the "right and the imperative duty of Congress to prohibit in the Territories" those twin relics as excesses of the opposing political party.

Barbarism itself had a racial and cultural meaning that furthered a paradigm of difference, established the "other," and generated sentiment to subdue or remove the savage element. Referring to polygamy as barbaric, Republicans aligned the Mormons with southern slaveholders, who often kept slaves as sexual concubines, in their rhetoric.[4] As Americans engaged in debates over federal authority to regulate the territories, many in the South feared the results of the approaching election that could make a Republican the most important decision-maker for the future of the territories.

During this time of political unrest, parties often identified some menace to republicanism as part of their ideology and made efforts to tie that menace to opposing parties. Ostensibly, these efforts were designed to reform flaws in the American political process to preserve republicanism and keep the power in the hands of the people.[5] The North and the South, Republican and Democrat viewed the other as corrupting republicanism.[6] By the mid-1850s, widespread disagreement existed among parties and between sections over the ideological heritage of and what constituted a threat against republican government.[7]

The Republicans first publicly demonstrated their fears of subversion of republicanism in the western territories in their 1856 presidential platform. In the middle and later years of the 1850s, both Mormons and southern slaveholders utilized the argument of local sovereignty to defend their respective domestic institutions—polygamy and slavery—in accordance with the language of the Kansas-Nebraska Act. Republicans argued that if slaveholders insisted that sovereignty granted them the sole right to legislate on slavery, they must also agree that the Mormons could demand the sole right to legislate on plural marriage. In doing so, Republicans played off the growing public aversion toward Mormon plural marriage to attack slavery and popular sovereignty. Republicans insisted on the supremacy of national sovereignty over the territories as indicated in the Constitution and in laws such as the Northwest Ordinance, and against "squatter sovereignty" that permitted the possibility of a plural marriage social structure and the expansion of slavery. Republicans wanted to contain slavery and, therefore, perform a gradual defeat of the institution. If slaveholders could control the western territories, Republicans feared, they would control the national government and subvert republicanism. The apparent "slavocracy" then perceived in American politics was ready to take over in newly acquired and conquered lands.

Republican thought also viewed Mormonism as a conspiracy against republican government. Rhetorically aligning Mormon Utah with the slave South allowed Republicans to imperil the concept of popular sovereignty and expose it as a situation-based political sham. The territories were open game. The West was the future of the nation and the young political party was determined to prohibit slavery's expansion by any means necessary. Connecting slavery to a practice and people as unpopular as Mormon plural marriage was a brilliant way to make an emphatic argument against popular sovereignty.[8]

The Republicans used the West and the "twin relics" trope skillfully to portray the sectional conflict in terms of republican principles. At Republican rallies during the 1856 campaign season, both antislavery and antipolygamy promoters claimed that adopting either Kansas or Utah as a state would bear heavily, perhaps conclusively, on the entire conflict between freedom and slavery. William Seward, a Republican from New York, claimed that slaveholders would turn the republicanism guaranteed in the Constitution into an aristocratic society. Seward and other Republicans described slavery in terms of enslavement to a type of government or control of the national government. In other words, they attempted to persuade Americans that slaveholders meant to control the government as an aristocracy or slavocracy, just as public opinion viewed Mormonism as an *imperium in imperio*. Both threatened to halt the growth of the empire of liberty.

The Republicans chose the explorer and former military governor and U.S. senator from California John C. Frémont as their presidential nominee. Speakers typically couched their antipolygamous rhetoric in terms of sovereignty and self-government. For example, on 18 September 1856, former Kansas governor Andrew H. Reeder gave a speech supporting Frémont. In his speech, he railed against slavery expansion and Mormon Utah. "On the western slope of the Rocky Mountains," Reeder began in his condemnation of the Latter-day Saints, "the people in one of our Territories have demonstrated their incompetency at least, for good self-government, by founding their social structure upon principles which poison and demoralize every fountain of civilization and good order, and having united Church and State in their government, their spiritual leader and civil governor claims to rule 'by divine right.'" Referring to Latter-day Saint leader and Utah's governor, Brigham Young, Reeder further exclaimed that he "placed himself upon the exploded authority claimed by emperors and kings, he repudiates allegiance to our common Constitution, and audaciously refuses to surrender his place at the call of the Federal Government."[9] In other words, Mormon society had spawned a tyrannical form of government, which, according to Reeder, opposed republicanism in the same way slavocracy did.

Reeder concluded his comments on Utah by challenging the manhood of the winner of that year's presidential election. He claimed, "A pusillanimous President, busied only with selfish aggrandizement, succumbs to the rebellion, and this Church and State potentate by divine right is left in power over a portion of our people." In essence, Reeder suggested that the incoming president, whether Democrat or Republican, would be perceived as an unmanly coward if he did nothing to diminish the power of Mormon sovereignty in the Great Basin. This rhetoric was almost certainly directed at the Democratic nominee, James Buchanan. During Buchanan's political career, opponents attacked him for being a bachelor, for having a "shrill, almost female voice," and for not wearing a beard. Political cartoons during the 1856 presidential election cast Buchanan doing women's work; one in particular displayed him as a seamstress. As sociologist Michael Kimmel argues, since 1840, "the president's manhood has always been a question, his manly resolve, firmness, courage, and power equated with the capacity for violence, military virtues, and a plain-living style that avoided cultivated refinement and civility. . . . Gender had become political currency, and subsequent campaigns continued to trade in manly rhetoric." The 1856 campaign proved no different.[10]

The Mormon question as raised by Reeder and the Republicans came at an inopportune time for the Democrats and their doctrine of popular sovereignty. The Democratic Party ticket for 1856, known as the Cincinnati Platform because the party's convention took place in the Ohio city that year, promoted strict construction of the Constitution, the sovereignty and equality of the states, the repeal of the Missouri Compromise line, and the right of the people of the territories to adopt their own institutions free from congressional interference. The Democrats encouraged aggressive expansion and endorsed popular sovereignty as found in the Kansas-Nebraska Act. They lauded the principle of congressional noninterference as the proper solution to slavery in the territories, thereby drawing a sharp line between them and the Republicans. Democrats believed that the Republican agenda pushed forward a clandestine effort to expand federal authority by restructuring government to allow federal interference in states and territories, particularly concerning slavery and its extension.[11]

The principle of territorial self-government, as pushed by the Democrats to balance sectional concerns over the opportunity for slavery's expansion in western territories, was a soaring political ideal and, according to Democratic rhetoric, demonstrated commitment to the republican tenet of popular rule. In James Buchanan, an ardent expansionist and nationalist at heart having served as secretary of state

FIG. 6. James Buchanan, Democratic presidential candidate, 1856. Courtesy of the Library of Congress, Prints and Photographs Division.

under James K. Polk, Democrats saw a presidential candidate that they could endorse because they believed in his ability to serve in the interest and for the good of the American people and the nation's republican institutions.[12]

The Democrat, Buchanan, won the 1856 election with 1.8 million popular and 174 electoral votes to Frémont's 1.3 million popular and 114 electoral votes and third-party candidate Millard Fillmore's 871,000 popular votes. Democrats also gained majorities in the U.S. House and Senate. Fears about a Republican ascendancy momentarily subsided.

Buchanan viewed his victory as the American people's endorsement of the Democratic Party's political ideals and the capacity of territorial constituents' ability for self-rule. He encouraged Congress to adopt a simple principle that the majority shall govern the settlement of domestic territorial issues. His inaugural address demonstrated his outward commitment to popular sovereignty as the great principle of free government to answer all territorial questions. The president focused his remarks on popular sovereignty as it related to slavery expansion. He stated, "The whole Territorial question being thus settled upon the principle of popular sovereignty—a principle as ancient as free government itself—everything of a practical nature has been decided. No other question remains for adjustment, because all agree that under the Constitution slavery in the States is beyond the reach of any human power except that of the respective States themselves wherein it exists." Because of popular sovereignty, Buchanan suggested that the slavery question should no longer occupy the public mind but that the people should divert their attention from it "to others of more pressing and practical importance." The president extended his discussion of local self-government in the territories. In a more general tone, Buchanan stated that "nothing can be fairer than to leave the people of a Territory free from all foreign interference to decide their own destiny for themselves, subject only to the Constitution of the United States." His speech also touched on his views of the power of government in the territories as he called for strict obedience to constitutional law. However, constitutional and other territorial laws contradicted the doctrine of popular sovereignty. No matter what the Democratic rhetoric was or what the president claimed, federal laws made the national government the ultimate authority in the territories.[13] Nothing had changed in that regard.

The president's inaugural speech focused on the western territories—it used the word "territory" significantly more than any other presidential inaugural to date. Buchanan's address stressed the importance of protecting and building a grand path and vital transportation routes linking the East and West, thereby indicating the need for greater federal influence in the West. He hoped that Congress would appropriate money toward the construction of a military road, which he viewed as "absolutely necessary for the defense of any State or Territory of the Union against foreign invasion." Without such infrastructure, he realized that the federal government could not afford the necessary protection to California and the western territories, particularly through those isolated regions in the Rocky Mountains. "I believe," the new president declared, "that many of the difficulties in the way, which now appear formidable, will in a great degree vanish as soon as the nearest and best route shall have been satisfactorily ascertained." Buchanan alluded here to the need for sending troops west to build up the federal infrastructure of the West as part of the ongoing process to create a transcontinental nation.[14]

Lodged in the path of United States' western expansion, the Mormons were perceived by most Americans as a subversive *imperium in imperio* threatening to halt progress and emigration across the plains, and take possession of that critical regional crossroads. Their presence obstructed nearly every path leading from the Great Plains to the golden lands of California. Utah Territory, therefore, became essential to controlling trade, commerce, defense, and travel in the West, a central space for the advancement of American institutions. As New York senator William Seward stated, the Latter-day Saints existed as an internal enemy entrenched within a territory "across the path which leads from our Atlantic to our Pacific settlements."[15] These sentiments, and others to follow, echoed James Polk's 1846 fears of the establishment of a Mormon protectorate or independent nation in the West.

The location of the territory was exacerbated by the rhetoric coming from its inhabitants. In January 1857, the Utah legislature wrote and sent to Washington a memorial asserting the right of the territory to "have a voice in the selection of our rulers, and that to deny the right is anti-republican and fraught with evil, not only to us who are unwisely and unjustly held in a Territorial capacity, but to every lover of

FIG. 7. Illustration from *Harper's Weekly*, May 1858, showing Salt Lake City and the extent of Mormon settlements therein. The road to the West, this image seems to suggest, went through the heart of Mormon country. Courtesy of the Library of Congress, Prints and Photographs Division.

American freedom." The January 1857 memorial was a demonstration of the Mormons' local sovereignty and their insistence that local control outweighed federal dictation. "We respect the General government and are at all times willing to observe the laws thereof," the memorial declared, "so far as they may be applicable to our condition in our Territorial capacity; we will resist any attempt of Government Officials to set at naught our Territorial laws, or to impose upon us those which are inapplicable and of right not in force in this Territory." Moreover, the Utah legislature stated, "we will not tamely submit to being abused by Government Officials, here in this territory; they shall not come here to corrupt our community, set at defiance our laws, trample upon the rights of the people, stir up the Indians and use the patronage of the Government to prejudice them against us and endeavor to influence the General Government against us, as a people, by their false statements and misrepresentations." The legislature concluded with a resolution stating, "We are a portion of the great American Republic; that we have rights civil, political and religious, in common with the rest of the States and Territories; that those rights are as sacred to us as they are to any other people, and that it is the duty of the Government to protect us in the peaceable enjoyment thereof, so far as it is in their power, and not to seek to annoy or distress us with either foreign appointments or by fastening upon our necks the yoke of tyranny and oppression, thus depriving us of those rights of freedom pertaining to every Republican Government and held sacred by every State and Territory."[16] The petition was ill timed coming on the heels of a tumultuous election that had brought Utah affairs directly into national political discourse. It was strongly worded and eventually engendered a hostile reaction in Washington, where officials saw it as Mormon intransigence. Nevertheless, it served as an expression of the Mormons' ongoing strategy to claim their rights and exercise local sovereignty.

Shortly after the election, however, the juxtaposition of popular sovereignty and the federal desire to establish control mechanisms in the West created a paradox for the Democrats. In early 1857, popular and congressional rhetoric supported federal action against the Mormons to deny them their independent sovereignty. In a January 1857 report based on the 1854 and 1855 requests from citizens of Carson Valley, Utah, to have that region annexed to California, Vermont Republican representative Justin Morrill, of the House Committee on the Territories, responded. Morrill's report recapped the petitions sent to Congress in late 1855, specifically mentioning the persecution described by Carson Valley citizens, the failure of territorial officials to administer justice for non-Mormons, and the petition of the valley's women describing the disgust they felt in raising their families among the plural marriage structure in Utah. Morrill claimed that his committee had little accurate information about the extent of these issues, but, he asserted, if the grievances exist in Carson Valley, "it may fairly be presumed that their force and offensiveness is not diminished where the sway of Mormon elders is supported by an overwhelming majority, and where the ecclesiastical leaders have the unlimited control over the political, civil, and religious action of their devotees." He recommended that Congress do something to arrest the antirepublican society of Utah. Extending the boundaries of California, already too large geographically in his opinion, would not remedy the problems with the Mormons and their governing capacity in the West. Morrill concluded that "some measure of wider scope is necessary to effect a radical cure of the moral and political pestilence which makes Utah the scandal of the American people." Since the Vermont representative wanted to alleviate the concerns of Carson Valley and the rest of the nation, he pushed a new measure, a bill for the prevention and punishment of plural marriage, which he thought to be of the utmost necessity and expediency.[17]

The next month, in a 23 February 1857 speech to the U.S. House of Representatives, Morrill insisted that the people of Utah Territory were hostile to republicanism and no longer recognized federal law, but obeyed only Brigham Young, who "desired a kingly government, in order to make their patriarchal institutions more homogenous." Morrill asserted that the sovereignty claimed by the Mormons was not properly subordinate to the federal government and that people instead insisted on their independent lawmaking capacity to control the local population. He further indicated that the United States could not count on conditional Mormon loyalty as it expanded its empire of liberty in the West. Morrill pointed out that Mormon theology permitted bondage through plural marriage as a biblical doctrine in his connecting of African and Indian slavery to Mormonism as patriarchal, nonrepublican institutions currently employed in Utah.[18] Likely based in the earlier reports from Utah's federal officials and public rhetoric on Utah affairs, Morrill also claimed, "Not less than four hundred Indians, children or adults, are today held in bondage in Utah under the pretense of apprenticeship," thereby making an implicit connection to the perceived subversive Mormon-Indian relationship in Utah.[19]

Morrill's contemporaries also feared Mormon-Indian relations, with some estimating that the Mormons "were in close alliance with 300,000 Indians" in the Great Basin.[20] Morrill criticized the Mormon system by listing a dozen territorial laws that endowed the governor with various forms of control and power that gave Young a monopoly over religious, political, and military components of the territory.[21] With this speech, Morrill highlighted the three main sites of contested sovereignty between the federal and territorial government, and each informed the other.

Morrill emphasized the peculiar character of the Mormon form of government. "The Mormons are quite as hostile to the republican form of government," Morrill declared. In the end, Morrill pushed for the congressional rejection of Utah laws; the reduction of the boundaries of Utah or complete annexation of the territory to adjoining geopolitical entities; and the establishment of a colonial-style government for Utah with non-Mormons to fill all federal offices supported by and sustained by U.S. troops. Morrill's statements echoed those of earlier visitors to Utah and political pundits. The operation of a nonrepublican form of government in Utah, according to Morrill and others, created an opportunity for the president to assert national sovereignty in the territory.[22]

While the Constitution allowed federal action in the territories against a nonrepublican form of government according to its fourth article, Morrill and others also highlighted the dilemma facing the U.S. government: assertive action to crush Utah's self-governing institutions would violate the Democratic Party's doctrine of popular sovereignty for the territories and further aggravate southern fears about the future of slavery. Public rhetoric from around the country during the early and middle months of 1857 demonstrates that this sentiment was reflective of national attitudes and was of particular concern for popular sovereignty's future.

Advocates of popular sovereignty became painfully aware that too zealous a crusade against Utah might backfire. If one relic of barbarism could be rendered criminal, that might open the door for federal power over the other. Political debate, particularly the contest of words between Abraham Lincoln and Stephen Douglas four months later, and newspaper coverage around the country highlighted this dilemma as well. In national newspaper coverage of Utah Territory from 1856 to 1858, the word "sovereignty" appeared in relationship to ideas about the political doctrine of popular, or squatter, sovereignty and to Congress's ability to assume sovereignty over the territories and often in a rhetorical connection to Kansas.[23]

Several newspapers, particularly Whig and Republican organs, voiced concerns that Utah emphasized the real lack of sovereignty held by the territories. The editor of the Philadelphia-based *North American and United States Gazette* published an article on "Mormondom" explaining that the sovereignty claimed by the people of a territory, any territory, was not wide and absolute as popular sovereignty advocates claimed, but quite limited.[24] People in the territories, the *Gazette's* editor soberly stated, "will have to bow to the supremacy of the Constitution, which will not allow them (sovereign as they boast themselves) to ordain a monarchy; or set up a state-church, which shall have in keeping the consciences of all men; or establish any institution which conflicts with the fundamental law of the country." The popular sovereignty ideal could not enable the sovereign existence of any system adverse to the United States' law and principles. The editor further warned southerners of throwing their support behind popular sovereignty because of the Utah case. "Much as the South may desire the introduction of a new slave State," the *Gazette* editor opined "that they will find it but poor policy to advocate the right of the people to set up the system of polygamy at their pleasure, on the ground of this principle of popular sovereignty.... The institution of slavery will gain nothing by making a twin sister of it, standing on the same platform, and clasping it in an affectionate embrace."[25] But would repudiating popular sovereignty in Utah strike a blow to the potential of slavery expansion in new territories? Even after the 1856 election had been decided, the worrisome connection between slavery and polygamous Utah remained prevalent in public rhetoric.

Other newspapers likewise indicated that Utah affairs upset the guiding principle of popular sovereignty. An article in the *Bangor*

Daily Whig and Courier, a Maine-based anti-Democratic organ, asked, "What *is* this popular sovereignty, if under it the Mormons may not keep as many wives as they please? It protects slaveholding, according to democratic doctrine; why not polygamy?" How could the newly elected president reconcile any such interference with the Democratic dogma, which Americans understood as denying "all right of the Federal Government to interfere with the institutions, or scarcely with the government of the Territories?" A *New York Herald* article likewise noted the paradox facing the country concerning the Mormons and local self-government. That article stated, "Politically and religiously, the Mormons have the whiphand of us, and know it. They know that the safety of the Union will not permit us to establish such a precedent as interference by Congress with the religious institutions of a Territory or State; and they are aware of the vantage ground which their adversaries give them by appealing to Heaven and the Scriptures to condemn their depravities.... If the apprehension of the South—that the Northern men will vote against the admission of every new slave State—renders Congress obdurate on this head, the only remaining resource of the administration will be to act upon the evidences of rebellion now before the world." The Salem, Massachusetts, *Observer* also alleged that the Mormons were making arrangements with southerners for the perpetuation of slavery and all domestic institutions through popular sovereignty.[26]

In April 1857, the *National Era* aptly summarized the Utah-popular sovereignty conundrum. An article in the Washington DC–based antislavery newspaper suggested that national leaders pushing popular sovereignty created the situation of "abominations that prevail in Utah" and if not for that doctrine Congress could act without repercussions to legislate on the territory's domestic concerns. "It is this false and mischievous doctrine," the article stated in reference to popular sovereignty, that enabled "the Democratic Party to wear two faces, so that it might secure the support of hostile sections, and to exempt the Slavery-Propaganda from Congressional interference." The article also decried the doctrine that held Congress back from action against Utah, the vile institution of polygamy, and the growing Mormon power, which the newspaper believed was mounting defiance to the United States. The *National Era* attacked Mormon social structure as the basis of political structure and concluded that Congress did have the power, despite popular sovereignty, to pass laws prohibiting plural marriage or other institutions that infringed on the rights of citizens. As soon as Congress made the discovery that it could legislate in this way against plural marriage—"the burning of women, and the drowning of children"—the article suggested, it might go a step further, "and forbid the enslaving of men, the whipping of women, and the selling of children." The president and Congress, the editorial asserted, should authorize a force to break up and disperse the Mormon form of government "just as it would in relation to any other alien attempt to appropriate a portion of our Territory." Ultimately, the *National Era* highlighted the crux of Buchanan's justification for federal action and control: the Mormon form of government, its Indian policy, and its social institutions were alien and abhorrent, or perceived as foreign in nature and as a threat to the United States' expanding influence in the West.[27] Buchanan said as much in a later proclamation when he described "the great mass of those settlers" in Utah acting under the influence of "leaders to whom they seem to have surrendered their judgment," as a "strange system of terrorism."[28]

Other Democratic and moderate voices supported active measures to control Utah not because of polygamy but because the territory belonged to the United States and was subject to the Constitution and the laws of the Union, which required a republican form of government. The *Washington DC Daily National Intelligencer* published a sensational article in April 1857 that questioned the character of the Mormon form of government as a kingdom within the republic, one that exerted substantial power and supported an aberrant social structure. It also included several quotes supporting the idea of a Mormon-Indian alliance. The *Intelligencer* article declared that the Mormons abused popular sovereignty but that nevertheless the doctrine allowed them greater autonomy than they could find as a state government. It stated, "They already have that which to them is far better, namely, a *willful perversion* of the democratic principle of self-government, declared in the Kansas-Nebraska bill, 'to regulate their own institutions in their own way.' This leaves them in a far better condition to propagate their *treasonable* designs than if they were existing under the form of a State government." While the statement was certainly hyperbole, the *Intelligencer* continued to insist that the Mormon government recognized federal laws only "as a form," while the power remained absolute in the head of the church, who was also the head of the state. The *Intelligencer* encapsulated the American concern about Utah Territory. It claimed that the Mormon version of popular sovereignty was a "perversion" because it promoted self-sustained theocratic autonomy. The article further recognized that the Mormons could hide behind the political rhetoric of the Democratic Party that would allow them to continue to exercise local sovereignty and control.[29]

Mormons enjoyed popular sovereignty, as did the slaveholders, Kansans, Nebraskans, and Oregonians, because it provided them a measure of self-government and sovereign rights that they used to establish their own laws and protect their lifeways. While Mormon ideas of popular sovereignty were similar to those of the rest of the nation, the same cannot be said for their ideas about republicanism. The Mormons envisioned Utah as a place in which they could operate a theocracy, or what they believed was "true Republicanism." However, the Mormons' combining of church and state inherent in its operation of a theocratic form of government made it nearly impossible for the nation's political leaders and pundits to trust their loyalty. As Secretary of War John B. Floyd wrote of the Mormons: "This people have claimed the right to detach themselves from the binding obligations of the laws which governed the communities where they chanced to live. They have substituted for the laws of the land a theocracy." Floyd believed, as did others in the presidential cabinet, the Mormons concentrated themselves in a remote and nearly inaccessible region of federal territory, from which they sent defiance to the sovereign power with a plan to "prepare for a successful secession from the authority of the United States and a permanent establishment of their own."[30]

The general idea of the American federal system reserved to the states any number of freedoms, securing to the people universal religious freedom, entire control of their local municipal affairs—including their law of marriage—and admitting the territories as states as soon as their population and form of governance met the accepted standards. An April 1857 *Harper's Weekly* issue, referring to the accepted standards of the nation, asked, "Now what qualification is there to this?" The answer: "There is, or as yet has been, but one—'The United States shall guarantee to every State in this Union a *Republican form of Government.*'"[31] Neither plural marriage nor Mormon Indian policy coincided with the American notion of a republican form of government.

In the spring of 1857, while settlers battled to promote their interests for slavery expansion or free soil in Kansas, the president and his cabinet made a decisive move in Utah to promote republicanism, build the national infrastructure, and assert federal sovereignty over the territorial population. Of the Mormon problem, papers such as the Richmond, Virginia, *Enquirer*, a politically neutral paper, believed the Mormons had no right to exercise self-government unless they relinquished their "barbarous code of laws" and conformed to "the usages of civilized society." The *Enquirer* further suggested that the "interests and honor of the people of the States" were threatened by Utah and recommended that the federal government "should energetically exercise the powers with which it is entrusted."[32] Among those powers was the guarantee of a republican form of government and the right of the president to protect U.S. lands against domestic violence. The operation of a theocratic government in possible rebellion to usurp U.S. lands meant that the federal government could legitimately and "energetically" exercise its constitutional power in sending the army to Utah to correct the power balance in the region that the Mormons had upset. Pennsylvania senator William Bigler informed the president that a *"universal sentiment"* against the Mormons demanded action. Similarly, political confidant Robert Tyler urged Buchanan to seize this Mormon question "with a strong fearless resolute hand," with the enticement that the "eyes and hearts of the Nation may be made to find so much interest in Utah as to forget Kansas!"[33] Popular sovereignty had problems in Kansas because the mechanisms of voting meant that the voice and will of the people did not always get a fair decision. In Utah, Americans perceived that the Mormons defied federal authority, and popular sovereignty did not allow for local control insubordinate to the national government. Kansans, who knew better than to attack the federal government, complained that the federal government's obsession with Kansas allowed for the growth of "King Brigham." The Lawrence, Kansas-based *Herald of Freedom* recommended that the White House focus on policing Utah and its troublemaking Mormon neighbors. The *Herald* blamed popular sovereignty:

> The great doctrine of Squatter Sovereignty, the nursling of that same administration, the political foundling of Cass, the pet of Douglas, and the darling of Pierce, has turned up to be a young giant in Utah. Brigham Young has adopted him, and the naughty child has learned to repeat the language of his venerable ancestor, that "new States have the right to shape their own destiny, by embracing or rejecting whatever institutions they please; that is, that the people have a right to regulate their own *domestic* institutions."[34]

Public opinion flamed against the Mormon operation of Utah Territory. The time had come to let them know that they were not as powerful as the American government.

The shared tendency of both Republicans and Democrats to create political "others" emerged as the Mormons became a common "non-American," "nonrepublican" enemy. Many justifications were introduced for interfering in Utah's local politics by the Democrats, but their inconsistency on the issue of popular sovereignty, especially its implementation, only served to further spur debate on the merits of this guiding principle. As the spring of 1857 approached, more newspapers and periodicals reported on the otherness of Mormons. Some of President Buchanan's close confidants and political allies suggested that acting against Utah's aberrant government with military force would unify the country. Such an idea seemed to suggest that as long as the Democrats could show the Mormons as unfit for republican self-government, their interference in territorial local politics would be construed as a responsible action rather than turning popular sovereignty into a farce.[35] With a move against Utah, the logic held, the president could distance his party from Republican anti–popular sovereignty rhetoric that tied plural marriage to slavery in hopes of maintaining sectional balance. However much Americans deplored Mormons and their social structure, political opponents of popular sovereignty saw the inherent contradiction in Democratic policy. The attempt to distance from plural marriage would distance the Democrats from slavery and raise the specter of federal power to prohibit all domestic institutions in the western territories, a possibility that southern interests had feared since even before the Wilmot Proviso in 1846.

Nevertheless, to uphold the constitutional promise of continuing republican government as new lands and people were integrated into the national whole, Buchanan's cabinet did not opt to repeal Utah's organic act. Rather, it opted for federal military action to restructure territorial authority and institute a republican form of government run by non-Mormon officers despite the potential problems such a move might cause concerning popular sovereignty. Buchanan began his presidential administration as a calculated scheming interventionist in the territories. He and his cabinet made a crucial decision to send the federal army to gain control of Utah, and almost simultaneously, he advocated the passage of a constitution permitting slavery in Kansas Territory.[36]

The Buchanan administration's mode of decision-making was collaboration. This was typically achieved through long discussions that

FIG. 8. The Buchanan administration, ca. 1859. From bottom left: Jacob Thompson, secretary of the interior; John B. Floyd, secretary of war; Lewis Cass, secretary of state; Howell Cobb, secretary of the treasury; Joseph Holt, postmaster general (assumed this position in 1859 replacing Aaron V. Brown); Isaac Toucey, secretary of the navy; and Jeremiah S. Black, attorney general. James Buchanan pictured in the center. Courtesy of the National Archives and Records Administration.

ended in consensus among the president and cabinet members. Buchanan's main goal as president was to uphold the Constitution. While Buchanan served as secretary of state in the James Polk administration, he observed that the president was vigorously active in extending American sovereignty and acknowledged California military authorities as a de facto government as long as they did not exercise power inconsistent with the provisions of the Constitution. Buchanan brought this previous experience and his ideals of strict construction of the Constitution to the White House. Since Buchanan sought for consensus among his cabinet, a quick examination of their views on popular sovereignty and Utah affairs is important to understanding the ideologies that informed the administration's ultimate decision to send troops to Utah.[37]

In January 1857, Secretary of State Lewis Cass, who had served as secretary of war and fielded Mormon complaints from their Missouri experiences in 1833 and 1834, wrote a letter indicating his preference to see the president stabilize problems in the territories and demonstrate that the federal government held sovereignty in the territories. Attorney General Jeremiah Black too supported a strict construction of the Constitution. He understood that the territories were wholly dependent upon Congress for their very existence, and he maintained that local territorial populations held little power.

In the spring of 1857, Black received influential letters from two federal officers who had recently left Utah: a letter of resignation from William W. Drummond, a justice of Utah's federal supreme court, and a letter from former Utah Territory chief justice John F. Kinney. Among the reasons he provided for leaving his post, Drummond suggested "all male members of the Church" resisted the laws of the country and that all Mormons looked to their prophet for the law to which they should abide. Drummond accused the Mormons of slandering federal officials and the executive branch when he complained that religious leaders in Utah daily disparaged the federal officers and the form of American government. Drummond held the Democratic

Party, though he numbered himself a Democrat, responsible for "the treasonable and disgraceful state of affairs that now exists in Utah Territory." The disgruntled judge finally indicated that a non-Mormon government with sufficient military aid would produce the desired results of control over government, Indian affairs, and society generally.[38]

Kinney similarly advised the White House on the state of affairs in the Great Basin. Among Kinney's six points in a letter he sent to Attorney General Black were that the "Mormons are inimical to the Government of the U.S." and that they send out men "every year for the ostensible purpose of converting the Indians but really to poison their minds against the government and Americans and also to make them their allies in case of any difficulty with the U.S."[39] Kinney closed his letter to Black declaring that federal officers needed to be sustained in the discharge of their duties by a military force. Those two elements, a non-Mormon government and a permanent military presence that would aid in the enforcement of federal law, both Drummond and Kinney believed, would change the dynamic enough to ensure the expansion of American sovereignty in Utah and in the West. In May 1857, though, Drummond expressed some discontent that Attorney General Black and the Buchanan presidential administration had not made an overwhelming show of federal force against the Mormons in Utah. The judge believed the cabinet to be "ignorant beyond comparison" because Buchanan, along with Cass, Black, John Floyd, and Jacob Thompson, thought "less than one thousand men would be amply sufficient to enforce the laws and also coerce the Mormons." The president and his cabinet, Drummond declared, did not "appreciate the power of the Mormons."[40]

A report from Secretary of War John B. Floyd confirmed his support of federal military action in Utah. He implied that the Mormons had prepared themselves for a successful secession from the authority of the United States in order to establish their own independent nation. Floyd was also influenced by an important letter from General

Winfield Scott in early 1857. Scott's letter emphasized the importance of women to crumbling the Mormon stranglehold over government in Utah. Of Utah society, Scott wrote, "No divisions of interest or sentiment is known to exist among the Mormons in respect to obedience to their Church or to the laws of the U. States. They are understood to be, *to a man*, on the side of the former & the two are utterly repugnant and antagonistic. The only hope of a schism rests on the women. They may create a party among the *American* men in favor of Christianity, law & order." Scott, in a way similar to observations made after the departure of Steptoe's troops from Utah in 1855, seemed to advocate warfare and control over the people in Utah through sexual conquest. This letter, a proposal to send a military force to Salt Lake City in the summer of 1857 to enforce obedience to the laws of the United States, suggested that occupying the city with an adequate force of men could have a desirable effect on the territory's women while simultaneously coercing the Mormons to submit to the sovereign authority of the United States. In essence, the ideas in this letter, certainly read by the president and the cabinet, confirm that sending the army to Utah for permanent settlement would conquer the Mormons on two fronts: "their" women, and by extension their familial structure and subversive political system.[41] Jacob Thompson, the secretary of the interior, also recounted the letters he had received from various commissioners of Indian affairs and that were in his files from the previous seven years' experience telling of Mormon efforts to align with Native Americans against the United States. He too did not object to using military force in a territory to uphold the Constitution and federal laws.

The early months of 1857 also brought changes to territorial Indian affairs. Congress went to work to enact legislation changing the dual responsibilities combined in the office of superintendent of Indian affairs and governor in the territories. Since the Northwest Ordinance, the responsibilities of the governors were primarily to administer the affairs of the territory and its white inhabitants. However, just following the enactment of the ordinance, in a resolution of 3 October 1787,

FIG. 9. This *Frank Leslie's* cartoon illustrates the federal government's hoped-for response of Mormon women to the coming of the soldiers, while one crowns Brigham Young with a book of law and order. From the author's collection.

Congress combined the office of superintendent of Indian affairs with that of the governor. This action established the pattern and precedent for the organization of new territories. The Department of State directed the territorial work of a governor, but his duties as an ex officio superintendent of Indian affairs came under the direction of the War Department and, subsequently, of the Department of the Interior. As Indian superintendent, the governor found himself in general required to act as the chief liaison officer between the Indian Office in Washington and the agents in the field and to implement the Indian policy of the federal government in his territory. The dual appointment gave one man immense power over two of the most significant facets of territorial life.

In this most important time and place for federal Indian affairs, territorial governors, such as Brigham Young, presided over the dealings, and the quarrels, of both the American Indians and the whites. Young used his dual office to try to conciliate Native peoples and keep them friendly with his religious followers. Implementing federal Indian policy in the territories, keeping the peace, and disbursing and accounting for federal funds, which amounted annually to many thousands of dollars, constituted the responsibilities and activities of the

Indian superintendent.[42] In Utah, the governor made efforts to reconcile these objectives. He undoubtedly advanced the interests of the Mormon civilian population. He also looked after Indian rights and welfare as they pertained to the LDS religion. The Mormons' Indian policy, though, diverged from federal Indian policy and even violated federal law by sending missionaries with potentially subversive messages to the area's indigenous population. In addition, Mormon Indian policy could not keep "the Indians at peace" any better than the government's policy. By the middle of the 1850s, the public and its officials perceived Utah as a striking example of the dual office appointment as bad strategy.

As early as 1854, the commissioner of Indian affairs recommended dividing the duties of Indian affairs from the governor. In his annual report of that year, Commissioner George Manypenny stated his concern that one man was both governor and superintendent of Indian affairs and therefore responsible for overseeing both the white and Indian populations in the western territories of New Mexico, Utah, Oregon, Washington, and Minnesota. He thought it more prudent, efficient, and harmonious to separate these responsibilities as had been done in Kansas and Nebraska Territories.[43] In March 1857, Congress finally took action on Manypenny's suggestion and authorized the discontinuance of the combined office in the aforementioned western territories.

On 3 March 1857, Congress passed the Indian Appropriations Act. In a significant development in territorial administration, the act officially divided the offices of governor and superintendent of Indian affairs in several territories, including Utah, Oregon, and New Mexico. Section 3 of the act provided a substantial reassertion of federal power over western territorial Indian policy by stipulating that the "superintendents of Indian affairs in the Territories of Oregon, Washington, Utah, and New Mexico, shall negotiate no treaties with any Indian tribes within said Territories, unless instructed thereto by the President of the United States." Both the 1857 Indian Appropriations Act and the 1834 Trade and Intercourse Act endowed the president with more power over the territories and in Native American relations. In addition to making the negotiation of territorial Indian treaties a presidential prerogative, the Appropriations Act placed the power to appoint superintendents of Indian affairs in the four western territories with the president.[44] One man no longer legally controlled the interests of both whites and Native Americans in Utah Territory.[45]

Indian administration was a focal point of federal activity in the West and at the center of national expansion. Nearly three decades of mainstream American public discourse characterized Mormons and Native Americans, separately and together, as a threat to U.S. control. Resulting partly from the assumed complicity of American Indians and Mormons as sinister allies in the Great Basin region, based in reports and correspondence from federal officers in the territory, President Buchanan made his decision to reaffirm the federal administrative structure concerning Indian affairs in Utah. The federal government accepted the numerous reports that demonstrated Mormon interference with federal Indian policy, particularly the Trade and Intercourse Act. Civil administrators were given primary responsibility for organizing, controlling, and directing settlement and expansion. Mormon civil administrators, particularly Brigham Young, however, directed territorial Indian policy in line with religious views by proselytizing to indigenous peoples, which, as James Buchanan believed, excited "their hostile feelings against the United States." The Buchanan administration decided to send the army to Utah in part because of the voluminous documents on difficulties with the Mormons concerning Indian affairs and because of the administration's belief that Mormon missionaries were breaking the laws of the United States by attempting to turn Native Americans into hostile enemies.[46] A restoration of federal authority in Utah Territory was therefore in order; this required that U.S. troops go to Utah Territory to enforce federal Indian policy.[47] The Mormons, primarily through their missionaries, had reportedly inflamed insubordination and discontent among Great Basin

Native peoples against American citizens and interests. Coupling the presidential authority granted in the recently passed Appropriations Act and the 1834 Trade and Intercourse Act, Buchanan's administration moved to sustain its legal position toward Native Americans and the territories with the necessary power and the means of enforcement.

Within Buchanan's cabinet, a consensus emerged that Utah's constituents were not capable of political autonomy and the federal government could not complete the transfer of sovereign capacity to Utah because of the reports of Mormon tampering with Indians and developing a nonrepublican form of government and social structure. The rhetorical consensus and legal precedents justified a controversial but legitimate federal action based in the president's power vested in him by the Northwest Ordinance, Kansas-Nebraska Act, and federal Indian laws. Thus, the federal government viewed the Mormons as a people incompatible to and irreconcilable with national republican identity, which required a push into Salt Lake City to break up their monopoly on the region. Buchanan's cabinet decided to pursue military action to ensure that new federal officers could perform their duties in extending the U.S. federal government's sovereignty in the territory.

On 28 May 1857, Buchanan ordered some 2,500 troops to Utah. In his first annual message as president, given on 8 December 1857, Buchanan provided his first public explanation for sending soldiers to permanently occupy Utah. The president explained his concern that as the head of church and state in Utah, Young held too much power and that his was a particularly antirepublican form of power. He stated: "Whilst Governor Young has been both governor and superintendent of Indian affairs throughout this period, he has been at the same time the head of the church called the Latter-Day Saints, and professes to govern its members and dispose of their property by direct inspiration and authority from the Almighty. His power has been, therefore, absolute over both church and State." Buchanan alluded to the nonrepublican form of government operating in Utah and continued in his remarks that as president the duty fell to him to ensure that this territory, in preparation for eventual statehood, had restored to it the supremacy of the Constitution and federal law. President Buchanan sent the U.S. Army to Utah Territory for several purposes, but one that he articulated in particular was the growing national fear that as superintendent of Indian affairs in Utah Territory, Brigham Young "has had an opportunity of tampering with the Indian tribes, and exciting their hostile feelings against the United States." As a part of redeeming the laws of the United States, which Buchanan suggested as the primary reason for the military action, came the vindication of national sovereignty and federal Indian policy, notably the sections of the Trade and Intercourse Act and the Appropriations Act that gave him the authority to do so. In order to achieve these ends and hoping to reverse the trend of what had been ineffective territorial management and governance to date, Buchanan appointed a new governor, Alfred Cumming of Georgia, who had previously served as a superintendent of Indian affairs in St. Louis, as well as new judges and a new superintendent of Indian affairs for Utah in accordance with the Indian Appropriations Act. He sent with these officers a military force for their protection, and to aid as a *posse comitatus*, in case of need, in the execution of the laws.[48]

The *posse comitatus* model was well entrenched in America's legal tradition, dating from the Judiciary Act of 1789. Congress passed legislation on 3 March 1807 that made it lawful in cases of insurrection or obstruction to federal laws for the president to call out the militia or U.S. armed forces if necessary. This law's phraseology echoed Article IV, Section 4, of the Constitution, but it went a step further by bestowing ultimate authority on the president to call out federal troops for civil duty. In the case of a federal territory, the *posse comitatus* was controlled from the executive office, and the army retained its regular chain of command. The *posse comitatus* model maintained internal security. As the historian Joan M. Jensen notes, the "national army could be used as a posse comitatus against a growing number of white citizens who opposed the laws of the land." The army was at the disposal of the president and could be used in various ways, including in the interference of domestic institutions in the territories.[49]

In a later message endorsing the proslavery Lecompton Constitution in Kansas, Buchanan used similar rhetoric about the *posse comitatus* on the violation of law that had kept the Territory of Kansas in a state of nearly open rebellion against the government. He discussed the refusal of Kansans to submit to lawful authority and stated that the people's boycott of the election demonstrated their deplorable character and the need for federal intervention. Since those people boycotted the vote and the Lecompton Constitution was passed, Buchanan suggested that a general spirit against its enforcement "will prove fatal to us as a nation." "It is the same spirit which has produced actual rebellion in Utah," Buchanan stated. The safety of the nation consists only, he further remarked, "in obedience and conformity to law." He argued that popular sovereignty had been exercised through the ballot-box, that the Lecompton convention was legally constituted, and that if the people refused to vote it was not for them to complain that their rights had been violated. A *posse comitatus* was also ordered to Kansas to combat those who opposed the Lecompton law.[50]

The threat of Mormon independent sovereignty represented by their nonrepublican government, plural marriage family structure, and Indian policies proved so troubling to national leaders of the Democratic Party that they were willing to expose the shortcomings in their doctrine of popular sovereignty to restrain that threat. Despite his 1856 presidential platform pledge and the rhetoric of his inaugural address to not interfere in the territories, James Buchanan sent the army to Utah to extend republicanism and federal influence over Utah Territory.

Just two weeks after Buchanan made that decision, on 12 June 1857, Stephen A. Douglas, one of the most prominent proponents of the Democratic doctrine of popular sovereignty, gave a speech at Springfield, Illinois, on sovereignty in the territories. Although he was unaware of Buchanan's decision at the time, Douglas too criticized Utah's form of governance and society and the Mormons' tampering with Native peoples. The Illinois senator characterized Mormonism as a disgusting cancer on the body politic. Independently of one another, Buchanan and then Douglas advocated greater federal authority over territorial affairs in Utah.

Douglas's Springfield speech spoke to the Supreme Court's recent *Dred Scott* decision, bleeding Kansas, and Utah, three of the most volatile matters of the day concerning popular sovereignty. The senator spent precious little time on Kansas because "little need be said at the present," as he endorsed the 6 March 1857 *Dred Scott* ruling that the federal government had no authority to prohibit slavery in the territories. Even if territorial residents voted to deny slavery expansion within its borders, the *Dred Scott* decision clearly decreed those same territorial residents could not exercise such power and that the federal government would not assist them in any attempt to prohibit slavery in the territory. Said more simply, *Dred Scott* affirmed the right of slaveholders in the territories. Though Douglas supported the Supreme Court ruling, it flew in the face of popular sovereignty and the power of local self-government to decide domestic institutions. The Illinois senator's remarks on Utah Territory also contradicted the Democratic platform of popular sovereignty. Douglas argued that the "Mormon government" operated a nonrepublican form of government based on its peculiar institutions and allegedly subversive alliances with Indian tribes. Congress, he thought, had the right to repeal the territory's organic act, remove it as a geopolitical entity, and assert federal sovereignty over that jurisdiction. Douglas further asserted that the federal government could repeal the organic act on the grounds that the Mormons disavowed their allegiance to the United States and they were "alien enemies and outlaws, unfit to exercise the right of self-government." The Illinois senator and chairperson of the Senate Committee on Territories emphasized that Mormons were incapable of exercising popular sovereignty in the territory and that they only sought statehood to "protect them in their treason and crime, debauchery and infamy."

Furthermore, he argued that to protect them in their "treasonable" and "bestial" practices by allowing them to govern themselves would be a disgrace to humanity and civilization and potentially fatal to American interests in the West. Douglas advocated no temporary policy or halfway measures, but decisiveness in Utah. His proposal to repeal the Utah territorial organic act, abolish the territorial government, and bring the territory in line with republican institutions met with applause from the many Democrats in the audience.[51]

An occasional ally to the Mormons during their sojourn in Illinois in the 1840s, Douglas had a long familiarity with the group and its difficulties. He served as a state supreme court justice in Illinois and rendered a decision in one of Joseph Smith's extradition cases in that state. Douglas declared the writ of extradition issued by the state of Missouri invalid and therefore set Smith free from bond and extradition to Missouri in 1841. Douglas and Smith had other interactions, and in 1843, Douglas even suggested that the Mormons go west to Oregon and establish their community in that place away from persecution. During the next decade, however, he reconsidered. He had received letters from Utah Latter-day Saints, including Brigham Young, demonstrating their desire for autonomous self-government according to the doctrine of popular sovereignty, especially as contained in the Utah Organic Act and the Kansas-Nebraska Act.[52]

The Kansas-Nebraska Act when examined closely was meant to determine, through popular sovereignty, the acceptance, or not, of slavery in the new territories. Sections 14 and 32 of the Act stated: "It being the true intent and meaning of this act not to legislate slavery into any Territory or State, nor to exclude it therefore, but to leave the people thereof perfectly free to form and regulate their domestic institutions,"—which included among other things property, family affairs, education, morality, public health, and slavery—"in their own way, subject only to the Constitution of the United States: *provided*, that nothing herein contained shall be construed to revive or put in force any law or regulation which may have existed prior to the act of sixth of March, eighteen hundred and twenty, either protecting, establishing, prohibiting, or abolishing slavery." However, the vague or ambiguous language of "domestic institutions" in the Kansas-Nebraska Act allowed the Mormon leadership to read its own version of popular sovereignty into the act, one that permitted its theocratic form of government and plural marriage. Other politicians and pundits also noticed the enigmatic phrase "domestic institutions," which they believed gave the people of the territories freedom and sovereignty similar to that of a state. In a letter to Douglas, Brigham Young claimed that the Mormons should not be exempt from popular sovereignty and the enjoyment of self-government given the Kansas-Nebraska guarantee that the people of a territory had the right to choose and regulate their own domestic institutions in their own way. Brigham Young expressed to Douglas his belief that the people of Utah Territory had the right to make their own choices as to who governed them.[53] The Illinois senator disagreed.

Douglas asserted that the federal government could repeal the organic act because Mormons were not capable of self-government. They were unfit citizens of a territory operating a nonrepublican government and as such could never earn statehood as an equal political entity with the other states of the Union. Only citizens, and not "alien enemies," could vote and operate a government under the Constitution, and Douglas proclaimed that granting the Mormons sovereignty would only provide them with an "invincible shield to protect them in their treason and crime, debauchery and infamy." Douglas agreed with the president in using "all the military force necessary to protect the officers in discharge of their duties, and to enforce the laws of the land." In other words, he advanced the idea of bringing the territory "under the sole and exclusive jurisdiction of the United States." To Douglas this was not a moral issue, but a legal one. Douglas did not believe that morality had anything to do with the right to repeal an organic act of a territory. Rather, in the Utah case, because an antirepublican government and an "alien" population resisted the authority of the United States,

Congress could and should abolish that territorial government and make it operate under the same system of laws that operated in "Kansas, Nebraska, Minnesota, and our other Territories."[54]

Within two months of delivering the speech, Douglas received several letters of approval for his stance on Utah. Many came from those intimately knowledgeable about the territory's history. The first territorial surveyor general in Utah, David H. Burr, remarked, "Your views of affairs in Utah are correct and your suggestions relative to the course to be pursued is the true one; and I hope & trust, will be carried out by the administration. My residence of more than two years among the Mormons, has made me thoroughly acquainted with too much of this villany, and the newspaper accounts fail to give a full & correct picture of the state of affairs in that Territory." Likewise, Benjamin G. Ferris, a former territorial secretary in Utah, received a copy of the speech and responded with great interest. Ferris thanked the senator for the speech, and in return he sent Douglas a copy of his book about the Mormon community entitled *Utah and the Mormons*. Ferris, an outspoken critic of the Mormon community, referred Douglas to pages "368–9 where I have ventured to suggest some remedies for the unfortunate state of things in Utah. Your proposition to repeal the organic act strikes me as altogether the most efficatious and I greatly wonder it did not occur to me." Charles J. Faulkner, a Democrat from Virginia and the House Committee on Military Affairs chair in 1857, similarly approved of the speech and asserted, "It will unquestionably become our duty in the next Congress to take some decisive steps in relation to *Utah*." Faulkner further suggested that he had heard of no better solution to this difficult problem than those delivered in Douglas's Springfield speech.[55]

A "Mr. Buck" from Omaha, Nebraska, also read Douglas's speech in the newspaper and responded. This Nebraskan observed, "Your views on Utah will be hailed here with great pleasure, here upon the border where we see more of them and of their infernal acts." T. P. Andrews, deputy paymaster general of the U.S. Army on sick leave from

Fort Leavenworth, also wrote to Douglas. He described the problems the army faced in Kansas and added that many of his colleagues at Fort Leavenworth read the speech closely. The consensus, according to Andrews, was that Douglas's ideas for Utah were the "true & wise exposition of the course the gov't should pursue towards Brigham & his deluded followers. I did not hear a single intelligent officer of the Army that did not express an ardent wish the gov't would act on the same principles, action by Congress *first*; & the use of the Army *afterwards*." William Wick from Indianapolis wrote that unless the nation subscribed to Douglas's designated plan, "then Utah matters will trouble us terribly." Wick continued, "No government ought to expose itself to the defeat which must necessarily follow effort to enforce decent laws in Utah, as a Territory. To admit it as a State, with a Mormon population would overwhelm the Democratic Party probably, and is for that and other reasons not an admissible idea." Wick observed that the Mormon question could divide the Democratic Party; therefore, he concurred with Douglas's proposition for Utah Territory. As these six letters indicate, people from all sections of the nation backed Douglas's proposition, feeling it essentially right and not at all inconsistent with the doctrine of popular sovereignty.[56]

Douglas's speech, however, gave the Republicans and anyone else concerned about popular sovereignty reason to pause. Detractors indicted Douglas for promoting national sovereignty over Utah Territory and for even arguing against his own doctrine that idealistically guaranteed to "each State and Territory the right to do as it pleases on all things, local and domestic, instead of Congress interfering." This speech coupled with Buchanan's decision to send the federal army to Utah created a political nightmare for the Democrats. They claimed to protect the threats to republicanism found in Utah and that they were therefore not acting against popular sovereignty. However, these ideas and actions privileged national sovereignty over local autonomy as the Republican Party platform declared just a year earlier in 1856.

Democratic actions in Utah provided Republicans with a new, tangible example to further attack the opposing party as hypocrites.[57]

Douglas had many detractors. The most important critique came from Republican up-and-comer Abraham Lincoln. Lincoln gave a speech in Springfield fifteen days after Douglas. Although the *Dred Scott* decision constituted the largest part of his speech, Lincoln spent nearly as much time discussing Mormon Utah as he did bleeding Kansas. He condemned Douglas's popular sovereignty idea, calling it "squatter sovereignty," and uncovered the contradictions put forth by the Illinois senator relative to local self-government and states' rights. Lincoln said, "The Mormons ought to obey the law as all good citizens do and should." However, the future emancipator stated, "If it prove to be true, as is probable, that the people of Utah are in open rebellion to the United States, then Judge Douglas is in favor of repealing their territorial organization, and attaching them to the adjoining States for judicial purposes. I say, too, if they are in rebellion, they ought to be somehow coerced to obedience; and I am not now prepared to admit or deny that the Judge's mode of coercing them is as good as any." However, Lincoln wanted an important question answered. If the Mormons desired to "live without law—without records—without Courts, and I thought the sacred right of Squatter Sovereignty secured to every people the right of the people to live as they pleased. Now, why deprive them of this fundamental right?—that is the question." Why then, he asked, did the senator presently back down from his beloved doctrine? "This thing of Squatter Sovereignty was never anything but a humbug," Lincoln asserted, because it was designed to extend slavery to the West. Lincoln used Douglas's renunciation of the Mormon version of popular sovereignty to attack the expansion of slavery by the same principle.[58]

The Republicans claimed that the Democrats had sold out to slavery. Republicans did not disagree with the government's power over the territory but made a direct connection to the overarching issue of self-government and slavery. Believing in the ability of the government to interfere in the territories when necessary, Lincoln also suggested that the federal government ought to coerce the Mormons to obedience to the Constitution and laws of the United States. Lincoln continued by attacking Douglas's backtracking on his "beloved principle." He stated, "To be sure, it would be a considerable backing down by Judge Douglas from his much vaunted doctrine of self government for the territories; but this is only additional proof of what was very plain from the beginning, that that doctrine was a mere deceitful pretence for the benefit of Slavery. Those who could not see that much in the Nebraska Act itself, with forced Governors, and Secretaries, and Judges on the people of the Territories, without their choice or consent... There is nothing in the United States Constitution or law against polygamy? And why is it not a part of the Judge's 'sacred right of self government' for that people to have it, or rather to *keep* it, if they choose?" Plural marriage was not outlawed by any federal legislation, and Lincoln employed this illustration to demonstrate that neither Douglas nor any other Democrat ever answered such an important question.[59]

Lincoln, whose speech, like Douglas's, was published in most of the major national newspapers, saw a grave inconsistency in squatter sovereignty demonstrating that the Mormons had not used the doctrine according to the Democratic plan. With this speech, he rephrased the very quandary that Representative Justin S. Morrill articulated four months earlier. Assertive and explicit legislative action to crush Utah's domestic institutions would violate the Democratic Party's doctrine of popular sovereignty and aggravate southern fears about restrictions on the future of slavery expansion and threats to slavery's very existence. For the Democrats, according to Republican orators, popular sovereignty was the guiding and only acceptable doctrine of the nation, unless a group of people used it contrary to or inconsistent with their designs for slavery extension. While that may have been the case, the Democrats acted in defense of popular sovereignty as it related to slavery but were quick to assert imperial control over an undesirable, foreign government and population in the West.

Another critical eye on the proposal to repeal Utah's Territorial Organic Act came from a lawyer with a pen name of M. McConnel. He disagreed with Douglas's Springfield speech on constitutional grounds. McConnel believed that Douglas overstated the power of the federal government because of ambiguities related to the territorial provisions in the Constitution.

The lawyer highlighted an important problem that the nation grappled with in western territories: whether territories under popular sovereignty had the same rights as those of a state. McConnel felt that Douglas's suggestions about Utah granted the federal government too much power to legislate over a local entity and that if it could repeal laws in or over an entire territory then it could do the same to a state according to the popular sovereignty principle that placed territories on the same sovereign plane as states.[60]

McConnel, however, seems to have missed the most crucial part of Douglas's reasoning for abolishing Utah Territory. Douglas asserted that a nonrepublican form of government operated by alien enemies existed in the Great Basin. The Constitution, according to the same clause as put forth by McConnel, guaranteed to each state in the union a republican form of government. As a condition of tutelage, on the way to statehood, the Constitution required Utah to have a republican government. Douglas and others imagined Utah as operating an alternative governmental system; therefore, decisive action to uphold the Constitution was constitutional. Nevertheless, McConnel's analysis and indication of uncertain constitutional principles echoed Abraham Lincoln's description of the inconsistencies in popular sovereignty. The main difference for Douglas was that he did not consider southern slaveholders as antirepublican, alien enemies, as he did the Mormons in Utah. That nuance, however, did not stop his detractors from emphasizing the Utah case as a major contradiction to the ideal of popular sovereignty.

More criticism of Douglas's supposed reversal came via the press. Newspapers in New York, Chicago, Boston, Washington DC, St. Louis, and other major population centers published Douglas's speech. The *Chicago Daily Tribune* called Douglas two-faced in a 16 June 1857 editorial. To blot Utah out as one of the organized territories of the United States and to repeal its organic law, the paper stated, was to suggest that the general government would hold the whole and sole jurisdiction over any territory or state in the union. With the power to repeal an organic act, regulate, and legislate for a territory, the federal government could reverse the measures of self-government at any time. Douglas had apparently abandoned the great fundamental principle that every people ought to possess the right of forming and regulating their own internal concerns and domestic institutions in their own way. "Hereafter, then, when the *Times* and other organs of the Pro-Slavery party set up their customary howl over the abominations of Mormonism," the editorial declared, "it will be well to suggest that they also charge Mr. Douglas with the folly of being the active agent in getting them permission to work these abominations with entire impunity. Without his now abandoned Squatter Sovereignty—the rankest political humbug upon which a small demagogue was ever wrecked—Mormonism, in its present shape, would never have been." Douglas's new position on Utah indicated that sovereignty did not lie with the people, but in the form of the territory; and even the sovereignty of the territory was so precarious a possession that Congress or the president could remove it without ceremony. Similar to other critiques, the *Tribune* writer feared the potential growth in federal power that would allow the government to prohibit slavery expansion and even go so far as to wholly remove states' rights.[61]

Who held sovereignty in a territory was the crux of most of the rhetorical responses to Douglas's speech. Prior to Douglas's speech, a writer in the antislavery *National Era* described "the miserable doctrine of squatter sovereignty" as one that shuts Congress out of the territories and prevents the electorate from having a say in the destiny, character, and institutions of vast territories. Following the speech, a *National Era* article stated, "It thus appears from Mr. Douglas's own exposition, that this vaunted right of the people of the Territories to govern themselves is not what he used to call it, an 'inherent right of self government,' but merely a privilege, that Congress may give or take away as it pleases." Popular sovereignty in Kansas and slavery expansion in western territories generally served as the backdrop to this discussion. Although the Kansas-Nebraska Act unquestionably provided for the possibility of slavery in western territories under the phrasing of domestic institutions, the Utah case served as a foil for antislavery and anti–popular sovereignty critics.[62]

In response to his critics, Douglas argued that he was no hypocrite because he maintained that the government could not interfere in a territory regarding slavery, which position he had long advocated. It could, however, interfere with theocracy or any other threat to the growth of republican government. Nevertheless, his speech condoning federal government action in a territory created a backlash against his policy. One periodical called Douglas's doctrine an "absurdity and, to get around it, he is obliged to claim for Congress far more extensive powers than were ever exercised or even contemplated before." A *National Era* article added the following ominous question for the nation to consider: "If Congress can strip a Territory of its vaunted sovereignty, why not a State? For the sovereignty of the one is as inherent as the other; and if Congress can punish the inhabitants of a dismantled Territory for bestial practices, why not also the inhabitants of a State? And if it can, what security is left for Slavery—an institution as bestial as Polygamy, and to which a larger number are addicted." The *National Era* article further asserted that "the question as to government of Utah, however, has fairly broken [Douglas's] constancy down." It, along with the other critiques, suggests the complications introduced by popular sovereignty in Utah and the general idea that the Democratic doctrine espoused of equating territorial autonomy with that of a state.[63]

A *Harper's Weekly* article likewise focused on the problems wrought by repealing organic acts. It stated:

This scheme of repealing Territorial Acts is open to grave objections. Suppose a new Territory carved, in any future year of grace, out of New Mexico, and organized on the basis of the Kansas and Nebraska acts; suppose that Territory peopled with slaveholders, and prepared for admission to the Union with a Slave Constitution; and suppose a Congress strongly imbued with hostility to the extension of slavery; how convenient a precedent this scheme of Senator Douglas's would be for the passage of an Act repealing the Territorial Act of the new Territory, and leaving the offending slaveholders in the attitude of "alien enemies!"

This 4 July *Harper's* article viewed Douglas's idea of extending federal power over the Mormons in Utah as a potentially dangerous precedent. Yes, Mormons were viewed as un-American, alien enemies because of their perceived desire for independence and hostility toward republican government by the president, by Douglas and others in Congress, and by most of the nation. But extending federal control over an American territory presented more fundamental and important questions. Might the revocation of a territorial government also apply to Kansas? What would happen if the federal government, populated by Republicans, moved to control or extend its influence to repeal a territory's decision to allow slavery? This article suggested that it might turn slaveholders into "alien enemies" by forbidding slavery in new territory. Hearkening back to debates over the Wilmot Proviso wherein southerners expressed intent to secede from the United States at the prospect of prohibiting slavery in the western territories, this article and others feared that southerners might secede from the Union and become an independent nation. The article concluded with the suggestion that a temperate exercise in firmness and time, "without violating any such vital principle as the inherent sovereignty of the people of each and every separate community within the United States," would end the ultimate difficulties with Utah and save the balancing principle of popular sovereignty, "which underlies all our institutions."[64]

Douglas said popular sovereignty did not apply to Utah; it was only to be used in particular times and circumstances. But such backpedaling on the political philosophy that was to guide and balance the nation on slavery could not reverse the damage that Utah affairs brought to national political stability.

In the end, most viewed Douglas's "new Territorial policy" to make national sovereignty full and absolute over the territories as unwise. The Richmond, Virginia, *Examiner*, a Democratic southern newspaper, opined that this should "be general, and embrace all the Territories" since it allowed the country to revert to its early territorial policy "and no longer pursue the vain effort to erect popular government in the Territories before yet the family takes root, society is formed, a community is established, and a wholesome public opinion has asserted its supremacy over the people." The *Examiner* indicated that popular sovereignty was an ineffective scheme, and because of its contingent nature it would be "prostituted everywhere, resulting in all the Territories in as arrant a humbug and farce as it has done in Kansas and Utah." In both Kansas and Utah the scheme of popular sovereignty had not worked as intended by its founders. The *Examiner* concluded,

> It is clear that to leave the serious business of government to crude and half-organized communities, composed of people without any settled interests or views, is about the same as throwing a raw and inexperienced youth upon the world without guidance or control. In such a condition of premature independence, Utah has grown up insolent, rebellious, heathenish, and unmanageable. This is one of the fruits of the disastrous compromise of 1850, as Kansas is the result of the same policy, as carried out in the repeal of the Missouri Compromise. But these froward youngsters, Utah and Kansas, have grown to such a size as to make it difficult to deal with them.[65]

The equilibrium on western issues was crumbling, and federal authority was taking center stage in national discourse.

Another newspaper feared the result of absolute federal control over territorial governance. Responding to the *Examiner*'s editorial, the *Philadelphia North American and United States Gazette* stated: "This is the ancient Roman pro-consular system revived. The post of Governor of a territory would be exalted under it to a degree of power and importance hitherto unknown in the United States. The Examiner proposes to allow the settler no exercise of sovereignty, by elections, or in any other mode, until the time arrives for organizing a State government. This would abolish the territorial legislatures and all the offices and officers of local selection, leaving the very simplest outline of laws and government under the regulation of Congress." Though the federal government indeed had sovereign authority over the territories, questions remained as to how it would exercise that authority. Exacerbated by vacillation in the territorial policy of the Democratic Party, some wondered how greatly such a policy "to subject Utah to the rule of officers appointed by the President with the approval of the Senate, and to allow the settlers no participation in the government," would influence the party's future political maneuvering. Douglas's implicit renunciation of popular sovereignty in Utah provoked more intense public debates about the role of popular sovereignty in the territories. His Springfield speech suggested a refocusing of power in the federal government despite the pervading states' rights ideology. The flip-flopping and uncertainty presented by Stephen Douglas's and President Buchanan's verbal commitment to federal non-interference in Kansas but using federal force to establish national sovereignty over Utah created more questions about authority and rights in the territories than it gave answers to territorial affairs in the West.[66]

The Mormons began discussing Douglas's speech in late August 1857, after they had already learned of the president's decision to send the army to Utah. Brigham Young and *Deseret News* editor Albert Carrington prepared an editorial in response. On 30 August, at a public gathering in Salt Lake City, Young read Douglas's remarks and the official Mormon response to it. Wilford Woodruff, in attendance for the public reading of these two documents, wrote in his journal that Douglas's speech on Utah was "contemptible."[67]

The Mormon response to Douglas appeared in the *Deseret News* in early September. It consisted of two full pages with four full columns on each page disputing Douglas's several claims about the character of Utah's government and people. The Mormon paper considered Douglas's statement pure hyperbole and "a gross and palpable lie," particularly regarding his pronouncement that aliens, or foreigners, constituted 90 percent of the territorial population. "Without being fully in possession of the statistical information requisite," the *Deseret News* article insisted, "it is safely within bounds to state that foreigners bear a very much smaller proportion to the number of native born and naturalized citizens in Utah than they do in many, if not all, the principal cities in our Union." They considered Douglas's portrayal hypocritical and wondered if he or other politicians considered the disproportionate numbers of foreigners in other American cities an alien threat. The Salt Lake City paper suggested that only one-quarter of the citizens of St. Louis were American and asked, "What 'appropriate remedy' will the Senator apply to that 'evil' in St. Louis?" The LDS church's First Presidency and all levels of leadership within the church, according to this report, were composed solely of native-born Americans. Furthermore, it proclaimed, "the Territorial Assemblies and the Territorial offices have invariably been filled, with very few exceptions, with NATIVE BORN Americans." Mormon rhetoric maintained that the leaders of the church and those filling civil offices were primarily Americans and deserved their rights from the government.[68]

The *Deseret News* article also combated Douglas's claim that Young and other Mormons were forming alliances with Indian tribes in the region and stimulating them to acts of hostility against those who supported U.S. authority. It further argued that Young did nothing with Indians "except certain friendly talks, parental counsels, mutual lawful agreements, and present makings, all enjoined by the Governmental duties of his office, and for which he has been justly and highly commended by the Hon. George W. Manypenny." Regarding national Indian affairs, the *Deseret News* indicated that inconsistencies existed in the objectives and rewards for the people of the territories. "The wantonly abusing and slaughtering of Indians in Oregon and Washington Territories," according to the Mormon statement, "can be rewarded with hundreds of thousands of dollars of Government money, but the kindest and most conciliatory treatment towards them in Utah, strictly in compliance with Department instructions and with a greater trial of patience and expenditure of PRIVATE means than has ever been practiced elsewhere, meets with the vilest misrepresentation by a Senator of these United States." The Mormon report dismissed the idea of a Mormon-Indian alliance as a wild incantation done for political advancement and as "a lie too absurd to deserve even a denial, for the citizens of Utah know their rights and duties too well to transcend their bounds, neither have they a desire or occasion for transcending them, either in this or any other matter."[69]

The Mormon response described a colonial situation in Utah. The rhetoric from Douglas and the action from Buchanan to establish a military control in the territory to them represented an effort to gain ultimate control and cause a loss of sovereignty among the people of the territory. To Douglas's suggestion of Congress applying the knife and cutting the Mormons out of Utah and the American union, the *Deseret News* stated Douglas was merely "advocating the old English colonial policy for officering a people at the point of the bayonet, and in the next breath... recommending the extermination of that people." Indeed the British had a long history of controlling or dispossessing peoples "at the point of the bayonet" and the United States had, since it won its independence, sought to be recognized as the successor to Britain's North American empire.[70] The Mormons saw this as a form of imperial control to enforce an unequal power relationship in the territory by advocating and then sending a large, armed force with a class of officers to the territory. "Would any American dare risk advising," the *Deseret News* editorial questioned, "the wholesale extermination of any class of our citizens other than 'Mormons,' even though their acts had proceeded to the extent of civil war, as in Kansas? No."[71]

Young and Carrington's response to Douglas's speech closed with a diatribe labeling the senator's ideas on Utah oppressive, illegal, and unconstitutional. The report queried, "What 'practices and institutions of the 'Mormon' government' are 'infamous and disgusting'? for you have not told us. We do not get drunk, for that is a civilized and Christianized 'practice and institution', we lay no claim to it. So also of whoredom, fornication, adultery, profane swearing, lying, . . . gambling, law-breaking, murder and the whole dark catalogue of civilized and Christianized 'practices and institutions' so popular and prevalent in the world." Douglas abandoned popular sovereignty, the "only enlightened and liberal policy" for the government of the territories, according to the lengthy Mormon rebuttal. In an early August 1857 letter, Brigham Young likewise suggested that the Democrats were acting against their principles of self-government when it came to Utah. "Although the Government was not excessively friendly to us, as a people," Young wrote to his confidant Horace Eldredge, "we supposed that those principles enunciated as a platform, by the Cincinnati convention would certainly be extended to this Territory." Acting against those principles, Young argued, would prove a precedent "contrary to every rule of justice, and in direct opposition to the principles of the 'Constitution.'"[72]

Ultimately, the Mormons defended their believed right to local sovereignty and domestic arrangements with the argument that if they could be punished for their private institutions, so too could slaveholders. Orson Pratt explained, "Undertake to deprive the people of this one domestic institution," polygamy, and you can deprive them of all others upon the same principle. Mormons believed that the same Constitution that protected the right to self-government also protected religious freedoms and liberties.[73] However, the Republican "twin relics" platform tied what Mormons viewed as religious freedom to barbarism and the excesses of the slave party. Herein lay the confusion. The popular sovereignty doctrine may have protected the right of a local body to determine domestic institutions according to the Kansas-Nebraska Act and Democratic Party rhetoric, but it did not supersede the constitutional rights of Congress to override territorial legislation and ensure republicanism. Popular sovereignty ideals also did not supersede the president's authority to appoint territorial officers and enforce federal law. Utah affairs and the ambiguity of popular sovereignty magnified the questions of whether the U.S. federal government could interfere with the local institutions of a territory and under what circumstances.

The president and his cabinet determined that Mormons in Utah were failing to operate within the dual sovereignty of the United States. In Utah, national sovereignty and settler sovereignty could not accommodate each other and as a result, the specter of an armed conflict was raised. Determined to ensure obedience to federal law in Utah, Buchanan sent the army to that territory and asserted, perhaps as a shot at sectional divisions and as a warning for Kansas, "This is the first rebellion which has existed in our Territories; and humanity itself requires that we should put it down in such a manner that it shall be the last."[74] The president's action was legitimate and fell in line with the legal statutes put forth by the Constitution, the Northwest Ordinance, subsequent territorial legislation, and national Indian policy. However, because of the doctrine of territorial self-government and the questions surrounding it, the actions of the federal government exercising power in a locality suggested a turn toward the ascendancy of national sovereignty in the West. At that politically contested time, however, such a trend toward federal power did nothing to alleviate sectional concerns. It was not a politically savvy maneuver.

5 The Utah War and the Westward March of Federal Sovereignty, 1857–1858

In the summer of 1857, the army began its march to Utah. Accompanying the army, President James Buchanan had appointed and sent new federal officials to govern the territory, including Alfred Cumming as the new governor and Jacob Forney as the new superintendent of Indian affairs. Both men were to replace Brigham Young, who had served in those dual roles since 1850. The new appointees and the army marched to Utah to promote national sovereignty and the enforcement of federal law over the territory, assume control over the territory's Indian affairs, and accelerate white westward expansion.[1] While the army and new federal officials traveled west to the edge of the Great Basin, Congress debated the merits of enlarging the army in Utah specifically and what that meant for federal authority in the territories more generally. These early 1858 congressional discussions placed Utah affairs alongside the ongoing crisis in Kansas over the Lecompton constitution. The Utah War emerged at an inopportune time for Buchanan and the Democrats as they attempted to balance and manage the expansion of federal sovereignty in Utah without imperiling local choice for slavery in Kansas.

With the Mormons' potentially subversive government, social structure, and relationship with the region's indigenous peoples blocking a crucial path to American republicanism, progress, and expansion, Buchanan saw an opportunity to expedite and enlarge the federal government's presence along vital transportation routes in the West. The army's orders were to take up a commanding position in the heart of Mormon Utah "for the performance of the ordinary military duties of security and protection upon our frontiers, and also, if necessary, to aid in the enforcement of law" and to support public peace.[2] As a *posse comitatus* the army fell under the direction of and was to act in conformity with the instructions of the chief executive magistrate, or governor, of the territory. Though not originally assigned to lead the command, General Albert Sidney Johnston took the lead after General William Harney remained in Kansas to support the federal troops mediating problems between proslavery and free-soil settlers in that territory.[3] With the strategic stationing of the army in the Great Basin to support the new non-Mormon federal officials, the Democratic president made a strong show of force that introduced a significant non-Mormon population and promised to restrict Mormon sovereignty. The use of federal power in Utah, however, engendered more debate over the question of the future use of federal power in the territories.

After the army began its march to Utah from Fort Leavenworth, Kansas, in July 1857, Captain Stewart Van Vliet, an assistant quartermaster, received an order to proceed with an advance company ahead to Salt Lake City to procure provisions and determine the availability of supplies and forage along the route and in Utah Territory. Van Vliet's orders also directed him to scout the area around Salt Lake City to find a suitable location replete with wood, water, and grazing lands for a military camp. Above all Van Vliet's was to "treat the inhabitants of Utah with kindness and consideration."[4] Van Vliet had previous contact with the Mormons at Winter Quarters in Nebraska and had treated them well, which made his diplomatic mission to inform the people of Utah of the army's intentions more likely to succeed. The captain arrived in Utah on 8 September 1857 with a letter from the

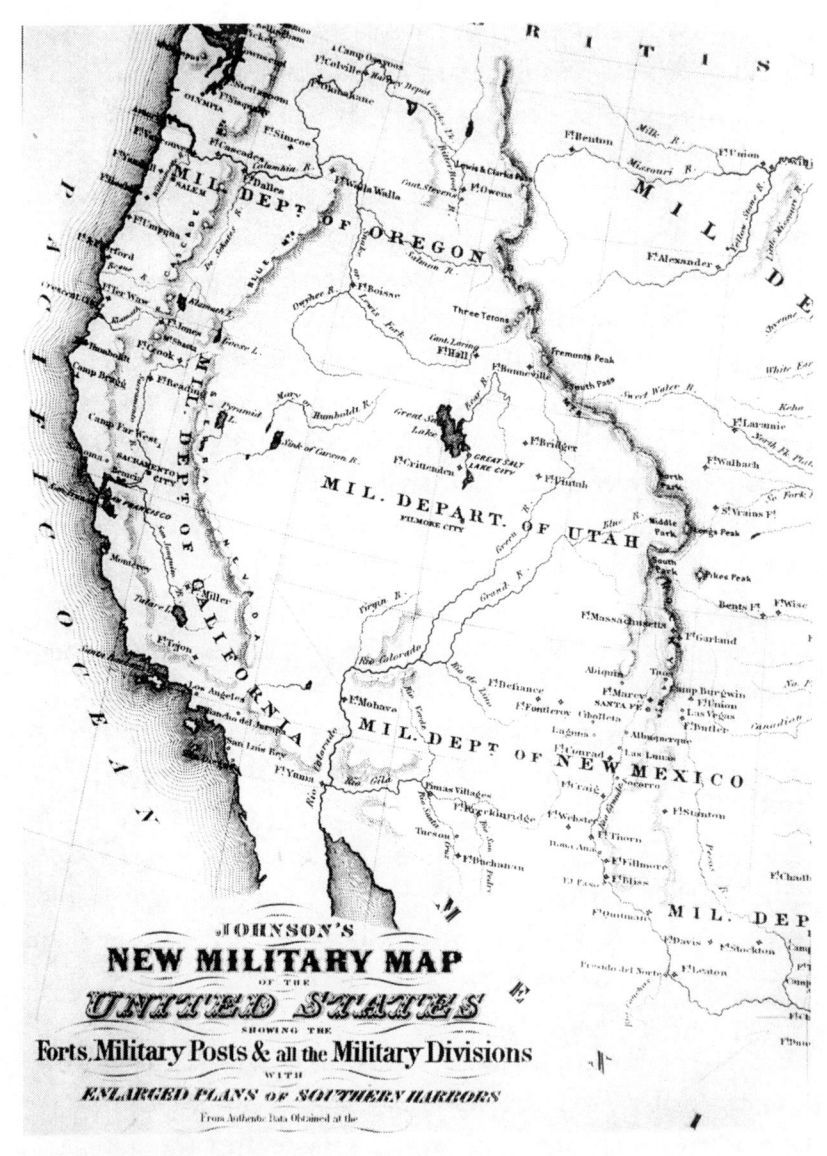

FIG. 10. Map of the West divided into various federal military departments, including Utah, ca. 1860. Used by permission, Utah State Historical Society.

commanding officer to Brigham Young.[5] Nothing in either the letter or Van Vliet's written orders indicated that Young would be replaced as governor or that the Mormons were considered to be rebellious to the United States. Instead Van Vliet communicated to the Mormon leader that the federal government had opted to form Utah Territory "into a Military Department, similar in all respects to the Military Department of New Mexico, the Pacific, and other geographical Military districts."[6] Establishing a new military district in the Great Basin with new army camps in Utah would help facilitate the development of federal infrastructure so important to promoting settlement and expansion in the West and would fulfill presidential objectives of protecting the United States' pacific possessions. By the time of Van Vliet's arrival, however, Young and the Mormons had already heard that the army was coming to the Great Basin.

Word of the president's decision to send an army initially reached Utah in late June 1857 via two Mormon mail contractors who had heard the rumor when they were farther east. Brigham Young and the Mormons, about to celebrate the tenth anniversary of their arrival in Utah, were immediately incensed and eventually made the information known at a public gathering on 24 July.[7] William Carruth, a Mormon then living in Utah, remembered that "inteligance reached us that the U States were sending out 25 hundred troops to Utah to bring the people as they say into subjection, and enforce officers on the people contrary to there choise."[8] Carruth appears to have understood the coming of the army in terms of sovereignty: the troops were to protect federal officials in the exercise of national sovereignty at the expense of local self-determination. The *Deseret News*, the LDS church's Salt Lake City newspaper, published scathing statements on the federal government's decision. Still asking for the affirmation of their self-government, the Mormon newspaper described its people as obediently and valiantly upholding the Constitution and laws of the country. The Mormon community could not understand why the federal government would not allow the people of Utah to govern themselves, eventually suggesting that the "tyrannical Administration is totally disregarding those laws," referring to the Constitution and indirectly to popular sovereignty, "in its efforts to destroy every man, woman and child that will not 'RENOUNCE MORMONISM.'"[9] Recalling prior persecutions, Young and his fellow church members labeled this episode another example of "mobocracy" from the states. They concluded that another Missouri or Illinois mob was moving on the territory to annihilate them and their religion.[10]

Brigham Young paid close attention to national newspapers. He read in them a persecutory spirit and believed that the Buchanan administration desired to ruin Mormonism. That objective, according to Young, was the real intention of the government. "If, therefore," Young wrote in his journal, "persecution and death must come, we concluded that we might better make the job cost our enemies all in our power by selling our lives and liberties as dearly as possible."[11] As Mormons had at various times during earlier persecutions, Young and the Mormon organ again began differentiating church members from Americans, whom they now considered enemies. The Mormons' own conceptions of self vacillated from loyal, Constitution-loving Americans to an oppressed and persecuted people that viewed Americans as enemies. For example, Rachel Woolsey Lee recorded the contents of a patriotic Fourth of July speech in her diary. She wrote that Isaac Haight, a Mormon leader and mayor of Cedar City in southern Utah, lauded James Buchanan as a "man of very liberal sentiments" who "intended to carry out the Spirit of the Constitution." About six weeks later, Lee's diary entry of 17 August 1857 provides the content of another speech from a Latter-day Saint leader. Lee wrote that George A. Smith "delivered a discourse on the Spirit that actuated the United States toward this people—full of hostility and virulence."[12] In a discourse given in November 1857 in Salt Lake City, Mormon apostle John Taylor similarly complained that the federal government had "sent an armed force contrary to law and right and to the principles that ought to prevail in the United States."[13] Taylor stated that the government interfered with the Mormons "because of the kingdom of God. . . . It is not polygamy that they are so horrified at."[14] The combined church and state of Mormon theocracy was now, more than ever, considered by Mormons to be "higher, and its laws . . . so much more exalted than those of any other nation" including those of the United States. Taylor and others made a semantic distinction in their minds between belief in and loyalty to the Constitution and sovereign institutions of the United States and fealty to the government and those operating it.[15]

What appears to have been the collective psychological effect of twenty-five years of prior persecutions caused the Mormons to build a resistance movement, believing armed defense as their only way to end the maltreatment they had suffered and that they believed they would continue to suffer. As the early settlers who established a sovereign position in their adopted homeland, the Mormons attempted to maintain that position by force of arms. As early as 11 August 1857, Brigham Young's diary noted his course of action. On that day, he "fixed [his] determination not to let any troops enter this territory. And unless the Government assumes a more pacific attitude to, declare emigration by the overland route Stopt, And make every preparation to give the U.S. a Sound drubbing."[16] Eighteen days later, on the morning of 29 August, Young instructed Daniel Wells, a counselor in the church's presidency and commanding officer of the territorial militia, to write a gubernatorial proclamation declaring Utah under martial law and refusing individuals to pass into or out of the territory without express written permission.[17] Though his diary entries suggest an immediate response to developing circumstances, Young's martial law declaration may have been years in the making. Young wrote to his nephew John R. Young, then proselytizing in Hawaii, on 4 September 1857. The Mormon leader stated, "We had determined years ago, if a mob again attacked us, whether led by their own passions, or unconstitutionally legalized by the general government, or by the government of any of the states, or territories, that we'll resist their aggressions by making an appeal to God and our own right arms, for that protection which has been denied us by Christianized and civilized nations."[18] These sentiments illuminate the Mormon mindset as Captain Van Vliet entered Salt Lake City in early September 1857.

Van Vliet's visit consisted of many meetings and conversations with Young and other Mormons. He likely heard the agitated messages of the Mormon leaders and worked to quell their intense opposition to the arrival and stationing of an army in their midst. His diplomacy did not work. By the time he returned east to his detachment, six days after his arrival on 8 September, Captain Van Vliet was convinced that the Mormons would resist the entry of the troops.[19]

During this period of tension, violence broke out in southern Utah Territory. On 11 September 1857, approximately 120 California-bound emigrants from Arkansas and Missouri were killed at Mountain Meadows near Cedar City. Mormon settlers in southern Utah, some disguised as Indians, perpetrated this brutal massacre. This horrific event had begun several days earlier, as the emigrants were under siege before the main attack occurred. Several noteworthy scholars have written about the massacre in great depth.[20] Therefore, this important and appalling event receives little attention here. While one could read into the massacre an exercise of Mormon sovereign authority in response to the coming of the army, it figured little in the federal government's effort to assert its sovereignty over antebellum Utah. That was already well in motion in early September. Nevertheless, the massacre came to symbolize Mormon savagery in the national media in the years and decades following the Utah War. The incident also seemed to add fodder to the idea of a subversive Mormon-Indian alliance, as the press later portrayed Mormons and Indians as having worked together to execute this ghastly crime.[21] The massacre likewise offered another, later opportunity for the federal government to encroach on the Mormons as investigators probed the crime for decades after it went unpunished. Violence in the territory was real, whatever the motives behind the Mountain Meadows massacre.[22]

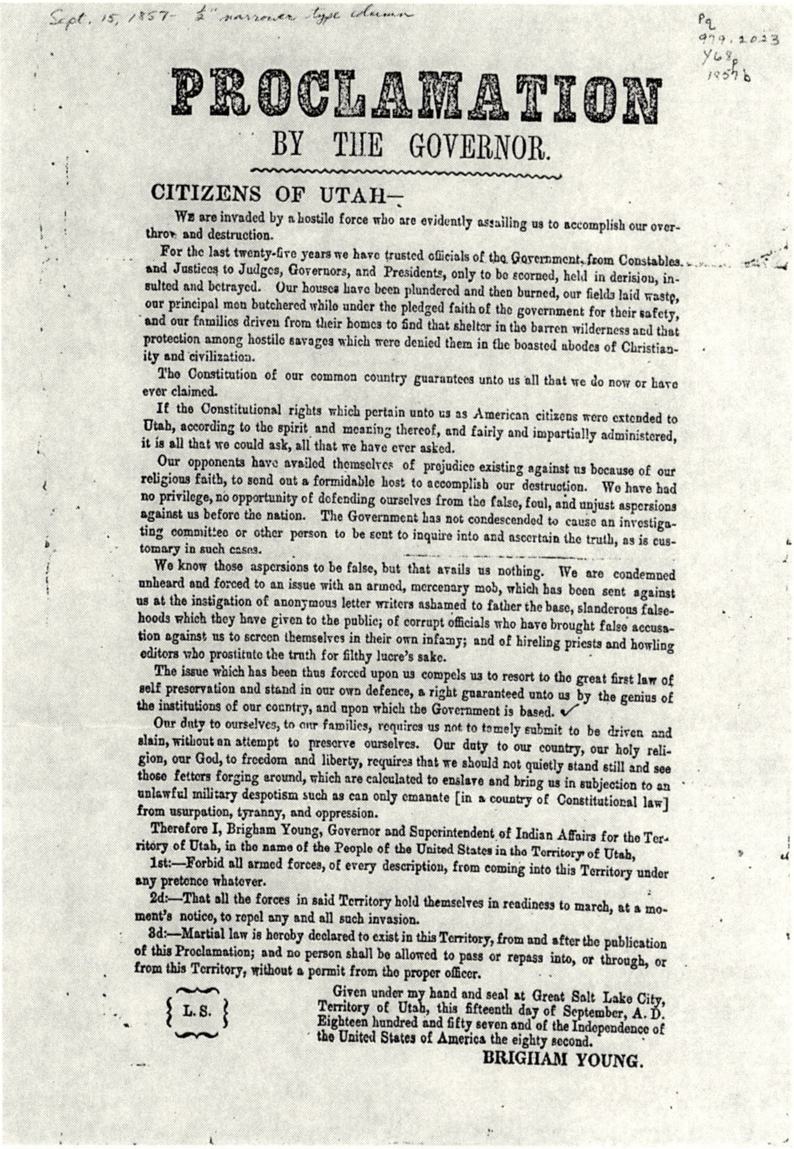

PROCLAMATION
BY THE GOVERNOR.

CITIZENS OF UTAH—

We are invaded by a hostile force who are evidently assailing us to accomplish our overthrow and destruction.

For the last twenty-five years we have trusted officials of the Government, from Constables and Justices to Judges, Governors, and Presidents, only to be scorned, held in derision, insulted and betrayed. Our houses have been plundered and then burned, our fields laid waste, our principal men butchered while under the pledged faith of the government for their safety, and our families driven from their homes to find that shelter in the barren wilderness and that protection among hostile savages which were denied them in the boasted abodes of Christianity and civilization.

The Constitution of our common country guarantees unto us all that we do now or have ever claimed.

If the Constitutional rights which pertain unto us as American citizens were extended to Utah, according to the spirit and meaning thereof, and fairly and impartially administered, it is all that we could ask, all that we have ever asked.

Our opponents have availed themselves of prejudice existing against us because of our religious faith, to send out a formidable host to accomplish our destruction. We have had no privilege, no opportunity of defending ourselves from the false, foul, and unjust aspersions against us before the nation. The Government has not condescended to cause an investigating committee or other person to be sent to inquire into and ascertain the truth, as is customary in such cases.

We know those aspersions to be false, but that avails us nothing. We are condemned unheard and forced to an issue with an armed, mercenary mob, which has been sent against us at the instigation of anonymous letter writers ashamed to father the base, slanderous falsehoods which they have given to the public; of corrupt officials who have brought false accusation against us to screen themselves in their own infamy; and of hireling priests and howling editors who prostitute the truth for filthy lucre's sake.

The issue which has been thus forced upon us compels us to resort to the great first law of self preservation and stand in our own defence, a right guaranteed unto us by the genius of the institutions of our country, and upon which the Government is based.

Our duty to ourselves, to our families, requires us not to tamely submit to be driven and slain, without an attempt to preserve ourselves. Our duty to our country, our holy religion, our God, to freedom and liberty, requires that we should not quietly stand still and see those fetters forging around, which are calculated to enslave and bring us in subjection to an unlawful military despotism such as can only emanate [in a country of Constitutional law] from usurpation, tyranny, and oppression.

Therefore I, Brigham Young, Governor and Superintendent of Indian Affairs for the Territory of Utah, in the name of the People of the United States in the Territory of Utah,

1st:—Forbid all armed forces, of every description, from coming into this Territory under any pretence whatever.

2d:—That all the forces in said Territory hold themselves in readiness to march, at a moment's notice, to repel any and all such invasion.

3d:—Martial law is hereby declared to exist in this Territory, from and after the publication of this Proclamation; and no person shall be allowed to pass or repass into, or through, or from this Territory, without a permit from the proper officer.

{ L. S. }   Given under my hand and seal at Great Salt Lake City, Territory of Utah, this fifteenth day of September, A. D. Eighteen hundred and fifty seven and of the Independence of the United States of America the eighty second.

BRIGHAM YOUNG.

FIG. 11. Proclamation by Brigham Young, 15 September 1857. This document was the most tangible and overt demonstration of Mormon resolve to maintain sovereignty and rebel against the authority of the federal government. Courtesy of the Church History Library, Salt Lake City, UT.

Just four days later, Brigham Young, still acting as territorial governor, issued a formal, public proclamation of martial law. That 15 September 1857 proclamation forbade all armed forces from entering the territory and mandated that the citizens of the territory should hold themselves in readiness to repel any such invasion.[23] In the proclamation, Young maintained that he had not been officially informed of the army's advance or of his being replaced as governor. Young declared that Latter-day Saints had not been extended their constitutional rights and he was determined to have those rights of self-government for his people. The Mormon leader then pronounced, in something hearkening back to American revolutionary rhetoric, that the "great first law of self preservation" required his people to stand in their own defense against what he considered "unlawful military despotism."[24] More importantly, Young's declaration signaled to Mormon men the need to protect women and family and by extension their religion and society. Young and the Mormons decided to stand their ground, to fight to maintain their political autonomy and social customs against the efforts of the federal government to end their home rule. Young ordered the territorial militia, also known as the Nauvoo Legion, to prepare itself to defend the Salt Lake Valley and resist the coming of the federal troops. The proclamation was widely circulated and sent to military and ecclesiastical leaders throughout the territory.[25] Young's proclamation signified a tangible and outward act of rebellion by the Mormon people against the sovereignty of the federal government.

The *Deseret News* and the *Millennial Star*, the Mormon-run newspaper in England, printed many articles, editorials, and reports that highlighted the federal government's poor treatment of Utah. Both periodicals claimed that the people of the church were American citizens, born and raised, who understood and governed themselves in accordance with the Constitution. In what could be read as a perfectly American response to the federal invasion, and in the fashion of the revolutionary generation, the Mormon newspapers emphasized that the people of Utah would not "ever tamely bow to tyranny in any shape."[26] Analogous to Young's martial law declaration that emphasized the condemnation of slanderous individuals, corrupt federal officials, and "howling editors who prostitute the truth for filthy lucre's sake," the Mormon papers also viewed the military action against Utah as a political machination brought about by "the lies of hypocrites, the howlings of corrupt editors, and the rottenness of officials."[27] Mormon rhetoric encouraged the entire federal government to reconsider its use of force and adhere to the Democratic Party platform and the promises made by the president in his inaugural address of noninterference in the territories. The Latter-day Saint press wanted to see the Mormons receive the rights of popular sovereignty and local self-government that it believed was "applicable to *Territories* as to States." The Mormons had adopted a broad interpretation of popular sovereignty and, just as had others in the United States, saw the problems for the Democrats if they acted against local self-government with a show of federal force in Utah.[28]

As Young prepared and then delivered his martial law proclamation, he and other church leaders initiated several protective policies. One of the more significant was calling "all the Saints and Elders" who were out on proselytizing missions back to Utah to prepare for a war. Young personally wrote to church members in San Bernardino, California suggesting that they return for their safety. If the United States commenced hostilities in Utah, Young warned that the Californians would also turn against them and force them from the state.[29] Samuel Miles and other missionaries in northern California received an assignment from George Q. Cannon in San Francisco to travel immediately to Utah, though Miles did not arrive until early January 1858.[30] By calling all Mormon men from their colonized outposts to Salt Lake City to protect the religious family, the church leader hoped to coordinate and demonstrate to the incoming troops a formidable Mormon manhood.[31] At the same time, pulling back preachers diminished the Mormon sphere of influence in the region, at least temporarily. Young aimed to prevent what he saw as the failure of manhood that occurred in the ravenous murders perpetrated against his people in Missouri and Illinois. Mormon men understood that they must take up arms in the protection of women, family, home, and religion.[32]

Based on their experiences with army men like Sylvester Mowry in the preceding years, the Latter-day Saint men again grew anxious at the prospect of army men winning the affection of Mormon women and disrupting their social system. As the army moved west in the late summer of 1857, Mormon leaders predicted scenes of rapine and plunder and feared that disease, pollution, and the rape of Mormon women would occur once the troops arrived in the territory.[33] In a letter to a Mormon confidant in the states, Brigham Young wrote: "Col. Johnston and his command are at Fort Bridger, and so far as we can learn are more angry, if possible, than they were last fall, not having enjoyed the anticipated pleasure of debauching our wives and daughters and wickedly reveling in our houses and upon the fruits of our labors."[34] Latter-day Saint men sought to prevent not only attacks on women and family but also those on their own manhood as they rallied to stop the raping of the Mormon people. Mormon militiamen obeyed instructions from the Nauvoo Legion leaders to watch the army's movements by passing as strangers and riding into their camp. Such tactics would help the Mormon militiamen learn if it was in fact their intention to push their way into Salt Lake City, take and murder Brigham Young and all the leading men, and defile Mormon women and prostitute them at their pleasure. Under the trying circumstances, Mormon militiaman Barney volunteered his services to defend his wives, children, and religion.[35] U.S. Army officer John Wolcott Phelps also suggested, in a journal entry, that those in the Mormon army "had been told and believed that we were a mob coming upon them to destroy both women and children."[36] The idea that the army was coming to seduce Mormon women echoed the concerns arising from the army's sojourn in Salt Lake City in 1854–55. That notion would also become part of the way Mormons chose to remember the Utah War. For example, in a later Mormon novel about the war, a Mormon man was enraged when he heard "the wicked threats of the dissolute officers concerning the fair daughters of his people."[37] While Mormon men dreaded the army men as an incoming threat to their manhood, religion, and family structure, *Harper's Weekly* printed images of Mormon men arming their women with weapons to fight the army, indicating that Mormon men were not man enough to fight their own battles.[38] This public image matched with others to highlight the weakness of Mormon men, the strength of American men, and the believed ease with which the army would conquer the Mormon community.

During the fall of 1857, the army train of soldiers and supply wagons stretched from Fort Leavenworth in Kansas past Fort Laramie, then in Nebraska Territory. As more soldiers reached the Rocky Mountains in September, they met harsh weather conditions and confronted Mormon guerillas along the way. Captain Stewart Van Vliet rejoined the army as it approached South Pass in present-day Wyoming. In October, Van Vliet received word from Brigham Young, in the form of a letter with a copy of his martial law proclamation included, that the Mormon leader was forbidding the army from entering the territory and directing them to return to the States via the same route they entered. The captain delivered the message to Colonel Edmund Alexander, the officer in command of the advance troops. Alexander replied that the troops were in the territory according to the orders of the president to establish a military post near Salt Lake City and that their future movements and operations would depend on orders issued from military authority in Washington.[39]

Assistant Adjutant General Fitz-John Porter, who had graduated from the U.S. Military Academy in 1845 and served in the U.S.-Mexico War in 1847, was among the troops en route to Utah. Porter kept a journal of his experiences.[40] In it, the native of Portsmouth, New Hampshire, wrote of the devotion he felt to his country in upholding the nation's power and authority as significant to the honor and welfare of the country. He equated the Mormons with traitors and advocated dealing with them as a foreign nation. The United States, a powerful nation, he believed, would not be made weak by the Mormons. He wrote of the army's mission to enforce the interests of the country and the important issues of power and conquest in Utah. On 15 October 1857, Porter wrote in his journal that the U.S. troops had reached South Pass and would soon make the Mormons feel their power. "We will conquer them," Porter declared.[41]

Porter and his army mates regarded Brigham Young's martial law proclamation as proof positive of open rebellion. Meanwhile, Young continued to send notices to the army to leave the territory, warning them of the dangers of colliding with Mormons, whom he then referred to as good American citizens. The adjutant general considered Young's proposition to lay down arms and return to the east as an insult to the army's martial manhood. "He must suppose we are a set of pusillanimous cowards," Porter vented, "to retire at his beck and call. But he will find us made of 'sterner stuff' than the subjects he wields and moulds." The army would follow through on its orders, Porter triumphantly wrote, because an "American Army never recoils."[42] By the end of October, as the army arrived at and decided to make arrangements for establishing winter quarters near Fort Bridger, Porter lamented that "we will not be able to do anything towards conquering them this fall."[43] Porter's journal entries provide a window into the troops' mindset as they entered Utah. They wanted to conquer and extend national power over the Mormons, thereby proving the strength of American manhood. Indeed, the army and its soldiers were key in establishing and maintaining federal sovereignty in Utah.

From the army's arrival in Utah Territory in September to the winter break beginning in December, no major battles occurred. Minor skirmishes amounted to a tactical standoff. The Mormon militia employed guerrilla tactics to harass the army. Mormon soldiers, acting on orders from Salt Lake City, stampeded military animals, intercepted army supply trains, burned the grasses and foraging lands, and blocked the canyons all as part of their strategy to cut off provisions and leave the army stranded in the mountains.[44] Lewis Barney wrote in his journal, "Our orders from the commanding officers was to harass the Army, keep them awake and not let them sleep night or day, stampede their stock, burn every patch of grass that would burn, but not fire a gun only in self defence."[45] Similarly, U.S. Army captain John Wolcott Phelps described the Mormon tactic of setting the grass on fire and his command's subsequent engagement in preventing the spread of fires. Phelps, a radical abolitionist and later a general in the Union army during the Civil War, detested the Mormon tactics and advocated the use of force to suppress them.[46] By the time winter arrived, the Mormons had burned over fifty wagons loaded with food and equipment, drove off hundreds of oxen and beef cattle, and forced the army to reconsider its move to enter Salt Lake City.[47] Some 2,500 Mormon militiamen spent the winter encamped in strategic canyons and mountain passes along the Wasatch front to watch the troops and prepare to resist their invasion.

Mormon women also helped in preparations and supported those in the canyons aggravating the U.S. soldiers. The Relief Society transitioned from aiding Native Americans to providing materials for the Mormon soldiers. Mothers and sisters gathered food and clothing. They knitted homemade socks and long, thick-knitted overcoats to send with the men to the mountain passes. Priscilla Merriman Evans wrote that her Relief Society in the Spanish Fork second ward, which was organized one day after Brigham Young issued the martial law proclamation on 15 September 1857, collected food and clothing to aid in the defense of their territory.[48] Margaret Clawson similarly recalled, "My mother, who was indefatigable worked in the Relief Society in the fifteenth ward. She went voluntarily through the ward getting contributions of warm clothing for the brethren who were in the mountains and badly in need of them; she sat up many nights knitting wooline stockings to protect them from the inclemency of the weather; she contributed her time and what little means she could spare for their comfort."[49] Mormon men and women banded even closer together and threw their full support behind their church leadership to fight in defense of their homeland and way of life.

Reports of Mormon tactics reached the eastern press by October 1857 and further enflamed popular opinion that the Mormons existed in a state of rebellion against the United States. The Utah War filled columns in newspapers across the nation. A Wilmington, Delaware, mill worker named John Comly Past, an avid newspaper reader, wrote in his journal, "I see by the Papers that the Mormons are in open rebellion to the National Government they have been robing [sic] supply trains and murdering the escorts as well as instigating the Indians to plunder Emigrant trains and murder the people accompanying them. If the reports are true that come to as it is high time that their nest of iniquity was broken up and the knavish leaders sent to *Hades* and their poor deluded followers scattered amongst people who would show them the egregious folly of the course they have been pursuing."[50] Highlighting Mormon guerilla tactics proved their disloyalty and the wisdom in Buchanan's decision to send the troops to extend federal authority over Utah and its peoples.[51]

Having already battled Mormon guerillas along the route, facing heavy snow and difficult mountain passes filled with militiamen determined to resist their passages, the army, led by Colonel Alexander, gathered approximately 125 miles northeast of Salt Lake City near Fort Bridger. The army would have to wait until the spring of 1858 to enter the Salt Lake Valley, but it took advantage of its long winter near Fort Bridger, an outpost previously owned and controlled by Mormons. In advance of the army's arrival, some Mormons burned it down. Upon reaching the Black's Fork of the Green River at a main diversion point for the Oregon and California Trails through the Continental Divide, the army established the makeshift Camp Scott just south of the old trapper's fort. The improvements to the area prompted the army to maintain soldiers there and to reconstruct Fort Bridger as a strategic outpost. The soldiers would face a miserably cold and snow-filled winter with low supplies and rations. When General Johnston arrived at Camp Scott in the fall he kept the soldiers active, educated, and well practiced in tactical exercises.[52] New Utah governor Alfred Cumming arrived at Camp Scott with his wife, Elizabeth, around 20 November 1857 and worked quickly to establish his administration and exercise his duties as territorial executive. Elizabeth noted the not-so-monumental occasion. "We must stop here all winter where there is wood and water," she wrote before noting simply that "Alfred has made this the seat of gov[ernment]."[53] Cumming immediately interacted with non-Mormon men and officers "nearly all day—arranging for the future," according to Elizabeth's observations.[54] A new era in territorial administration started quietly.

Having heard the great many rumors of Mormon and Indian complicity, upon their making winter camp, soldiers and the new federal officials reached out to representatives from the regional tribes to ascertain their loyalty or neutrality in hopes of preventing attacks on more than one front. General Albert Sidney Johnston met with some regional Native leaders. Letters between military men and camp followers observed some of the army-Indian interactions. At one meeting, W. M. F. Magraw and James Bridger witnessed as Johnston advised Shoshone leaders Washakie and Little Soldier "to stay clear of the existing difficulties as the government did not wish them to connect themselves to Mormon troubles." Nevertheless, Johnston apparently told the Native leaders that if they wanted to connect themselves with the army, he or any of his men could use their services as guides, herders, or scouts, for which he would pay them. At this point, according to the observers, "Wash-a-kee and Little Soldier stated that they regard the Mormons as their worst enemy."[55] Witnessing the large army trains equipped with large quantities of food and arms streaming into their homelands probably induced the indigenous leaders to consider the potential war atmosphere and navigate the situation to serve their best interests, using the conflict to their advantage. Upon his arrival in

FIG. 12. Chief Washakie (center) and other Shoshones. Used by permission, Utah State Historical Society.

Utah Territory in November, new superintendent of Indian affairs Jacob Forney immediately met with as many Native representatives as he could. Similar to Johnston, Forney wanted to determine whether the Great Basin's indigenous peoples would assist the Mormons in the event of armed conflict.

Mormons also conducted visits and sent communications to Native peoples. It is unclear to what extent Mormons approached regional Native groups regarding such an alliance, or vice versa; it seems, however, some overtures were made. In mid-August 1857, Dimick Huntington met with various bands of Utes and Goshutes spreading the message that the army would kill the Mormons and then all of the Native peoples. Huntington told the Utes and Goshutes he met with that "they and the Mormons was one." In early September 1857, Huntington and Young encouraged Anterro, a leader of the Uintah Utes, to "be at peace with all men except the Americans."[56] On 1 September

1857, Mormon Indian missionary Jacob Hamblin brought Kanosh, the Pahvant Ute leader, with several of his band to visit Brigham Young in Salt Lake City. After this meeting, Young's diary reads, "A Spirit Seems to be takeing possession of the Indians to assist Israel. I can hardly restrain them from exterminating the 'Americans.'"[57] It seems clear that Mormons were attempting to form alliances with regional Native peoples against the coming army, though the exact nature of the alliance, including its size and strength, is not known. In the end, the alliance failed to materialize.

Still, Indian affairs continued to complicate the federal-territorial relationship in Utah. On 8 April 1857, President Buchanan appointed James W. Denver as the nation's commissioner of Indian affairs.[58] Prior to the arrival of Jacob Forney, Denver and Brigham Young conducted little correspondence, but they exchanged a few intense letters on Indian policy and the role of the army in Utah. Young, writing on 12 September with vouchers for expenditures on Indian affairs, reported that Native raiders had taken the lives of many emigrants and a great deal of property. He stated that the reason for the widespread raiding was the abhorrent practice of overland travelers "shooting at every Indian they could see." Because of that practice, he suggested, "the Indians regard all white men alike as their enemies, and kill and plunder whenever they can do so with impunity, and often the innocent suffer for the deeds of the guilty." Young's equivocating statement implicitly dismissed the ideas of a Mormon-Indian alliance by likening all white people in relation to indigenous people. He continued, "It is hard to make an Indian believe that the whites are their friends, and that the Great Father wishes to do them good, when, perhaps, the very next party which crosses their path shoots them down like wolves. This trouble with the Indians only exists along the line of the traveled west, and beyond the influence of our settlements." The Mormon leader further expressed his concern over the coming of the army. Though white settlers in other frontier territories typically requested military protection, the governor considered the stationing of the army in Utah superfluous. He considered its stationing in Utah to be counterproductive, even dangerous, because it created more volatility in relations with regional Indians. The Mormon leader feared that the army would excite the area's Native population to violence against the territory's white inhabitants. Young offered a thinly veiled threat when he stated, "The troops must be kept away, for it is a prevalent fact that wherever there are the most of these, we may expect to find the greatest amount of hostile Indians, and the least security for persons and property."[59]

In his response, Denver emphasized the necessity of stationing troops in the territory because of the lingering accusations that Mormons had violated the federal Trade and Intercourse Act. Denver informed Young that "the department has information from reliable sources that, so far from encouraging amicable relations between the Indians and the people of the United States outside of your own immediate community, you have studiously endeavored to impress on the minds of the Indians that there was a difference between your own sect, usually known as Mormons, and the government, and other citizens of the United States; that the former were their friends and the latter their enemies."[60] Denver then remarked on the movement of the troops to Utah informing Young that the president directed the army's march, and, the commissioner fumed, "it is fair to presume that he would not send them to Utah Territory unless there was a necessity for so doing." Furthermore, Denver noted that troops were required to preserve the peace and to subjugate the region's Native peoples.[61] In his vehement response to Young, Denver could muster no reason why one would think that persons and property should be any less secure in the neighborhood of the troops.

Denver also responded to an earlier complaint from Young that the federal Indian office failed to issue proper instructions and adequate financial arrangements to Utah. "It could never have been intended," the commissioner replied, "when the appropriations were made by Congress, that the money should be used in arousing savages to war against our own citizens, or to enable a subordinate officer to carry on treasonable practices against his government. The rule of this office is to withhold annuities from the Indians whenever they place themselves in a hostile or antagonistic attitude towards the government, and I know of no reason why the same rule should not be applied to you at this time."[62]

In addition, Denver suggested that he could think of no reason why peaceable citizens should object to the army's presence. "If it is your intention to preserve peace," Denver informed the Mormon leader, "the troops will not interfere with you; but if you intend otherwise, then it is necessary that the troops should be on the ground to enforce" laws and Indian policy. The commissioner expressed regret that such a state of affairs existed and he believed that the president made the decision to send the army to the territory with "great reluctance . . . to require the strong arm of power compel obedience to the law." Denver concluded by lambasting Young's tenure as governor and superintendent of Indian affairs. He believed that Young as "a subordinate officer" to the federal government overextended his authority and used "his official position to injure one portion of his fellow-citizens, and to alienate another portion from loyalty to their government." The existence of these facts, particularly the perceived relations between the Mormons and Indians, Denver indicated, forced the president's hand to send an army since he had "no alternative left but to crush out rebellion, and for this purpose all the powers of the government are placed under his control."[63] Denver and Young's exchange emphasized the power of the president in the territorial relationship and that a primary purpose for sending the army resulted from Mormon activities among the Indians.

The Mormon efforts to woo Indian allies also caused reverberations in neighboring territories. Late in 1857, Denver wrote to James Collins, superintendent of Indian affairs in New Mexico, explaining why the president and the army were involved in Utah. Collins was to do his best to keep the Indians in his jurisdiction quiet, sparing no efforts to prevent them from attacking the army. If he could not control them, he was to direct their attacks against the Mormons and their Indian allies, "those savages who may take up arms against our people." Denver explained: "You are therefore instructed to use every endeavor in your power to effect this object, if it is necessary that you should visit them in person you are required to do so, and to use all funds in your hands, applicable to such a purpose, if requisite, in making presents or otherwise for the purpose of conciliating them."[64] The commissioner of Indian affairs directed Collins to keep a vigilant eye on Native movements, to proceed with great caution and delicacy so as not to excite the minds of the Indians. Above all Collins was to keep the Indians "on good terms with our citizens."[65] Denver, like the president and others, continued to operate under the impression that a subversive Mormon-Indian alliance of significant numbers existed in the Great Basin.

In discussing the movement of troops to Utah, the popular imagination went wild speculating on the strength of the Indian-Mormon alliance. An initial report from Lieutenant General Winfield Scott to John B. Floyd estimated that the Mormons had "8,000 males (between 16 & 65) capable of bearing arms. We will, however, take the number at the low figure of 7,000, without including Indian allies."[66] The lieutenant general did not speculate on the numbers, but indicated that the Mormon-Indian alliance not only existed, but was formidable. The Mormons, allied with Indians, press reports intimated, would ravage, rob, plunder, and murder Americans at their pleasure. The *San Francisco Daily Evening Bulletin* provided an unconfirmed report that "On the 23d of December, a party of 700 or 800 Comanche and Cheyenne Indians were encountered on their way from Salt Lake City to their homes, about 80 miles from Fort Laramie, accompanied by about twenty Mormon leaders. These Indians, who had been led to believe that the Mormons had 80,000 fighting men well equipped for service, were to be employed in the spring, under Mormon influence, in harassing and cutting off supply trains sent to the relief of Colonel Johnston."[67] The Norristown, Pennsylvania, *Register* worried that the Mormons had "20,000 Indian allies, whom they are ready to furnish with arms and horses in an emergency. These Indians are partially instructed in the Mormon religion—enough to make them superstitious in regard to the God of a superior race, yet modifying none of their ferocity."[68]

Indian and Mormon complicity was also feared in the Pacific Northwest. In 1855, coming on the heels of the success of the Southern Indian Mission, Brigham Young called for the establishment of an Indian mission in Oregon Territory on the Salmon River to proselytize to the Nez Percé, Shoshone, Bannock, and Flatheads. The missionaries established Fort Limhi and had some success in converting Native peoples, including Shoshones.[69] From Fort Limhi as a base of operations the Latter-day Saint missionaries could reach out and preach to a variety of tribes. This prospect flummoxed non-Mormons and some in the press who feared that the Mormon influence would grow among the many Indians of Oregon.[70] Statements from the army stationed in Oregon acknowledged that Mormons sent emissaries among the Indians of the Pacific Northwest to incite them to band together against the United States.

At this time of unrest, Brevet Brigadier General Newman S. Clarke, of the Department of the Pacific based in San Francisco, California, forwarded a letter written by Captain Ralph Kirkham, who had served in the Rogue River and Yakima Wars in the fall and winter of 1855–56, as evidence of the Mormon-Indian alliance. In connection with the movement of troops to Utah, Kirkham wrote, "The Snakes tell our Indians that they are well supplied with ammunition, and that they can get from the Mormons any quantity that they wish; and they further tell our Indians that the Mormons are anxious to supply them, to wit: the Nez Percés, the Cayuses, and Walla-Wallas, with everything that they wish. I would not be surprised if the Mormon influence should extend to all the tribes in our neighborhood, and if they are determined to fight we may have trouble among the Indians on the coast again."[71] Another letter written in November 1857 by George Gibbs of Washington Territory reported his understanding that Mormons had

Defiant Attitude of Brigham Young and yᵉ Indians towards yᵉ Uncle Sam.

FIG. 13. April 1858 *Yankee Notions* cartoon illustrating the American perception of a Mormon-Indian alliance against the federal government during the Utah War. Courtesy of W. Paul Reeve.

gone from Washington to southern California to gain influence over all the western tribes. "It is not to be doubted that the Mormons have cultivated friendship with the Indians, and it is scarcely doubtful that, in the recent exodus of the Mormons from San Bernardino, they have been accompanied by Indians." Clarke also wrote to the defense headquarters in the nation's capital. He recommended "instant measures calculated to detach Indians from Mormon influence. As an initial step toward that end," Clarke suggested "that headmen or chiefs be invited to visit Washington. As an inducement they should receive presents to a generous extent."[72] The Mormons had apparently offered indigenous peoples large quantities of arms, ammunition, cattle, and horses as a reward for assistance, and army officers recommended similarly extravagant entreaties.[73] The potential threat of the Mormons tampering with and attempting to ally with Native peoples all over the West was indeed a frightening prospect for federal officials and the army on the ground.

The idea of a Mormon-Indian alliance gained more credence during the Utah War. One *New York Herald* editorial argued that the Mormons "are in collusion with the many adjacent Indian tribes," and with such an alliance could divide and conquer any U.S. forces sent there by burning the grass, cutting off the army's provisions, stampeding the cattle, diverting their attention, and generally delaying their march.[74] Another newspaper reported, likely in connection with Brigham Young's spring 1857 visit to Fort Limhi, that Young and "350 of his followers are now on a visit to the Indians in the north part of the Territory—the Bannaks, Flatheads, and Nezperces—it is supposed for the purpose of uniting them with his own forces against the general government. If the matter comes to blows, Brigham will stop the emigration across the plains, and take possession of the country."[75] The Nashville, Tennessee, *Daily News* also discussed the closeness of "numerous bands of the Piute Indians, who were well armed, pretty comfortably attired, and apparently on very good terms with the Mormons. They likewise passed through bands of the Utes, who were living close to the settlements. Many of the Indians spoke tolerably good English. There is no question that the Mormons in all the settlements are fully posted on the war question and the Indians seem quite as much interested."[76] Enlisting Indians in a regional war was not a new tactic; indeed the British and French used such tactics throughout the eighteenth century. The perception that Brigham Young could call thousands of Natives to his side in a battle against the United States generated great fear and justified the federal government's removal of Young as both Indian superintendent and governor. Government officials, the press, and those connected with both perceived the Mormons as having incredible tribal influence.[77] Linking the two unpopular groups in the public mind exploited prejudices to malign both Indians and Mormons.

In late 1857 and early 1858, Brigham Young corresponded with regional tribal leaders, but his letters do not paint the portrait of a steadfast martial alliance. In November, Young explained in a letter to Washakie that the army was coming to fight the Mormons. Young articulated his desire to see the Shoshone remain neutral and expressed hope that Washakie and his band would not join the Americans in fighting against the Mormons. Young could not be sure of what actions the Shoshone or any other Native band would take at this time of conflict. The Mormon leader's letter indicates that neither he nor his followers could have controlled the Shoshone. It also suggests that their alliance, if they had one at all, was in flux.[78] Communications between Washakie and General Albert Johnston suggest that at the time of the army's arrival at Fort Bridger, contention existed between the Mormons and Shoshone, despite any proselytizing successes at Fort Limhi. If Young did indeed control the Indians and could call tens of thousands of Native allies to arms as the American public believed, this and other letters do not so indicate.[79]

Other letters portray a different relationship. For example, in January 1858, Arapeen, a Ute leader, wrote to Young to ask why the Americans were coming to fight the Mormons and the Indians. Arapeen proposed to fight against the troops. Via an unknown interpreter, the Ute leader stated, "Tell them that I am not afraid of them I know how to fight & I under stand all about the mountain tell the Americans that I have got a plenty of Powder & lead Guns & caps & I now how to use them & that they must not come on my Land to shead blood.... If they will not hear good counsil they will find me & my men a verry formidable fo."[80] The next month, Arapeen sent another letter to Young that declared his intent to fight with the Mormons against the army. The Ute leader told Young that the army had tried to "hire the Indians to take the Mormon Cattle & Horses in the Spring," though Arapeen encouraged his people to avoid the army and that type of behavior. Arapeen then stated, "If the americans come here and want to drive the Mormons from this land I will geather all the indians from the sorounding mountains and fight them untill they will be glad for peace."[81] While Arapeen seemed willing to form an alliance with the Mormons to fight the Americans, or to fight them outright, the LDS leader evidently did not take Arapeen up on his offer. Although Mormon missionaries had delivered messages that were considered damaging to the federal government's relationship with Great Basin Native peoples, these letters place significant doubt on the idea of a widespread Mormon-Indian conspiracy. They instead demonstrate the varied relationships between Mormons and Native peoples and the contingencies of events as they occurred. Furthermore, the letters to Young and to Washakie shed light on the decisions of Native Americans to act according to their best interests during the Utah War. Nevertheless, the perception of a subversive military alliance between Mormons and Indians remained entrenched in the American public mind.

In early December 1857, Buchanan delivered his first annual message to Congress and to the American people, which included a section on the decision to send federal troops to Utah Territory. In his first public remarks on the decision to send the standing army to Utah, Buchanan highlighted Brigham Young's despotic power over church and state. A show of strength, the president suggested, would prevent bloodshed and restore and maintain the authority of federal law. Buchanan also emphasized the growing national fear that as superintendent of Indian affairs in Utah Territory, Young "has had an opportunity of tampering with the Indian tribes, and exciting their hostile feelings against the United States."[82] Young needed to be replaced so that he would no longer govern the population and could no longer license Mormon missionaries to go preach and teach Native peoples and so that he was no longer responsible for governing white-Indian relations, a focal point of federal activity in the territories.

In the Buchanan administration's official report on the intelligence that informed the decision to order a military expedition to Utah Territory, nearly a third of the number of documents contained in the report concerned Indian affairs. Those forty-six documents described the "policy pursued by the Mormons," which the then-acting commissioner of Indian affairs Charles Mix believed "aimed at the establishment of an independent Mormon empire" by inciting Indians to malicious activities against all non-Mormons in the territory in direct violation of the Trade and Intercourse Act.[83] In his cover letter to the "copies of all papers on file in the Indian office," Mix singled out the claims of Jacob Holeman and Garland Hurt. Mix reiterated what Holeman had stated in 1851, that "Brigham Young 'made use of his office as superintendent and of the money of the government to promote the interests of his church.'" The acting commissioner also summarized Hurt's 1855 correspondence and emphasized that the Mormons intended "to teach them that the Indians were the rightful owners of the American soil, that it had been wrongfully taken from them by the whites, and that the Great Spirit had sent the Mormons among them to help them recover their rights."[84] In a private letter not included in the official report, the former Utah Territory chief justice John Kinney similarly advised the White House on the state of affairs in the Great Basin. Among Kinney's six points were that the "Mormons are inimical to the U.S. Government," and that they send out men "every year for the ostensible purpose of converting Indians but really to poison their minds against the government and Americans and also to make them their allies in case of any difficulty with the U.S."[85] This letter demonstrates that Buchanan and his cabinet knew of and had received documents additional to those printed in the official report that the public and Congress were not aware of when they acted. The Buchanan administration decided to send the army to Utah in part because of the voluminous documents on difficulties with the Mormons concerning Indian affairs and because of the administration's belief that Mormon missionaries were breaking the Trade and Intercourse laws of the United States by attempting to turn Native Americans into hostile enemies.[86] A restoration of federal authority in Utah Territory was therefore in order; this required that U.S. troops go to Utah Territory to enforce federal Indian policy. Executing or enforcing federal law in the territory was the key motive in sending the army to Utah. The federal government believed that Utahans had failed to uphold federal law. Among the laws that its officers perceived as violated were federal Indian laws: laws that empowered the president to send an army against people acting contrary to them.

By January 1858, with the Utah War still hotly disputed, even California governor John Weller made the connection between Mormons and Indians several times in his Inaugural Address. In discussing overland emigration to the Pacific coast, Weller depicted the Mormons and Indians as an alliance that threatened immigration to the Golden State.[87] Weller, like the rest of the nation, believed that the army could diminish the power of the Mormon-Indian alliance and make the region safe for continued American expansion. While the army on the ground ascertained the extent of the Mormon influence over regional Natives, the press in the East propagated the idea of Mormon efforts to persuade tribes to join them. Nevertheless, the government and the press maintained that the army's presence in Utah would dissolve any alliance and render the region safe. In other territories and to protect national expansion interests, the federal government introduced the army and built forts as part of a designed plan for control; in this case that largely meant that they act as law enforcers for Indian affairs.[88]

Early in 1858, Mormon legislators took advantage of the winter and its attendant military stalemate. They attempted to refocus the discussion about the Utah War around their believed right to self-determination. On 6 January 1858, members and officers of the legislative assembly of Utah Territory adopted a memorial to Congress requesting the right to select "their rulers" because previous experience and the current situation with the army presence did not bear a resemblance to the free voice and desire of the people, "as ever should be the only course in a republican government."[89] "Cannot American citizens," the memorialists asked, "upon American soil, be heard" by the parent government in their own defense, according to their political and social desires? The Mormon petitioners believed that the federal government usurped their authority and had sent a soldiery to the territory to reenact "the horrid scenes of Missouri and Illinois." Again identifying as good, loyal Americans, Mormons claimed that in a republican form of government, established by the founders, "and such as ours still professes to be, the officers are and should be the servants of the people, and not their masters, dictators, or tyrants." The petitioners spoke with the same rhetoric as Americans had in defense of republicanism.[90]

The Mormon memorial again raised the idea of the administration's actions as imperial and tyrannical against law-abiding citizens. The document argued that Utah adopted a republican constitution and form of government in 1856 and petitioned to be admitted into the Union as a free, sovereign, and independent state. Unfortunately, "prejudice was so strong against us that our delegates found no member of Congress willing to present and advocate our position."[91] The memorial asked Congress to include Utah as a free and self-governing entity because the territory's citizens had demonstrated their love of liberty. The memorialists again vehemently denied that they were alien enemies as Senator Stephen A. Douglas and others had suggested. Rather, they warned that continued actions of force against them would turn them into enemies. They added that they were well armed and had no confidence that the U.S. Army coming to Utah was a harmless demonstration intended for their own good. Rather, they believed that the troops came with the objective "to destroy the leaders of our people" and they threatened "to take out lives and to sport, at pleasure, with our wives and daughters." The Mormon request ended powerfully and concisely: "Give us our *constitutional rights*, and we are at home."[92] The memorial reached Washington in the spring and, like earlier Mormon appeals and requests for statehood, received little attention in the halls of Congress.

As the calendar year turned to 1858, however, Congress did discuss and debate the Mormons, popular sovereignty, and the raising of additional military detachments for Utah. Potential pitfalls in establishing, communicating, and outfitting the army in Utah created a congressional call for additional regiments and in that process, the proposal that Stephen Douglas laid out in his June 1857 Springfield speech to repeal Utah's Organic Act resurfaced. Regarding the proposal to repeal Utah's Organic Act and on the question of sovereignty in the Great Basin, South Carolina congressman Laurence M. Keitt noted "there are three schools upon the question." Referring to the doctrine of popular sovereignty and attacking Douglas's reversal on the idea, the South Carolinian opined, "One thinks that, by some geological property in the dirt, or some pneumatic essence in the air, the people of a Territory are vested with indefeasible sovereignty. That school cannot consistently vote to repeal or abolish the territorial act." "There is another school," Keitt stated, "which believes that Congress is sovereign; that it can establish what form of government it pleases in a Territory; that it can build up classes and distribute titles to anybody. It believes in the omnipotence of the Federal Government." That class, perhaps referring to the Republican Party's view on federal power, held that the federal government had the power to control territorial law and governments. The last class believed that the federal government should act in the best interest of states.[93] With his comments, Keitt submitted the key question facing the nation. It was a multifaceted question that brought various answers, which were contingent upon one's interests: what rights of self-government did the people of the territories hold? It did not have a one-size-fits-all resolution despite what the peddlers of popular sovereignty were trying to sell to the American public.

Settlers in territories such as Utah, Oregon, and Kansas demanded complete self-government, the popular election of all territorial officers, and the removal of congressional veto from territorial legislation according to the dictates of the Kansas-Nebraska Act. In essence, they wanted the federal government largely removed from the territorial system. But the presidential administration did not take itself out of territorial affairs. Rather, it placed itself in the thick of territorial matters and attempted to exercise greater control. Buchanan's policy to use forceful military intervention in the territory placed national sovereignty over local sovereignty and set a precedent for presidential use of the military and federal regulation in local matters.[94] Many in the United States soon recognized, however, that by meddling with the Mormons and their local social and political institutions, the federal government could also interfere with and jeopardize contested social institutions elsewhere if it so chose. Congress and the public began discussing further the constitutional and legal merits of the Utah War, as the movement to suppress the Mormons by force became a factor in the fight over the South's peculiar institution. It did so by raising serious questions concerning federal authority in the territories, not to mention the exercise of expanded powers generally, that would have larger ramifications for the territories in the West.[95] For instance, the publicly accepted use of greater power in Utah meant that the president or Congress could protect slavery's existence in the territories. But it also meant that if a president or Congress opposed slavery, the same power used to protect the institution could defeat and use force to prohibit its existence.

While one might expect divisiveness over popular sovereignty and the exercise of federal power in the territories between Democrats and Republicans, fissures opened at the time of the Utah War within the Democratic Party as President Buchanan attempted to bring Democrats together by pushing through the admission of Kansas as a slave state under the proslavery constitution fraudulently drawn up in Lecompton.[96] Buchanan's decision to send an army to Utah and his active endorsement of a slave state constitution in Kansas demonstrated his desire to dictate the future of the territories, popular sovereignty be damned. In January 1858, newspapers, including the *New York Herald*, commented on the irony in the Democrat's flip-flopping position on popular sovereignty in Utah and Kansas. In an article titled "The Approaching Conclusion of the Kansas Comedy," the *Herald* considered it farcical that the federal government maintained the military in Kansas "to enforce the doctrine of 'popular sovereignty,'" only to uproot it to carry out the same design to control "the 'popular sovereignty' saints of Utah."[97] In spite of all the problems in Kansas, the

Herald chided, "this Kansas imbroglio has substantially worked out its own solution" of becoming a "free State with a slave State constitution." That contradiction, the *Herald* suggested, was the only solution that could come from popular sovereignty in Kansas.[98] The *Deseret News* saw in the federal government's administration of Kansas and Utah a striking contrast. In Kansas popular sovereignty failed and truly threatened to produce dangerous sectional feuds and the specter of a great Civil War. Still the president sought its speedy admission as a sovereign slave state. Meanwhile, in Utah, where the people's voice was one, the federal government decided the people were traitorous and sent "every engine of oppression" to humble them. In other words, the federal government refused to allow popular sovereignty to take its course in both western territories.[99]

The Democratic president watered down the party's commitment to popular sovereignty and apparently bowed to southern pressure by "attempting to ram slavery down the throats of Kansans despite the wishes of the local majority."[100] Still, many maintained the party line. Democratic representative James F. Dowdell of Alabama followed the president in the Kansas constitutional crisis. In his message in the congressional debate over Lecompton, he reflected, "Now, shall we presume to violate the sovereignty of a State, by polling her masses to ascertain whether the voice spoken by her convention is the truly expressed will of the people? To do so, would be to exercise arbitrary power." Unlike Douglas and his acolytes, Dowdell did not view the rights of the territories in the same manner as the rights of the states. The Lecompton convention, in his estimation, was a political body, duly invested with power to make and ordain a constitution.[101]

Lecompton, however, marked a turning point for the Democratic Party as two of its main figureheads, Buchanan and Douglas, split over slavery and popular sovereignty. While the two appeared to agree that Mormons in Utah incorrectly interpreted the popular sovereignty doctrine and were not capable of republican self-government, they differed sharply over Lecompton. Douglas believed that Buchanan overstepped his authority and acted contrary to his rule of true popular sovereignty by offering presidential backing to the proslavery constitution. He strongly opposed the passage of the Lecompton Constitution. So did Republicans, who denounced the president's support for Lecompton as the denial of local majority rule in Kansas and as subversive to republican government. The Democratic Party hid behind a legalistic definition of popular sovereignty, which suggested that the people voted and passed a certain constitution, but likewise evaded the doctrine's true democratic promise, as not all of the people's voices were heard. Kansas voters rejected the Lecompton Constitution in a 4 January 1858 referendum providing solid evidence that the constitution did not reflect the will of the people.[102]

Utah affairs added to the crisis unfolding before politicians. Popular sovereignty had utterly failed in that territory. The Mormons interpreted and applied popular sovereignty to protect their theologically based political system, religious practices, and engagement with Native peoples, which was seen as unacceptable by even the staunchest supporters of the Democratic doctrine. The Mormons not only were deemed unable to govern themselves but also were preparing to prevent the federal government from exercising sovereignty over them. In December 1857, Buchanan requested additional standing regiments and an enlarged armed force for Utah.

Questions regarding the president's use of force and war-making authority, however, and Congress's position relative to the territories, primarily its ability to repeal territorial laws and legislate for them, caused a stir among politicians. On 26 January 1858, Democratic senator Robert Toombs of Georgia questioned the president's power to make war and wondered whether Buchanan's actions gave the executive too much authority. Toombs stated, "Congress, which alone has the power to make war, has not spoken; and it is very certain, unless our country has undergone a silent revolution, that the President cannot make that war. It is very certain, that unless the Senate and House of Representatives intend to go on in the downward path of vesting all the powers of government confided to the legislative department in the executive, this war does not exist in contemplation of law."[103] Toombs believed that the bill gave the president too much authority and power in a republican form of government.[104] Conversely, New York Republican senator William H. Seward, who would later serve as Abraham Lincoln's secretary of state, voted in favor of the increase: "With a view to save life, to save the public peace, and to bring the Territory of Utah to submission to legal instituted authorities without bloodshed, I favor the increase of force which is to be sent there and for no other reason."[105] Seward suggested that in Utah the government entered into a new experiment in territorial governance entirely distinct from the whole line of previous experience. Seward saw in the Mormon religious and political constitution two fundamentally troubling elements: resistance to federal law and authority, and a lust for independence, power, and dominion.[106] In line with Republican thinking, the New York senator approved the expedition and its expansion of federal authority over the western territories.

At the end of a discussion on popular sovereignty and slavery in Kansas, Republican representative John Thompson of New York chimed in on the debate over Kansas and the Lecompton Constitution. He asserted that an issue confronted the nation "even before the affairs of Kansas" that required immediate action. "For the first time since the organization of this Government," Thompson observed, "we are called upon to authorize the increase of the Army, ostensibly for the purpose of being employed against the people of one of our territories." Thompson used the term "ostensibly" because he did not consider Mormons citizens, but rather a heterogeneous nation consisting of aliens from Germany, Sweden, Denmark, Scotland, England, and Australia who repudiated the paternity and power of the federal government and bolstered a theocratic polity. Therefore, the army should exercise the federal government's power in Utah. Thompson attacked Mormon leader Brigham Young, calling him a despot who grew "desperate enough to declare openly his defiance of the General Government." The

Republican complained about the use of thousands of troops in Kansas Territory, "under the pretence of maintaining law and order, and compelling a free people to vote or refrain from voting under the roar of United States artillery," when more troops were needed in Utah, ironically to force a people into a particular governing archetype. Common to messages on Utah, Thompson attacked the Mormon religion and imagined Mormons as "others" by connecting their religion to the "Mohammedans" and their having a "Koran of Mormonism."[107] The connection to the Islamic faith was a common rhetorical trope used by nineteenth-century Americans to offend and demonstrate the otherness of Mormons.

Thompson likewise added gender and racial politics into his discussion. He declared that plural marriage defrauded women in their rights, "as long as man is capable of honor, or woman of love, so long will this licentious system which degrades her into a plaything of idle dalliance, or a breeding animal for children" lost in the "shameless contentment of herding in droves like swine, beneath the roof of a creature who regards her as at once menial, mistress, and slave." Not only did Thompson imagine Mormon men as inhuman and therefore necessary to control, but he also made specific connections between Mormon women and slaves, thereby further attaching the twin relics of barbarism pronounced in the Republican's 1856 platform to the Utah War.

Thompson proceeded to suggest a course of action in Utah. "I would pass a law making polygamy a crime in the Territories," he declared, "and then send a force sufficient to scatter every harem to the four winds." He further suggested that an armed force should apprehend Brigham Young and other church leaders to "secure to the inhabitants a republican form of government, and see that they enjoy their freedom without the heel of a despot." Thompson sought to stop the spread of Mormonism and its political influence, a matter he believed more important than any financial cost it might accrue. Though he had attacked Democratic responses to popular sovereignty in Kansas and

Utah, Thompson concluded with his hope that "this may not become a party question—a shuttlecock for political partisanship." Instead, he advocated increasing military forces through volunteers to deal with what he considered a common threat to the nation and its planned westward expansion. His one caveat was that volunteers be disbanded after they quelled the Mormon problem.[108]

Unusual support for the military increase came from Mississippi fire-eater, former secretary of war, and then-chairperson of the Senate Committee on Military Affairs Jefferson Davis. In a February 1858 speech to Congress, Davis emphasized the pressing issue of western geography and exercising control over the western inner-empire by adding to and supplying the army of occupation. Growing and maintaining the army in Utah, in Davis's estimation, would force the Mormons to withdraw from their rebellious ways and submit to the laws of a republican government.[109] Furthermore, Davis commented on the importance of controlling the geographic position of Utah, particularly "to keep in check the Indians who surround" the territory. The Mormons, he declared, had already stimulated the region's indigenous population to hostility and held control of a mountain region full of the main emigrant routes. The army had to establish itself in the Great Basin, Davis opined, to provide protection to emigrants and settlers. "I do not see how we are to look forward," Davis asserted, "from any possible conclusion of this Mormon difficulty, to a reduction of the Army."[110] The former secretary of war wanted a permanent increase of the army to provide the necessary military presence to expand federal infrastructure in the Great Basin West.

Davis's speech concluded with another glimpse into the importance of establishing a federal military presence in Utah as a strategic node in a network for control. He mentioned that troops in Utah could provide quick and great aid to the ongoing Indian fighting elsewhere in the region, including Oregon, Washington, and New Mexico.[111] With the military entrenched in Utah, the federal government would have a stronger, more efficient, and capable network for protection, promoting American settlement and expansion, and supporting federal authority against internal and external security threats.

Davis denied emphatically the power of the federal government to coerce or invade a state, but understood that territories did not occupy the same constitutional position as states because of their status as federal dependencies. Furthermore, he stated that when a territory rebelled against the federal government, it remained in that government's power to put down the insurrection and compel obedience.[112] As a proponent of states' rights, Davis articulated a key component to the misunderstanding on sovereignty, as the Constitution held, that territories did not occupy the same position as states. Davis stated:

> I do not admit, as I have never subscribed to the doctrine of squatter sovereignty that the Government of the United States has no more power in a Territory than in a State. I hold that the Territories are dependencies of the Federal Union; they are in a condition of pupilage, to be governed by the States, the property of States; and that if men, either foreign or native, should aggregate themselves upon a Territory of the United States, and raise the standard of rebellion against the Government, and in defiance of its laws, it is not only within the power, but it is the plain, palpable duty of the Government to put down such an insurrection, and to compel obedience.[113]

Davis reiterated his point on the relationship between national and state government: "The federal government has no power to invade the limits of a State there to attempt the coercion of its people."[114] Though he made a careful distinction about the difference between states and territories, Davis's statement on Utah and the power of the federal government to quell rebellion provides an eerie foreshadowing of the federal government's response to put down insurrection in the South during the 1860s.

Charles J. Faulkner, Democratic representative from Virginia, also gave a speech in favor of increasing the army permanently in early

March 1858. Eight months earlier Faulkner wrote to Douglas applauding his stance against popular sovereignty in Utah and in favor of repealing the territory. Now he advocated raising a large and permanent force to handle the exigency which had arisen in Utah because he did not think an inexperienced soldiery could perform well enough to achieve the goals of the campaign. Faulkner gave a brief historical lesson on the usage of volunteer forces sent to Oregon and Washington in the mid-1850s to fight Indian tribes, forces he suggested were ineffective and economically burdensome.[115] He believed the necessities of armed police in the country required the addition of five regiments to the regular army, though this proposition had received little encouragement in the House Committee on Military Affairs. He warned that the actual strength of the army, at about thirteen thousand men, was not able to successfully police and defend the vastness of the country. Not only could the standing army not control the Indians of the West, the force was inadequate to serve as the "military police to guard your line of communications between the Mississippi valley and the Pacific ocean, covering something like nine thousand miles of emigrant route."[116] The vast continental nation needed a larger standing army, according to the representative. Faulkner quoted a report from the secretary of war that stated, "If there is a higher duty than another devolved upon a well regulated government, it is to afford perfect protection to its citizens against outrage and personal violence; *yet this great obligation is not performed by the government of the United States.*" Faulkner invoked the congressional requirement to uphold the Constitution in providing for the protection of the lives and property of the country's people. Regardless of the Utah situation, he declared, "it is the duty of Congress to increase the military force of this country."[117] Senator Alfred Iverson of Georgia likewise called for the increase in the regular force for the present exigency of the Utah war and "for permanent employment hereafter."[118]

Faulkner likewise gave his opinion that the Mormons professed "some wild and treasonable ideas of the doctrine of 'popular sovereignty.'" The Virginia congressman complained that the Latter-day Saints had asserted "their right to the soil, their right to elect all their own officers and to manage their own affairs, in utter contempt and defiance of the authority of this government." Faulkner highlighted the problems with Mormon sovereignty and the need for the federal government to quash its existence. Fearing an outbreak of hostilities and buying into the idea of a Mormon-Indian alliance, he combined the Mormon and Indian problems and stated that the Mormon rebellion added another element to the existing need to defend the "Indian frontier." He advocated a firmer control over the Indians and over the territories generally to maintain the supremacy of national law, and enforce the rights of the federal government in that territory.[119] Asserting the supremacy of federal authority in the territories, Faulkner presented a long-range view to establish defense and control over the West.[120] His commentary and many others demonstrate the imperial behavior of the United States, a behavior that sought to extend the empire of liberty and remove or control the administration of government in the western territory. That imperial behavior also added to the federal government's authority and purview.

Other southerners in Congress, however, feared the result of adding military strength if the Republicans should win control of the government's military in the future. Some were concerned that a growth in the army might lead to greater federal power, particularly in the territories, which could have forcefully prohibited the expansion of slavery.[121] In congressional debate surrounding the increase of the standing army during the Utah War, Senator Andrew Johnson of Tennessee stated that the sending of the army to act against local sovereignty would end states' rights and that state sovereignty would crumble before the central government. He further suggested that if the standing army be enlarged, to "tell the States to beware for their sovereignty is at an end."[122] Johnson argued that the president did not ask for an additional force for a standing army, but rather an additional imposing force to prevent the shedding of blood in Utah. He suggested that volunteers would serve just fine in answering the call of the president, and then the proper authorities could dismiss the volunteers when the difficulties ceased. A June 1858 *Harper's Weekly* article likewise recounted the continuing problems of Utah Territory in the discussion on local self-governance and slavery expansion. "A singular and almost unaccountable indifference to the constitutional and legal bearings of this question," the *Harper's* article proclaimed, "has been hitherto displayed by a school of politicians which might have been expected to regard it with earnest attention. Hardly any notice seems to have been taken of the inevitable bearing which any legislation on the subject of polygamy would have on the graver topics of slavery and popular sovereignty. One is at a loss to explain an inattention seemingly amounting to blindness."[123] The school of politicians almost certainly referred to the Democratic Party. The *Harper's* article and congressional discourse underscore the concerns that Americans shared about the potential growth of federal power.

The congressional debate over adding military regiments continued in February and into the early spring of 1858. Senator William Gwin from California also favored adding five regiments to the regular army to give the president the aid he needed and to protect the interests of California. Gwin, like Representative Faulkner, did not believe "the military force of the United States, as it is organized at present ... meets the wants and emergencies of the section of the country where those Indians are located whom they are intended to keep in subordination."[124] The California senator cut to the heart of the matter and admonished his colleagues to endow the president with the power to call out a force of either volunteers or regulars for this emergency to relieve, sustain, and support the forces in Utah or in any emergency.[125] Adding forces for Utah, Gwin proposed, would allow Buchanan to "carry out his policy; but he cannot do it unless an addition is made to the military establishment of the country." Gwin concluded that Congress should make the best use of this time of necessity to increase the army permanently, if that was the nation's intent.[126] Albert G. Brown, senator from Mississippi, repeated the idea that "if you send volunteers to fight the Mormons you will have civil war beyond all question." His reasoning suggested that volunteers coming from the states of Mormon enemies, particularly Illinois and Missouri, would bring an immense war. "I want no war," Brown contended; "I want no bloodshed. If you will send no volunteers to Utah, you will have no war. There is no necessity for it. Brigham Young and his followers do not mean to fight. They will not fight you unless you force war on them."[127] The debate on Utah and raising additional military forces continued on and off until April when both houses of Congress agreed on a compromise and authorized the president to call two regiments of volunteers for the purpose of quelling disturbances in the Territory of Utah, for the protection of supply and emigrant trains, and for the suppression of Indian hostilities on the frontier. The total number of volunteers could not exceed 740 men.[128] Men in Florida and across the country were ready to heed the call, some with a continuing zeal "to crush out the 'relic of barbarism' that pollutes the fair soil and clime of Utah."[129]

The matter of Mormon plural marriage and morality continually crept up in these and other debates over Utah in early 1858. Mormons combated the prevalent American rhetoric of the evils of plural marriage by pointing out that large-scale prostitution and extramarital affairs occurred in the states. The Mormons were not the only ones who made these counterarguments. Senator Andrew Johnson stated that the nation needed to clean itself of the "practical polygamy" ongoing in some of the cities of the Union. Johnson asked his fellow legislators to look closer to home. Did polygamy, in the form of extramarital affairs, exist nowhere else, he asked? Speaking frankly, Johnson stated, "There is more practical polygamy now in many of the cities of this Confederacy than there is in all Salt Lake. Then, before we get so fierce, so rampant, and so willing to run these misguided and deluded people into the mountains, into the caverns and the gorges, as hiding places, I think we should be a little considerate, and see if we cannot correct the evil which lies at our own door."[130] Johnson espoused reform-minded ideals common in the antebellum era. While the senator sought to reform the sexual impulses of the Mormons and American urbanites by comparing both groups' practice of promiscuity, the Mormons incessantly sought to use the prostitution comparison to their defense.

Typical Mormon thoughts on the subject stated that prostitution and moral rot resulted from monogamy, as did adultery, abortion, and divorce. Mormons glorified procreation as the sole aim of sexuality. They also sought to strengthen families and church membership through sex.[131] Despite American popular opinion that Mormon men enslaved women in polygamy, some LDS women argued vigorously in favor of the multiple wife system. Mormon women accepted the practice because they believed the doctrine was essential to their and their husband's eternal salvation; they viewed it as honorable and believed that plural marriage could give women a sense of pride and significance within the Mormon community.[132] A non-Mormon woman living among the Latter-day Saints, the new governor's wife, Elizabeth Cumming, wrote to a family member about Mormon cohesiveness, particularly on the part of the women. She stated, "Such *devotedness* to their religion as they evince is instruction on more ways than one. The spirit of martyrdom here lives and has its being—Here one sees the power of *faith* and how faith may be abused. The Mormon ladies talk a great deal about the religion. They live it, they feel it. Every act almost of their lives is mormonized." Cumming further wrote of Mormon women, "They have an infinity of arguments in favor of polygamy. They are 'in favor of it on moral, physical, and religious" grounds because it led them to spiritual exaltation in the hereafter.[133]

Mormon rhetoric emphasized that women in polygamous societies were typically guaranteed to have a husband and provider, while monogamous societies more often left women without the same support structure and raised the rate of prostitution. The *Western Standard*, a California newspaper edited by Mormon George Q. Cannon, published a critique of monogamy in one of its pre–Utah War issues.

Cannon wrote the piece and argued that the "genius of Christian monogamy is to encourage prostitution; because it forbids plural marriages, yet compels no man to marry, and thus debars thousands of females from gratifying the strongest instincts of their nature, which are comprehended in the sacred names of 'wife' and 'mother.' . . . The result is, the country is cursed with the most dreaded of all curses, prostitution."[134] Americans, and especially Protestant women, had many reasons to oppose prostitution, but the main one centered on the notion that all sexuality that took place outside of the family generated deep concerns about social order. While Mormons promoted their ideal that plural marriage kept all sexuality within the family, most outsiders failed to see it that way and rather considered it a highly organized system of mass prostitution.

In the end, the congressional discussion about Mormons and Utah in early 1858 led to a modest increase in temporary, volunteer troops. The debates in Washington also generated discourse on federal power. Based upon adherence to the Constitution as they understood it and not upon favoritism toward their section of the country, congressmen debated the merits of the Utah War. For some, such as Jefferson Davis, the use of the troops in a territory did not stand in the same relation to constitutional questions as the use of troops in a state. Some understood the relationship of the federal government to the territories and to states, while others feared the precedent set in Utah. Tennessee senator Andrew Johnson believed that such actions would end states' rights and that state sovereignty would crumble before the central government. Northerners and southerners alike feared that adding military strength in the West would result in a trend toward the waning of local autonomy generally.

Near Fort Bridger, as spring 1858 approached and with military aid, Governor Alfred Cumming thought to give the Mormons the chance to peacefully submit to the authority of the United States.[135] He began making preparations to meet with the religious leaders on their turf.

The new governor hoped his proximity and cool demeanor would convince the Mormons to abandon their ideas of resistance. Meanwhile, in Washington, the longtime Mormon ally Colonel Thomas L. Kane met and corresponded with President Buchanan to seek a peaceful end to the Utah troubles. In a letter to Kane, Buchanan demonstrated his admiration for the colonel's strong conviction, but he also stated his position that the Mormons understood the intentions of the federal government toward them and if they did not, his December 1857 annual message should have disabused their minds. "Its views therein expressed," the president explained, "have undergone no change. These sentiments were expressed in sincerity & truth, & I trust that your representation of them was met with the success you anticipate. I hope that the people of Utah may be convinced ere it is too late that there exists no duties of higher obligation than those which they owe to their country."[136] Buchanan held Kane in high regard and felt confident in him, but he would not send any agent to visit the Mormons. Kane's father, Judge John K. Kane, did not think Thomas would succeed in brokering a peace, particularly if the Mormons assailed the troops, which he believed would bring the wrath of the entire country on Utah as the American people would never be satisfied "while a Mormon community survives on this continent."[137] Although he held little hope for successful negotiations because of the Mormons' insistence on self-government, Kane traveled to Utah to see if he could help end the difficulties between the Mormons and the federal government and its army.[138]

Kane sailed from New York City just as the calendar turned to 1858. By way of San Francisco and wagon travel via the Old Spanish Trail to Salt Lake City, Kane met with Mormon leaders in late February 1858. Kane attempted to persuade Brigham Young of peace when the two met briefly before the Pennsylvanian departed for the army base at Camp Scott. In a 15 March 1858 letter, Kane recommended to Buchanan to impress upon the Utah constituents a conviction that they could rely upon American laws and the administration by instituting a territorial judiciary that would try any offender justly and impartially.[139] The perceptive Kane also asserted that he felt no satisfaction "that our officers will be able to control their soldiers—much less their disorderly retinue of Camp followers and attendants (and keep them from committing excesses and offenses against the laws)." Kane worried that he could not persuade the Mormons that juries would not contain their enemies.[140] He thought it best to impress upon the people that they could rely on the laws and the administration with no prejudiced juries, to clearly delineate the powers and relations between them and the officers. In a reversal of thought on the Mormon-Indian alliance, Kane also encouraged Buchanan to consider giving specific instructions to Utah's superintendent of Indian affairs and several Indian agents "to use the utmost circumspection in their dealings that they may not be misrepresented as bestowing gifts or using other influences to stir up the savages to war against the Mormons."[141]

In March, Kane approached the encamped U.S. troops. Dismissing his Nauvoo Legion escort, he entered the camp alone. As he came forward, shots were fired and a bullet from one of the guards nearly hit him. Incensed, Kane brushed aside General Albert Johnston's later apology and engaged Alfred Cumming to share his counsel. Cumming responded, "The storm, so long impending, is now ready to burst upon the deluded inhabitants of this territory; and whilst it is my duty to enforce unconditional submission to the authority of the United States, yet, in the performance of that duty I would gladly temper justice with mercy, and prevent the unnecessary effusion of blood—especially I would shield women and children from the sufferings incident to civil war." Cumming appreciated Kane's work and thought "it is desirable [he] should continue to exert [his] influence in teaching a rebellious population that both duty and policy indicate the necessity of immediate submission to the United States, and dictate an appeal to its clemency for immunity from past offences."[142] The mediator Kane convinced the newly appointed governor he would be safe if he rode into Salt Lake City without military escort. Doing so, Cumming was graciously received by Young, who transferred the records and seal of the governor's office to him in April, marking a peaceful transfer of power. Perhaps Young saw the futility in his endgame. The United States, a nation bent on manifest destiny and expansion, would not permit an independent sovereignty within its borders. It had also become all too clear that the Mormons would not have the sovereignty, peace, or isolation they desired when they arrived in the Great Basin in 1847. Nevertheless, he was not yet ready to completely submit to the new authority figures in the territory.

Still distrustful of government intentions, Brigham Young and the Latter-day Saints had already begun a massive evacuation from their homes in the Salt Lake Valley and prepared to "move south." In the early spring, Mormon leaders, still with plans to maintain their sovereign power to conduct governmental and social affairs in their own ways and fearing violent persecution and debauchery from the army, ordered their followers in northern Utah to board up their homes and close up their farms to move south toward Provo. The northern settlements would be burned before the army came if Young gave the order. Mormons in the south were encouraged to build up the roads and help the incoming population get settled. The move began in earnest in late March and continued until July 1858. In numbers, but not in distance, the move dwarfed the earlier Mormon flights from Missouri and Illinois: about thirty thousand people moved fifty miles or more south in short order. It proved a harrowing experience for many Mormons who packed up their meager belongings and food into wagons. For example, Cynthia Jane Park Stowell had to remain in her home in the Ogden area until she gave birth to a child on 14 April 1858. With the move south ongoing, she left her home with her newborn baby a week later, "with one wagon and two yoke of steers." Cynthia's husband, William, had been captured by U.S. soldiers the previous fall, leaving only Saphronia, one of William's plural wives, and twelve children to travel on their own.[143]

After receiving word of the army's poor condition that winter, the president worried that the Mormons might attack and destroy the army before additional forces could be mustered at an even more severe political cost. Just as hastily as he had sent the army, Buchanan sought a rapid end to the intervention. While Governor Alfred Cumming and freelancer Thomas L. Kane attempted to persuade Mormon leaders to cease resisting the approaching army, the president sent an official party to negotiate peace with the Mormon population. As peace commissioners he sent Lazarus W. Powell of Kentucky and Benjamin McCulloch of Texas to Utah armed with a blanket pardon on 6 April 1858 to mark the official end to the Utah War once the Mormon people accepted the decree. Before any major confrontation between the U.S. Army and the Mormon militia occurred, Buchanan offered "a free and full pardon to all who will submit themselves to the authority of the federal government."[144] The pardon appeared to be in line with Buchanan's first annual message which indicated the president's desire to prevent bloodshed and ensure that the people of Utah upheld the Constitution and respected the federal law that governed the territory. It also warned that any who persisted in rebellion would receive no further leniency.[145] According to one periodical, the presidential pardon confirmed that Utah Territory belonged to the "United States and is subject to the control of the National Legislature, by the powers vested in him by the Constitution and laws" because it forced the Mormons to unconditionally surrender to the authority of the federal government.[146]

Offering to all Utah citizens who submitted to the authority of the U.S. Constitution and national laws as administered by federal officials a pardon, the president appeared satisfied with the prospect for national control of the territory. That prospect appeared even greater as the army moved to execute "the orders of Government," to march into Salt Lake Valley, establish a military post, and ensure, as President Buchanan spelled out in his annual message, the restoration and maintenance of "the sovereignty of the Constitution and laws over the

Territory of Utah."[147] The arrival of the army in the territory created a new series of dynamics for the three entities. On the federal side, the army's presence allowed the president a renewed opportunity to establish federal control over the region. Stationing an army in Utah to support federal appointees and supervise the administration of national law and Indian affairs had long been advocated, and the government was about to establish two military bases. But, as the next few years would reveal, the many layers of territorial governance and divergent opinions of the various arms of the federal government in Utah made managing sovereignty in that or any western territory fraught with difficulties. On the Mormon side, the army and non-Mormon appointees dealt a significant blow to their insular community. Likewise, for Native peoples, the new federal presence meant another entity to navigate in an already complex landscape.

6 The U.S. Army and the Symbolic Conquering of Mormon Sovereignty

President Buchanan's pardon signaled his satisfaction that the army and federal officials would capably enforce national sovereignty in Utah. The army played an important, and multifaceted, role in promoting American expansion across the continent; it often served as the harbinger of American institutional development. Once established in the Great Basin territory, the army made symbolic shows of its power and advanced strategic efforts to expand federal infrastructure in the West. The army built forts in strategic locations, conducted explorations, built and defended roads, offered a nuclei for town building, enforced the law, and attempted to subdue Native peoples.[1] The army's presence and seating of new government officials made an enduring intrusion on Mormon sovereignty, one that the president declared would not be "withdrawn until the inhabitants of that Territory shall manifest a proper sense of the duty which they owe to this Government."[2] However, the federal officials were not unified. In the end, the ineffective coordination between the various federal officers, communication delays between Utah and Washington, and the nation's growing sectional conflict revealed the imperfect nature of territorial governance and the problems the Buchanan administration faced in fully achieving sovereign control.

Within days of the 6 April 1858 pardon, Lazarus Powell and Benjamin McCulloch, the peace commissioners assigned by James Buchanan, had left Washington for Utah. They, like Alfred Cumming, James Denver, and other federal officials, sought to demonstrate to the Mormon people that if they wished to live in peace under the Constitution and laws of the United States, they should desire a portion of the army to be located in the territory. The army, according to Powell and McCulloch, would protect the Mormons from Indian depredations, afford them a market for their surplus products, and "protect, and not injure, all true, loyal, and patriotic citizens."[3]

Before the peace commissioners arrived in Utah, new territorial governor Alfred Cumming made the trip from Camp Scott to Salt Lake City. Cumming too wanted to make peace overtures and simultaneously have his and the federal government's authority acknowledged by the people. On 25 April 1858, while the majority of the Latter-day Saints were moving from their homes and heading south, the new governor attended a meeting at the Salt Lake City tabernacle, where he spoke and outlined the course of his administration and the reason for the coming of the army. Cumming declared his authority, having been appointed by the president with the consent of the Senate, to be the governor of Utah. Cumming told the congregation that while a large body of armed men sat waiting to enter the valley, they were not sent to destroy the Mormons, "but to protect them from the lawless savage." This appeared to be a departure from the typical Mormon-Indian alliance rhetoric. Perhaps the governor was speaking to the larger idea of federal protection for American expansion, in which he was indicating that Mormons could be a part if they would prove their loyalty to the United States. Cumming also indicated his intention to cooperate with LDS church leaders in all future moves hoping that this would allow the people to gain confidence in him and the federal government.[4]

Mormons were not yet fully assured by the new governor and so indicated at the 25 April meeting. Latter-day Saint Gilbert Clements suggested that the real question at hand "was whether we would tamely submit to vassalage, or whether we would stand up for our rights." "We would not have been here," Clements stated, referring to the Mormons' move to the Great Basin, "if we had had our constitutional rights."[5] Mormon leader John Taylor stood and reiterated a common Mormon trope of oppression when he suggested that "A standing army is only for tyrants." The Mormon congregation also questioned the main object of the government, wondering if the army intended to "put down" plural marriage. If so, an unnamed Mormon shouted, demonstrating that community's understanding of the sectional complications facing the nation incidental to Utah affairs, it "would be just as right for the north to put down the slavery in the south."[6] Another in the crowd moved topics again to the idea of Mormon-Indian relations. He echoed the Mormon position that their contact with Native peoples had been in line with civilizing them, but "since the approach of this army [the Indians] had measurably returned to their old practices." The crowd declared that they could not "receive Gov. Cumming unless he will use his influence to have that army withdrawn and present us in a favorable light to this nation."[7] The meeting ended with no resolution. The Mormons' move south continued.

The conflict between the territory and national authority remained in flux. The non-Mormon citizens in Utah's western Carson Valley took advantage of the opportunity presented by the Utah War to renew their petitions to Congress to create a new territory over the western part of Utah. Carson Valley citizens William Ormsby and Martin Smith claimed that the people of western Utah had no civil or political power; they could not protect themselves against perceived Mormon-instigated Indian raids, they had no legal mechanisms in place, and they could make no application for "the redress of grievances."[8] The two men concluded their plea by highlighting the Mormon "treasonable defiance to federal authority, that our danger from them and their Indian allies is much greater than attends citizens of any other State or Territory. By the present condition of things, and unless there be, at this session of Congress, a territorial government organized, the citizens of that great basin will be, as they have been, constrained to do illegally, for their own protection, that which should be done under legal authority."[9] In a reversal of the Mormon experience in Ohio, Missouri, and Illinois, it was non-Mormons requesting government protection against the majority population.

The possibility of creating a new territory in the West from Utah Territory had long been discussed. Vermont representative Justin Morrill had proposed to realign Utah's borders in early 1857 based on the early Carson Valley citizens' requests, and suggested circumscribing "the boundaries of the Territory, and give the inhabitants much narrower limits." He also proposed cutting up the territory and annexing it to adjoining territories and states.[10] Stephen Douglas, in his June 1857 Springfield speech, also advocated removing the Mormon ulcer, while others in Congress discussed dividing Utah up among the neighboring territories of Nebraska, Kansas, Oregon, and New Mexico.[11] By May 1858, the House Committee on the Territories issued a report on the potential of organizing a new territory. From the many petitions sent from Carson Valley, the House committee report concluded "that the establishment of a territorial government would tend to protect the public mails travelling within and through it; make safe and secure the great overland route to the Pacific as far as within its limits; restore friendly relations with the present hostile Indian tribes; contribute to the suppression of the Mormon power by the protection it might afford to its dissatisfied members; and, in the present exigency in that region, might be, and almost certainly would be, of material aid to our military operations." The potential in these aims satisfied and impressed the House Committee on the Territories, which then supported the passage of a bill for the formation of a new territory called Nevada.[12]

Before the resolution of the Utah War, in June 1858, the Boston-based *Flag of Our Union* encouraged Congress to create a new territory by clarifying to its readership that the applicants for the establishment of Nevada "are not Mormons, but American citizens." The paper indicated that the Mormon authorities had always been inimical to the Carson Valley citizens, who, the paper declared, had suffered much from the vindictive persecution. The paper reiterated the idea that those in Carson Valley did not have proper civil government and that the people were easy "prey to the hostile Indians set on by their persecutors," the Mormons.[13] In rhetoric similar to one of Buchanan's justifications for sending the military to Utah, the *Flag of Our Union* reported that the Carson Valley citizens' appeal called for the establishment of a republican government and to protect the people against the threat of a Mormon–Indian alliance, which remained entrenched in popular opinion. "The Indian population of this part of Utah is estimated at one hundred to one hundred and fifty thousand," the paper estimated, "the greater part of whom have been stirred up to hostility against the white settlers by the machinations of the Mormons. These fiends in human shape mingle with the Indians, pretend to admit them to their sect, take their females as supernumerary wives, and use the influence thus acquired to inflame their hatred against our citizens." The idea of a Mormon-Indian threat remained. The *Flag of Our Union* concluded its report by admonishing Congress to "repair the great blunder of Mr. Fillmore's administration, so far as possible, by cutting off the sound part of Utah, and erecting it into a separate territory."[14] Former Utah supreme court justice Perry Brocchus likewise believed that "justice and humanity demand the immediate organization of a government over that region" to protect them against the peculiar domestic relations and remove them from Mormon tyranny.[15] However, given the political climate and the ongoing national problems over territorial governance, Congress did not organize western Utah as Nevada Territory until March 1861; that would only be the first change to Utah's external boundaries since its creation in 1850.

Back in Utah, in early June, the peace commissioners, Lazarus Powell and Benjamin McCulloch, arrived and presented Mormon leaders with the president's pardon of 6 April 1858 as the official document to subdue Mormon power and redirect their loyalty to the United States.[16] Powell and McCulloch's efforts proved fruitful. On 12 June 1858, just five days after arriving in the territory, Powell and McCulloch informed General Albert Johnston that the "chief men of the Territory" would yield obedience to the Constitution and laws of the United States and that they would cheerfully consent to the implanted civil officers of the territory in performing their duties. The peace commissioners also reported that the Mormons would make no resistance to the army of the United States. The LDS leaders accepted the pardon and reversed their decision to move south. The houses, fields, and gardens of the Utah population were left unsecured by the massive move; the Mormon leaders asked that the army and its animals avoid destroying the unattended property. Powell and McCulloch asked Johnston to restrain his command and to keep the animals from grazing on civilian farms to demonstrate the army's respect for the people and their property.[17] The peace commissioners sent a report back to the secretary of war stating, "Since the arrival of the army in the valley the apprehensions of many of the people here that the army would not respect their persons and property have greatly diminished. The Mormons express their gratification at the admirable order observed by the army since it reached the valley of the Great Salt Lake."[18]

In their reports, Powell and McCulloch congratulated the presidential administration. After having arrived in the territory, they became "firmly impressed with the belief that the presence of the army here, and the large additional force that had been ordered to this Territory, were the chief inducements that caused the Mormons to abandon the idea of resisting the authority of the United States. A less decisive policy would probably have resulted in a long, bloody, and expensive war."[19] The Mormons unanimously accepted President Buchanan's pardon and voiced loyalty to the federal government to satisfy the peace commissioners, new federal appointees, the army, the president, Congress, and the court of public opinion. The *Valley Tan*, a non-Mormon newspaper, later published an article stating that the Mormon acceptance of the pardon and "acquiescence has been further and fully evidenced by the conduct and acts of the people since that time."[20]

About the same time that the peace commissioners wrote to the military authorities about the Mormons' submission, James Buchanan prepared a message to Congress communicating Alfred Cumming's report of his interactions with the Utah population during April and May. The new Utah governor had written to Secretary of State Lewis Cass about the speech he had given in the Salt Lake City tabernacle on 25 April, in which he outlined the federal government's intent in the territory. Cumming stated, "I informed them that I had come among them to vindicate the national sovereignty; that it was my duty to secure the supremacy of the Constitution and the laws; that I had taken my oath of office to exact an unconditional submission on their part to the dictates of the law."[21] Upon beginning his gubernatorial term, Cumming announced that the territory was open and viable for settlement by the American public, though he thought the territory required a larger armed force to "chastise the Indians" and to protect the property of the inhabitants.[22] Cumming concluded his letter by noting that before long he hoped "to announce that the road between California and Missouri may be travelled with perfect security by teams and emigrants of every description."[23] The territory's superintendent of Indian affairs Jacob Forney sent a similar message when he triumphantly stated, "This route to California is now free from all danger" from Indians and Mormons.[24]

The federal officials' statements pacified and satisfied the president. If the dispatching of the army had achieved nothing else, Governor Cumming's official announcement and Forney's declaration encouraged the president that the overland route from the Great Plains through Salt Lake City to the Pacific was safe for emigrants and protected by a substantial federal force. The critical geographic crossroads through Utah were now under federal military supervision. Buchanan had won a key facet in his war.

President Buchanan's statement to Congress confirmed "that our difficulties with the Territory of Utah have terminated, and the reign of the Constitution" was restored. In a congratulatory tone, he immediately rescinded the need "to make any appropriation for the purpose of calling into service the two regiments of volunteers authorized by the act of Congress approved on the 7th April last, 'For the purpose of quelling disturbances in the Territory of Utah, for the protection of supply and emigrant trains, and the suppression of Indian hostilities on the frontier.'" Buchanan spoke gratefully at "this satisfactory intelligence from Utah, because it will afford some relief to the treasury at a time demanding from us the strictest economy."[25] The president believed that his decisive action brought misguided people to their senses and that the presence of the army and functioning non-Mormon government officials would convert them into good, republican citizens with true allegiance to the Constitution and laws of the United States.[26] He also saw fruits emerging from the larger tree of western expansion. Non-Mormon federal officials backed by the army could enforce the supremacy of national law in the territory. The army could regain control over Indian affairs. The establishment of military posts in Utah could protect emigrant routes and accelerate the process of American settlement in the West. In the middle of 1858, with this statement to Congress, Buchanan had convinced himself, and possibly others, of the success of the war. Conceivably bowing to political pressure and providing an acknowledgment of the problems caused by his use of federal power in the territory, the president declared triumph over Utah, signaling an end to that episode and thereby hoping political opponents and pundits would move on from it and its attendant complications.

Many Mormons, however, did not see their acceptance of the president's pardon as the unconditional surrender of their local rights. They viewed it as a temporary appeasement. Latter-day Saint Lewis Barney wrote of the Mormon submission to peace, stating, "President

Buchanan finding himself in the wrong wished to have the trouble settled if possible honorably to himself. He sent the peace commissioners to arrainge for peace, and treat with the Mormons, as they would with an foreign powere or Nation."[27] Barney blamed the federal government for denying them the opportunity to determine their own interests and elect their own governing officials. This became a common memory for the Mormons: the Americans came as a mob to continue persecuting the religious community. Barney's account also offers an interesting insight into how he believed the United States dealt with Utah Territory. He described the peace offering as a treaty with a foreign power to control the terms for future existence. Brigham Young reportedly called it a filibustering operation by Buchanan that was intended "to go and take possession of the Mormon improvements." Young also said "the political pulse of the United States is to annex the whole world." Young further questioned the tangible benefits of protection provided by the army, particularly concerning warfare with the region's Native peoples.[28] Brigham Young and his fellow Mormons were forced to submit to federal authority and viewed the Utah War as a move to expand American power and control over the territory and Mormon sovereignty. Buchanan viewed it the same way and said as much when pardoning the Mormon people. "It is mere madness," he stated, "to suppose that with your limited resources you can successfully resist the force of this great and powerful nation."[29]

After Utahns accepted Buchanan's pardon, the army executed "the orders of Government," to march into the Salt Lake Valley and establish a permanent military post in the Great Basin.[30] By 8 July 1858, the army began to set up its post in Cedar Valley. This was a strategic location. It sat approximately forty-five miles southwest from Salt Lake City on the northwest side of Utah Lake nearly equidistant to Provo and within a short march to the territorial capital of Fillmore. General Johnston did not think the Mormons sincere in their professions of loyalty and

FIG. 14. The U.S. Army marching through Salt Lake City in 1858. The army carried the American standard in its mission to assert federal sovereignty over Utah Territory. From the author's collection.

peace.[31] Still, he made every effort to leave the people and their social practices alone as long as they abided by the law and direction of the new federal officials. With that in mind, Johnston thought it wise for the army to maintain some distance from the major centers of Mormon population to prevent, as much as possible, incidents and excitement between the troops and citizens.[32] By 10 July, the post, known as Camp Floyd in honor of the secretary of war, John B. Floyd, became the official headquarters for the newly created military Department of Utah. Until this time, a military department overseeing the Great Basin did not exist; the fort filled a major, strategic need to promote the success of the civil authorities, maintain law and order, and watch with vigilance the movements of Native peoples. From the fort, the army could supervise both the Mormon and American Indian populations and ensure a safe traveling route to the Pacific settlements. Mormons and Native Americans would soon acknowledge Camp Floyd as a symbol of federal authority.[33] With troops in Utah the army detachments in the West could mobilize more quickly and efficiently.

Buchanan's administration also introduced a substantial non-Mormon population to Utah by establishing military quarters in the territory as a step to occupy and render the region safe for settlement and expansion by loyal Americans.[34] It was hoped that the protection afforded by the military would enable a well-regulated government to administer the law while the soldiers provided the order. In the territories, it was the duty of the federal government to afford protection to its citizens against personal violence, yet, according to Floyd, prior to the arrival of the army in Utah, "this great obligation is not performed by the government of the United States. For a large portion of the year, scarcely a week elapses without bringing to us intelligence of some Indian massacre, or outrage more shocking than death itself; and it most frequently happens that these acts go unpunished altogether, either from the want of troops for pursuit, or from their remoteness from the scenes of slaughter, which renders pursuit useless."[35] Creating a military department with two strategically located outposts at Fort Bridger, on the territory's northern border and along the main east-west overland route, and Camp Floyd, in the heart of the territory along Utah's primary north-south route, fell in line with the secretary's overall design. Floyd and others in Buchanan's cabinet desired to establish "a line of posts running parallel with our frontier, but near to the Indians' usual habitations, placed at convenient distances and suitable positions, and occupied by infantry, would exercise a salutary restraint upon the tribes" to punish aggression, or repress any spirit of insubordination. Such a line of defense, the secretary believed, would constitute a perfect protection to the settlements.[36] Camp Floyd and Fort Bridger soon occupied commanding positions on important lines of travel and in proximity to principal Mormon settlements. These posts facilitated transportation, commerce, and communication. By 1858, the U.S. military presence in New Mexico and Utah was becoming more conspicuous and effective and added to the strength already present in Oregon, Washington, and California.

As early as May 1858, John B. Floyd directed the establishment and fortification of a depot and military reservation at Fort Bridger. Floyd recommended to the president that "a tract of land in Utah, 'commencing at a point five miles due north of the north east corner of Fort Bridger, running thence due west seven miles thence due south twenty five miles thence due east twenty miles, thence due north twenty five miles, and thence back to the point of departure,' be reserved from sale for military purposes." On 21 May 1858, Buchanan approved the recommendation thereby creating a military colony at Bridger. About one year later, on 22 June 1859, Floyd requested the enlargement of "tracts of land at Fort Bridger and Camp Floyd, Utah," for military purposes. The next month, in July 1859, the president signed off on the enlargement of the military lands adding strategic growth to the Department of Utah.[37] Beginning with the Utah War until the Civil War, the largest concentration of the U.S. Army was found in Utah.[38]

Fort Bridger became a central location on the primary trail to the Pacific for information, medical supplies, and arms. Alfred Cumming suggested that all overland travelers report at Bridger for the most current information on traveling conditions and Native American movements.[39] Fort Bridger also housed a medical department under the direction of Assistant Surgeon Thomas M. Getty, to maintain a "necessary hospital to receive the sick left at this post."[40] A medical department served as a welcome sight and aided tremendously in serving the sick and afflicted overland travelers to the Pacific. The army stockpiled its arms at Fort Bridger and made it a clearinghouse for the transportation of arms and ammunition to other forts in the West. Soldier G. E. Gould wrote to his brother about the quantity of arms and the fortification of Fort Bridger. On 24 September 1858, from Bridger, he believed that the Mormon difficulty had not yet seen its final conclusion and noted, "We have now thirty pieces of artillery—24 pieces of light artillery—nine and twelve pounders—six pieces of heavy twenty-four and thirty-two pounders all brass guns—You would hear more noise in one day here, when the whole army is at target practice than you would there in a dozen fourth of July's." To this soldier, Fort Bridger had become a new military fortress.[41] Bridger indeed became an imposing feature with twenty-foot-high rock walls that spearheaded the many trails that overland travelers passed heading to California, Oregon, Washington, Utah, and New Mexico.[42] Removing Fort Bridger from Mormon control and reestablishing it as an army foothold on the main diversion point for trails to the Pacific Coast proved a tangible victory in the Utah War.[43]

Near a flowing spring in the Cedar Valley, a small party of Mormons settled a town named Fairfield in 1855 east of the spring's headwaters and on the north side of the spring-produced creek. Camp Floyd was constructed on the southwest side of the spring. Near the town of Fairfield where a pasture and ample supply of water and fuel existed, large warehouses, barracks, mess halls, stables, officers' quarters, and blacksmith shops were built. At Camp Floyd, hundreds of fine adobe one-story buildings, stabling and store rooms, officer's quarters, and a large parade ground at the camp were constructed by soldiers, as well as Mexican and Mormon laborers with lumber supplies bought from members of the LDS church.[44] By the end of 1858, Kirk Anderson began publishing the *Valley Tan*, a new voice for news, gossip, and non-Mormon thought in the territory as a competitor to the *Deseret News*. Not only did the Utah War introduce a substantial and permanent army population into the territory, but it also brought nearly three thousand camp followers. This group consisted of women, teamsters, and wagon masters. The women, though many were officers' wives, served the army as cooks and laundresses. Other women joined the soldiers as they occupied Utah, including Mormon and Indian women, prostitutes, actresses, peddlers, and barmaids.[45] The camp followers were confined to a small area between the Mormon settlement and the military base known as Frogtown. These men and women were spectacles, awful, yet fascinating to the Mormons, who believed them sinners of the worst sort: fornicators, murderers, and thieves. Brigham Young cursed the place, particularly when it overtook some faithful Latter-day Saints with carnal vice. The urban community that grew up around the military base boasted some seventeen saloons and much gambling.[46]

The army outposts established at Bridger and Camp Floyd were two strategic points for federal militarized surveillance and control of the region.[47] From Fort Bridger and Camp Floyd, the army could operate more seamlessly in the making of new routes and roads, constructing bridges, grading hills, and creating new efficient routes not only between the two military points but also to various points in the region. With the army protection in place, the president recommended that Congress authorize a land office in the territory to further encourage white American settlement. The military reservations at Fort Bridger and Camp Floyd, on the two major arteries of travel through Utah Territory to the Pacific, further demonstrated the president's commitment to managing Native relations and promoting expansion in the region.[48] With the presence of the army, civil authorities touted the newfound authority of and protection offered by the federal government. All peoples could now travel the western road from the Missouri River "with perfect security by teams and emigrants of every description" as Alfred Cumming had hoped.[49] The army presence in Utah at these two strategic locations gave vital federal protection to routes through the intermountain West.

The military forts became the recognized symbols of federal authority in Utah, and the raising of the U.S. flag at those army fortifications represented another form of the symbolic conquering of Mormon sovereignty. Prior to 1857, several reports over the previous ten years detailed Mormon efforts to suppress the flying of the American flag in Utah settlements. One overland traveler gave a detailed account of events at which Mormons attempted to prevent the raising of the stars and stripes in the territory. The account stated,

In 1849, the United States flag was raised on the 4th of July by some California emigrants in a neighborhood about fifteen miles north of the [Salt Lake] city but was hauled down again the same day by order of the mormons. In 1850, about one hundred and sixty emigrants raised the U. States flag again in the same neighborhood, determined, at all hazards, to maintain it. Some mormons said it must come down; but there being about 3000 emigrants in the valley at the time, ready, if necessary, to defend it with their lives, the mormons deemed it prudent to allow the flag to stand. In the city, also, in 1850, the United States flag was raised on a cottonwood tree. Some mormons said it must come down. The emigrants told them that they would have to kill them first. The mormons did not persist in the demand.[50]

Whereas reports indicated that Mormons raised their own flags and did not allow the flying of the American flag in the territory, the raising of the stars and stripes by the U.S. Army demonstrated the symbolic conquering of the Mormon people. Lafayette McLaws, an infantry officer from Georgia who served in the U.S.-Mexico War and as an officer in the Department of Utah, called 9 November 1858 a "gala day with us here at Camp Floyd."[51] Indicating his belief that no finer army for its size existed above the Army of Utah, McLaws continued, "A magnificent flagstaff having been recently erected near the center of the camp, the star-spangled banner was that day run up for the first time, with all appropriate honors." At noon, all the bands struck up at once "The Star-Spangled Banner," and with a salute of thirty-three guns and amid the cheers of officers and men, up the pole went the nation's flag, which, according to McLaws, the army was sent out to plant and maintain in Utah. "Every friend of humanity will," McLaws wrote, "rejoice that the raising of it was so peaceably accomplished, after all the threats, to the contrary, that were rung into our ears by vociferous Saints last Fall and Winter."[52]

The raising of the American flag on an opponent's land had long symbolized victorious occupation. For example, even in error, as when U.S. commodore Thomas ap Catesby Jones, believing that Mexico and the United States were at war, triumphantly raised the Stars and Stripes after he occupied Mexico's California capital at Monterey in the fall of 1842.[53] The United States, when it actually went to war with Mexico, ended its conquest with a flag raising. McLaws, who also served in the U.S. Army during the U.S.-Mexico War, compared the Utah victory to the American conquest at the Battle of Chapultepec. He reveled in the thought that the glorious American flag floated in triumph over the last of the Mexican strongholds then and now it reigned supreme over the Mormons.[54] McLaws's observations underscored the role the army was to play, having been "sent out to plant and maintain" the American flag in Utah, or to ensure the establishment and maintenance of federal sovereignty in the vast western territory. He also directly connected the Utah campaign to imperial maneuvers during the U.S.-Mexico War, suggesting that the planting of the flag in Utah would result in the continued expansion of American sovereignty and empire of liberty.

McLaws promoted national expansion and American power at this moment, but, paradoxically, he eventually chose a different nation to support just two years later. McLaws, General Albert Johnston, and others fought on the Confederate side of the Civil War. They switched their imperial loyalties to the Confederate States of America and attempted to destroy the power and authority that they had helped build for the United States over the previous two decades. This provides insight into what it meant at that time to be an American. In the 1850s loyalties and allegiances were, to a high degree, still taking shape and contingent upon the political climate, particularly surrounding the contentious issue of slavery. Nevertheless, while Americans were growing more divided and loyalty to the United States remained in flux in the mid- to late 1850s all seemed convinced that the federal government should extend its authority over the Mormons in Utah.

The presence of the army, then manned by officers and individuals who would later appear in the Civil War on opposing sides, symbolically ended the Mormons' machinations for an independent sovereignty. In the Utah War, the army extended the federal government's authority and control over the Mormons in Utah. From the federal government's perspective, planting the non-Mormon army in Utah restored the "reign of the Constitution and the laws" in the territories and brought peace to the nation, if momentarily.[55] For the local population that consisted of Native Americans and Mormons, on the other hand, peace was far from reality.

Though strategically stationed on the periphery of Mormon settlements, the army's presence in Utah was pronounced and inescapable. The non-Mormon influx provided an economic boon for the Mormon community.[56] Mormon laborers were hired for seventy-five dollars a month plus rations as carpenters and bricklayers to aid in the ongoing construction at Camp Floyd.[57] Because of a favorable winter harvest, trade with merchants, and laboring for the army, "a degree of general prosperity attends every interest of the Territory," wrote Young, which instilled in him the belief "that the strenuous efforts our enemies are now making in certain quarters will not soon again be able to interrupt the peace, quiet and general prosperity of our young and thriving territory."[58] Some Mormons obtained contracts with the army to sell to them meats and cheeses, as well as candy for the Camp Floyd Theater.[59] Brigham Young wrote to George Q. Cannon that the only benefit he could see to the army presence in Utah was a greater access to materials and the potential for newfound wealth for the church. "They brought a large amount of money, goods, mules, wagons, iron, etc., articles much needed in our Territory," Young penned, "and a large portion of which has already been scattered among the people, adding Much to their comfort and present and future prosperity. How long Government may see fit to retain an army of immense expense in a locality where its services have no opportunity for benefiting the country, we neither know nor care, for through the above enumerated local profits arising from their presence are very convenient."[60] Non-Mormon freighter Richard Thomas Ackley indicated that the army desired to buy foodstuffs from the Mormons because it was cheaper than hauling it over one thousand miles, in spite of the high prices the Mormons charged.[61] Nevertheless, the Mormons continued to rail against the maintenance of an army presence in Utah as "a source of great irritation to the Mormons, and a no less unfailing source of expense to the country." The *Deseret News* added that the presence of the army was "subversive of the true progress of republican government" even though many of the "'Mormons' have found rich pecuniary reward in the 'presence' of the 'Utah expedition.'"[62]

The symbolic conquering of Utah also renewed a physical component to federal-territorial relations as soldiers and Mormons again lived in close proximity to one another. Camp Floyd and the military presence in the territory brought permanent unwanted elements that proved Mormon fears about renewed intimate interactions between army men and Mormon women. Mormon observers noted a rise in gambling, saloon going, and "wickedness of every name and kind" occurring in Salt Lake City and Utah generally. Faithful Latter-day Saint Charles Bailey wrote of some of the changes introduced by the army in his journal. Bailey bemoaned:

> Camp Floyd was full of Rotenness And evil of every discripsion And am Sorry to Say our people of both Sexes Mixed up with them largely And oh how bad it did look to see young Laides whos Parents where faithful Saints And Still there girls and Some of the wives of the faithful men who had died true to the faith And young Men falling into the ways of the Low Gentiles and Some of the fathers and Mothers Mixing up with them.... A great Many of our people lots of Men who performed good Missions Abroad And held Responsible

Possissions in the Church And bore faithful testimonies to the truth And then in A few weeks find them with the drunkard And Mixing up with the ungodly and denighing the work of the Lord.[63]

With the influx of strangers, a few of the Mormon people absorbed more or less of the worldly atmosphere, and some became very restless and finally drifted into the camp itself. So while the camp meant a symbol of American authority, it also meant a symbol of corruption for the Mormons. The permanent presence of the United States and significant numbers of non-Mormon men worried the Mormon community by keeping carnal temptation real and close.

Interactions between the sexes comprised an important aspect of relations with the arrival of the army in Utah as it had with the Steptoe detachment in 1854–55. Keeping Mormon women away from the army men again became a major concern for the Mormon community. The idea of sexually conquering Mormon women occurred to the federal soldiers in 1858, as it had with Lieutenant Sylvester Mowry four years earlier. At Camp Floyd, one sergeant in the U.S. Army, when asked by a Mormon man of the thousands of men in the army how many would "abstain from seducing the women" reportedly responded he thought "about fifteen." The Mormon man then quipped, "These are the kind of men Buchanan has sent to put things to right in Utah."[64] Soldiers represented a tangible threat to Mormon masculinity and, by extension, their society. The same thought of sexual and masculine conquest by the U.S. troops over the Mormons, reminiscent of Winfield Scott's idea that the only hope for a schism in the Utah population rested with the women, also ran through the minds of some at *Harper's Weekly.* On May 22, 1858 *Harper's* printed a cartoon on the end of the Utah War. The cartoon, entitled "Frightful Scene of Carnage and Desolation at the Sack of Salt Lake City by the United States Troops," displayed U.S. Army men conquering the Mormon capital in more ways than one. The fear of the Mormons, in this image, is realized as comely Mormon women flock to their manly liberators while the con-

FIG. 15. Entitled "Frightful Scene of Carnage and Desolation at the Sack of Salt Lake City by the United States Troops," this *Harper's Weekly* cartoon provides a representation of the American idea that Mormon women would flock to the army men, who would arrest Mormon power and sovereignty. From the author's collection.

quered men sit disheveled and physically weak on the ground. Their long, pale, and unhealthy faces demonstrate their feeble and incapable manhood. The manhood of the nation would not endure Mormonism any longer, and this image emphasized the triumph of American manhood.

Although the press glorified the triumph of American army men, in a few real cases, soldiers did win the favor of Mormon women. If Mormon men had difficulties policing interactions between Mormon women and soldiers in 1854 when there were only a couple of hundred, it would be next to impossible to regulate with some 2,500 army men stationed in the territory. Indeed, Mormons had good reason to worry about sexual relationships between "their" women and non-Mormon men. Assistant Forage Master Elon John Farnsworth wrote to his friend, "I am to attend a ball here tomorrow night They are grand affairs one woman and 25 men is the average all the women that we have are either soldiers wives transported from the states or Mormon women who have run away from their *Harems*."[65] He further wrote of his fixation on one Mormon woman: "I have come across a Mormon lass here that takes my eye a little better than anything that I ever saw before. She is the daughter of one of the Mormon Prophets here and a prettier lass never lived and I think of taking the beauty away with me if I can steal her away from her parents. Her father has got over thirty wives and about seventy five children. This is one of the oldest she is eighteen."[66] Farnsworth did not provide a name, nor do subsequent letters reveal the outcome of his desire. Still, his mentality of stealing away a Mormon woman was common among military men, due to the minimal non-Mormon female company. This is not to suggest that all movements were unidirectional. At least one soldier became a Mormon during the Utah War. The boundaries between the groups were certainly porous.[67]

President Buchanan lauded the efforts of the army in his second annual message to Congress, which he delivered on 6 December 1858. The president opened his remarks on Utah with a congratulatory declaration of success. "I am happy to inform you," Buchanan stated, "that the governor and other civil officers of Utah are now performing their appropriate functions without resistance. The authority of the Constitution and the laws has been fully restored and peace prevails throughout the Territory." "The march of the army to Salt Lake city, through the Indian Territory," he asserted, "has had a powerful effect in restraining the hostile feelings against the United States which existed among the Indians in that region, and in securing emigrants to the Far West against their depredations. This will also be the means of establishing military posts and promoting settlements along the route," to expand federal influence.[68] The president's specific mention of the effect of the military on Indian affairs in Utah was significant. In an early draft of his message, Buchanan stated that the march of the army had a "happy" effect on Indian relations, but he changed the wording to "powerful," likely to demonstrate the importance of that action in protecting federal law and extending federal sovereignty in the territory. The president's second annual message reveals one of his desired outcomes in sending the army to Utah. Indian administration was a major focal point of federal activity in the West. As a part of this process, the federal government, through the army, reclaimed national sovereignty over Indian affairs, a vital facet of federal activity in the West. Because of the Utah War, the army established two major military posts in Utah Territory for surveillance, protection, and the promotion of settlement. At the end of 1858, with the new governor in place and the army stationed in Utah Territory, the president felt satisfied that the federal government now controlled that critical geographic crossroads and its peoples.[69] While the federal army compromised with the LDS church leadership to establish its camp beyond the advantageous thirty-mile range outside of Salt Lake City, it positioned itself well within striking distance of the city and on an important route of travel south from the city to southern California and New Mexico, not to mention the presence it maintained at Fort Bridger and on the Oregon Trail. Just a few months after the arrival of the army and new federal officials in Utah, the government's officers reported their perceived success in controlling the territory, its arteries of travel, and its Indian affairs. The president remained content with the immediate outcome in Utah.

Following their arrival in the territory, members of the U.S. Army continued to see the possibility of a Mormon-Indian alliance. General Johnston's right-hand man, Captain Fitz-John Porter, wrote in his journal on 30 October 1858 of his encounters with Great Basin American Indians. He told "them I was a man of their great father—the President at Washington. They tell many stories of the Mormon doings and sayings all of which we find confirmed by their acts. These Mormons are a vile set they have strived to put the Indians against us to steal our horses and beef, to burn the grass, and destroy us. They have

FIG. 16. Utes, including Arrapene, a soldier, and an interpreter on the outskirts of Camp Floyd, ca. 1859. Used by permission, Utah State Historical Society.

tried to impress the Indians that no people are so powerful as they, that the armies of the U.S. were like so many sticks and as easily broken."[70] The army sought to prove that notion wrong.

Contrary to the trend of national reports of a Mormon-Indian coalition, and because of the army's presence in Utah, Mormons began to fear the effects of an army-Indian alliance against them.[71] Mormon general authorities believed the army engaged in rousing up the "Indians to war against us."[72] The religious leaders claimed to have followed a policy of keeping the Native population neutral in case of armed warfare.[73] Without reporting which newspapers, one Mormon leader stated that he had read in the "last papers received from the States loud boasts of having secured the Utah and other Indians as allies against the 'Mormons.'" However, the Mormons believed that the army had hired "all the reckless and unprincipled Indians of the mountains" with "new guns, blankets, clothing, ammunition, paint, etc., to steal, rob, murder and do anything else that can be done to destroy" them.[74] The presence of the army in Utah Territory elicited a response from the Mormons that echoed the horror felt by non-Mormons in the eastern states. Rachel Lee heard news "that the Utahs had turned with the Americans.... But the Piedes are favourable as yet."[75] George A. Smith succinctly suggested that the army and new federal Indian agents "have sent messengers to all the peaceable Indians to incite them to deeds of rapine and bloodshed. A number of scattering settlements have been attacked and innocent blood stains the skirts of the present administration, whose agents have procured the murders."[76] He stated that the present efforts of the presidential administration in sending an army to incite violence against peaceable citizens crushed the nation's glorious institutions and, again invoking an imperial example, that it reenacted "barbarism more cruel than that inflicted by the King of Great Britain, through the hands of the red men upon the scattered settlements of the colonies, in the war of Independence."[77] Smith concluded with a lament that experience demonstrated to him "that Indians like Congress men and government officials have their price."[78] Smith's letter alluded to not only the potential of an American-Indian alliance against the Mormons but also the Mormon trope that government officials abused their power in exercising a system of colonialism, rather than republicanism in the territory, to dominate the religious group.

Perhaps the most plausible example of army-Indian action against the Mormons occurred in late February 1858 at the Latter-day Saint outpost of Fort Limhi in Oregon Territory. On the morning of 25 February 1858, hundreds of Bannock and Shoshone attacked, killing two, wounding five, and seizing some two hundred head of cattle, thirty horses, and other animals. This attack helped precipitate the eventual abandonment of that fort by the Mormons.[79] In the middle of March 1858, Andrew Love heard the news of the conflict near the Salmon River. He wrote, "We hear from the Northern Settlements Salmon River that the Indians have attacked our settlement killing two of our Brethren &

wounding five & driving off some 200 head of cattle."[80] Pleasant Green Taylor, a Mormon who had preached at the Fort Limhi mission, recalled, "The Government of the United States sent an army to Utah and a small number of them were sent up to Idaho to stir up strife and contention with the Indians against our people." His reminiscence further stated, "About the first of January fourteen soldiers came into the country and called the Indians together and paid these Indians to go and steal our cattle, also to kill all the Mormons. Making them believe that we were there to take possession of all the country, thus causing great hostilities with the Indians toward us."[81] A. J. Allen wrote in his journal on 13 April 1858, "Last night the indians stole 100 head of horses from Bro Neils hird ground, the Indians that were steeling at samon river has came to Cash valley and stolen 70 bushels of wheat. The people are leeving that give Indians a chance to steel. We believe the U.S. officers at Bridger are putting them up to it."[82] The *Deseret News* edition of 14 April 1858 included an article titled "Another Murder by Indians," in which the Mormon organ recounted the massacres and robberies perpetrated by Indians since the arrival of the military. It further stated, "The current rumor that the army have offered the Indians $150 for every 'Mormon' they will bring into Col. Johnston's camp, can be PROVED in court . . . that the Indians . . . openly avowed it to be their design to take the stolen animals to the U.S. army."[83] In a recommendation to President Buchanan, Thomas Kane wrote, "I think it would be well to issue instructions to our Indian agents to use the utmost circumspection in their dealings that they may not be misrepresented as bestowing gifts or using other influences to stir up the savages to war against the Mormons."[84] In a reverse of prior public opinion, it was the Mormons who now feared the possibility of an Indian alliance with the army. Though Mormons were thought to have cultivated deep and long-lasting alliances with all the Great Basin and Pacific Northwest Native peoples, these records demonstrate that Native peoples were their own diplomatic agents, and were, as individuals and groups, in demand as allies, but feared as enemies.

In April 1858, after the *Deseret News* published reports of perceived army-Indian complicity at Fort Limhi, several of the army and civilian officers responded. General Albert Johnston wrote to Governor Cumming in response to Mormon complaints against the army inciting Indian attacks against them. He penned the following in a letter dated 21 April: "I regret to learn that acts of depredation have been committed by the Indians on the inhabitants of the valley.... Other hostile acts perpetrated on Salmon river and other places have been inquired into by me. Inclosed you will receive a letter from Dr. Forney, superintendent of Indian affairs; also the affidavits of B. F. Ficklin, John W. Powell, and C. Jackson, which show that no act of hostility or annoyance has been committed on Salmon river, or Bannack creek or any other place by the Indians in consequence of the instigations by any one connected with the army."[85] Benjamin Franklin Ficklin, the army officer in charge of troops reconnoitering near the Salmon River, denied the allegations that he and other federal officers purposely instigated the attacks at Salmon River and on other Mormon settlements in early 1858.[86]

The same day, Indian Superintendent Jacob Forney responded directly to the *Deseret News* article's allegation in a letter to the governor. According to the letter:

> The article in question does injustice to the Indians with whom I have had intercourse, and very great injustice to those who are intrusted with the management of Indian affairs in this Territory. The policy adapted and strictly adhered to, in all my intercourse with Indians thus far, has been to avoid inciting them against the Mormons, either person or property. It is the manifest design of the person or persons who have fabricated the reports in question to impress upon the public that presents have been lavished upon the Indians, to incite them against the Mormons. I can speak confidently for the tribes inhabiting this portion of the Territory, that no

such bribes were necessary to secure their loyalty to the government. So far as the Indian department in this Territory is concerned, and legitimate representatives of the government, this article (Deseret News) is false and slanderous.[87]

Forney and Ficklin continued to insist that no federal officer did anything to induce the Native peoples to interfere with the Mormons in any manner. Ficklin stated, "On the contrary, I took every opportunity to tell all Indians and whites whom I met with on my trip . . . that Colonel Johnston did not desire, and would not permit, any interference from Indians." He continued by suggesting that the attack on the Salmon River Fort, by Bannacks and Shoshones, "was induced by Mormons furnishing a party of Nez Percés arms and ammunition to make war" on the Bannacks and Shoshones.[88] To add to the problem of Mormons supplying the Nez Percés for war, according to Ficklin's report, the Shoshone leader Washakie claimed that the Mormons failed to pay the Shoshone properly for land usage in Shoshone homelands. Washakie also charged the Mormons with constantly attempting to prejudice him and his people against the federal government and all persons who were not Mormons. Ficklin's report added to the existing notion that Mormons violated federal Indian laws.[89]

Notwithstanding the soldiers' insistence that they did not incite Indian violence against them, Latter-day Saints maintained that the army remained a nuisance in causing more Indian disturbances than it stopped. In a letter to confidant Horace Eldredge, Brigham Young mentioned the Salmon River murders "and the various depredations of the Indians in driving off stock, of which you are already aware, six of our people have been killed by them during the summer" by Shoshones provoked by the army. Young complained, "Nothing has been done about it in either case. . . . Indeed, we fear, as it is that by their tampering with the Indians we shall be involved in a war with them; but we trust that we may through the kind providence of the Lord steer clear of it."[90] Perhaps the Mormons had something to fear in a perceived army-Indian alliance. At the very least, the permanent army presence meant that regional Native tribes could navigate relations with whites in different ways. They also had to compete with more people for scarce resources, which raised the probability of "Indian depredations" on others in the territory.

Native groups acted as their own agents in navigating this difficult terrain and probably let each side think them allies at different times when it best served their needs. Still, as Mormon Indian interpreter Dimick B. Huntington wrote to the church offices on 21 June 1858, "the Indians are very much disappointed that peace was restored; they expected to come in here and while the Mormons and soldiers were fighting, they would have a chance to rob and plunder."[91] A large-scale battle between Mormons and federal troops could have served the interest of local indigenous groups, as it would have provided access to more goods and an opportunity to play both sides for the largest gain.

After the Mormons accepted the president's pardon, the soldiers still wanted to fight and with the directives to secure the routes of travel against Indian depredations, the army shifted its focus to subduing the regional Native population. In the fall of 1858, General Johnston organized several campaigns directed at Indian homelands.[92] The American Indians of the Great Basin resisted and remained a major force in the area; they proved more formidable to control than perhaps the army thought.[93]

While the federal army presence in Utah both frustrated and provided some tangible benefits to the Mormon community, the lion's share of benefits accrued for the federal government as it expanded the development of infrastructure in this previously inaccessible region. Almost immediately after it set up camp, the army reconnoitered for the best road locations and ease in facilitating the best possible transportation of goods, information, and people. The army improved routes for heavily loaded trains and in working on the roads; they avoided "as much as possible all steep grades, short turns, stony grounds, &c."[94]

The Utah War and establishment of strategic posts in the territory demonstrated the transportation and communication pitfalls in the region.[95] Because the federal government saw an even greater need for railroad expansion to the West based on this expedition, it acted quickly to appropriate funds for the surveying and construction of military and wagon roads. The House of Representatives established a committee to determine the wagon road, railroad, and telegraph to the Pacific and in 1857 the secretary of the interior established a Pacific Wagon Road office to direct public works in that region. All of this could be more easily facilitated now with the army entrenched in Utah.

Because of the acquisition of the West in 1848, protection of the Pacific region grew in importance. Should war break out with a foreign or domestic power, the federal administration understood that its communication and commercial interests would be interrupted "and the unity of our Confederacy" might break. However, with the army in Utah, the federal government began to use the territory as a staging ground for explorations, surveys, and construction of more efficient routes to other points west. In this way, Camp Floyd and Fort Bridger became important nodes on a communication and infrastructure network that would facilitate communication, movement, protection, and settlement with benefits to both public and private interests. Such projects would enable effective transportation of troops, military arms, carrying of mails, and the opening up of a vast extent of country to settlement, which mutually benefited the government and the people.

The army, especially the corps of topographical engineers, played a key role in developing the infrastructure of the West. On their march to Utah, the U.S. troops had built bridges along the way and left men to guard them as a means of facilitating future travel and transport.[96] While advantageous railroad routes remained at the forefront of federal thoughts, military and other roads gained urgent attention for "special and prompt opening and occupation." Secretary of war Floyd argued, "If the railroad were, to-day, completed from El Paso to the line of California, a strong and urgent necessity would still remain for maintaining and keeping open at least two of the other routes, for the passage of emigrants and the transportation of military stores to vast regions of our country accessible only by these routes."[97] Buchanan's administration helped promote occupation and the federal presence in the West and used the Utah War to further access and control the region.

The exact location of new posts and the direction of road-building corps were decided according to the discretion of local commanders, thereby preventing mistakes and miscalculations from Washington, although they had to receive permission to move forward with their plans from the secretary of war and the president. General Johnston understood the importance of developing roads to connect places, to gain knowledge of the land and peoples, and to increase mobility. He wrote to Major Irvin McDowell about the transportation corps. Johnston believed transportation issues were of the highest interest to the government "in respect to the mobility of our troops and economy of administration of the business of the quartermaster's department."[98] Upon his arrival for early reconnaissance in Utah, army officer Stewart Van Vliet remarked, "There is but one road running into the valley on the side which our troops are approaching, and for over fifty miles it passes through narrow canons and over rugged mountains, which a small force could hold against great odds."[99] One of the first tasks for the transportation corps was to open a new road from Fort Bridger to Camp Floyd via Salt Lake City. A more efficient route would fulfill the objective of increasing mobility and communication to, not to mention the protection of, the major army posts.

Johnston entrusted Captain James H. Simpson, chief of the army topographical engineers, with a task to survey and construct the road. Johnston ordered Simpson's corps to proceed from the Cedar Valley and survey Timpanogos Canyon east of Lehi for a wagon road to connect Camp Floyd with the army supply depot at Fort Bridger, thus skirting the Mormon capitol.[100] Assistant Adjutant General Fitz-John Porter delivered the instructions:

> With a view of ascertaining the practicability of opening a wagon road to Fort Bridger, the commanding general directs you proceed to-morrow to examine the route to that place known as the Provo or Timpanogos route. It is represented that the main obstacle to success has been overcome by the Mormons opening a road some eight miles up the Provo river. Little, however, of the features of the country beyond is known except through Lieutenant Beckwith's report, so that your attention will be principally directed to the facilities and difficulties presented by the remaining portion of the route for the movement of trains (pack and wagon) and bodies of troops, camping places, as well as the resources of the country for fuel, grass, and water.

The instructions also requested that Simpson survey other routes from White Clay Creek and Yellow Creek to the main Salt Lake Road for practical driving.[101]

In his report to Johnston and the secretary of war, Simpson described the outcome of the exploration. According to Simpson,

> The only wagon route from Fort Bridger to the valley of Great Salt Lake City which the people of this Territory, emigrants to and from California, and Indian traders have, up to the opening of the new route, been in the habit of travelling, has been that by Echo canon and the Big and Little mountains. This route has always been very objectionable, both on the score of the deficiency of grass and its exceedingly rough, mountainous character; but as there was none other than that by Soda Springs, which required a detour of about one and a half degree of latitude out of the way, there was no alternative.

Simpson developed the new route successfully with fair grades over the mountain divides and in a location with good access to grass, water, and timber fuel. Simpson declared that the new route was far superior to the old road because it provided a shorter and more efficient road. Since the opening of the road, Simpson reported,

Nearly all of the government as well as contractors' trains have been travelling it, in whole or in part, in preference to the old one. The agent of the contractors, Messrs. Russell, Majors & Co., (Mr. Garrison,) has informed me that some of the trains left Fort Bridger by the new route after others which had taken the old, and the former had reached Camp Floyd and been discharged before the arrival of the latter. There is no doubt that a great deal of draught and beef stock has been saved by the opportune opening of the new route, and to it I think must be attributed no little portion of the success which has attended the efforts of the contractors in getting in their trains before winter.

The new route proved good for "bringing pack animals and herds of cattle into the Great Salt Lake valley *early* in the spring and *late* in the fall."[102] Simpson also highlighted the military benefits and features of the new route. Three canyons sat along the road, and the chief of topographical engineers stated that the army would need to seize and fortify the Timpanogos and White Clay Creek canyons in case of an emergency or battle to maintain transportation along the route.

Following the successful construction of a new route between Fort Bridger and Camp Floyd, the topographical engineers also explored in the southwest direction of Camp Floyd in search of the best routes through the desert country to California, doing so "to establish a military post on the most eligible road to California."[103] With continued interest in the most central road across the continent, Simpson opted to head west from Camp Floyd along a route first scouted and used in 1855 by Howard Egan, a Mormon who drove his livestock from the Salt Lake Valley to California, to cut a direct wagon road from the army fortification to California. With much of the basic work of discovery accomplished by 1840, exploration in the American West entered into a new phase concerned with the problems of settlement on the widest possible scale, and the federal government assumed responsibility for launching expeditions into the far West designed to aid its citizens in the conquest and development of the region.

On 2 May 1859, Captain Simpson, accompanied by a topographical party and more than a dozen wagons, made an extensive reconnaissance across the Great Basin from Camp Floyd in Utah to Carson City and Genoa at the base of the Sierra Nevada Mountains. His sixty-four-member company included an artist, a geologist, a wheelwright, a blacksmith, teamsters, twelve six-mule wagons, scientific apparatus, and an escort of twenty soldiers. Over the next three months, Simpson's party traveled more than eleven hundred miles and opened a new route that slashed approximately three hundred miles off the distance to California. By the time he returned to Camp Floyd, Simpson had laid out such an improved route that the Chorpenning Mail Line and the Russell, Majors, and Waddell Company adopted it instantly. The distance from Camp Floyd to San Francisco was now roughly 750 miles. By the old Humboldt and Carson River route, the distance to San Francisco from the Salt Lake Valley was 1,065 miles.[104] Captain Simpson reported that the new route had a very favorable character in terms of grade, water, timber, and grass. The proposed new and very direct route created a new era in wagon road traveling between the states and California. But it was not suitable for a railroad, and the search for a transcontinental railroad route persisted.[105]

High-ranking military officials, such as Lieutenant General Winfield Scott, praised the work of the army in Utah. Scott wrote to John B. Floyd, "The opening of new roads in that region and the prospect of getting a route to the Pacific better and shorter 200 miles, than any now in use, with plenty of water, grass, & fuel, are facts of general interest to the nation as well as to the army."[106] The War Department, in keeping with the U.S. Army's role in western exploration, travel, and settlement, promptly approved the expedition that developed a crucial section of the nation's overland transportation network. The new routes promoted increased travel and correspondence between the Atlantic and the Pacific states. The successful operation of this great enterprise, government officials hoped, would produce an almost continuous line of settlements extending across the continent "and this now isolated Territory will be brought into more familiar contact with other portions of the country."[107] An overland stage station was established at Camp Floyd in 1859 and operated along the new Simpson route until the late 1860s. The Pony Express Station operated from 3 April 1860 to October 1861 along the same route. The U.S. Army did much to forge a new infrastructure in the region by opening up these new roads and routes while gaining a deep knowledge of the landscape.

Although the army made progress in regulating Indian affairs, building roads and otherwise expanding military infrastructure, and symbolically conquering the Mormons, discord between the governing body, the judicial body, and the troops emerged in 1859. The tangible benefits and successes brought by the Utah War were tempered by ineffective coordination and the variant nature of governmental aims from the federal entities on the ground in Utah. Unlike the Kansas situation, in which governors and troop commanders were synchronized in their goals, Alfred Cumming clashed with General Johnston and federal judges in Utah.[108] Such was the imperfect nature and implementation of territorial government in Utah after the Utah War. As early as April 1858, Elizabeth Cumming observed differences in purpose among the army and her husband. She heard "floating rumors" against her husband for trying to establish peace with the Mormons before word of President Buchanan's pardon proclamation reached the Great Basin. The army had hoped for a chance of promotion if a war took place, Elizabeth wrote, explaining that ambition "would be destroyed if you succeeded in peaceably establishing your government."[109] After the acceptance of peace, the governor's wife remarked that "the feeling of the army is anything but friendly to the Mormons," and notwithstanding the obedience of the citizens and the good discipline of the army, "half a dozen generals ... threaten the 'peace' so lately concluded."[110] One observer suggested that the principal reason for distrust of Cumming by others, particularly those in the army, was the Georgian's apparent antislavery stance "and as the majority of our national appointees are Southerners, this is inpalatable."[111] The people sent to colonize and bring Utah into order were not singular in purpose, which soon exposed the flaws of managing federal sovereignty in antebellum American territories.

Perhaps the most crucial source of division and discord was between Cumming and the judiciary over the aid of soldiers in law enforcement. From the Mormon perspective, not long after the establishment of Camp Floyd the "Government judges commenced their vexatious persecutions against the leading men of the church" by arranging for their arrest with the army's assistance. Again, Mormon persecution rhetoric grew. Church members made themselves the other and constructed an identity by again differentiating themselves from Americans. The Mormons prepared to defend themselves against the judges and the army.[112] Governor Cumming attempted to maintain peace but could not convince the Department of Utah's military officials to steer clear of judicial requests for police measures. General Johnston believed that theocracy still reigned in Utah and the "juries still rendered verdicts according to Church instructions." The general wanted to support the administration of federal law.[113] Newspaper reports emerged in the East that detailed problems in the judicial system in Utah, including an incident in which Mormon and non-Mormon members of a jury pulled revolvers on each other over witness testimony. The *Washington Union* described the problems as unsettling to the state of affairs in the territory, charging civil officers with poor judgment and intemperance in conduct and the supreme court judges "with attempting to embarrass the settlement of affairs by delaying action of the President's amnesty, and thereby exasperating, rather than conciliating the Mormons."[114] The *Union* suggested that the federal officials on the ground in Utah did not properly carry out the president's directives, thereby fumbling rather than grasping control over Utah.

Clashes between all three branches of the federal effort to control Utah came to a decisive head in March 1859. On 6 March 1859, John Cradlebaugh, the associate supreme court justice for Utah whom

Buchanan appointed in June 1858, summoned a grand jury and issued warrants for the apprehension of a large body of Mormon men, including nearly forty participants implicated in the Mountain Meadows Massacre, for trial at Provo. Cradlebaugh targeted Mormon men because he believed when "Indians commit crimes they are not so discriminate as to save children; they would not be so particular as to save the children and kill the rest."[115] Cradlebaugh requested that the army secure and hold the suspected criminals under armed guard, as no jail existed in the area. Without military aid, the offenders would go free. Accordingly, a company of infantry went to Provo to guard prisoners and witnesses. Mormon citizens regarded this as a military occupation and a "direct interference with the municipal regulations, while others, perhaps a small minority of the residents, insisted that the presence of the troops was an absolute necessity."[116] Mormon Andrew Love described Judge Cradlebaugh as "a Man Set Apart to do a dirty work, he is raising all the hell he can" among the territory's people. Love also commented on officials in civil government and the army, as well as the judiciary's unwillingness to "Carry Out President Buchanans peace Measures, but appear determined to raise the Devil if possible by goading This People beyond endurance." Love viewed the events surrounding this investigation and grand jury an invasion of Mormon rights. Such a move, he wrote, inspired the Mormons "with a doubt as to the real intention of the Government towards us as a People."[117]

The governor visited Provo and decided that the civil authorities could maintain the peace. He requested that General Johnston withdraw the troops back to Camp Floyd. General Johnston, in a memo to the governor on 22 March 1859, refused the request, citing the federal judge's appeal for armed assistance in administering the law. Johnston also suggested that he had no obligation "to conform to your suggestions with regard to the military disposition of the troops of this department, except only when it may be expedient to employ them in their civil capacity as a posse." He declared he would not recall his troops.[118] Two days later the territorial marshal requested an additional two hundred troops to aid in maintaining order against the many citizens trying to assist offenders in evading arrest and trial.

On 27 March 1859, Alfred Cumming issued a proclamation. With one company of U.S. infantry stationed at the courthouse in Provo, and another ten companies of infantry, artillery, and cavalry stationed near the courthouse, the governor stated that the presence of soldiers not only terrified the inhabitants and disturbed the peace of the territory but also subverted the ends of justice by causing intimidation of witnesses and jurors. Since the movement of troops was made without consultation with the governor, a movement that he believed opposite "to both the letter and spirit of my instructions," Cumming publicly protested the military movement. In his proclamation, Cumming also published the exact instructions given him by the president. The instructions described his duty to maintain peace and good order, to faithfully execute the laws, and for the army to support by power and authority the civil officers in the performance of their duties. Cumming boldly declared that the army was to act in conformity with the instructions given by him as the chief executive magistrate of the territory."[119]

After hearing of these problems in Utah, on 6 May 1859, John B. Floyd clarified the instructions to the Department of Utah. To maintain the peace restored to the territory, Floyd wrote to General Johnston, "the judicial administration of the laws will require no help from the army under your command. If the service of the United States troops should be needed under any circumstances, it could only be to assist the executive authority in executing the sentence of law or the judicial decrees of the court." The secretary emphasized that only a written application by the governor could call out the troops.[120] With no jail or armed presence to hold the prisoners, they were released. Buchanan's administration reiterated and made explicit what it had said when it first sent the army: the troops were at the disposal of the governor only as a *posse comitatus*. Still, neither Judge Cradlebaugh nor General Johnston agreed with the direction from Washington and considered Cumming guilty of mismanagement.[121] Cradlebaugh wrote to James Buchanan in June 1859 to express his displeasure with the implementation of federal governance in Utah. "It is much to be regretted," the judge stated, "that there is not more coincidence of view and harmony of action between the judges and executive of Utah. Without such concert the laws can neither be affectively nor worthily administered: with such concert the many atrocious crimes that have been committed could be [redressed] and although the perpetrators might not be punished through action of juries—yet something in the way of establishing the Supremacy of the Laws for the future might thereby be achi[eved]."[122] Cradlebaugh had wanted to prosecute the perpetrators of the Mountain Meadows Massacre and with Cumming's refusal to allow soldiers to aid in the investigation that effort largely ended. Though there were differing accounts coming from Utah's federal officials, the Buchanan administration ultimately backed the governor and remained tepidly satisfied with his management of territorial affairs. This would not be the last time Cradlebaugh lambasted Buchanan's handling of Utah.

In February 1860, based on the events in the Cradlebaugh court and in what he considered an unnecessary assemblage of a military force at Provo, Cumming wrote to Lewis Cass. Cumming stated that "perhaps one of the strongest reasons which prevent the administration of law in Utah, is a conviction generally held by the people of this Territory that the minds of the U.S. Judges are so blinded by prejudice against them, that Mormons can hardly expect a fair and impartial decision in any case where they are concerned." Many LDS church members believed that "there is a *strong desire* on the part of the U.S. Judges to convict a prisoner of a crime, if that prisoner be a Mormon, and especially if he should happen to be a person of importance in the community." Cumming further suggested that the "residence of the Chief Justice at the headquarters of the army, evidencing, they maintain, both dislike and distrust of the people towards whom it is his duty as judge to maintain an impartial and unbiased attitude."

Cumming expressed to Cass that the U.S. judges in Utah frequently expressed their opinion that the entire Mormon community had forfeited their rights to self-government "and that martial law is not only desirable, but necessary."[123] With this attitude, the governor indicated, the judicial system could not maintain the impartial and unbiased attitude required of its justices in administering the law. Mormons indeed feared the combination of the judiciary and military against them. For example, Rachel Lee wrote that she and others believed that the soldiers maintained their original intent to "destroy us."[124]

The next month—March 1860—Cradlebaugh was back in his native Ohio, where he gave an address to the citizens of Circleville on Utah affairs. According to the *New York Times*, the former Utah judge spoke to expose the policy of the Buchanan administration. Cradlebaugh stated that he concurred entirely with the views expressed by Senator Stephen A. Douglas in his 1857 Springfield speech. The judge thought "that the appropriate course for the Administration to have pursued would have been to procure 'the absolute and unconditional repeal of the organic act—blotting the Territorial Government out of existence— upon the ground that they are alien enemies and outlaws, denying their allegiance and defying the authorities of the United States.'"[125] Summarizing the judge's address, the *Times* underscored Cradlebaugh's opinion that the Mormons remained disloyal to the United States and their main leaders "hurled anathemas against the President, the Government, and the people of the United States," while Buchanan responded with a free pardon. Cradlebaugh called the pardon an "ill-advised act of grace" that was met with derision and scurrilous reproach as the Mormon community publicly reviled the administration and all federal officials. The judge jested at "Mormon gratitude" and lamented, referring to the Provo court incidents, that the army was not used properly to uphold the administration of law and establish federal authority in Utah.[126] Complete federal authority had not been established in Utah in part because of the lack of unification in purpose by the civil government, the military, and the judiciary.

The permanence of the army in Utah introduced new dynamics to a series of relationships. It brought unwanted elements into Mormon society. The army sent out a corps of engineers to develop new routes and gain a greater familiarity with the territory. The officers' reports provided new information about the land and encouraged non-Mormon settlement. The army also had many encounters with local Native Americans. The soldiers disrupted previous Mormon policies with the indigenous peoples, and despite their purpose to quell disturbances and render the region safe, armed confrontations with Indians continued to plague the Great Basin. The army presence provided a measure of control, but the many non-Mormon federal officials could not coordinate their activities. Utah's territorial governor, Alfred Cumming, repeatedly quarreled with General Albert S. Johnston and members of the territorial supreme court. Despite these divisions among the non-Mormons and government officials, the symbolic conquering of Utah Territory represented by the Utah War and the establishment of military posts there continued the process of reasserting federal power and rearranging the governing structure in that western territory. The army in Utah was meant to be a permanent intrusion in local sovereignty, though federal administration at times proved ineffective. Though the Utah War was largely viewed as a political misstep, it had material benefits for the nation's trajectory of westward expansion. Buchanan felt a measure of satisfaction from instituting a new governor and federal officials that were to restore national law and sovereignty to the territory and to gain the upper hand in Indian affairs. The U.S. Congress would soon add another measure of control over Utah and all other western territories. The Morrill Anti-Bigamy Act outlawed plural marriage in the territories and made monogamy the law of the land. In the intervening years, the problems engendered by Utah affairs continued to raise questions about federal power and the exercise of sovereignty in the West. In these myriad ways, the Utah example showcases the imperfect and uneven nature of federal efforts to manage territorial government in antebellum America.

7 To 1862

The Codification of Federal Authority and the End of Popular Sovereignty in the Western Territories

With the Buchanan administration's decision to send the army to Utah in 1857, the federal government demonstrated that it would take an active role in the affairs of its western territories. By the end of 1862, especially with the passage of landmark federal legislation that year, the federal government had strengthened its presence and more fully cemented its sovereign control over the territories; the laws and actions that took place in the territories, especially in Utah, confirmed the aggressive and involved role the federal government would take in shaping both the political and social institutions and the infrastructure of the nation. Indeed, as one historian has noted, "In 1861, most westerners were occupied peoples" as some ten thousand federal troops supervised the American West.[1] The four years between the arrival of the army in Utah and the passage of the 1862 laws brought significant change to the western territories. The popular sovereignty experiment in the territories had ended. That defunct principle had been a liability in the decisive election of 1860 for its main proponent, Stephen A. Douglas. The 1860 election seated a Republican president, Abraham Lincoln, and, coupled with the eventual secession of southern states, bolstered the Republican Party's control of the nation. In early 1861, the federal government created two new territories that significantly diminished Utah's boundaries. Later that year, by executive order, President Lincoln created a new, large reservation for Utah's Native American population that would provide the federal government a stronger position in its Indian affairs in Utah. Though the army stationed in Utah had departed incident to the Civil War, a new federal military contingent from California established itself on the mountain bench overlooking Salt Lake City in October 1862. More importantly, in 1862 Lincoln signed a series of path-breaking laws, including the long-debated Pacific Railroad Act and the first federal marriage law found in the Morrill Anti-Bigamy Act, signaling the extension of federal supremacy over the territories. At the same time, Mormon sovereignty, in the way the religious group envisioned its unfettered local self-government in the 1840s, had largely ended. Federal officials were then in the process of separating Native Americans from Mormon influence, the army had established a permanent fortification right in the heart of the Mormon capital city, and a federal law had been passed legislating against the Mormons' religiously based family system. Though Mormons, particularly Brigham Young, continued to contest federal power, by 1862 the federal government had developed its rightful role as legislator and was implementing, if imperfectly, its strategy for sustaining national sovereignty in the western territories and its authority over Utah.

With Republicans at the helm of Congress and the presidency in the early 1860s, Utah Territory experienced great change. The Republican congress and President Buchanan, two days shy of leaving office, approved a measure to organize the territory of Nevada on 2 March 1861. Approximately one-third of western Utah Territory was cut off to create Nevada; the Carson Valley citizens finally got their long-hoped-for new and non-Mormon local government. Just three days before creating Nevada, Congress passed and Buchanan signed an act to create Colorado Territory, which cut off the eastern quarter of Utah Territory. In addition, Congress renegotiated the boundaries of Nebraska Territory in 1861, trimming more land away from Utah. Still, it was the creation of Nevada and Colorado that diversified the government over the Great Basin West. These territories and their new governments ensured greater independence for non-Mormons in the area by tripling the number of federally appointed authorities over the vast region. It put into motion the process that the House Committee on the Territories had suggested in 1858.[2] By creating new territories out of Utah, the federal government put itself in a better position to extend its sovereignty to protect the people, to strengthen its Indian relations, and to further suppress any remaining Mormon power in the region.

Indian affairs had long been a focal point of federal activity in the West and were part of the rationale to reclaim national sovereignty in the Utah War. In the early 1860s the federal government redoubled its efforts to control its Indian affairs in Utah Territory and in the West more generally. Though Jacob Forney and Alfred Cumming had lauded their success in controlling Indian affairs just three years earlier, both had left their federal offices in Utah, creating a power vacuum that the Mormons attempted to fill.[3] In 1860 one federal report noted that Utah's Indian affairs were "unpromising" because of the departure of the federal agents, the vastness of the territory and homelands of the Indians, the lack of goods and game for Indian sustenance, and the renewed influence of the Mormons on Indians.[4] Federal Indian agents had established three small Indian reservations, or farms, in Utah at Spanish Fork in Utah County, in San Pete County, and at Corn Creek in Millard County near Fillmore City. The reported twenty-four thousand Native peoples inhabiting these reservations were "entirely surrounded by a large Mormon population," who had diminished the natural game of the region, leaving the Native population nearly destitute and impoverished in their circumstances, which, according to government reports, forced them into constant contact with whites in search of the necessaries of life.[5] Not only did the 1860 annual Indian report from Utah sound quite similar to Garland Hurt's exasperated reports from 1855; it also included rhetoric of a revival of the idea that Mormons encouraged Indians to violent attacks against non-Mormon whites.[6] With the threat of a Mormon-Indian alliance renewed and with too few officers to patrol and police the vast Utah

Territory, Indian agents called for change. They supported the removal of the Indians to a more remote location for their protection, for easier supervision and control, and to eventually eradicate the Mormon influence over the indigenous population.[7]

The commissioner of Indian affairs, William P. Dole, heard the agents' concern and likewise recommended the creation of a reservation far away from Mormon settlements and to concentrate in a manageable area the Indian residents who had since "scattered themselves in various portions of the Territory in search of the means of subsistence."[8] When it came to Indian affairs, generally Dole advocated a militarized policy to concentrate Indians on reservations.[9] His recommendation for Utah did not deviate. Dole informed Caleb B. Smith, the secretary of the interior, that Utah's Indian agents had held interviews "with some of the chiefs of important tribes," who had apparently stated to the agents their desire "to come under treaty relations, and to cede their lands to the United States, thereby securing to themselves quiet homes, and the means of comfortable subsistence."[10] From the information he had received, Smith also saw the benefit of the reservation and sent a proposal to President Lincoln to form the reservation. On Smith's recommendation, Lincoln began the process of markedly altering the physical and social landscape of Utah when he issued an executive order on 3 October 1861 to create the Uintah Indian Reservation deep in the mountains southeast of Salt Lake City.[11] The executive order established a reservation that kept Utah's Indians away from Mormon influence and prohibited Mormon settlement in the area, thereby extending federal authority over the territory's Indian affairs. The year following Lincoln's executive order, Utah's Indian agents described the "greatest advantage" of the new reservation: "its remoteness from white settlements, being separated from them by the Uintah mountains on the north, the Wausatch range on the west, and bounded by the deserts of Colorado river on the south and east."[12] The location of the reservation moved Native peoples away from the primary overland travel routes and new telegraphic communications, which also served the interests of the federal government. Moving Indians away from Mormon influence and white settlement was a vital shift in sovereignty, as it ultimately provided closer supervision of Native peoples and greater federal control in this vital sphere of western expansion. Such a move simultaneously promised to end the threat of the long-feared Mormon-Indian alliance.

By the end of 1862, the commissioner of Indian affairs stated that the movement to completely separate the main population of Utah's Native peoples onto the Uintah reservation had gained momentum, though the Indians continued to want and some were still in a "state of restlessness" because of Mormon interference.[13] It took time for federal officials, with assistance from Brigham Young and other Mormons, to negotiate formal treaties in 1865 that curtailed the remaining vestiges of Native sovereignty. Many Native peoples, including leaders such as Washakie and Peteetneet, favored a treaty, as they apparently understood that the survival of their people depended on their choosing to give up their homelands and remove to the reservation. It took Ute leaders, including Sanpitch and Sowiette, longer and with more coercion, but they ultimately signed a treaty to relinquish claim to their homelands and move to the reservation.[14] The same year as the aforementioned reservation treaty, an Ute leader known as Black Hawk led a resistance movement against the Mormons. The Mormon-Indian conflict lasted, intermittently, until 1872. During the course of those years, Mormon power in actual military might was exposed and the limitation of their influence with the Utes was seen. In the end, it was federal power that triumphed when the U.S. army stationed in Utah, which had purposely let the conflict ensue, abruptly put an end to the Utes' resistance.[15] Nevertheless, the plan and process that ushered in the removal of many of Utah's Native peoples to reservation lands was well underway following Lincoln's 1861 executive order, which exhibited the supreme role of the federal government over the territory's Indian affairs.[16] The ending of the Black Hawk War confirmed federal power in Utah.

With the creation of the Uintah reservation and the move toward Indian removal came the call for another federal military post in Utah Territory on the reservation "to maintain order, and to protect the Indians and the officers of government, and the reservation itself, from intrusions by white settlers."[17] The Fort Uintah post was short-lived and Fort Duchesne would not be established on the reservation for another two decades, but a group of military volunteers from California on orders from Washington arrived in Utah Territory in 1862 and established a different fortification, this time overlooking the heart of Mormondom in Salt Lake City.

In his fourth annual message on 3 December 1860, President James Buchanan stated that Utah was "now comparatively peaceful and quiet" when compared with its state of affairs in 1857. He lauded his policy to bring the Mormons into subjection to the Constitution and the nation's laws that he believed "was pursued with eminent success." At that moment, from Buchanan's perspective, there was an army to ensure the enforcement of law, "to keep the Indians in check and to protect emigrant trains on their way" to the Pacific.[18] However, with the onset of the Civil War and the departure of Utah's federal officials, including the governor, Alfred Cumming; and the army from Camp Floyd, renamed Camp Crittenden, the policy of the federal government temporarily lost its momentum. The army's departure from Utah provided the Mormons with an enormous economic windfall, receiving some four million dollars' worth of supplies for one hundred thousand dollars in payment.[19] As Mormon William Carruth noted, the sale occurred at a "great sacrifice to the government" and "thus ended the war of extermination on the Mormons."[20] Indeed, the army and the camp—both meant to be permanent fixtures in Utah—were now gone.

Following the army's departure from Camp Floyd, a small glimmer of hope for a resurrection of Mormon sovereignty emerged. But not for long. Rumors of Brigham Young's despotism resurfaced.[21] The federal government still questioned the loyalty of the Mormons and had come to understand that to maintain its authority and sovereignty in Utah

FIG. 17. Camp Douglas on the mountain bench overlooking Salt Lake City proudly flying the American flag, 1864. Used by permission, Utah State Historical Society.

required a military presence.[22] In October 1862, Patrick Connor and a new military contingent arrived from California and established Camp Douglas, a 2,500-acre fortification named for the Illinois senator Stephen A. Douglas, whom the Mormons had come to despise, on the east bench overlooking Salt Lake City and the seat of Mormon power.[23] The creation of that U.S. military infrastructure and the reinforcement to Fort Bridger, still in federal hands, resumed the sound policy of the federal government begun in 1857 to supervise Mormons, to ensure the observance of federal law and order, and to protect and continue to develop trails and communications with its excellent vantage point. Camp Douglas, later renamed Fort Douglas, remained a permanent fixture on the Utah landscape and once again deflated Mormon hopes for local self-government.[24]

Connor encouraged non-Mormon immigration to Utah and the enlargement of the military force there to punish lawbreakers. In particular, Connor had sought to forcefully prosecute violators of a recently passed federal antipolygamy law. Still, in the midst of the Civil War, President Lincoln and other high-ranking military officials feared that the ongoing war would encourage another Mormon rebellion and ordered Connor to avoid confrontations with the Mormons "for any cause whatever." Lieutenant Richard C. Drum warned that a "war with the Mormons would be the opportunity which our domestic enemies would not fail to improve, and it is not too much to say that at this time such a war would prove fatal to the Union cause."[25] Though federal officials still considered the Mormons as unloyal inhabitants, the stationing of a substantial military force ensured that a Mormon rebellion would not occur, just as such a force had in 1858. This time, however, the federal military presence would remain in Utah to protect federal sovereignty and strengthen the government's infrastructure and interests in the Great Basin begun with the arrival of the soldiers in the Utah War.

Following the federal display of power in the Utah War and despite the eventual victory of the antislavery majority in the battle over constitutional conventions in Kansas Territory, popular sovereignty grew untenable as a guiding doctrine for the territories. National sovereignty or federal authority over the territories ruled the day as the rhetoric of local autonomy grew stale. Even southerners recognized the power of the federal government and called for its protection of slavery in the territories, but to no avail.[26]

Though his beloved political doctrine was largely defunct in late 1859, Stephen Douglas nevertheless attempted to rescue the principle of territorial self-rule as a part of his 1860 presidential campaign. "Under our complex system of government," Douglas stated in a September *Harper's* article, "it is the first duty of American statesmen to mark distinctly the dividing line between Federal and Local authority."[27] The line had been blurred on this grave political question that was contributing to ongoing sectional conflict. Unfortunately for

Douglas he was the one muddling the line with his 1857 commentary on Utah and his waffling loyalty to the Democrats over the Kansas Lecompton constitution, which left many believing that the senator again discredited his own local rights philosophy "by attempting to dictate to Kansas how they should ratify their own constitution."[28] In 1859, he tried to clarify his stance. He explained that Congress had power to create and confer authority upon a territory, but it could not exercise power over domestic affairs and the internal polity of a territory unless they affected "the general welfare of the Republic," as he believed was the case in Utah.[29] Douglas's article attacked the Republican ideas of national control over the territories as "repugnant to the spirit and genius of our complex system of government; because it effectually blots out the dividing line between Federal and Local authority which forms an essential barrier for the defense of the independence of states and the liberties of the people against Federal invasion."[30] The Republican ideology, Douglas argued, would make the federal government too strong. The Illinois senator's nebulous claims about the dividing line of authority offered too little clarification on the topic. He could not recover from his past statements and actions, and perhaps the whole popular sovereignty idea had, from its origins, tried to do too much and could not be the all-encompassing doctrine that Douglas envisioned. In a divided sovereignty, then as now, difficult questions of local versus national authority did not have easy answers or outcomes.

Douglas's writing rang hollow. Many individuals from all over the political spectrum attacked or questioned Douglas's effort to save his beloved platform, as they had criticized his 1857 Springfield speech that illuminated the popular sovereignty contradiction. In an impassioned published pamphlet, George Ticknor Curtis, a former politician and lawyer who served as co-counsel for Dred Scott in his Supreme Court case in 1857, railed against the Illinois senator. Upon such a grave constitutional question as the division of sovereign power, Curtis could not comprehend how Douglas's amorphous dogma equating territorial sovereignty to state sovereignty could lead him to the White House. The territories, Curtis reminded his readers, were not legally entitled to all the rights of self-government, and the establishment of certain social institutions, such as polygamy, "which might be against the will of Congress and the entire policy of a Christian civilization," showed the shortcomings in Douglas's plan.[31] In the end, Curtis believed that the dividing line was already well established. States were sovereign and territories were not.

The Democratic U.S. attorney general, Jeremiah S. Black, also responded to Douglas's "dividing line" article. In Black's view, as was apparent in the Buchanan administration's decision to send the army to Utah, the territories did not have an uncontrollable and independent power over their own internal affairs. Douglas's reasoning for believing in the equal sovereignty of states and territories was, according to Black, "entirely erroneous." Furthermore, Black noted that Douglas's flip-flopping on the popular sovereignty issue was damaging the Democrats heading into the crucial 1860 election. Citing Douglas's earlier statements concerning slavery in Kansas, the attorney general stated, "Popular sovereignty in the last Congress meant the freedom of the people from all the restraints of law and order: now it means a government which shall rule them with a rod of iron. It swings like a pendulum from one side clear over to the other." Black also highlighted Douglas's 1857 speech on the Utah Territory. In a somewhat mocking tone, Black wrote,

> Utah is as much a sovereign State as any other Territory, and as perfectly entitled to enjoy the right of self-government. On the 12th of June, 1857, Mr. Douglas made a speech about Utah, at Springfield, Illinois, in which he expressed his opinion strongly in favor of *the absolute and unconditional repeal* of the organic act, *blotting the Territorial government out of existence*, and putting the people under the sole and exclusive jurisdiction of the United States, *like a fort, arsenal, dock-yard, or magazine.* He does not seem to have had the

least idea then that he was proposing to extinguish a sovereignty, or to trample upon the sacred rights of an independent people.[32]

What Black made clear was that Douglas's reversal on Utah had irreparably harmed the viability of popular sovereignty as a political concept. Douglas could not shake his previous support for federal intervention in Utah. That action had blurred the line of authority he was so desperately trying to clarify.

The Illinois senator understood the strategic decision made in 1857 as it related to territorial governance and the Mormons' sovereign capability. The Mormons appeared to control a large space on the primary east-west overland route to the Pacific and threatened American expansionist plans in the promotion of their own schemes that would have had a negative impact on the "general welfare of the Republic." From the debates of the Kansas-Nebraska Act in 1854 through the 1860 election, detractors of popular sovereignty criticized Douglas for promoting a localist philosophy that protected Mormon plural marriage in the same fashion that it protected slavery. Republicans never endorsed popular sovereignty, and their 1856 party platform tied slavery and plural marriage together, which forced Democrats, including Douglas, to reconcile local control with disapproval of plural marriage. While Douglas tried to distance himself from one of the twin relics in his 1857 Springfield speech and found the exercise of federal power in Utah justified, for his popular sovereignty principle, the speech was shortsighted. Playing politics in 1857 backfired on Douglas in 1860 when Republicans argued that the issue was either complacency with Mormon debauchery if they sided with Douglas, or "Congressional intervention and the one wife system" with Lincoln leading the way.[33] The nation ultimately voted for Lincoln and the Republican Party, which encouraged federal control in the territories.

More than that, popular sovereignty under the national microscope was proved untenable. It was a proposed solution to the particular political problem of slavery's expansion in the territories. But popular sovereignty needed to be versatile and accommodating of a pluralistic nation. For the doctrine to be successful, it needed to be welcoming and inclusive of multiple sovereignties and domestic institutions. Yet it could not even accommodate the differences over slavery, so it could not be the hoped-for guiding principle to balance the country. Popular sovereignty meant different things to different people and to the unpopular body of Mormons in Utah it meant the protection of their government, familial structure, and Indian relations. Not everyone agreed with Douglas's, or the president's, justification for exercising federal power in Utah or with the Democrats' wavering on their commitment to federal noninterference in the territories. Douglas was a good salesman and popular sovereignty sounded like a good idea, but it failed in practice to allow for and integrate multiplicity, which ended up damaging the Democrats' political power as the nation teetered on the brink of crisis.

During the mid-1800s, there were repeated moments of passionate talk about the need for a national law of marriage and for uniformity.[34] Serious legislative efforts to define marriage in the territories first emerged in the mid-1850s. Even before the Utah War began, key pieces of legislation designed by federal authorities to put down the power of the LDS church, and in particular its despised doctrine of plural marriage, were being constructed. A founding figure in the Republican Party, Justin S. Morrill, who represented Vermont in the House of Representatives, highlighted the dilemma facing the U.S. government in the Utah question. He suggested that something must be done to prevent Mormon self-governance because of church members' practice of plural marriage.

Morrill first wrote federal antipolygamy legislation in 1856, and he gave a speech in early 1857 to sway support for the bill. Morrill's speech depicted the Mormons as stealthily, under cover of the Constitution, establishing polygamy and using religion as a shield for maintaining barbarism in a civilized country.[35] His comments demonstrated that assertive and explicit legislative action to crush Utah's domestic institutions would violate the Democratic Party's doctrine of popular sovereignty for the territories and further aggravate southern fears about the future of slavery. Political debate, particularly the debates between Abraham Lincoln and Stephen Douglas four months later, as well as newspaper coverage around the country, highlighted this dilemma.[36] After the Civil War began, and with no opposition from southern states' rights interests, Morrill pushed through national legislation to combat alternative marriage and family structures and further federal control over the territories. Morrill urged Congress to make plural marriage, or any marriage other than that of one man to one woman, a violation of federal law. Doing so would strengthen republicanism and American-style order in Utah and would extend federal control over the territory that had started with the Utah War.[37]

The path leading to the passage of legislation outlawing alternative marriage took a few more turns as politicians in Washington continued to press the issue. In March 1860, the House Committee on the Judiciary made a report accompanying a bill to "punish and prevent the practice of Polygamy in the Territories of the United States." The report, like so much rhetoric that preceded it, singled out Mormon savagery and barbarism, stating, "Whatever differences of opinion may exist as to whether marriage is a civil or canonical contract, the whole civilized world regard the marriage of one man to one woman as being alone authorized by the law of God." The Committee on the Judiciary suggested that even before the nation's birth, the people of the colonies never tolerated this marital arrangement, nor did the people of the several states recognize or permit this type of union since, even though the Constitution did not explicitly prohibit the relationship. The committee report succinctly suggested that marriage was "the foundation of civil society," and related to it was "the interests of education and the prosperity of civil government." The House Judiciary Committee, like Stephen Douglas, targeted the Utah Territorial Organic Act and the question of Mormon local sovereignty.[38]

Allowing plural marriage to continue there, the Committee on the Judiciary's report stated, would continue to grow the unrest over territorial issues as the nation headed closer to its breaking point. "Whatever 'vexed questions' may exist in regard to the power of Congress," the committee wrote in reference to popular sovereignty, "to legislate as to other subjects affecting the Territories, it is conceived that no difficulty can arise as to the right to control the legislation of Utah and other Territories similarly situated, because the authority to do so is expressly reserved in the organic acts creating said Territories." Just as the Constitution and other foundational documents stipulated, and as arguments had gone before and during the Utah War, the Judiciary Committee demonstrated that the federal government indeed held the power over the territories.[39] The committee concluded that it was within the legitimate power of Congress to prohibit polygamy in the territories by legislative enactment.

In a rehearsal of another long-standing argument against Mormon sovereignty, the Judiciary Committee then targeted the church's governing system. The committee characterized Mormon governance as a "hierarchy obnoxious to the spirit of our institutions" with such "monstrous powers and arrogant assumptions" that directly contradicted American republican governance. For these legislators, the form of government practiced in Utah remained the crux of the problem because it allowed the LDS church to possess the power and authority to "originate, make, pass, and establish rules, regulations, ordinances, laws, and customs, and criterions for the good order, safety, [and] government," according to church covenants. The committee recommended the passage of the antipolygamy bill to reform the territory's antirepublican marital and governmental system. Such reformation was possible because of the presence of a non-Mormon governor and the army already in the territory thanks to the Utah War. However, the bill did not pass, largely because of continuing debates over local versus federal authority in the territories and questions about the future of slavery in U.S. territories. As Representative Laurence M. Keitt of

South Carolina stated, "If you allow Congress to declare polygamy in the Territories to be a crime, and to punish it, where will you stop?"[40] North Carolina representative Lawrence D. Branch perhaps stated the concern even more clearly when he called attention to the 1856 Republican Party platform: "If we render polygamy criminal, it may be claimed that we can also render criminal that other 'twin relic of barbarism,' slavery."[41] The nation was on the brink in the spring of 1860 and Congress was not willing to push it over the edge for polygamy legislation, no matter how deplorable nearly everyone found the practice.

On 24 April 1860, a month following the introduction of the 1860 plural marriage legislation, Stephen C. Foster of Maine built on the desire to end plural marriage and delivered a speech in the House of Representatives on "Republican Land Policy."[42] Foster argued, "The only way to render the abolition of polygamy effectual is to encourage the settlement of the Territories as rapidly as possible. To effect this result, no plan could be better devised than the homestead bill which lately passed this body, but which, I fear, is doomed to hang up for a long time in the other wing of the Capitol, if it ever passes that body. If such a law were passed, a very few years would suffice to fill the Territories with population, and to overwhelm the polygamists of Utah beneath the advancing tread of Christian civilization." Foster believed that "three measures of Republican policy which admirably harmonize with each other, and co-operate for the common defence and the general welfare of the Union" were "the homestead for actual settlers on the public lands, the construction of a Pacific railroad, and the suppression of polygamy." These three seemingly independent measures, the Maine representative claimed, would convert the West "into smiling fields and peaceful homes for millions of Christian families," and the influx of population would serve as "the only sure remedy for polygamy."[43] That "sure remedy" was not passed while a Democrat sat in the White House. But following the Utah War, both Congress in

1858 and the presidency in 1860 changed from Democratic to Republican control.

By 1862, the federal government was ready to administer the remedy. With the nation ensnared in the Civil War, Republican president Abraham Lincoln signed a series of bills into law that would further facilitate the expansion of federal power in the West. On 20 May 1862, Lincoln signed the Homestead Act, opening up federal lands in the West to independent farmers and families. Though it diminished federal land holdings, it encouraged western migration according to the Jeffersonian ideal that extended the vision of the empire of liberty. Just a month later, Congress passed and Lincoln signed a statute outlawing slavery and involuntary servitude in U.S. territories, making good on the first half of the Republican promise of 1856 to prohibit the "Twin Relics of Barbarism" in western territories.[44] On 1 July 1862, President Lincoln signed the Pacific Railroad Act, which further promoted western migration as well as quicker transportation and communication from coast to coast. That act promoted the construction of the transcontinental railroad that would aid the federal government in its postal, military, and economic purposes and growing its power over the West. Seven days later, on 8 July 1862, Lincoln signed the Morrill Anti-Bigamy Act, introduced by Republican Justin Morrill and which outlawed plural marriage in western territories. It was the first federal law regulating marriage in the United States. The Morrill Act was thus the fulfillment of the Republican agenda to criminalize the twin relics. It was one of a series of landmark laws enacted in the late spring and early summer of 1862, all of which emboldened the federal government's control of the West and officially ended popular sovereignty.

Taken as a whole with other legislation passed in the spring and summer of 1862, the Morrill Act further extended federal reach and, in some cases, purview over aspects of western society and development. With that legislation, Morrill and the Republicans integrated law, order, and control in their efforts to reconstruct what they saw as a corrupt society in Utah.[45] The law unambiguously railed against alternative marriage by preventing and punishing polygamy in the territories. When the constitutionality of the Morrill Act was challenged, the Supreme Court eventually decided, "Mormon polygamists had no constitutional right to engage in a form of marriage directly prohibited by Congress."[46] This law, though it required subsequent strength and better enforcement in the decades that followed its passage, determined to make western territories into good republican units. In many ways, these 1862 acts brought full circle the 1853 railroad surveys during which Captain John W. Gunnison was killed in Utah. Those surveys were valuable in the planning and in the eventual binding of California and the West to the rest of the nation through a transportation route that James Buchanan noted in his inaugural address in 1857 was "absolutely necessary." These 1862 pieces of legislation would help bring to fruition the expansionist dreams of past presidents and administrations to develop a transcontinental nation filled with loyal American settlers.

Meanwhile, Mormon legislators renewed their efforts to gain sovereign recognition from the federal government. They continued their fight to govern themselves. Mormons still deeply distrusted the federal government, which they viewed as not abiding by its constitutional mandate to protect American citizens in the exercise of their rights. In the aftermath of the Utah War, Mormon organs continued their anticolonial, anti-imperial rhetoric against the United States in hopes of gaining autonomy. Utah's citizens increased their petitions to admit Utah into the Union as a sovereign state. They reiterated earlier claims that Mormons believed in and ran a republican form of government. Because that idea remained in question the Utah citizens emphasized that they would secure a republican form of government in the territory if the federal government would remove its military presence there.[47] Mormon leaders read the news and hoped that Congress would at least pass a bill authorizing the territories to elect their own governors, judges, and other officials. The Utah Legislative

Assembly sent a memorial asking Congress to "amend the Organic Act of the Territory of Utah as to extend to the people of this Territory the right of the elective franchise, authorizing them to elect their own Governor, Judges, Secretary, as well as other officers." They believed that the appointing of strangers as officers over the citizens of the United States in territories was a lingering tenet of British colonial rule and a direct infringement upon the rights of self-government. As Mormon rhetoric had stated for the past decade, the American territorial system was imperial.[48]

In what seems to be an incredible irony, at a time when eleven states had left the Union to form their own, the Mormons again attempted to prove their loyalty to join the United States as a sovereign state. In a June 1862 memorial to Congress, the assembly of Utah led by John Taylor begged for admission into the Union as the state of Deseret. Again, claiming the "inherent, inalienable, and constitutional rights guaranteed to every American citizen," Taylor and the other Mormon legislators called the current territorial organization inadequate and unable to meet the needs of the local population.[49] In another memorial, Daniel Wells also asked "for admission into the federal Union as a 'free and sovereign State,'" as he re-presented what he considered a "genuinely republican" constitution for the state of Deseret. Wells argued for local self-government, maintaining that that autonomy was "an inherent right of every American citizen; nay, that it is the birthright of every man, bequeathed to him by the Almighty Dispenser of all good gifts." He complained that the "citizens of Utah enjoy not this right" and that the "executive and judicial departments of the Territory are made up of strangers alike to her customs, her history, her wants, and her interests."[50] The Mormons again attempted to identify themselves as good Americans, as such an identification then suited their renewed interest in obtaining sovereign statehood. Wells concluded by requesting the federal government to recognize the Mormons' sovereign capacity and remove the territorial government and its colonial despotism.[51] This effort to achieve state sovereignty, like earlier attempts, failed. Unbeknownst to the Mormon delegation, the Republican-led federal government had already passed the Morrill Anti-Bigamy Act. The passage of that federal marriage law ensured that the Republican-led federal government, with its continuing mission to see the prohibition of the "twin relics of barbarism" in the territories, would not admit a Mormon state that approved of polygamy, even if they claimed loyalty to the Union. During and especially following the Civil War, the Mormons' practice of plural marriage haunted their effort toward achieving full self-government. It was the Mormons' religious refusal to abide by federal marriage law that created a lasting conflict between the religious group and the nation for the remainder of the nineteenth century.

Before Utah was made a territory, members of the LDS church governed themselves through the already-established organization of the church, including its court system. They especially wanted to have the courts under their control so that they could protect Mormon institutions such as plural marriage. But with the federal anti–alternative family law, the army again stationed in the territory, the separation of whites and Indians, and the litany of federal appointees governing the territory, Mormon aspirations for full self-government had largely been defeated. The 1862 Morrill Anti-Bigamy Act made monogamy the law of the land by providing penalties for persons found guilty of bigamy, invalidated territorial laws incorporating the LDS church, and made it unlawful for religious organizations in the territories to hold real property over fifty thousand dollars.

The first federal marriage law was not effectively enforced. With Mormon juries and district court judges, coupled with federal directives to avoid confrontation with the Mormons during the Civil War, officers were hamstrung in prosecuting the law. Nevertheless, federal efforts to prohibit plural marriage and enforce its version of proper American citizenship continued as the government slowly strengthened the instrumentalities of the marriage law to force change on the Mormon people during the twenty-five years following the Morrill

Act.[52] In 1867 the Utah Territorial Legislature asked Congress to repeal the Morrill Act, which prompted renewed debates about better enforcing federal law in the territory. George F. Edmunds, encouraging a stronger response against polygamy in Utah, echoed Stephen Douglas's antebellum remarks on Utah when he argued in 1873 that the federal government must exercise "sovereign dominion . . . over territory it has acquired" and thus more forcefully apply its power to legislate for Utah.[53] Congress accepted Edmunds's argument and the next year passed the Poland Act, which was designed to bolster the Morrill Act. The Poland Act altered Utah's judicial system, thereby diminishing the jurisdiction and role of territorial probate courts and their Mormon judges and giving more power to federal authorities over civil and criminal cases. It also gave federal officials greater power over the selection of jurors.[54]

Mormons continued to practice plural marriage, believing that the Morrill law violated their First Amendment rights to the free exercise of their religion. Crusading against the 1862 marriage law, George Reynolds, the private secretary to Brigham Young, agreed to stand trial to test the constitutionality of that law. In 1879, the U.S. Supreme Court ultimately issued its noteworthy decision in *Reynolds v. United States*. Chief Justice Morrison R. Waite gave the majority opinion that plural marriage was not republican and stated, "Laws are made for the government of actions, and while they cannot interfere with mere religious belief and opinion, they may with practices."[55] In the end, Waite and the Supreme Court upheld the 1862 Morrill Act deciding that no individual or religious group had the constitutional right to engage in a form of marriage directly prohibited by Congress. The 1879 ruling by the Supreme Court prepared the way for more heavy legislation against the practice of plural marriage. In 1882, the passage of the Edmunds Act, another series of amendments meant to strengthen the Morrill Act, facilitated more convictions by criminalizing polygamy and cohabitation with more than one woman, which proved much easier to prove than demonstrating a religious marriage had taken place. In addition, the Edmunds Act disenfranchised individuals convicted of polygamy to foster non-Mormon voting majorities in the territory and made belief in plural marriage a criterion for challenging and dismissing jurors in trials for polygamy crimes. Finally, the act changed the election process by making a federally appointed board of commissioners responsible for directing elections.[56] These provisions of the Edmunds Act continued to shift political power and to bring Utah Territory more fully into conformity with the "moral philosophy and social institutions of the rest of the country."[57]

The capstone marriage legislation passed by Congress was the Edmunds-Tucker Act in 1887. This act, in addition to the marriage laws that had already been enacted, dismantled the economic and political power of the church dissolving its corporate status and removing its control over property valued over fifty thousand dollars. It also replaced all local probate judges with federal appointees and disenfranchised all women in Utah, a devastating move against female equality and the church because Mormon women had typically voted in favor of plural marriage and governance by church leaders since 1870. The government also provided the personnel and financial backing to enforce the law. Federal officials and U.S. marshals arrested hundreds of Mormons who practiced plural marriage. Open, public practice of plural marriage became infeasible for Mormons.[58] Federal law finally established supremacy over both church and family and thereby changed the nature of both. In 1890, Mormon president Wilford Woodruff announced that the church would no longer sanction new plural marriage relationships. Those changes finally allowed Utah to achieve sovereign statehood in 1896. It was a slow process for the Mormons to gain that level of autonomy, and they gave up much to get there.

The Civil War era ushered in a triumph of nationalism over local rights that was unmistakable in the federal government's relationship with its western territories. The 1857–58 Utah War was an early part of that ascendancy, and by 1862 federal authority was strengthened substantially in the territories with the passage of crucial laws granting homesteads, endorsing and subsidizing a transcontinental railroad, and prohibiting plural marriage. These laws, the creation of a new, separated Indian reservation, and establishment of a permanent military fort in the heart of Mormondom continued the ongoing federal directive to more strongly subjugate Utah, and the western territories more generally, into national sovereignty and in line with the country's social institutions. After the Civil War the struggle in Utah continued as Mormons persisted in their religious practice of plural marriage in spite of a federal law they believed to be unconstitutional. The struggle over sovereignty entered a new stage focused almost solely around the federal effort to eliminate plural marriage. While territorial governance continued to be inefficient in some arenas and it took the federal government some three decades to extinguish plural marriage, federal authority was not going away and would only grow in strength in Utah and the west. The nearly thirty years that followed the passage of the Morrill Act revealed a federal government growing in power and exercising its authority to the point of finally overcoming the determination of a cohesive religious group to practice its faith.

Conclusion

The federal government's relationship with Utah Territory had been troublesome since 1850, but in the summer of 1857, just months after his inauguration, James Buchanan ordered some 2,500 troops of the standing U.S. Army to Utah Territory. The troops had strict instructions to establish a post at or near Salt Lake City and to establish national sovereignty through a new governor and federal officials that would occupy, observe, and police the territory and its peoples. The federal government's control over executive and judicial appointments in the territory, backed by a military force, and its veto authority over local legislation undoubtedly undermined the concept of popular sovereignty that the Democrats had pushed to maintain national balance on the ever-contentious issue of slavery expansion. Events as they unfolded in Utah revealed the fundamental flaw of that localist political philosophy. The federal government's management of early Utah can and should be seen as part of the nation's broader territorial policy to establish national sovereignty, republican government, control over Indian affairs, and infrastructural development in the West.

In the United States' national experience, the army consistently advanced and defended national interests. The army was, and remains, the federal government's most visible agent of empire. It was central to the westering experience and in federal efforts to establish authority across the North American continent. It had an important role in ensuring national security and in fostering national development and white settlement by constructing military roads, improving the land, promoting railroad construction, and developing communications. The primary reason for stationing troops in the West was to control other peoples, regulate their political and cultural institutions, and facilitate travel and communications on overland travel routes.[1] Though Buchanan's administration did not drop the hammer on the Mormons as swiftly and as strongly as it could have, by sending the army, it simultaneously diminished Mormon power and altered the course of sovereignty in the Great Basin. The action known as the Utah War also unveiled the real relationship between the federal government and its western territories.

The Utah War was the antebellum period's most influential display of federal power. It reversed Buchanan and the Democrats' commitment not to interfere with territorial social institutions. While the president's maneuver was in line with his constitutional and legal authority, the Utah War nevertheless became a significant political problem for Buchanan's administration and his political party because of popular sovereignty. Affairs in Utah Territory challenged the Democratic notion of popular sovereignty and federal noninterference in territorial domestic institutions. While Americans desired to eliminate the Mormon question that ominously clouded the American territorial experiment, they soon realized the entirely painful political consequences of employing federal authority and troops in stifling the popular will and the domestic institutions of Utah. The Utah War clarified that the federal government, whether the president and his cabinet or Congress, did have authority over the territories and could choose to act with force, if necessary, to manage sovereignty in spite of prominent party rhetoric. Such action, though, signaled to the nation that local choice and self-government were not as sacrosanct as Americans may have thought. Utah affairs simultaneously demonstrated the contingent and precarious nature of local self-government in antebellum America and the inconsistent, uneven, and shifting construction of an intercontinental empire.

In part because of the Buchanan administration's handling of the Mormon question, which was a political move to distance popular sovereignty from the Republican Party's "twin relics of barbarism" rhetoric, the specter that Congress or the president would regulate slavery in the territories was prominently raised. The same federal authority shown in Utah could be used to justify interference in Kansas or any other territory to act either for or against slavery, depending on the political party in the White House. Such contingency could not hold a nation that was tearing along its sectional lines.

While the American territorial system guaranteed to the federal government final say over the territories, many observers of the Utah situation viewed it as inconsistent with the principles of American republican governance and especially popular sovereignty. The federal government opted for direct control in the territories as an empire over its colonies, and although many suggested that Utah offered a different case because the people of the territory were exotic others, the Republican Party's platform connecting slavery and polygamy meant that advancing control over one meant the potential of advancing federal prohibition over the other. The doctrine of popular sovereignty stood as a middle ground against northern demands for congressional exclusion of slavery, and southerners insisted on federal noninterference in the territories. However, with the federal actions in the territories, direct interference destroyed that middle ground and pointed toward the trend of growth in federal power. Discussions and disagreements over federal power in the West had significant reverberations on the politics of the East, North, and South as the prospect for slavery's expansion looked even bleaker.

Utah Territory played an important, although largely overlooked, role in the national debates over sovereignty in the antebellum era. The case of Utah in nineteenth-century America offers a unique opportunity to examine the complex relationship between sovereignty and territory. At the end of 1858, new Utah governor Alfred Cumming explained to the Mormon people the real relationship between the federal government and the territories as one of parent and colony. Cumming stated: "The Government of the Territories has been characterized by certain individuals as a relic of barbarism and a system of oppression. These cavilers should remember that the patriots and sages, whose memory they profess to revere, not only achieved our independence, and framed the Constitution, but inaugurated also the system of Territorial Government.... All communities of freemen possess an inherent right of revolution and self-government;—but communities, like individuals, have their periods of infancy and tutelage, preceding those of matured strength and independent action."[2] The Mormons had established a new sovereign order that was not perceived to be loyal to American interests in the West. Mormon interests did not focus on the state, and though the Mormon leaders occasionally sought affirmation to govern themselves within the United States, they were not seen as having the capacity to do so because of their theocratic political ideals, plural marriage social system, and Indian policies. The Mormons needed to be better monitored and mentored through careful observation and "tutelage" under federal authority to ensure that they would become a good, loyal American people. The Buchanan administration decided to promote republican institutional expansion at the expense of the political realities to secure its hold on the Great Basin lands and to demonstrate that a territory was indeed the extension of American national sovereignty. This maneuver effectively curtailed the alternative Mormon sovereignty and the church leaders' aspirations for self-rule, at least momentarily, though it also proved the difficulties of implementing and administering national sovereignty in the western territories at a time when territorial politics over slavery expansion kept the nation on the edge of civil war. The Utah War, nevertheless, began to tip the balance toward a federal government that would impose its will in local territorial and state affairs even while raising questions across the nation about the propriety to do so. Such questions about the exercise of federal authority over local activities did not vanish in the nineteenth century; they remain and resonate with Americans, who continue to debate and puzzle over the limits of federal power as had their forbearers.

With the onset of the Civil War, the federal presence in Utah abated but was not lost and even emerged stronger in 1862 and beyond. The implementation of federal authority brought an immediacy of change to both Mormons and Native peoples, with the latter ultimately, though begrudgingly, agreeing to remove from their immediate, well-trod homelands to a distant reservation as a means of self-preservation. The self-rule that the Mormons had desperately sought when they went to the Great Basin in the late 1840s had faded, and the remaining struggle over marriage was the last vestige of the sovereignty battle. However, this fight over sovereignty died hard. The saga over marriage in Utah continued for three more decades as federal authorities eventually enforced a national definition of monogamous marriage in the territories. In Utah, beginning with the Utah War and the 1862 Morrill Anti-Bigamy Act, the federal government implemented its plan for active involvement to control western territorial affairs.

Westward expansion had long tested the permanence of the American Union. Different groups of people had different interests and competing visions for the future of the West. Though loyalty was essential in the territorial experiment, the allegiance of territorial inhabitants and those carefully watching the western opportunities for slavery was hardly inevitable. In the antebellum 1850s, the Mormons' allegiance and ability to govern themselves were highly doubted, and in Utah the federal government demonstrated that it would use military and legal threats to negotiate the parameters of the relationship between the nation and its territories. Managing Utah affairs proved the sovereign power of the federal government, one that would only expand and be more forcefully used to rein in and reconstruct the South during and after the Civil War and in the later Indian wars in the West. In all of these cases, the federal government's use of its power ensured the permanence of the American Union. The West, already regarded as vital to America's growth and prosperity, became a proving ground for the development of national authority; the Utah territorial experience demonstrated a significant component of that expansion and evolution.

NOTES

INTRODUCTION

1. In referring to the members of this religious group, this book will use the terms "Latter-day Saints" and "Mormons" interchangeably. In addition, this book will simplify the full title of the church to "LDS church."
2. Fritz, *American Sovereigns*, 1–9. For more information and analyses on early popular sovereignty and American constitutional tradition see Levin, *Representing Popular Sovereignty*; Wood, *Radicalism of the American Revolution*; Morgan, *Inventing the People*; Conkin, *Self-Evident Truths*; Lutz, *Popular Consent and Popular Control*.
3. While some scholars of Utah and Mormon history have explored facets of sovereignty and the Mormon question, especially in the postbellum era, the antebellum story has largely been neglected. For some pertinent studies, see Gordon, *Mormon Question*; Lyman, *Political Deliverance*; G. Larson, *Americanization of Utah for Statehood*.
4. "House of Representatives—Nebraska Bill," *New York Times*, 26 April 1854; Childers, *Failure of Popular Sovereignty*, 248.
5. For a complete discussion of Kansas, see Etcheson, *Bleeding Kansas*.
6. Etcheson, "Goose Question," 63.
7. Thomas Jefferson to George Rogers Clark, 25 December 1780, in Boyd, Cullen, Catanzariti, Oberg, et al., *Papers of Thomas Jefferson*, 4:237–38. For more on Jefferson's ideas about American empire see also Onuf, *Jefferson's Empire*; and Tucker and Hendrickson, *Empire of Liberty*.
8. Thomas Jefferson to James Madison, 27 April 1809, quoted in Lawson and Seidman, *Constitution of Empire*, 1.
9. Onuf, *Jefferson's Empire*, 7.
10. U.S. Const. art. IV, secs. 3, 4.
11. John B. Floyd to James Buchanan, 5 December 1857, in U.S. House of Representatives, 35th Congress, 1st Sess., "Report of the Secretary of War," 3–4.

12. Lamar, *Far Southwest*, 8; Grandin, "The Liberal Traditions in the Americas," 70.
13. Biber, "Price of Admission," 120.
14. George A. Smith, "Reminiscences of the Jackson County Mob, the Evacuation of Nauvoo, and the Settlement of Great Salt Lake City," 24 July 1854, in *Journal of Discourses*, 2:23–24. Parley P. Pratt referred to the Great Basin as an "Empire of Liberty." Pratt also used that phrase to describe the United States. See Pratt, "The Angel of the Prairies," 17–18. One of the goals of the Latter-day Saint Council of Fifty was to "hunt a spot somewhere on the earth where no other government has jurisdiction and cannot interfere with us and there plant our standard." Mormon leaders came to believe the Great Salt Lake region was that very spot. See Minutes, 11 April 1844, Council of Fifty, Nauvoo, Illinois, in Grow et. al., *Joseph Smith Papers: Administrative Records*, 88.
15. Orson Hyde, "Self-Government—Constitution of the United States—Church Government, etc.," *Journal of Discourses*, 6:157–58.
16. John Taylor, "Kingdom of God or Nothing," in *Journal of Discourses*, 6:19–20.
17. Taylor, "Kingdom of God or Nothing," 18.
18. Taylor, "Kingdom of God or Nothing," 22–25.
19. "Remarks, by President Brigham Young, Bowery, Sunday Morning, September 13, 1857," *Deseret News*, 23 September 1857.
20. Brigham Young, Minutes, 5 April 1844, Council of Fifty, Nauvoo, Illinois, available in Grow et. al., *Joseph Smith Papers: Administrative Records*, 82, 84. Six days later at a meeting of the Council of Fifty, Joseph Smith and Sidney Rigdon both emphasized the council's intent to establish a "theocracy according to the will of Heaven." Minutes, 11 April 1844, Council of Fifty, Nauvoo, Illinois, available in Grow et. al., *Joseph Smith Papers: Administrative Records*, 88.
21. Brigham Young, "Human and Divine Government," in *Journal of Discourses*, 6:342; see also Mason, "God and the People," 359.
22. See Bigler and Bagley, *Mormon Rebellion*, 8–9.
23. Holt, *Political Crisis of the 1850s*, 161–64, 176–80; Hicks, "Republican Religion and Republican Institutions," 204–5.
24. Holt, *Political Crisis of the 1850s*, 4–5.
25. See Blackhawk, *Violence over the Land*; Prucha, *Indian Policy in the United States*; Wooster, *Military and United States Indian Policy*.
26. Lea, *Annual Report*, 12.
27. Sylvester Mowry, "List of Camps and Distances from Great Salt Lake City, Utah Territory, to Fort Tejon, California," 12, MMCU. Mowry stated that

several hundred Indians that he encountered had received the same education. See also Steptoe to Manypenny, 5 April 1855, in U.S. House of Representatives, "Utah Expedition," 178–79. Steptoe pled to the commissioner of Indian affairs for full support in establishing consistency in Indian administration in Utah. Great Basin Indians, Steptoe declared, did not understand their relationship with the federal government and instead believed the Mormons were the ultimate source of authority in the territory. See also Hurt to Manypenny, 30 August 1856 in U.S. House of Representatives, "Utah Expedition," 179–81.

28. In the 1840s and 1850s Mormons believed that God commanded some of His servants, whom they believed themselves to be, to marry additional wives. While some sources suggested that Joseph Smith knew about the principle of polygamy as early as 1831 and may have married a plural wife in the mid- or late 1830s, the practice was not generally adopted until 1841 and not made public until 1852. See Hedges, Smith, and Anderson, *Journals*, 2:xxv–xxix. In 1853, the LDS church-run newspaper, the *Seer*, published the principles behind plural marriage. See "Plurality of Wives," *The Seer* (Washington DC) January 1853, 12–13.

29. Cultural historians and postcolonial theorists have used the concept of the "other" to examine how a dominant group develops an identity by reducing a minority or foreign group to a stereotyped representation that opposes the dominant group's core values. The "other" is an individual or community that is perceived as unable to belong to mainstream society for a variety of reasons including different race, nationality, religion, political ideology, or sexual orientation. The constructed inferiority of the "other" provided justifications for the mainstream to act politically, legally, or martially against minority groups. See Said, *Orientalism*; Said, *Culture and Imperialism*; Bhabha, *Location of Culture*; Fanon, *Wretched of the Earth*; and Todorov, *Conquest of America*.

30. An outpouring of malevolent literature aimed at the Mormons in the mid-nineteenth century suggests that that religious group functioned as "other" for mainstream Americans. Representations of Mormons presented a range of un-American activities and attitudes. See Givens, *Viper on the Hearth*; Fluhman, *"Peculiar People"*; Reeve, *Religion of a Different Color*; Grow, "Whore of Babylon," 164.

31. See K. Smith, *Dominion of Voice*.

32. The conflict in Utah in the 1850s has been known by many names. Some labeled it a "so-called war" because of the paucity of bloodshed and the lack of a congressional declaration of war. Mormons remember it as an army of persecution or "Johnston's Army." By associating the army with its leader

and not the federal government, Mormons could later position themselves as victims of another persecution, while remaining good American citizens when it suited them. The official name, the Utah Expedition, was a name used by the army and was often used in official documents to reference the army sent to Utah. Nevertheless, the conflict in Utah was indeed a war and will be labeled as such in this study.

33. James Buchanan, "First Annual Message," 8 December 1857.
34. Buchanan was an ardent expansionist who believed in spreading the doctrine of democracy and enlarging the republic's influence continentally and globally. James Buchanan, Inaugural Address, *New York Times*, 5 March 1857. See also Binder, *James Buchanan and the American Empire*, 10.

1. IMPERIUM IN IMPERIO

1. Fliegelman, *Prodigals and Pilgrims*, 3–5, 200–201.
2. Pomeroy, *Territories and the United States, 1861–1890*, xvii–3.
3. Watson, *Liberty and Power*, 6, 44.
4. Gienapp, "Crisis of American Democracy," 113.
5. Berkhofer Jr., "Northwest Ordinance," 45; Onuf, *Statehood and Union*, xiii.
6. "An Ordinance for the Government of the Territory of the United States North West of the River Ohio," in Hill, *Journals of the Continental Congress*, 334–39; "An Act to Organize the Territories of Nebraska and Kansas," *Statutes at Large* 10 (30 May 1854): 278.
7. Lawson and Seidman, *Constitution of Empire*, 3.
8. Ostler, "Empire and Liberty," 203.
9. Wood, "Evangelical America," 360.
10. Joseph Smith History, vol. A-1, 5, in Davidson, Jensen, and Whittaker, *Histories*, 2:222.
11. Wood, "Evangelical America," 379; MacKay, Dirkmaat, et al., *Documents*, 1:xxvii.
12. A revelation given through Joseph Smith indicated the Mormon belief that the Constitution and the founding of the United States were inspired by God. A revelation in Mormon terms "generally refers to messages expressed in the first-person voice of Deity that Joseph Smith dictated to his scribes." See Jensen, Woodford, and Harper, *Revelations and Translations*, 1:ix. For the text of the revelation, see Smith Jr., Cowdery, Rigdon, and Williams, *Doctrine and Covenants*, sec. 97, 239–40. As early as 1835, LDS scripture revealed that "governments were instituted of God for the benefit of man." Furthermore, Smith declared that the Mormon people believed "that all men are bound to sustain and uphold the respective governments in which they reside, while protected in their inherent and inalienable rights by the laws of such govern-

ments." As for the Mormon belief in America as God's country in the most literal sense, on 20 July 1831 Smith claimed to have received revelation from God that Independence, Missouri, would become the "New Jerusalem" and the place for the second coming of Jesus Christ. These revelations can be found in current LDS scripture called *The Doctrine and Covenants*, secs. 57: 1–2 and 134: 1, 5.

13. See Bushman, *Believing History*, 25, 47; see also Bushman, "Book of Mormon and the American Revolution," 3–20; and Godfrey, "'Seeking after Monarchal Power and Authority,'" 15–37.
14. See Givens, *Viper on the Hearth*; Fluhman, *"Peculiar People"*; Reeve, *Religion of a Different Color*; Grow, "Whore of Babylon," 164.
15. Jennings, "Zion Is Fled"; Dirkmaat et al., *Documents*, 3:186–98; Walker, "Seeking the 'Remnant,'" 13–20.
16. For more on the Jackson County difficulties in 1833, see Dirkmaat et al., *Documents*, 3:xvii, xxvii–xxxii; Isaac McCoy, Statement, 28 November 1833, in *Daily Missouri Republican*, 20 December 1833; and Lund, "Society of Like-Minded Men," 169–200.
17. For more on Mormon efforts to receive restitution and protection from Missouri authorities, see Davidson, Jensen, and Whittaker, *Histories*, 2:203–88; for more on redress petitions to the federal government, see Johnson, *Mormon Redress Petitions*.
18. Letter to the Church in Clay County, Missouri, 22 January 1834, in Dirkmaat et al., *Documents*, 3:407–12; Edward Partridge et al. to Andrew Jackson, 10 April 1834, WWP, CHL; "The Mormons' So Called," *The Evening and the Morning Star*, Extra, February 1834, 1–2, CHL.
19. Grimsted, "Rioting in Its Jacksonian Setting," 366; Prince, "Great 'Riot Year,'" 1–19.
20. Allen, "Joseph Smith vs. John C. Calhoun," 78–79.
21. Lewis Cass, letter to A. S. Gilbert et al., 2 May 1834, WWP, CHL.
22. For more on Mormon movements in Missouri, see Romig and Riggs, "Reassessing Joseph Smith's 'Appointed Time,'" 27–49.
23. For more on Missouri Executive Order 44 and the 1838 Mormon War in Missouri, see LeSueur, *1838 Mormon War in Missouri*; and Baugh, "Call to Arms."
24. Wiebe, *Self-Rule*, 54; Ryan, *Civic Wars*, 131; Grimsted, *American Mobbing*; Gilje, *Rioting in America*.
25. These ideas culminated and are encapsulated in Joseph Smith's 1844 presidential platform; see Joseph Smith, "General Smith's Views on the Powers and Policy of the Government of the United States" (Nauvoo: John Taylor, 1844).

26. Wilentz, *Rise of American Democracy*, 320–60; Watson, *Liberty and Power*, 117–31.
27. Howe, *What Hath God Wrought*, 584–85.
28. Joseph Smith and Elias Higbee, letter to Hyrum Smith and the High Council, 5 December 1839, Letterbook 2: 85, JSC, box 2. For more on states' rights issues and the division of power at various government levels, see, for instance, McDonald, *States' Rights and the Union*.
29. Smith and Higbee to Hyrum Smith and the High Council, 5 December 1839, JSC.
30. Kimball Jr., "Wall to Defend Zion," 491–97; Kimball Jr., "Nauvoo Charter," 66–78; Bushman, *Joseph Smith*, 412–16; Leonard, *Nauvoo*, 91–92, 101–19.
31. Fluhman, *"Peculiar People,"* 96; and Flanders, *Nauvoo*, 284.
32. "Life in Nauvoo," *New York Daily Tribune*, 28 May 1844.
33. Ford, *A History of Illinois*, 232.
34. Joseph Smith, Journal, 2 November 1843, JSC. Henry Clay (Whig from Kentucky), John C. Calhoun (Democrat from South Carolina), Richard M. Johnson (Democrat from Kentucky), Martin Van Buren (Democrat from New York), and Lewis Cass (Democrat from Michigan) constituted the five candidates in the U.S. presidential election of 1844 to whom Joseph Smith wrote. James K. Polk (Democrat from Tennessee) and James Buchanan (Democrat from Pennsylvania) were also candidates. Polk, not regarded as a candidate until just before the Democratic Party convention in May, eventually won the 1844 presidential election. Joseph Smith, Letter to Henry Clay et al., 4 November 1843, JSC, box 2.
35. Three candidates responded to Smith. They were Henry Clay, John C. Calhoun, and Lewis Cass. Joseph Smith, Journal, 27 December 1843, JSC; Joseph Smith, Journal, 15 May 1844, JSC; Henry Clay, Letter to Joseph Smith, 15 November 1843, JSC, box 3; John C. Calhoun, Letter to Joseph Smith, 2 December 1843, JSC, box 3; Lewis Cass, Letter to Joseph Smith, 9 December 1843, JSC, box 3.
36. Cass to Smith, 9 December 1843, JSC, box 3; Joseph Smith, Journal, 2 and 4 November 1843, JSC.
37. Calhoun to Smith, 2 December 1843, JSC, box 3.
38. McDonald, *States' Rights and the Union*, 122.
39. For more on the Smith and Calhoun correspondence, see Allen, "Joseph Smith vs. John C. Calhoun," 73–92.
40. Smith here is referring to the division of power in the federalist system and the Constitution's federal supremacy clause (Article VI, Section 2.) Joseph Smith to John C. Calhoun, 2 January 1844, JSC, box 2.
41. Joseph Smith, Journal, 21 December 1843, JSC; "Memorial of the Constituted Authorities of the City of Nauvoo in Illinois Praying to Be Allowed a Territorial

Form of Government," 21 December 1843, JSC, box 4; Cong. Globe, 28th Cong., 1st Sess. 482 (1844).
42. "Highly Important from the Mormon Empire on the Mississippi," *New York Herald*, 21 May 1842.
43. Joseph Smith, Journal, 21 December 1843, CHL; "Memorial of the Constituted Authorities of the City of Nauvoo in Illinois Praying to Be Allowed a Territorial Form of Government," 21 December 1843, JSC, box 4; Cong. Globe, 28th Cong., 1st Sess. 482 (1844).
44. Cong. Globe, 28th Cong., 1st Sess. 482 (1844).
45. At an 18 April 1844 meeting of the Council of Fifty, Joseph Smith closed his remarks by saying that the only difficulty with the Constitution of the United States was that it "lacks the power to carry the laws into effect" and that it needed to be altered "so as to make it imperative on the officers to enforce the protection of all men in their rights." See Hedges et al., *Journals*, Vol. 3: *May 1843-June 1844*, 231 and Grow et. al., *Joseph Smith Papers: Administrative Records*, 129.
46. Joseph Smith, "The Globe," *Times and Seasons*, 15 April 1844. As early as 27 August 1843, Smith publicly declared his belief that God giving the law to the people and the people abiding by that law was the perfect law and form of government. Joseph Smith, Journal, 27 August 1843, JSC.
47. Joseph Smith to the Globe, 15 April 1844, SDP, box 42.
48. Allen, "Joseph Smith vs. John C. Calhoun," 83.
49. "General Smith's Views on the Powers and Policy of the Government of the United States," *Nauvoo Neighbor*, 8 May 1844; see also Wicks and Foister, *Junius and Joseph*; Poll, "Joseph Smith and the Presidency, 1844"; and Hickman, "Political Legacy of Joseph Smith," 17-36.
50. *Nauvoo Expositor*, 7 June 1844.
51. For more on the destruction of the *Nauvoo Expositor*, see Bushman, *Joseph Smith*, 539-42; and Oaks and Hill, *Carthage Conspiracy*, 14-58.
52. In antebellum America, politics as well as ethnic, racial, and religious animosities provided the most frequent provocation for mob activities and riots. See Howe, *What Hath God Wrought*, 431. Thomas Ford spent twenty pages in his history of Illinois on the history of mobbing in the state. He provided much depth on the mobs in Alton in 1837 against the Presbyterian reverend Elijah P. Lovejoy, "which resulted in the destruction of an abolition press, and in the death, and in the death of one of the rioters and one of the abolitionists" (Ford, *History of Illinois*, 232-52).
53. Ford, *History of Illinois*, 249.
54. Ford, *History of Illinois*, 250-51.
55. Hyrum Smith and Joseph Smith to Brigham Young and the Twelve Apostles, 17 June 1844, JSC, box 2.

56. Order to Hosea Stout, General Orders, 17 June 1844, NLR; Jonathan Dunham to Nelson Higgins, 17 June 1844, NLR; Nauvoo Legion, History, NLR.
57. Correspondence from Nauvoo to Washington DC took approximately two and a half weeks in travel time. See Orson Hyde to Joseph Smith, Nauvoo, 25 April 1844, JSC, box 3; Orson Hyde to Joseph Smith, 26 April 1844, JSC, box 3; Joseph Smith, Journal, 13, 16, and 21 May 1844, JSC.
58. Ford, *History of Illinois*, 291; Thomas Ford to J. B. Backenstos, 29 December 1845, BYC.
59. Bennett, *Mormons at the Missouri*, 6.
60. "Message of the President of the United States," App. to Cong. Globe, 28th Cong., 1st Sess. 1–4 (1843); "President's Message," *Nauvoo Neighbor*, 27 December 1843.
61. Joseph Smith, Memorial to Congress, 26 March 1844, CPL.
62. Van Wagenen, *Texas Republic and the Mormon Kingdom of God*, 3.
63. Van Wagenen, *Texas Republic and the Mormon Kingdom of God*, 6.
64. Smith, *General Smith's Views on the Powers and Policy of the Government of the United States*.
65. Orson Hyde to Joseph Smith and Others, 11 June 1844, JSC, box 3.
66. Dinger, "Joseph Smith and the Development of Habeas Corpus in Nauvoo, 1841–1844," 142–44.
67. "Nauvoo Legion," *Times and Seasons*, 15 May 1841.
68. According to scholar Bruce Van Orden, "Beginning in 1854 Douglas's opponents in Illinois, remembering that he had been identified as a friend of the Mormons, charged that his Kansas-Nebraska bill and popular sovereignty were to be used by Douglas to bring Utah into the Union as a polygamous state. To these opponents, polygamy was a fate even worse than slavery.... Douglas himself came to realize that the charges that he was defending polygamy were becoming dangerous politically." Van Orden, "Stephen A. Douglas and the Mormons," 369.
69. Hyde to Smith, 26 April 1844, JSC, box 3; Fremont, *Report of an Exploring Expedition*; "Military and Geographical Surveys West of the Mississippi," *Nauvoo Neighbor*, 19 March 1845.
70. Hyde to Smith, 26 April 1844, JSC, box 3.
71. Veracini, *Settler Colonialism*, 68.
72. "The Mormons," *Times and Seasons*, 1 December 1845. This was not the first time that the Mormons had been accused of establishing an independent empire, and it would not be the last. Some earlier newspaper articles focused on Joseph Smith being crowned as the "Mormon King." See "Life in Nauvoo," *New York Daily Tribune*, 28 May 1844; "Report of Gov. Ford," *Ottawa Free Trader*, 10 January 1845.

73. Young became the Mormon Prophet approximately two years after Joseph Smith's death during a succession crisis that caused some of the faith to follow different leaders. Young claimed that the power and authority to lead the LDS church rested in the Quorum of the Twelve Apostles, over which he was the presiding officer. The majority of the LDS voted to have Young lead them. In 1847, at his direction, the Twelve Apostles reorganized the church presidency with Young chosen as the faith's president and prophet. Young became the presiding officer over the entire LDS church. See Turner, *Brigham Young*, chap. 5; Esplin, "Emergence of Brigham Young,"189–92; Arrington, *Brigham Young*, 115–29.
74. James K. Polk, Diary, 3 June 1846, in Quaife, *Diary of James K. Polk*, 445–46; Dirkmaat, "Enemies Foreign and Domestic," 141.
75. Brigham Young to James K. Polk, 9 August 1846, BYC.
76. Manuscript History of the Church, 13 July 1846, vol. 16, 46. See also Arrington, *Brigham Young*, 128 and Dirkmaat, "Enemies Foreign and Domestic," 158.
77. Orson Hyde to Joseph Smith, 26 April 1844, JSC, box 3.
78. For Oregon, see Johannsen, *Frontier, Union, and Stephen A. Douglas*; for Kansas, see Etcheson, *Bleeding Kansas*; and for Nebraska, see Kammer, "Public Opinion Is More than Law," 309–24.
79. "Public Notice," *Messenger and Advocate*, August 1836.
80. D. Morgan, *State of Deseret*, 23.
81. Smith, Journal, 8 December 1843, JSC; Hyrum Smith et al., Memorial to U.S. Senate and House of Representatives, 21 December 1843, in USSC, RG 46.15, NARA.
82. Journal History, 19 July 1849, CHL.
83. "Memorial signed by members of the Legislative Assembly of Utah to the President of the United States," 29 September 1851, in U.S. House of Representatives, Message of the President of the United States, Transmitting Information.
84. Deseret (State) Papers, 3 December 1849, MS 2918, folder 7, CHL.
85. Deseret (State) Papers, 7 February 1851, MS 2918, folder 9, CHL.
86. Johannsen, *Frontier, Union, and Stephen A. Douglas*, 2–3.
87. Johannsen, *Frontier, Union, and Stephen A. Douglas*, 4–7, quote from p. 7.
88. Journal History, 28 June & 10 October 1848, CHL. See also Morgan, *State of Deseret*, 29.
89. State of Deseret, Constitution, art. II, secs. 1 & 2, CHL.
90. U.S. House of Representatives, Message of the President of the United States, Transmitting Information, 25.
91. Memorial, 29 September 1851, in U.S. House of Representatives, Message of the President of the United States, Transmitting Information.

92. Thomas L. Kane to Franklin Pierce, 3 September 1854, in BYC.
93. Furniss, *Mormon Conflict*, 10, 22–29; George A. Smith, Journal, 14 January 1851, CHL.
94. See Furniss, *Mormon Conflict*, 21–27; see also Walker, "Affairs of the 'Runaways,'" 1–43; Walker and Grow, "People Are 'Hogaffed or Humbugged,'" 1–52.
95. "Report of Messrs. Brandebury, Brocchus, and Harris to the President of the United States," 19 December 1851, in *Report from the Secretary of State*, App. to Cong. Globe, 32nd Cong., 1st Sess., 87 (1852).
96. Quoted in Walker, "Affair of the 'Runaways,'" 35.
97. *New York Herald*, 10 January 1852; Brocchus, *Letter of Judge Brocchus*, 21.
98. Derr and Davidson, *Eliza R. Snow*, 433–34.
99. U.S. House of Representatives, Message of the President of the United States, Transmitting Information, 8–9. See also U.S. House of Representatives, Misc. Doc. No. 58.
100. U.S. House of Representatives, Message of the President of the United States, Transmitting Information, 8–9.
101. B. D. Harris to Millard Fillmore, 12 January 1852, in U.S. House of Representatives, B. D. Harris to Millard Fillmore.
102. "Utah—Public Buildings—Further Appropriations; Letter from the Secretary of Treasury," in U.S. House of Representatives, Misc. Doc. No. 58.
103. Walker, "Affairs of the 'Runaways,'" 39.
104. See Walker, "Affairs of the 'Runaways,'" 1–43; Walker and Grow, "People Are 'Hogaffed or Humbugged,'" 1–52; Alexander, "Carpetbaggers, Reprobates, and Liars," 215–19; Dirkmaat, "Enemies Foreign and Domestic," 365–95; Furniss, *Mormon Conflict*, 21–29.
105. B. Madsen, *Exploring the Great Salt Lake*, xvi–xvii.
106. J. J. Abert, Col. Corps of Topographical Engineers to Captain Howard Stansbury, Philadelphia, PA, 11 April 1849, War Department, Topographical Bureau, Letters Issued, Vol. 2, 202–3, RG 77.4, National Archives, Washington DC.
107. B. Madsen, *Exploring the Great Salt Lake*, xiv. Stansbury's official report was entitled "U.S. Congress, Senate, *Exploration and Survey of the Valley of the Great Salt Lake of Utah*, by Captain Howard Stansbury," U.S. Senate, *Exploration and Survey*.
108. B. Madsen, *Exploring the Great Salt Lake*, 800–801.
109. Gunnison, *Mormons*, 150.
110. Gunnison, *Mormons*, 136–37.
111. Gunnison, *Mormons*, 23.
112. Gunnison, *Mormons*, 138, 154–55.
113. Henry Sterling Bloom to Eliza Ann Bloom, 23 July 1850, Henry Sterling Bloom Gold Rush Letters, CSL.

114. Henry Bloom to Eliza Bloom, 24 July 1850.
115. Henry Atkinson Stine, Journal of Henry Atkinson Stine on His Overland Trip to California from St. Louis to Sacramento 4 May 1850 to 25 October 1850, CSL.
116. Stine, Journal, 11 August 1850.
117. Unruh Jr., *Plains Across*, 302–15.
118. For more on sexual assault of Mormon women by non-Mormons at Hawn's Mill in Missouri, see Rogers, "To the 'Honest and Patriotic Sons of Liberty,'" 58–61.
119. "Highly Important from the Mormon Empire on the Mississippi," *New York Herald*, 21 May 1842.
120. "The Mormons," *Cleveland Evening Herald*, 23 January 1844.
121. "Gov. Brigham Young to Be Deposed," *Nebraska Palladium*, 25 October 1854.
122. In the early 1850s, of the members in the LDS church's two main governing bodies, the First Presidency and the Quorum of the Twelve Apostles, only John Taylor was not born in the United States. He was born in England and then immigrated to Canada before moving to the United States in the mid-1830s. See Gibbons, *John Taylor*, 5–12. For one detailed account of outsider rhetoric, see "News from Utah," *Frank Leslie's Illustrated Newspaper*, 9 May 1857.
123. Lamar, *Far Southwest*, 76–81. Widespread prejudices existed among easterners toward the Hispanic, Catholic population, thanks largely to the general ignorance about conditions in the Southwest, racism, and later reports and rhetoric of Indiana senator Albert Beveridge, all of which coalesced to prevent New Mexico's statehood. R. Larson, *New Mexico's Quest for Statehood*, 244–45.
124. Grow, "Whore of Babylon," 141–42. See also Bunker and Bitton, *Mormon Graphic Image*, 75–94.
125. "General Epistle of the First Presidency," 22 September 1851, Journal History, CHL; "Extract of a Letter from a Judicial Officer of the Government," at Great Salt Lake City, 20 September 1851, in U.S. House of Representatives, Message of the President of the United States, Transmitting Information, 6; *New York Herald*, 18 October 1851; *New York Herald*, 8 November 1851.
126. "Affairs in Utah," *North American and United States Gazette*, 13 June 1853. "The Mormons," *Raleigh Register*, 23 November 1853, stated that Young's imperious rule over both church and state was the "law of its life." This publication likewise complained that Young claimed for himself divine authority to rule the people of Utah Territory, not only in spiritual matters but also in their temporal concerns.
127. "Affairs in Utah," *North American and United States Gazette*, 13 June 1853.

128. "Affairs in Utah," *North American and United States Gazette*, 13 June 1853.
129. "The Mormons," *Raleigh Register*, 23 November 1853.
130. "Mormons," *Raleigh Register*, 23 November 1853. In "The Mormons," *Glasgow Herald*, 17 October 1855, the author similarly described the American fear of a Mormon kingdom developing into an independent sovereignty within the U.S. borders. It stated, "Certainly, the most extraordinary anomaly of modern times is the kingdom of the Mormon chief—an *imperium in imperio*—an establishment of polygamy of the epoch of Jacob" in the midst of "the institutions of the highest civilization of the nineteenth century of the Christian dispensation."
131. The 1787 Northwest Ordinance and later the Compromise of 1850 and the 1854 Kansas-Nebraska Act maintained that the federal government held the ultimate sovereignty over the territories and the people therein by controlling appointments to various offices and veto power over legislation.
132. Etcheson, "Great Principle of Self-Government," 16.
133. McDonald, *States' Rights and the Union*, 167.
134. "Utah and Popular Sovereignty," *National Era*, 30 April 1857.
135. Clayton, "Speech," 17–18.
136. Charles Sumner, "The Nebraska and Kansas Bill," App. to Cong. Globe, 33rd Cong., 1st Sess., 268 (1854). For more on the debate in the House of Representatives, see Cong. Globe, 33rd Cong., 1st Sess. 1092–1114 (1854).
137. Augustus Hall, Circular Letter to the Electors of the First Congressional District of Iowa, May 5 1856, p. 7, Augustus Hall and John Fitch Kinney Collection, box 3, NSHS.
138. The *Salem Oregon Statesman* insisted that people of the territory should choose from among them their governor, their judges, and all their officers, and that they should make their own laws subject to no disapproval "by a distant, and essentially foreign power." *Oregon Statesmen*, 17 March 1857.
139. Brigham Young, "The Constitution and Government of the United States—Rights and Policy of Latter-Day Saints," 18 February 1855, *Journal of Discourses*, 2:170; George A. Smith, "Celebration of the Fourth of July," 4 July 1854, *Journal of Discourses*, 6:365. See also Smith, "Reminiscences of the Jackson County Mob, the Evacuation of Nauvoo, and the Settlement of Great Salt Lake City," 24 July 1854, *Journal of Discourses*, 2:24.
140. Johannsen, *Frontier, the Union, and Stephen A. Douglas*, 16, 20.
141. Young to Douglas, 29 April 1854, SDP, box 42.
142. United States, "An Ordinance for the Government of the Territory of the United States North West of the River Ohio," 336; "An Act to Organize the Territories of Nebraska and Kansas," 278.

2. INTIMATE CONTACT

1. Asa Whitney was an indefatigable New York merchant and transcontinental railroad promoter who in 1849 published *A Project for a Railroad to the Pacific* and wrote other memorials to Congress to encourage the federal government to take up the project. Thomas, *Iron Way*, 37–40; Goetzmann, *Army Exploration in the American West*, 283–84; Meinig, *Shaping of America*, 6.
2. Bell is quoted in Meinig, *Shaping of America*, 1; Journal History, 31 January 1854, CHL; "Railroad Meeting," *Deseret News*, 2 February 1854; Patty Bartlett Sessions recorded in her journal having attended the mass meeting about the railroad with thousands of others at the Tabernacle. Smart, *Mormon Midwife*, 31 January 1854, 200; see also Brigham Young to Stephen A. Douglas, 29 April 1854, SDP, box 42.
3. Beckwith, *Report of Exploration of a Route for the Pacific Railroad*, 10, USHS.
4. Beckwith, *Report of Exploration of a Route for the Pacific Railroad*, 72–73, 82–83; Simmons, *Ute Indians*, 95–96.
5. Beckwith, *Report of Exploration of a Route for the Pacific Railroad*, 82–83.
6. Letter from the Secretary of War, 6 January 1854, Exec. Doc. No. 18, USHS.
7. See Morgan, *State of Deseret*, 23–29; Thomas, *Iron Way*, 37–40.
8. Samuel Stokely, Letters of Declination, 14 July 1852 and 2 August 1852, RG 59, entry 767, box 4.
9. Edward J. Steptoe to George W. Manypenny, 5 April 1855, in U.S. House of Representatives, "Utah Expedition," 178–79; Sylvester Mowry, "List of Camps and Distances from Great Salt Lake City, Utah Territory, to Fort Tejon, California," 12, MMCU; Garland Hurt to George W. Manypenny, 2 May 1855, in U.S. Department of the Interior, Commissioner of Indian Affairs, *Annual Report, 1857*, 306.
10. Flake, *Politics of American Religious Identity*, 9; Doctrine and Covenants, Sec. 132:1, 34–38; Daynes, *More Wives than One*, 131; Shipps, *Mormonism*, 61.
11. Daynes, "Mormon Polygamy," 135; Theodore Parker to Charles Sumner, 8 December 1854, TPP, reel 2.
12. Daynes, "Mormon Polygamy," 134–35, 140.
13. See Hedges, Smith, and Anderson, *Journals*, 2:xxv–xxix.
14. Cornwall, Courtright, and Beek, "How Common the Principle?" 149; Daynes, *More Wives Than One*, 101; Bennion, "Plural Marriage, 1841–1904," 122–25.
15. Theodore Parker to Charles Sumner, 8 December 1854, TPP, reel 2.
16. "Plurality of Wives," *The Seer*, January 1853, 12–13.
17. Daynes, *More Wives than One*, 49; Friedman, *Crime and Punishment in American History*, 127–32.
18. Daynes, *More Wives than One*, 4–5.
19. Hoyt and Patterson, "Mormon Masculinity," 72.

20. Hoyt and Patterson, "Mormon Masculinity," 73–75; See Doctrine and Covenants, Sec. 84; Orson Pratt, "A Revelation on the Patriarchal Order of Matrimony, or Plurality of Wives: Given to Joseph Smith, the Seer, in Nauvoo, July 12th, 1843," *The Seer*, January 1853, 7–11; see also Hardy, *Solemn Covenant*, 16–17 and Daynes, *More Wives than One*, 72–73.
21. Eliza R. Snow revised her original minutes of Joseph Smith's 28 April 1842 teaching to the Female Relief Society in Nauvoo. Her revision was written in Joseph Smith's history, which was then printed in the *Deseret News* in September 1855. That printed history indicated that the founding Mormon leader taught the following: "He spoke of delivering the keys of the Priesthood to the church, and said that the faithful members of the Relief Society should receive them in connection with their husbands, that the Saints whose integrity has been tried and proved faithful, might know how to ask the Lord and receive an answer." The idea that women shared the priesthood with men through marriage continued to be taught in Mormon society by many individuals for the remainder of the nineteenth century. (See "A Book of Records, Containing the Proceedings of the Female Relief Society of Nauvoo," Nauvoo Relief Society Minute Book, 34–37, CHL, 11 November 2015, http://josephsmithpapers.org/paperSummary/nauvoo-relief-society-minute-book?p=31#!/paperSummary/nauvoo-relief-society-minute-book&p=34; Joseph Smith, History, 1838–1856, vol. C-1, addenda, 39, CHL, 11 November 2015, http://josephsmithpapers.org/paperSummary/?target=X292E6172-5559-444F-AC9C-F19EC545E79F#!/paperSummary/history-1838-1856-volume-c-1-addenda&p=39; "History of Joseph Smith," *Deseret News*, 19 September 1855; East Bountiful Ward, Relief Society Minutes, 14 November 1876; Franklin D. Richards, Discourse, 19 July 1888, in *Woman's Exponent*, 1 September 1888, 52–54.
22. Journal History, 18 October 1854, CHL; see Derr, Cannon, and Beecher, *Women of Covenant*. The idea of republican motherhood placed women in a separate, domestic sphere but required them to be educated and instill in their progeny republican values and a sense of civic duty. See Kerber, *Women of the Republic* and Robbins, "'Future Good and Great of our Land,'" 562–91.
23. Dudley, Relief Society Minutes, 24 January 1854, BYU; Smart, *Mormon Midwife*, 10 June 1854, 206. See also R. Jensen, "Forgotten Relief Societies, 1844–67," 105–25.
24. Daynes, *More Wives than One*, 197. For more on plural marriage and popular sovereignty, see Gordon, *Mormon Question* and Talbot, *Foreign Kingdom*.
25. MacKinnon, "Sex, Subalterns, and Steptoe," 227–28.
26. Sylvester Mowry to Edward J. Bicknall, 17 September 1854, Sylvester Mowry Letters, CHL.

27. This is Mary Jane Ayers Young, sometimes known as Mary Ann Ayers Young. See MacKinnon, "Sex, Subalterns, and Steptoe," 232–34; Daynes, *More Wives than One*, 277.
28. Mowry to Bicknall, 17 September 1854.
29. LaRhett L. Livingston to James G. Livingston, 27 October 1854, LaRhett L. Livingston Letters, Beinecke Library.
30. Mowry to Bicknall, 17 September 1854.
31. Sylvester Mowry to Edward J. Bicknall, 31 December 1854, Sylvester Mowry Letters, CHL.
32. Mowry to Bicknall, 31 December 1854.
33. Mowry to Bicknall, 31 December 1854.
34. Sylvester Mowry to Edward J. Bicknall, 27 April 1855, MMCU.
35. Remy and Brenchley, *Journey to Great Salt Lake City*, 206–7.
36. Mowry to Bicknall, 27 April 1855, MMCU.
37. Givens and Grow, *Parley P. Pratt*, 278.
38. Mowry to Bicknall, 27 April 1855, MMCU.
39. Mowry to Bicknall, 27 April 1855, MMCU; Rufus Ingalls to Nancy Butterfield, 17 April 1855, BYC.
40. See Young, "The Priesthood and Satan—The Constitution and Government of the United States—Rights and Policy of the Latter-Day Saints," 18 February 1855, in *Journal of Discourses*, 2:182.
41. LaRhett L. Livingston to James G. Livingston, 7 February 1855, LaRhett L. Livingston Letters, Beinecke Library.
42. Mowry to Bicknall, 7 February 1855, Sylvester Mowry Letters, CHL; see also Journal History, 6 February 1855, CHL.
43. Young, "The Priesthood and Satan—The Constitution and Government of the United States—Rights and Policy of the Latter-Day Saints," 18 February 1855, in *Journal of Discourses*, 2:182. Young gave some similar remarks in an 8 July 1855 speech, "The Kingdom of God," in *Journal of Discourses*, 2:312–13; see also Mowry to Bicknall, 7 February 1855, Sylvester Mowry Letters, CHL.
44. Young, "The Priesthood and Satan," 18 February 1855, in *Journal of Discourses*, 2:183.
45. MacKinnon, "Sex, Subalterns, and Steptoe," 239; Heber C. Kimball to William Kimball, 29 May 1855, Journal History, CHL; Hawthornthwaite, *Mr. Hawthornthwaite's Adventures*, 12; *The Mormon*, 15 September 1855; see also Fielding, *Unsolicited Chronicler*, 219–33. The historian Laurel Thatcher Ulrich has recently noted that the number of Mormon women leaving with the army was perhaps "a little more than a dozen," though she also makes the compelling point that "it really doesn't matter whether there were a hundred or a dozen runaways. Enough women left to reinforce prejudices and fears on all sides." Ulrich, "Runaway Wives," 5.

46. *Brooklyn Daily Eagle*, 12 September 1855.
47. Hawthornthwaite, *Mr. Hawthornthwaite's Adventures*, 12; *The Mormon*, 15 September 1855.
48. Horowitz, *Attitudes toward Sex*, vii; Kimmel, *Manhood in America*, 5–7; Rotundo, *American Manhood*, 120; "The Mormon Question: Shall We Admit into the Union an Anti-Christian and Barbarous State?" *Christian and Advocate Journal*, 19 July 1855; "Utah and Popular Sovereignty," *National Era*, 30 April 1857; "The Mormons," *Harper's Weekly*, 25 April 1857. For secondary works depicting Mormon manliness in the American mind, see Bitton and Bunker, "Double Jeopardy," 184–202; and Kerstetter, *God's Country, Uncle Sam's Land*, 44. Kerstetter writes, "Non-Mormons in the Victorian United States believed the entire social order rests on men's abilities to control their desires. Polygamy smacked of unbridled sensuality, which many feared would undermine morality, the foundation of civilization and of the nation's social order. In addition, given its connotations of slavery, it threatened to debase women and womanhood, who were supposed to be the glue that held American homes together."
49. Cott, *Public Vows*, 3.
50. Fluhman, *"Peculiar People,"* 122–23.
51. Kimmel, *Manhood in America*, 46; M. Jones, *Performing American Identity*, 53.
52. Foster, *Women, Family, and Utopia*, 156; Hardy and Erickson, "'Regeneration—Now and Evermore!,'" 40–61; see also Hardy, *Solemn Covenant*; Pratt, "A Revelation on the Patriarchal Order of Matrimony, or Plurality of Wives: Given to Joseph Smith, the Seer, in Nauvoo, July 12th, 1843," *The Seer*, January 1853, 13.
53. Slater, *Fruits of Mormonism*, 86–87.
54. Marr, *Cultural Roots of American Islamicism*, 187.
55. Marr, *Cultural Roots of American Islamicism*, 187. For other critiques of Mormon plural marriage and its connections to Islamic imagery see Slater, *Fruits of Mormonism*, 86–87; Ellen Kinney Ware, "Crossing the Plains in 1854: A Retrospect," 72–73, in Augusts Hall and John Fitch Kinney Collection, box 4, NSHS; Fluhman, *"Peculiar People,"* 115–18; Givens, *Viper on the Hearth*, 4–6, 97–152; Berman, *American Arabesque*, x–xi.
56. "Shall Utah Come into the Union as a State?" *Chicago Tribune*, 14 August 1858; "Utah and the Mormons," *Frank Leslie's Illustrated Newspaper*, 26 September 1857; "Mormon Emigrants," *New York Times*, 26 May 1855; "The Mormon Question: Shall We Admit into the Union an Anti-Christian and Barbarous State?" *Christian and Advocate Journal*, 19 July 1855; "The Mormon Question," *Circular*, 15 March 1855; "Utah and Popular Sovereignty," *National Era*, 30 April 1857; see also Berman, *American Arabesque*, x–xi.

57. Lyon, "No Government Bounty to Polygamy," 1–2.
58. "The Mormon Question: Shall We Admit into the Union an Anti-Christian and Barbarous State," *Christian Advocate and Journal*, 19 July 1855.
59. "The Mormon Question," *Circular*, 15 March 1855; "The Mormons in Utah," *National Era*, 28 June 1855; "The Mormons," *Christian Advocate and Journal*, 8 March 1855; "The Mormon's Wife," *Putnam's Monthly*, June 1855, 641–49; "The Mormons," *Harper's Weekly*, 25 April 1857. See also Cott, *Public Vows*, 7; Brown, *Good Wives, Nasty Wenches*, 126–27; Okin, *Women in Western Political Thought*.
60. Gordon, *Mormon Question*, 81.
61. "The Mormons, Shall Utah Be Admitted into the Union," *Putnam's Monthly*, March 1855.
62. Gordon, *Mormon Question*, 81.
63. "The Mormons, Shall Utah Be Admitted into the Union," *Putnam's Monthly*, March 1855; Berman, *American Arabesque*, 31–48.
64. "The Mormons," *Putnam's Monthly*, March 1855.
65. "The Mormons," *Putnam's Monthly*, March 1855.
66. "An Act Defining the Boundaries of Carson County, and Providing for the Organization Thereof," 17 January 1854, Chapter 65, in *Acts, Resolutions and Memorials*, 1855, 261. This act authorized the governor to appoint judges who were to organize the county and hold elections for "various county and precinct offices." For the judiciary, see "An Act Relating to the United States Courts for the Territory of Utah," chap. 62, in *Acts, Resolutions and Memorials*, 1855, 258; see Bowers, *Sagebrush State*, 7–9.
67. Journal History, 18 January 1855, CHL; "Carson Valley," *Daily National Intelligencer*, 15 November 1855.
68. James C. Fain et al., "Petition of the Citizens of Carson Valley Praying for the Annexation of Utah Territory," 23 November 1855, HR 34A, 10 July 1856, Documents, NA box 104 of TP box 326, TRG 233.
69. L. M. Allen, Sarah Hartshorn, et al., "Petition of L.M Allen and Others of Carson Valley, Utah Terr. Praying for the Annexation of That Portion of Utah Terr. to the State of California," 5 December 1855, Documents, NA box 104 of TP box 326, TRG 233; Thomas Nelson, "Polygamy in Utah," App. to Cong. Globe, 36th Cong., 1st Sess., 194 (1860); "Mormon Emigrants," *New York Times*, 26 May 1855.
70. Fain et al., "Petition of the Citizens of Carson Valley Praying for the Annexation of Utah Territory," 23 November 1855; William M. Ormsby to Stephen A. Douglas, 12 February 1858, SDP, box 15; "Proposed New Territory," *Daily National Intelligencer*, 10 October 1857.
71. "Affairs in Utah," *North American and United States Gazette*, 13 June 1853; "Mormons," *Raleigh Register*, 23 November 1853.

3. MISSIONARIES TO THE INDIANS

1. For more on the historiography of Mormon-Indian relations see Jones, "Saints or Sinners?," 19–46. For more on Mormon Indian policies see Christy, "Open Hand and Mailed Fist," 215–35; Christy, "Walker War," 395–420. See also Bigler and Bagley, *Mormon Rebellion*. Additional studies on individual federal Indian agents and superintendents in Utah include D. Morgan, "Administration of Indian Affairs in Utah, 1851–1858," 383–409; O'Neil and Layton, "Of Pride and Politics," 236–50; Eckman, "Brigham Young's Indian Superintendency"; Bigler, "Garland Hurt," 149–70; Coates, "Brigham Young," 428–52.
2. Farmer, *On Zion's Mount*; Walker, "Wakara Meets the Mormons," 224; Simmons, *Ute Indians of Utah, Colorado, and New Mexico*, 91.
3. Van Hoak, "Waccara's Utes," 309–30; Walker, "Wakara Meets the Mormons," 215–37; Jones, "'Redeeming' the Indian," 220–41.
4. Alley Jr., "Prelude to Dispossession," 104–23; Heaton, "'No Place to Pitch Their Teepees,'" 35.
5. Blackhawk, *Violence over the Land*, 253–54.
6. See Walker, "Affairs of the 'Runaways,'" 1–43; Walker and Grow, "People Are 'Hogaffed or Humbugged,'" 1–52; Alexander, "Carpetbaggers, Reprobates, and Liars," 215–19; Dirkmaat, "Enemies Foreign and Domestic," 365–95; Furniss, *Mormon Conflict*, 21–29.
7. Lea, *Annual Report of the Commissioner of Indian Affairs*, 12.
8. Jacob Holeman to Luke Lea, 28 November 1851, in U.S. House of Representatives, "Utah Expedition," 129.
9. Holeman to Lea, 28 November 1851, in U.S. House of Representatives, "Utah Expedition," 128–30; Jacob Holeman to Luke Lea, 28 December 1851, in U.S. House of Representatives, "Utah Expedition," 133–36.
10. Young to Fillmore, 20 October 1851, in U.S. House of Representatives, Message of the President of the United States, Transmitting Information, 7–8.
11. Grua, "Memoirs of the Persecuted," 88.
12. *The Evening and the Morning Star*, July 1832; *Latter Day Saints' Messenger and Advocate*, November 1835; Book of Mormon, 3 Nephi 20:22.
13. Bushman, *Joseph Smith*, 94; see also Vogel, *Indian Origins and the Book of Mormon*, 30.
14. Bushman, *Joseph Smith*, 99. Indeed, the LDS church's newspaper reflected on Book of Mormon teachings that made known "the choice people of this continent," the American Indians. That article lauded the federal government's efforts to remove Indians to the West as part of the prophesied gathering of the scattered people. *Latter Day Saints' Messenger and Advocate*, January 1836. An earlier article in the church's newspaper also depicted Indian removal as leading to the fulfillment of Book of Mormon prophecies. See "Indian Treaties," *The Evening and the Morning Star*, January 1833.

15. Brooks, "Indian Relations on the Mormon Frontier," 2.
16. For Book of Mormon passages relative to Native American redemption, see 2 Nephi 30 and 3 Nephi 16 and 21; see also Ashurst-McGee, "Zion Rising," 111–55, 387. For more on the revelations on and early Latter-day Saint missions to the "Lamanites," see MacKay, Dirkmaat, et al., *Documents*, 1:9, 177–90, 200–205.
17. The LDS church-run newspaper in Jackson County, Missouri, *The Evening and the Morning Star*, paid attention to Indian treaties and removal, but it saw that process as part of the fulfillment of the prophecy that "the time cometh that after all the house of Israel have been scattered and confounded ... the Lord God will proceed to make bare his arm in the eyes of all the nations, in bringing about his covenants and his gospel unto they which are of the house of Israel. Wherefore, he will bring them out of captivity, and they shall be gathered together to the lands of their inheritance." Non-Mormon residents of Jackson County viewed these ideas as threatening. "Indian Treaties," *The Evening and the Morning Star*, January 1833.
18. Richard W. Cummins to William Clark, 15 February 1831, William Clark Papers, vol. 6, 113–14.
19. Isaac McCoy, Statement, 28 November 1833, in *Daily Missouri Republican*, 20 December 1833.
20. In July 1836, Missouri residents were upset by the large numbers of Mormons immigrating to Clay County and alarmed at the possibility of a Mormon-Indian alliance. Clay County citizens feared the Mormons' open declarations "that the Indians are a part of God's chosen people, and are destined, by heaven, to inherit this land, in common with themselves." Eventually negotiations between the Latter-day Saints and other Clay County residents resulted in the Mormons leaving the county for the newly established Caldwell County in 1836. *Latter Day Saints' Messenger and Advocate*, August 1836.
21. Bagley, *Blood of the Prophets*, 23–37.
22. Walker, "Seeking the Remnant," 7, 21.
23. Farmer, *On Zion's Mount*, 81.
24. Christy, "Open Hand and Mailed Fist," 215–35.
25. *Deseret News*, 22 June 1854.
26. The idea that it would be cheaper to feed than to fight Native peoples can be traced back to at least the summer of 1851. Other Mormon leaders, including Jedediah Grant, a member of the LDS church's first presidency and the mayor of Salt Lake City, supported the formulated Indian policy. In a discourse of 2 April 1856, Grant noted that feeding and clothing the Indians would prove the cheapest way of fighting them and their ways. See Christy, "Open Hand and Mailed Fist," 231–35; *Deseret News*, 27 February and 2 April 1856.

27. George A. Smith, Journal, 2 January 1851, CHL.
28. Smith, Journal, 15 January and 8 February 1851.
29. Smith, Journal, 3 March 1851.
30. Smith, Journal, 4 March 1851.
31. Smith, Journal, 21 March 1851.
32. Walker, "Wakara Meets the Mormons," 224; Simmons, *Ute Indians of Utah, Colorado, and New Mexico*, 91.
33. Smith, Journal, 10 August 1851.
34. Conetah, *History of the Northern Ute People*, 41.
35. Brigham Young, Proclamation by the Governor, 19 August 1853, M12.
36. Young, Proclamation, 19 August 1853.
37. Christy, "Walker War," 411–12.
38. Brooks, *Journal of the Southern Indian Mission*, 3.
39. Brooks, *Journal of the Southern Indian Mission*, 19 May 1854, 30.
40. "Letter from Elder Henry Lunt," 29 December 1853, in *Deseret News*, 2 February 1854; Bean, Journal, 1 May 1855, CHL; Duke, Reminiscences and Diary, 17 July 1855, CHL; *Deseret News*, 16 March and 20 July 1854; Brooks, *Journal of the Southern Indian Mission*, 31; Brooks, "Indian Relations on the Mormon Frontier," 11.
41. Huntington, *Vocabulary of the Utah and Sho-Sho-Ne or Snake Dialects*, 1st ed., CHL; Turley and Rogers, "Found," 236–37; Compton, *Frontier Life*, 59; and Journal History, 28 February 1854, CHL.
42. Brooks, *Journal of the Southern Indian Mission*, 75.
43. *Deseret News*, 22 June 1854.
44. Brooks, *Journal of the Southern Indian Mission*, 85–86, 123.
45. Young to George W. Bradley, 13 June 1854, BYC; see also Coates, "Brigham Young and Mormon Indian Policies," 452.
46. Bigler, *Fort Limhi*, 48–49, 91.
47. Brooks, *Journal of the Southern Indian Mission*, 133.
48. Brooks, *Journal of the Southern Indian Mission*, 133.
49. Bean, Journal, 1 and 30 December 1855, CHL.
50. Rachel Lee, Diary, 27 April 1856, Huntington Library.
51. Smart, *Mormon Midwife*, 205–6. See also R. Jensen, "Forgotten Relief Societies, 1844–67," 105–25.
52. Sixteenth Ward Relief Society, Record Book, 1854, in Sessions, Diary and Account Book, CHL; Twelfth Ward Relief Society, Minutes, in Smith, Notebook, CHL; Ward Histories, Richard D. Poll Papers, box 77, MLSC; *Woman's Exponent*, July 1903, 6.
53. See R. Jensen, "Forgotten Relief Societies," 105–25; Derr, Cannon, and Beecher, *Women of Covenant*, 75–77.
54. Wolfe, "Settler Colonialism," 388.

55. Quoted in Coates, "Brigham Young and Mormon Indian Policies," 19.
56. Coates, "Brigham Young and Mormon Indian Policies," 19.
57. Journal History, 21 February 1855, CHL.
58. Veracini, *Settler Colonialism*, 67.
59. "An Act to Establish a Territorial Government for Utah," sec. 9, 9 September 1850; Homer, "Federal Bench and Priesthood Authority," 94–96.
60. "An Act Containing Provisions Applicable to the Laws of the Territory of Utah," *Acts, Resolutions and Memorials of the Legislative Assembly of the Territory of Utah, 1855*, chap. 64, 14 January 1854, 260–61.
61. Homer, "Federal Bench and Priesthood Authority," 89–110.
62. Hagan, *Reports of Cases Determined in the Supreme Court of the Territory of Utah*, vol. 1, 11–17; Brooks, *Diary of Hosea Stout*, 12 November 1855, 565; see also Homer, "Judiciary and the Common Law," 103–4.
63. Brooks, *Diary of Hosea Stout*, 8 February 1855, 550.
64. Homer, "Federal Bench and Priesthood Authority," 94–96.
65. Brigham Young, Discourse, 18 February 1855, *Journal of Discourses*, 2:182–83.
66. Love, Diary, 23 March 1855, BYU; Brigham Young to Jefferson Davis, 8 September 1855, printed in Walker, "President Young Writes Jefferson Davis about the Gunnison Massacre Affair," 159.
67. Love, Diary, 23 March 1855, BYU; Brooks, *Diary of Hosea Stout*, 26 March 1855, 553–54.
68. Edward J. Steptoe to George W. Manypenny, 5 April 1855, in U.S. House of Representatives, "Utah Expedition," 178–79; Edward J. Steptoe to Robert McClelland, 5 April 1855, M21.
69. Young to Davis, 8 September 1855, 160.
70. "The Mormon Evil," *National Era*, 24 May 1855.
71. "The Mormon Evil," *National Era*, 24 May 1855.
72. "The Mormons in Utah," *National Era*, 28 June 1855.
73. "The Mormons," *Christian Advocate and Journal*, 8 March 1855; "Life in Utah," *Sacramento Daily Union*, 2 May 1854. See the following articles and speeches that linked Mormons with Indians as uncivilized enemies conspiring against the United States: "The Mormon Question," *North American and United States Gazette* (Philadelphia PA), 26 June 1857; "The Mormon Question," *Lowell (MA) Daily Citizen and News*, 8 June 1857; William H. Seward, Speech of 26 January 1858, Cong. Globe, 35th Cong., 1st Sess. 413 (1858).
74. Young to Davis, 8 September 1855, 160.
75. Beckwith, *Report of Exploration of a Route for the Pacific Railroad*, 98.
76. William W. Drummond to Mrs. Gunnison, 27 April 1857 in Gunnison, *Mormons*, viii–xiv.
77. "From the Plains: The Emigrants—Battle between the Indians and Mormons—A Nobleman among the Redskins," *Ohio Observer*, 23 June 1852.

78. "The Mormons Exciting the Indians against the Americans," *Philadelphia North American and United States Gazette*, 20 January 1857.
79. "The Mormons and the Indians," *Bangor (ME) Daily Whig and Courier*, 22 May 1855.
80. For more on Mormon-Indian intermarriage figures see Kitchen, "Mormon-Indian Relations in Deseret."
81. Berkhofer, *White Man's Indian*, 155.
82. Coward, *Newspaper Indian*, 30–45. Coward suggests that newspaper representations of Indians served the interests of the majority white population "marginalizing Native American lives, documenting their differences, and affirming their inferiority and barbarity" resulting from ideological ethnocentrism, though he does not suggest what a connection or melding of a group with Indians suggested for the non-Indian group, see p. 62. See also Berkhofer, *White Man's Indian*, pt. 4.
83. Steptoe to Manypenny, 5 April 1855, in U.S. House of Representatives, "Utah Expedition," 178–79; Mowry, "List of Camps and Distances," 12, MMCU; Hurt to Manypenny, 2 May 1855, in U.S. Department of the Interior, Commissioner of Indian Affairs, *Annual Report, 1857*, 306; Gunnison, *Mormons*, 150.
84. Steptoe to Manypenny, 5 April 1855, in U.S. House of Representatives, "Utah Expedition," 178–79.
85. *Bangor (ME) Daily Whig and Courier*, May 22, 1855; *Christian Advocate and Journal*, 19 July 1855. W. Paul Reeve explores Mormon-Indian relations and the racialized social constructs of Mormons and Indians merging through their perceived alliances. See Reeve, *Religion of a Different Color*, chaps. 2 and 3.
86. Morgan, "Administration of Indian Affairs," 386.
87. Hurt to Manypenny, 2 May 1855, in U.S. Department of the Interior, Commissioner of Indian Affairs, *Annual Report, 1857*, 306.
88. Hurt to Manypenny, 2 May 1855, in U.S. Department of the Interior, Commissioner of Indian Affairs, *Annual Report, 1857*, 306.
89. The Trade and Intercourse Act, which became law on 30 June 1834, provided the principal legal base for regulating commerce and other interactions between American Indians and non-Natives in the United States at that time. A congressional act of 27 February 1851, which authorized Indian agents for the territories of New Mexico and Utah, also extended the provisions of the Trade and Intercourse Act to those geopolitical regions. *U.S. Statutes at Large* 9:586–87; Prucha, *Documents of United States Indian Policy*, 63 and 68. Prucha's edited volume contains the full text of the Trade and Intercourse Act, *U.S. Statutes at Large*, 4:729–35.
90. Jones, "Trial of Don Pedro León," 165–68.
91. Charles E. Mix, Memoranda for Secretary of the Interior, 15 August 1855, in U.S. House of Representatives, "Utah Expedition," 177–78.

92. Mix to McClelland, 10 July 1855, in U.S. Department of the Interior, Commissioner of Indian Affairs, *Annual Report, 1857,* 306.
93. Mix, Memoranda, 15 August 1855, in U.S. House of Representatives, "Utah Expedition," 177–78.
94. James Buchanan to U.S. House of Representatives, 26 February 1858, in U.S. House of Representatives, "Utah Expedition," 1.
95. Mowry, "List of Camps and Distances," 12, MMCU.
96. Mowry, "List of Camps and Distances," 13–14, MMCU.
97. Columbus L. Craig to David H. Burr, 1 August 1856, in U.S. House of Representatives, "Utah Expedition," 116–17.
98. Hurt to Elliott, 1 October 1856, M234, roll 898.
99. Elliott to Manypenny, 20 December 1856, M 234, roll 898.
100. Hurt to Young, 31 October 1856, in U.S. House of Representatives, "Utah Expedition," 189.
101. Hurt to Young, September 1856, in U.S. Department of the Interior, Commissioner of Indian Affairs, *Annual Report, 1857,* 305; *National Era,* 28 June 1855.
102. Prucha, *Indian Policy in the United States,* 37.
103. Letter to James Barbour, Secretary of War, 1 March 1826, Library of Congress, American State Papers, 2:653; Buckley, *William Clark,* 165–71.
104. R. Jensen, *Pawnee Mission Letters, 1834–1851,* xxx, 81; Extract from the *Annual Report of the Commissioner of Indian Affairs,* 25 November 1838, in Prucha, *Documents,* 72–73.
105. *Daily National Intelligencer,* 20 April 1857; see also *National Era,* May 24, 1855; *Philadelphia North American and United States Gazette,* 20 January 1857; Prucha, *Documents,* 91.
106. Prucha, *Documents,* 91.
107. "Editors of the National Intelligencer," *Daily National Intelligencer,* 20 April 1857.
108. Lorenzo Snow to Brigham Young, 13 August 1857, BYC. Verbiage from the letter is also quoted in Walker, Turley, and Leonard, *Massacre at Mountain Meadows,* 95.
109. Hurt to Young, September 1856, 230.
110. U.S. Department of the Interior, *Annual Report, 1854,* 14.
111. George W. Manypenny to Robert McClelland, 10 April 1854, in U.S. House of Representatives, "Utah Expedition," 165–66. An appropriations act was passed in 1851 that required all treaties with Indian tribes to be negotiated by officers and agents of the Indian department as designated by the president of the United States. Section 7 of that act states, "*And be it further enacted,* That all the laws now in force, regulating trade and intercourse with the Indian tribes, or such provisions of the same as may be applicable,

shall be, and the same are hereby, extended over the Indian tribes in the Territories of New Mexico and Utah." See *U.S. Statutes at Large* 9:586–87.

112. George W. Manypenny to Robert McClelland, 10 April 1854, in U.S. House of Representatives, "Utah Expedition," 166.
113. Garland Hurt to George W. Manypenny, 30 August 1856 in U.S. House of Representatives, "Utah Expedition," 179.
114. Prucha, *Documents*, 63, 68.
115. *U.S. Statutes at Large* 9:586–87.
116. Prucha, *Documents*, 64.
117. Prucha, *Documents*, 64.
118. Prucha, *Documents*, 65.
119. The act's tenth section read, "That the superintendent of Indian affairs, and Indian agents and sub-agents, shall have authority to remove from the Indian country all persons found therein contrary to law; and the President of the United States is authorized to direct the military force to be employed in such removal." In addition, the twenty-third section stated "that it shall be lawful for the military force of the United States to be employed in such manner and under such regulations as the President may direct, in the apprehension of every person who shall or may be found in the Indian country in violation of any of the provisions of this act." Prucha, *Documents*, 65–66. See also Mix to McClelland, 13 August 1855, in U.S. Department of the Interior, Commissioner of Indian Affairs, *Annual Report, 1857*, 307–8.
120. Brooks, *Journal of the Southern Indian Mission*, 25, 133; Bean, Journal, 1 and 30 December 1855, CHL.
121. Prucha, *Documents*, 67.
122. Prucha, *Documents*, 67.
123. Brooks, *Journal of the Southern Indian Mission*, 85–86, 123.
124. Faulkner, "Speech," 9 March 1858.

4. THE "TWIN RELICS OF BARBARISM"

1. Walker, "Buchanan, Popular Sovereignty, and the Mormons," 108–32.
2. For more on the Mormons' attempts to gain statehood, see Lyman, *Political Deliverance*, 7–9. For more on the Mormon reformation, see Peterson, "Mormon Reformation of 1856–1857," 59–87; and Sessions, *Mormon Thunder*, 262.
3. Holt, *Fate of Their Country*, 117; see also Etcheson, *Bleeding Kansas*, 89–138; and Stampp, *America in 1857*, 5–8.
4. R. Nichols, *Disruption of American Democracy*, 110; and Porter and Johnson, *National Party Platforms*, 27. "Some Considerations on the Utah Imbroglio—The Mormon Question," *San Francisco Daily Evening Bulletin*, 19 December 1857; Jacobson, *Whiteness of a Different Color*, 54; Fluhman, "Peculiar People," 103.

5. Holt, *Political Crisis of the 1850s*, 5.
6. Holt, *Political Crisis of the 1850s*, 6.
7. Morrison, *Slavery and the American West*, 159.
8. McDonald, *States' Rights and the Union*, 177; Stampp, *America in 1857*, 200; Kagan, *Dangerous Nation*, 231.
9. Reeder, "Speech of Governor Reeder at New Haven," 4. U.S. Const., art. IV, sec. 4, states, "The United States shall guarantee to every State in this Union a republican form of government, and shall protect each of them against invasion; and on application of the legislature, or of the executive (when the legislature cannot be convened), against domestic violence." Since territories were designed to become equal states in the Union, it was assumed that a republican form of government was required in the territories as well. See also Holt, *Political Crisis of the 1850s*, 190–211.
10. Reeder, "Speech of Governor Reeder at New Haven," 4; Kimmel, *Manhood in America*, 39.
11. Gordon, *Mormon Question*, 58–59.
12. Democratic Ticket, Newsclipping, SDP, box 9. John M. Eberman to James Buchanan, 6 June 1856 JBP, roll 26; Robert Tyler to James Buchanan, 24 May 1856, JBP, roll 26; Isaac Hengus to James Buchanan, 26 May 1856, JBP, roll 26. See also Binder, *James Buchanan and the American Empire*, 10.
13. Morrison, *Slavery and the American West*, 186; Buchanan, "Inaugural Address," 4 March 1857.
14. Buchanan, "Inaugural Address," 4 March 1857.
15. "The Mormon Question, *North American and United States Gazette*, 26 June 1857 and "The Mormon Question," *Lowell Daily Citizen and News*, 8 June 1857; Seward, speech, 26 January 1858, Cong. Globe, 35th Cong., 1st Sess. 413 (1858); Thompson, "Mormonism—Increase of the Army, 1; John B. Floyd to James Buchanan, 5 December 1857, in U.S. House of Representatives, Report of the Secretary of War, 1857, Exec. Doc. No. 2, 3 and 8. See also Bigler, "Lion in the Path," 4–21.
16. Memorial, 6 January 1857, Governor's Office Files, BYC; Brigham Young to George A. Smith and John M. Bernhisel, 3 January 1857, BYC, Letterbook 3:259.
17. Justin S. Morrill, Report No. 116, 34th Cong., 3d Sess., House of Representatives, 20 January 1857, 1–2, TRG 233; Morrill, "Utah Territory and Its Laws—Polygamy and Its License," App. to Cong. Globe, 34th Cong., 3rd Sess. 285 (1857); "The Mormons," *Harper's Weekly*, 25 April 1857; Winfield Scott to John B. Floyd, 26 May 1857, MSS A 458, USHS.
18. A territorial law permitted slavery in Utah. Acts, Resolutions and Memorials passed at the Several Annual Sessions of the Legislative Assembly of the Territory of Utah, Territorial Laws of Utah, "An Act in Relation to Service,"

chap. 17, sec. 1, 160. The law stated that slavery allowed in other states or territories was also binding in Utah Territory. Section 4 prevented any sexual intercourse between master and servant of the African race; it also dictated that no white person could have sexual relations with any person of African race.

19. Morrill, "Utah Territory and Its Laws," 287.
20. "News of the Day," *New York Times*, 21 April 1857.
21. Morrill, "Utah Territory and Its Laws," 285–87.
22. Morrill, "Utah Territory and Its Laws," 285.
23. For instance, see the following contemporary newspaper articles: "The Mormon Problem Must Be Solved," *San Francisco Daily Evening Bulletin*, 18 June 1857; "The Mormon Question," *New York Herald*, 3 May 1857; "Douglas on Utah: The Two Faces of the Little Giant," *Chicago Daily Tribune*, 25 June 1857; "Utah and Popular Sovereignty," *National Era*, 30 April 1857, 70; "The Mormons," *Harper's Weekly*, 25 April 1857; "The Question of the Mormons," *Harper's Weekly*, 4 July 1857; "News from Utah," *Frank Leslie's Illustrated Newspaper*, 9 May 1857. Another article from the same paper, "Utah and the Mormons," *Frank Leslie's Illustrated Newspaper*, 26 September 1857, also discussed the Mormon platform and the "degraded position they assign to women, the privileges they give to themselves, the implicit obedience they inculcate upon the converts, and the arbitrary right of altering the tenets of belief" among the entire population in Utah Territory.
24. "Mormondom," *North American and United States Gazette*, 19 December 1856.
25. "Mormondom," *North American and United States Gazette*, 19 December 1856.
26. "The Mormon Problem," *Bangor Daily Whig and Courier*, 18 April 1857; "The Mormon Question," *New York Herald*, 3 May 1857; "The Mormon Question," *Salem Observer*, 9 May 1857.
27. "Utah and Popular Sovereignty," *National Era*, 30 April 1857.
28. Buchanan, "Proclamation—Rebellion in the Territory of Utah," in Hafen and Hafen, *Mormon Resistance*, 332–37.
29. "The Modern Sodom," *Daily National Intelligencer*, 20 April 1857; "Editors of the National Intelligencer," *Daily National Intelligencer*, 20 April 1857.
30. "Remarks, by President Brigham Young, Bowery, Sunday Morning, September 13, 1857," *Deseret News*, 23 September 1857; John B. Floyd to James Buchanan, 5 December 1857, in U.S. House of Representatives, Report of the Secretary of War, 6–7, Exec. Doc. No. 2.
31. "The Mormons," *Harper's Weekly*, 25 April 1857.
32. *Richmond Enquirer*, 27 March 1857.
33. William Bigler to James Buchanan, 25 May 1857, JBP; Robert Tyler to Buchanan, 27 April 1857, JBP.

34. "The Mormons—Shall the Doctrine of Popular Sovereignty Be Applied to Utah?" *Herald of Freedom* (Lawrence KS), 27 June 1857.
35. Varon, *Disunion*, 14; Mullis, *Peacekeeping on the Plains*, 59–60. Mullis suggests that proslavery bands in the Bleeding Kansas episode, likely playing on the history of Mormons in Missouri, would rhetorically "Mormonize" abolitionists to turn out hordes of voters against them.
36. Buchanan, First Annual Message, 8 December 1857.
37. Gienapp, "'No Bed of Roses,'" 100; Lawson and Seidman, *Constitution of Empire*, 160 and 185; McDonald, *States' Rights and the Union*, 147. Many of the documents that influenced the Buchanan administration's decision are found in the official report, U.S. House of Representatives, "Utah Expedition."
38. Lewis Cass to Captain Robinson, 29 January 1857, Lewis Cass Papers, box 3; William W. Drummond to Jeremiah S. Black, 30 March 1857, in U.S. House of Representatives, "Utah Expedition," 212–14.
39. John F. Kinney to Jeremiah S. Black, 20 March 1857, in MacKinnon, *At Sword's Point*, pt. 1, 110.
40. William W. Drummond to Stephen A. Douglas, 16 May and 22 May 1857, SDP, box 7.
41. U.S. House of Representatives, Report of the Secretary of War, 5 December 1857; Buchanan, First Annual Message, 8 December 1857; Winfield Scott to John B. Floyd, 26 May 1857, MSS A 458, USHS.
42. Neil, "Territorial Governor as Indian Superintendent in the Trans-Mississippi West," 213–37; "Proclamation by the Governor," *Deseret News*, 27 February 1856. In this proclamation, Brigham Young called on the territorial militia to suppress all Indian hostilities in the territory for the "common preservation" of whites and Native peoples.
43. U.S. Department of the Interior, *Annual Report, 1854*, 14.
44. Indian Appropriations Act, 408.
45. Indian Appropriations Act, 408; John B. Floyd, U.S. House of Representatives, Report of the Secretary of War, 16 December 1857, 7.
46. Winfield Scott to John B. Floyd, 26 May 1857, MSS A 458, USHS; Charles E. Mix to Jacob Thompson, 22 February 1858, in U.S. House of Representatives, "Utah Expedition," 125.
47. Buchanan, First Annual Message, 8 December 1857; see also Rockwell, *Indian Affairs and the Administrative State*, 2–3.
48. Buchanan, First Annual Message, 8 December 1857.
49. J. Jensen, *Army Surveillance*, 12, quote from 20; Tate, *Frontier Army*, 81.
50. Buchanan, Message to Congress Transmitting the Constitution of Kansas, 2 February 1858, JBP, box 71.
51. "Kansas—The Mormons—Slavery: Speech of Senator Douglas: Delivered at Springfield, Ill, 12 June 1857," *New York Daily Times*, 23 June 1857. The *Times*

article contains the full text of Douglas's speech. Snippets or summaries of the speech are found in numerous newspapers published across the United States. Two of the better summaries come from the following papers: "Douglas on Utah: The Two Faces of the Little Giant," *Chicago Daily Tribune*, 25 June 1857; "Squatter Sovereignty Abandoned By Its Father," *National Era*, 16 July 1857.

52. Orson Hyde to Joseph Smith, 25 April 1844 and 26 April 1844, JSC; Brigham Young to Stephen A. Douglas, 29 April 1854, SDP, box 42. See also Bushman, *Joseph Smith*, 426–27, 518. For more on the idea of refuge for the Mormon community in the West, see Esplin, "'Place Prepared,'" 71–97.

53. "Act to Organize the Territories of Nebraska and Kansas," secs. 14 & 32, *U.S. Statutes at Large*, vol. 10, 227; Brigham Young to Stephen A. Douglas, 29 April 1854, SDP, box 42.

54. "Kansas—The Mormons—Slavery," *New York Times*, 23 June 1857.

55. David H. Burr to Stephen A. Douglas, 23 June 1857, SDP, box 8. Benjamin G. Ferris to Stephen A. Douglas, 1 August 1857, SDP, box 8. Charles J. Faulkner to Stephen A. Douglas, 4 July 1857, SDP, box 8.

56. J. A. W. Buck to Stephen A. Douglas, 24 June 1857, SDP, box 8; T. P. Andrews to Stephen A. Douglas, 1 July 1857, SDP, box 8; W. W. Wick to Stephen A. Douglas, 8 July 1857, SDP, box 8.

57. Johannsen, *Lincoln-Douglas Debates of 1858*, 48.

58. "Reply to Senator Douglas: Speech of Hon. A. Lincoln, of Indiana," *New York Daily Times*, 4 July 1857.

59. "Lincoln's Springfield Speech," *Chicago Tribune*, 29 June 1857; "Reply to Senator Douglas: Speech of Hon. A. Lincoln, of Indiana," *New York Daily Times*, 4 July 1857.

60. M. McConnel to Stephen A. Douglas, 2 July 1857, SDP, box 8.

61. "Douglas on Utah: The Two Faces of the Little Giant," *Chicago Daily Tribune*, 25 June 1857; "Squatter Sovereignty Abandoned by Its Father," *National Era*, 16 July 1857.

62. "Utah and Popular Sovereignty," *National Era*, 30 April 1857; "The Northern Press," *National Era*, 30 July 1857; "The *Charleston Mercury*," *Daily National Intelligencer*, 23 June 1857; "Squatter Sovereignty—Kansas and Utah," *Ripley (OH) Bee*, 6 December 1856.

63. "Squatter Sovereignty Abandoned by Its Father," *National Era*, 16 July 1857.

64. "The Question of the Mormons," *Harper's Weekly*, 4 July 1857.

65. The text of the *Examiner* article is found in "Mr. Senator Douglas on Utah, versus Kansas: Federal and Local Politics—A Municipal and a National Issue," *New York Herald*, 4 July 1857; "A New Territorial Policy," *North American and United States Gazette*, 6 July 1857.

66. "Mr. Senator Douglas on Utah, versus Kansas: Federal and Local Politics—A Municipal and a National Issue," *New York Herald*, 4 July 1857; "A New Territorial Policy," *North American and United States Gazette*, 6 July 1857.
67. Young, Diary, 30 August 1857, in Cooley, *Diary of Brigham Young*, 68; Kenney, Woodruff, Journal, 30 August 1857.
68. "Comments," *Deseret News*, 2 September 1857.
69. "Comments," *Deseret News*, 2 September 1857.
70. See Gould, *Among the Powers of the Earth*.
71. "Comments," *Deseret News*, 2 September 1857. See Gould, *Among the Powers of the Earth*; for an example of British control and dispossession see Faragher, *Great and Noble Scheme*.
72. "Comments," *Deseret News*, 2 September 1857, 205; Brigham Young to Horace S. Eldredge, 7 August 1857, BYP, USHS.
73. *Journal of Discourses*, 7:226.
74. Buchanan, *Mr. Buchanan's Administration on the Eve of the Rebellion*, 234.

5. THE MARCH OF FEDERAL SOVEREIGNTY

1. Cass to Cumming, 30 July 1857, BYC.
2. "Utah Affairs," State Department Territorial Papers, Utah Series, M12.
3. "The Utah Expedition," *North American and United States Gazette*, 23 June 1858.
4. Pleasanton to Van Vliet, 28 July 1857, in Hafen and Hafen, *Mormon Resistance*, 38.
5. Harney to Young, 28 July 1857, RG 393.
6. Harney to Young, 28 July 1857, RG 393.
7. Bigler, *Forgotten Kingdom*, 145; Cooley, *Diary of Brigham Young, 1857*, 49–53; Walker, Turley, and Leonard, *Massacre at Mountain Meadows*, 35–36.
8. Carruth, Autobiography and Journal, 29, CHL.
9. "What of Utah?" *Deseret News*, 3 February 1858; "Remarks," *Deseret News*, 5 August 1857; *Deseret News*, 14 October 1857.
10. Cooley, *Diary of Brigham Young*, 49; Barney, Journal, BYU; Luck, Journal, 4, USHS; Young to Eldredge, 3 December 1858, Brigham Young Papers, box 1, USHS; Hyde, "The Work of Reformation—The United States' Army—Labours of 'Mormon' Missionaries—Judgments of God, etc.," *Journal of Discourses*, 6:15.
11. Cooley, *Diary of Brigham Young*, 54.
12. Rachel Woolsey Lee, Diary, 4 July 1857 and 17 August 1857, Huntington Library.
13. Taylor, "The Kingdom of God or Nothing," *Journal of Discourses*, 6:20.
14. Taylor, "The Kingdom of God or Nothing," *Journal of Discourses*, 6:22.
15. Taylor, "The Kingdom of God or Nothing," *Journal of Discourses*, 6:24.

16. Cooley, *Diary of Brigham Young*, 58.
17. Cooley, *Diary of Brigham Young*, 68.
18. Young, *Memoirs of John R. Young*, 97.
19. Hafen and Hafen, *Mormon Resistance*, 49–50.
20. Among the studies to consider on Mountain Meadows are J. Brooks, *Mountain Meadows Massacre*; Bagley, *Blood of the Prophets*; Walker, Turley, and Leonard, *Massacre at Mountain Meadows*.
21. For the portrayals in the press, see Seefeldt, "Horrible Massacre of Emigrants!!: The Mountain Meadows Massacre in Public Discourse," available at http://mountainmeadows.unl.edu; see also Bunker and Bitton, "Illustrated Periodical Images of Mormons, 1850–1860," 90; and Reeve, *Religion of a Different Color*, 87–89.
22. The Mountain Meadows Massacre was not the lone episode of violence in Utah Territory during the Utah War. See, for example, Bigler, "Aiken Party Executions and the Utah War, 1857–1858," 457–76.
23. Young, "Proclamation by the Governor," 15 September 1857, USHS.
24. Young, "Proclamation by the Governor, 15 September 1857."
25. Cooley, *Diary of Brigham Young*, 80; Brigham Young Letterbook, vol. 3, 858–60, BYC.
26. "Governmental Treatment of Utah: (From the *Desert News*)," *Millennial Star*, 5 December 1857.
27. Young, "Proclamation by the Governor, 15 September 1857; "Governmental Treatment of Utah," *Millennial Star*, 5 December 1857.
28. "Governmental Treatment of Utah," *Millennial Star*, 5 December 1857.
29. Cooley, *Diary of Brigham Young*, 56.
30. Miles, Autobiography, CHL.
31. Cooley, *Diary of Brigham Young*, 58.
32. Griffin, Autobiography, USHS; Groesbeck, Autobiography, USHS; Jones, Autobiography, USHS; Barney, Journal, 77–78, BYU.
33. MacKinnon, "Sex, Subalterns, and Steptoe," 245; U.S. House of Representatives, Utah, Memorial, 17 March 1858.
34. Young to Eldredge, 5 April 1858, Brigham Young Papers, USHS.
35. Barney, Journal, 77–78, BYU.
36. Phelps, Diary Book A, 17 October 1857, John Wolcott Phelps Papers, box 1, USHS.
37. Gates, *John Stevens' Courtship*, 117.
38. *Harper's Weekly*, 28 November 1857.
39. Alexander to Young, 12 October 1857, in U.S. House of Representatives, "Utah Expedition," 84.
40. Eicher and Eicher, *Civil War High Commands*, 435.
41. Porter, Journal, 15 & 17, October 1857, Library of Congress.

42. Porter, Journal, 15 & 17, October 1857, Library of Congress.
43. Porter, Journal, 15 & 17, October 1857, Library of Congress.
44. "Elder Hyde on the Mormon Question," *New York Herald*, 1 December 1857; Bagley, Record Book, 3, BYU; Phelps, Diary, 1–5 October 1857, USHS.
45. Barney, Journal, 78, BYU.
46. Phelps, Diary, 5 October 1857, USHS; Kerstetter, *God's Country, Uncle Sam's Land*, 61.
47. Smart, *Mormon Midwife*, 23 & 28 November 1857, 250.
48. Evans, Autobiography, USHS.
49. Clawson, Reminiscences, CHL.
50. Past, Journal, 4 February 1858, NSHS. Past, from White Haven, Pennsylvania, spent his time working and attending temperance meetings, fraternal organizations, and gatherings of the White Haven Literary Society. In 1857 he moved to Wilmington, Delaware, remaining in mill-work. The next year he moved to Industriana, Minnesota. His journal contains his feelings on the hard times in the late 1850s, banks closing, business failures, men begging for work, economic failure in the South, and Mormon uprisings, among other contemporary issues.
51. "The Utah Expedition," *Milwaukee Daily Sentinel*, 18 November 1857; "Important from the Plains—News from the Utah Expedition," *New York Herald*, 12 November 1857; "The Military Expedition to Utah," *Daily National Intelligencer*, 16 December 1857.
52. Roland, *Albert Sidney Johnston*, 192–99.
53. Elizabeth Cumming to Anne, 28 November 1857, Alfred Cumming Papers.
54. Elizabeth Cumming to Anne, 28 November 1857, Alfred Cumming Papers.
55. Magraw and Bridger to Porter, 28 April 1858, 83 in U.S. House of Representatives, Report of the Secretary of War, 1858.
56. Huntington, Journal, 10 and 16 August, 1 September 1857, CHL.
57. Cooley, *Diary of Brigham Young*, 71.
58. Kvasnicka and Viola, *Commissioners of Indian Affairs, 1824–1977*, 70–73.
59. Young to Denver, 12 September 1857, BYC.
60. Denver to Young, 11 November 1857, M21, reel 58, 40; see also U.S. Department of the Interior, Commissioner of Indian Affairs, *Annual Report, 1858*, 312–13.
61. Denver to Young, 11 November 1857.
62. Denver to Young, 11 November 1857.
63. Denver to Young, 11 November 1857.
64. Denver to Collins, 24 November 1857, M21, reel 58, 74–75.
65. Denver to Collins, 24 November 1857.
66. Scott to Floyd, 26 May 1857, MSS A 458, USHS.
67. "Mormons and Indians," *San Francisco Daily Evening Bulletin*, 16 February 1858. Information from this article was printed originally in the *St. Louis*

Republican of 19 January and reprinted in "Important from the Plains—The Mormons Calling the Indians to Their Aid," *Ripley (OH) Bee*, 23 January 1858.

68. "Mormon and Indian Alliance," *Norristown Register and Montgomery Democrat*, 24 November 1857. The *Norristown Register* of 8 December 1857 also includes an article describing the contributions made by indigenous peoples to the Mormons in Utah, particularly in the extorting of money and cattle from overland emigrants.
69. Bigler, *Fort Limhi*, 48–55.
70. "Indians and Mormons," *Ripley Bee*, 7 November 1857.
71. Clarke to Thomas, 1 January 1858, 335–36, in U.S. House of Representatives, Report of the Secretary of War, 1858.
72. Clarke to Thomas, 1 January 1858.
73. Ginn, Diary, *Mormon and Indian Wars*, 62, USHS.
74. "Elder Hyde on the Mormon Question," *New York Herald*, 1 December 1857.
75. "The Mormon Question," *Lowell (MA) Daily Citizen and News*, 8 June 1857.
76. "The Mormons—Later from Utah," *Nashville Daily News*, 31 January 1858.
77. Bunker and Bitton, *Mormon Graphic Image*, 28.
78. Young to Washakie, 2 November 1857, BYC.
79. See also Young to Simons, 22 March 1858, BYC.
80. "Arrapine" to Young, 3 January 1858, BYC.
81. "Arapene" to Young, 28 February 1858, BYC. For a similar situation, see Hamblin, Diary, 23 December 1854, Jacob Hamblin Papers, CHL; and Compton, *Frontier Life*, 67–68.
82. Buchanan, First Annual Message, 8 December 1857.
83. Eighty-seven of 215 pages of the Buchanan administration's official report on the Utah War concerned Indian affairs. U.S. House of Representatives, "Utah Expedition," 124–28; Bigler and Bagley, *Mormon Rebellion*, 11.
84. Mix to Jacob Thompson, 22 February 1858, in U.S. House of Representatives, "Utah Expedition," 125.
85. Kinney to Black, 20 March 1857, in MacKinnon, *At Sword's Point*, pt. 1, 110.
86. Scott to Floyd, 26 May 1857, USHS; Mix to Thompson, 22 February 1858, in U.S. House of Representatives, "Utah Expedition," 125.
87. Weller, Inaugural Address, 8 January 1858, CSL; "The Mormon War," *New York Herald*, 28 April 1858. "Latest by Telegraph. The Indians of Utah Territory," *Nashville Daily News*, 31 January 1858. This Nashville article reported that the spread of Mormon influence over Indians had not reached Natives in California. It also declared that California military volunteers stood ready for service to advance against the Mormons from the west.
88. Satz, *American Indian Policy*, 278; Prucha, *Indian Policy in the United States*, vii.

89. U.S. House of Representatives, Utah, Memorial, 17 March 1858, 1.
90. U.S. House of Representatives, Utah, Memorial, 2.
91. According to a report of the Utah Commission in the 1880s, Utah Territory prepared a "State constitution and memorialize[d] Congress for admission into the Union. The convention assembled at Salt Lake City on 17 March 1856. Ten days later the constitution and memorial were adopted, and Hons. George A. Smith and John Taylor were elected delegates to present the same to Congress. The delegates proceeded to Washington and presented the memorial to Congress, but the record makes no mention of any action thereon." Report of the Utah Commission to the Secretary of the Interior, 1886, 79.
92. Utah, Memorial, 4–5.
93. Laurence M. Keitt, "Delegate from Utah," Cong. Globe, 35th Cong., 1st Sess. 170 (1857); Lawson and Seidman, *Constitution of Empire*, 121–23, 133–38.
94. "The Mormon War Question, 'W. W.' Versus 'Hawkeye,'" *San Francisco Daily Bulletin*, 14 January 1858.
95. Cumming to Cass, 2 May 1858, Thomas L. Kane Papers, box 14, BYU. Blair, Diary and Autobiography, 18, BYU.
96. McDonald, *States' Rights and the Union*, 183.
97. *New York Herald*, 27 January 1858.
98. *New York Herald*, 27 January 1858.
99. "Unfair Treatment of Utah," *Deseret News*, 2 June 1858.
100. Holt, *Political Crisis of the 1850s*, 204.
101. Dowdell, Message, 10 March 1858, Cong. Globe, 35th Cong., 1st Sess. 1057–58 (1858).
102. Etcheson, *Bleeding Kansas*, 167–68.
103. Toombs, Message, 26 January 1858, Cong. Globe, 35th Cong., 1st Sess. 407 (1858).
104. Toombs, Message, 26 January 1858, Cong. Globe, 35th Cong., 1st Sess. 407 (1858).
105. Cong. Globe, 35th Cong., 1st Sess. 518–19 (1858).
106. Seward, Message, Cong. Globe, 35th Cong., 1st Sess. 413 (1858).
107. Thompson, "Mormonism-Increase of the Army," 27 January 1858.
108. Thompson, "Mormonism-Increase of the Army," 27 January 1858.
109. Davis, "Speech," App. to Cong. Globe, 35th Cong., 1st Sess. 60 (1858).
110. Davis, "Speech," App. to Cong. Globe, 35th Cong., 1st Sess. 60 (1858).
111. Davis, "Speech," App. to Cong. Globe, 35th Cong., 1st Sess. 60 (1858); "News from New Mexico," *New York Herald*, 14 February 1858.
112. Hafen and Hafen, *Mormon Resistance*, 247; and App. to Cong. Globe, 35th Cong., 1st Sess. 55 (1858).
113. Davis, "Speech," App. to Cong. Globe, 35th Cong., 1st Sess. 54 (1858).
114. Davis, "Speech," App. to Cong. Globe, 35th Cong., 1st Sess. 55 (1858).

115. Faulkner, "Speech," 9 March 1858, 13, MLSC; see also "Bill to Raise Volunteers," 9 March 1858, Cong. Globe, 35th Cong., 1st Sess. 1007–10 (1858).
116. "Bill to Raise Volunteers," 9 March 1858, Cong. Globe, 35th Cong., 1st Sess. 1007–10 (1858).
117. Faulkner, "Speech," 9 March 1858, 7.
118. Iverson, 27 January 1858, Cong. Globe, 35th Cong., 1st Sess. 432–33 (1858).
119. Faulkner, "Speech," 9 March 1858, 8.
120. "Bill to Raise Volunteers," 9 March 1858, Cong. Globe, 35th Cong., 1st Sess. 1007–10 (1858).
121. Furniss, *Mormon Conflict*, 174.
122. Johnson, "Speech," 17 February 1858, Cong. Globe, 35th Cong., 1st Sess. 737–39 (1858).
123. "The End of the Mormon War," *Harper's Weekly*, 19 June 1858.
124. Gwin, "Speech," 18 February 1858, Cong. Globe, 35th Cong., 1st Sess. 759 (1858).
125. Gwin, "Speech," 18 February 1858, Cong. Globe, 35th Cong., 1st Sess. 759 (1858).
126. Gwin, "Speech," 18 February 1858, Cong. Globe, 35th Cong., 1st Sess. 759 (1858).
127. Brown, "Speech," 18 February 1858, Cong. Globe, 35th Cong., 1st Sess. 769 (1858).
128. An Act to Provide for the Organization of a Regiment of Mounted Volunteers, chap. 13, 35th Cong., 1st Sess., 7 April 1858, in Sanger, *Statutes at Large*, 262–63.
129. Hopkins to Perry, 23 January 1858, Series 2153, box 4, Florida Department of State, Division of Library and Information Services; Langley, *To Utah with the Dragoons*, 20.
130. Johnson, "Speech," 17 February 1858, Cong. Globe, 35th Cong., 1st Sess. 740–41 (1858).
131. L. Foster, *Women, Family, and Utopia*, 182–83.
132. Embry, "Effects of Polygamy on Mormon Women," 56–61.
133. Elizabeth Cumming to Anne, 24 September 1858.
134. Cannon, "Improvement of Our Species," *Western Standard*, 7 August 1857.
135. Elizabeth Cumming to Anne, 5 April 1858, Alfred Cumming Papers.
136. Buchanan to Kane, 31 December 1857, Thomas L. Kane Papers, box 14, BYU.
137. Kane to Kane, 4 January 1858, Thomas L. Kane Papers, box 14, BYU.
138. Kane was instrumental in negotiating with the Mormons. For much more on Kane see Grow, *"Liberty to the Downtrodden"* and Poll, "Thomas L. Kane and the Utah War," 112–35.
139. Kane to Buchanan, 15 March 1858, Thomas L. Kane Papers, box 14, BYU.
140. Kane to Buchanan, 15 March 1858, Thomas L. Kane Papers, box 14, BYU.
141. Kane to Buchanan, 23 March 1858, Thomas L. Kane Papers, box 14, BYU.
142. Cumming to Kane, 23 March 1858, Thomas L. Kane Papers, box 14, BYU.

143. Shurtliff, Autobiographical Sketch from his Journals, 97–99, USHS; Stowell, Biographical Sketch, CHL. For more on the move south, see also Smart, *Mormon Midwife*, 255–58 and Poll, "Move South," 65–88.
144. Buchanan, "Proclamation—Rebellion in the Territory of Utah," in Hafen and Hafen, *Mormon Resistance*, 332–37.
145. Buchanan, "A Proclamation—Rebellion in the Territory of Utah," in Hafen and Hafen, *Mormon Resistance*, 332–37.
146. "Utah Expedition," *Valley Tan*, 3 December 1858.
147. General Order no. 26, Headquarters, Department of Utah, Camp Scott UT, 5 June 1858, 154–55, RG 393; for similar instructions, see Lay to Harney, 29 June 1857, in U.S. House of Representatives, Report of the Secretary of War, 1857, 21.

6. CONQUERING MORMON SOVEREIGNTY

1. Tate, *Frontier Army in the Settlement of the West*, x; Wooster, *Military and United States Indian Policy*, 5.
2. Buchanan, "Proclamation—Rebellion in the Territory of Utah," in Hafen and Hafen, *Mormon Resistance*, 337.
3. Powell and McCulloch to Floyd, 3 July 1858, in U.S. House of Representatives, Report of the Secretary of War, 1858, 174.
4. LDS Journal History, 25 April 1858.
5. LDS Journal History, 25 April 1858.
6. LDS Journal History, 25 April 1858.
7. LDS Journal History, 25 April 1858.
8. Ormsby and Smith, "Carson's Valley," 2 February 1858 in U.S. House of Representatives, Carson's Valley, 2–3.
9. Ormsby and Smith, "Carson's Valley," 2–3.
10. Morrill, "Utah Territory and Its Laws," 23 February 1857, 284–90.
11. MacKinnon, "'Like Splitting a Man up His Backbone,'" 109.
12. U.S. House of Representatives, "Territory of Nevada," 5.
13. "A New Territory," *Flag of Our Union*, 26 June 1858.
14. "A New Territory," *Flag of Our Union*, 26 June 1858.
15. "Nevada Territory," *Daily National Intelligencer*, 7 June 1858.
16. Powell and McCulloch to Floyd, 3 July 1858, in U.S. House of Representatives, Report of the Secretary of War, 1858, 172–74.
17. Powell and McCulloch to A. S. Johnston, 12 June 1858, "[From the N.Y. Evening Post of July 22.] Letter from the Peace Commissioners to General Johnston," *Deseret News*, 1 September 1858.
18. Powell and McCulloch to Floyd, 3 July 1858, in U.S. House of Representatives, Report of the Secretary of War, 1858, 174; Buchanan, "Second Annual Message," 6 December 1858.

19. Powell and McCulloch to Floyd, 3 July 1858, in U.S. House of Representatives, Report of the Secretary of War, 1858, 174; Buchanan, "Second Annual Message," 6 December 1858.
20. "Utah Expedition," *Valley Tan*, 3 December 1858.
21. Cumming to Cass, 2 May 1858, in Alfred Cumming Papers.
22. "The Utah Expedition," *North American and United States Gazette*, 23 June 1858.
23. Cumming, Dispatch, in U.S. Senate, Message of the President, 7.
24. Forney, Report, in U.S. House of Representatives, Report of the Secretary of War, 1858, 565.
25. Buchanan, Message of the President, in U.S. Senate, Message of the President, 10 June 1858.
26. Buchanan, Message of the President, in U.S. Senate, Message of the President, 10 June 1858.
27. Barney, Journal, 81, BYU. Van Vliet to Pleasanton, 16 September 1857, in U.S. House of Representatives, Report of the Secretary of War, 1857, 26. Van Vliet wrote the following of Mormons being blinded by a history of persecution: "During my stay in the city I visited several families, and all with whom I was thrown looked upon the present movement of the troops towards their Territory as the commencement of another religious persecution, and expressed a fixed determination to sustain Governor Young in any measures he might adopt."
28. Young to Eldredge, 20 November 1858, Brigham Young Papers, USHS; LDS Journal History, 24 May 1858. The entry in the LDS Journal History discusses filibustering in Central America in comparison to the military engagements in Utah.
29. Buchanan, "Proclamation—Rebellion in the Territory of Utah," in Hafen and Hafen, *Mormon Resistance*, 332–37.
30. General Order no. 26, Headquarters, Department of Utah, Camp Scott, UT, 5 June 1858, 154–55, RG 393.
31. Johnston to McDowell, 22 April 1858, RG 393.
32. Johnston to Cumming, 19 June 1858 and Johnston to McDowell, 8 July 1858, RG 393.
33. Moorman, *Camp Floyd and the Mormons*, 81.
34. Buchanan, "Second Annual Message," 6 December 1858. Buchanan seemed so impressed that he "recommended that the benefits of our land laws and preemption system be extended to the people of Utah by the establishment of a land office in that Territory."
35. Floyd, Report of the Secretary of War, 4, in U.S. House of Representatives, Report of the Secretary of War, 1857.

36. Floyd, Report of the Secretary of War, 4-5, in U.S. House of Representatives, Report of the Secretary of War, 1857.
37. Floyd to Buchanan, 20 May 1858 & 22 June 1859, M127.
38. Blackhawk, *Violence over the Land*, 254 and Simmons, *Ute Indians of Utah, Colorado, and New Mexico*, 104.
39. Alfred Cumming to Lewis Cass, 12 May 1858, in Alfred Cumming Papers.
40. Fort Bridger—Special Order, no. 41 Headquarters, Department of Utah, Camp Scott, UT, 7 June 1858, 156, RG 393.
41. G. E. Gould to Frederick H. Gould, 24 September 1858, Letters from Camp Floyd, USHS.
42. Lee-Palfrey Family Papers, MMC 3329, box 4, Library of Congress.
43. General Order 50, Camp Floyd, 2 September 1858, RG 393.
44. Ackley, "Trip across the Plains in 1858," 43–44, USHS.
45. A. Godfrey, "Housewives, Hussies, and Heroines," 158.
46. Ackley, "Trip across the Plains," 45, USHS; Camp Floyd at Fairfield, Utah, 8 July 1858–27 July 1861, USHS.
47. Mormon observers noted the importance of the troops establishing large and permanent stations at Fort Bridger and in Cedar Valley. See the Journal of William Luck, 5 July 1858, USHS. See also Ackley, "Trip across the Plains," 26, USHS.
48. Floyd to Buchanan, 20 May 1858, "Fort Bridger," and Floyd to Buchanan, "Fort Bridger and Camp Floyd," 22 June 1859, M127. Buchanan responded with authorization in separate letters on 21 May 1858 and 14 July 1859, respectively.
49. Cumming to Cass, 2 May 1858, in U.S. House of Representatives, Cessation of Difficulties in Utah, 7.
50. Slater, *Fruits of Mormonism*, 83. For another overlander account on issues concerning the U.S. flag and Mormons, see also Henry Sterling Bloom Gold Rush Letters and Bloom Family Miscellany, MS 2315, folder 1, CSL.
51. McLaws, Letter Excerpts, 15 & 17 December 1858, USHS. While McLaws gave the date of 9 November for the flag-raising ceremony, Fitz-John Porter, the assistant adjutant general, stated that on 6 November 1858 at 11:30 A.M. the men would raise "the National Flag in Camp Floyd" in a special ceremony; see letter of that date in RG 393.
52. McLaws, Letter Excerpts, 15 & 17 December 1858, USHS.
53. "An Untoward Occurrence," *Washington Daily National Intelligencer*, 13 January 1843.
54. McLaws, Letter Excerpts, 15 & 17 December 1858, USHS; also printed in "Utah: From Our Own Correspondent," *New York Daily Tribune*, 16 December 1858.
55. Buchanan, Message of the President, in U.S. Senate, Message of the President.
56. For more on the economic benefits, see Arrington, *Great Basin Kingdom*, 196–99; and Moorman, *Camp Floyd and the Mormons*, 260–71.

57. Carruth, Autobiography and Journal, CHL.
58. Young to Kane, 14 January 1859, Kane Collection, box 1, SUL.
59. Thornton, Diary, USHS.
60. Young to Cannon, 3 November 1859, MS 7261, CHL.
61. Ackley, "Trip across the Plains," 27.
62. "The Army Occupation of Utah," *Deseret News*, 30 March 1859.
63. Bailey, Biography from his journal, 35, USHS. The spelling is maintained from the journal.
64. LDS Journal History, 18 May 1858.
65. Farnsworth to "Friend," 8 April 1859, Camp Floyd Letters, MLSC.
66. Farnsworth to "Friend," 8 April 1859, Camp Floyd Letters, MLSC.
67. Seifrit, "Charles Henry Wilcken," 308–21; "Romney Ancestor Fled Army, Joined LDS Church," *Deseret News*, 8 September 2007, available at http://www.deseretnews.com/article/695208290/Romney-ancestor-fled-Army-joined-LDS-Church.html?pg=all.
68. Buchanan, "Second Annual Message," 6 December 1858.
69. Buchanan, Notes, etc. regarding Utah, Manuscript Group 8, reel 53, JBP.
70. Fitz-John Porter, Journal, 30 October 1858, Library of Congress.
71. Rachel Woolsey Lee Diary, 11 April 1858, 66, Huntington Library.
72. LDS Journal History, 23 March 1858.
73. LDS Journal History, 5 April 1858.
74. LDS Journal History, 5 April 1858.
75. Rachel Woolsey Lee Diary, 11 April 1858.
76. Smith to Stenhouse, LDS Journal History, 5 April 1858.
77. Smith to Stenhouse, LDS Journal History, 5 April 1858.
78. Smith to Stenhouse, LDS Journal History, 5 April 1858.
79. Bigler, *Fort Limhi*, 30 & 275; Mann, *Sacajawea's People*, 22–25.
80. Andrew Love, Diary, 13 March 1858, BYU.
81. Pleasant Green Taylor, Family Record, CHL.
82. A. J. Allen, Journal, 13 April 1858, USHS.
83. "Another Murder by Indians," *Deseret News*, 14 April 1858.
84. Kane to Buchanan, 23 May 1858, Thomas L. Kane Papers, box 14, BYU.
85. Johnston to Cumming, 21 April 1858, in U.S. House of Representatives, Report of the Secretary of War, 1858, 77.
86. Bigler, *Fort Limhi*, 281.
87. Forney to Cumming, 21 April 1858, in U.S. House of Representatives, Report of the Secretary of War, 1858, 78.
88. B. F. Ficklin to Major Fitz-John Porter, 21 April 1858, in U.S House of Representatives, Report of the Secretary of War, 1858, 79.
89. Craven Jackson, Affidavit, 21 April 1858, 81 in U.S., House of Representatives, Report of the Secretary of War, 1858, 81. W. M. F Magraw and James Bridger

to Major Fitz-John Porter, 28 April 28 1858, in U.S. House of Representatives, Report of the Secretary of War, 1858, 82.
90. Young to Eldredge, 20 October 1858, Brigham Young Papers, USHS.
91. LDS Journal History, 21 June 1858.
92. Wooster, "Military Strategy in the Southwest, 1848–1860," 12.
93. "Utah," *New York Daily Tribune*, 16 December 1858; Langley, *To Utah with the Dragoons*, 123–32.
94. Canby to Jones, 23 September 1858, in U.S. Senate, Report of the Secretary of War, 2 March 1859, 16.
95. William Gwinn, Statement, 19 January 1858, House Select Committee on the Pacific Railroad, a proposed bill to aid the construction of the, HR35A-D23.14, 35th Congress, RG233; "Construction of a Railroad and Telegraphic Communication from the Atlantic to the Pacific Ocean," 24 July 1856, 34th Cong., House Select Committee on the Pacific Railroad papers, HR 34A—D24.4, RG 233.
96. Ackley, "Trip across the Plains in 1858," 24.
97. Floyd, 16 December 1857, in U.S. House of Representatives, Report of the Secretary of War, 1857, 13.
98. Johnston to McDowell, 20 January 1858, in U.S. House of Representatives, Report of the Secretary of War, 1858, 44.
99. Van Vliet to Captain Pleasanton, 16 September 1857, 26 in U.S. House of Representatives, Report of the Secretary of War, 1857.
100. Mormons were hired to work on the road. See Smart, *Mormon Midwife*, 259.
101. Porter to Simpson, 24 August 1858, in U.S. House of Representatives, Report of the Secretary of War, 1858, 145.
102. Simpson, Report and Map of Wagon Road Routes in Utah Territory in U.S. Senate, Report of the Secretary of War, 2 March 1859, 21.
103. Porter, "On Explorations Southwest from the Headquarters of the Department of Utah," in U.S. Senate, Report of the Secretary of War, 2 March 1859, 21.
104. Newsclippings, undated, William Lee Papers, CHL. One clipping in this collection has the title, "Arrival of Capt. Simpson and Party in Carson Valley—A new and short Wagon Road to Camp Floyd and Great Salt Lake City," but does not reveal a date or publisher. William Lee served as the "Assistant to Observer," on the road development mission. More data on Lee's observations during the exploration are found in the Lee-Palfrey Family Papers, Library of Congress. Captain James H. Simpson's journal and report from his explorations based out of Camp Floyd are likewise important for greater details and are found in US Army, Corps of Engineers Report, 1858–61, Library of Congress.
105. Goetzmann, *Exploration and Empire*, 231, 293.

106. Scott to Floyd, 30 October 1858, United States Indian Affairs Department, Correspondence, USHS.
107. Cumming, Governor's Message to the Legislative Assembly of the Territory of Utah, 13 December 1858, Alfred Cumming Papers.
108. Tate, *Frontier Army*, 85.
109. Elizabeth Cumming to Alfred Cumming, 21 April 1858, Alfred Cumming Papers.
110. Elizabeth Cumming to Anne, 9 July 1858, Alfred Cumming Papers.
111. Langley, *To Utah with the Dragoons*, 127.
112. Young to Kane, 14 January 1859, Kane Collection, box 1, Stanford University Library; Lewis Barney, Journal, 84, BYU.
113. Roland, *Albert Sidney Johnston*, 222.
114. "More Trouble with the Mormons," *Washington Union*, 8 February 1859.
115. The Mormon perpetrators of the Mountain Meadows Massacre spared most of the children in the overland party and brought them into Mormon households. "Charge," *Valley Tan*, 15 March 1859; for more on the warrants and Cradlebaugh's efforts to arrest Mormons involved in the Mountain Meadows Massacre, see Dotson to Cradlebaugh, 3 June 1859, in Bigler and Bagley, *Innocent Blood*, 223–24.
116. U.S. Senate, "Federal Aid," 97.
117. Love, Diary, 31 March 1859, BYU.
118. U.S. Senate, "Federal Aid," 97.
119. Cumming, Proclamation by the Governor of Utah Territory, 27 March 1859, Alfred Cumming Papers.
120. Floyd to Johnston, 6 May 1859, in U.S. Senate, "Federal Aid," 98.
121. Langley, *To Utah with the Dragoons*, 166.
122. Cradlebaugh to Buchanan, 3 June 1859, in Bigler and Bagley, *Innocent Blood*, 225.
123. Cumming to Cass, 2 February 1860, Alfred Cumming Papers.
124. Rachel Woolsey Lee, Diary, 17 July 1859, August, September, and October 1859, Huntington Library.
125. "Mormon Affairs: Address of Judge Cradlebaugh, of Utah, on the Condition of Public and Social Life in Utah," *New York Times*, 21 March 1860.
126. "Mormon Affairs: Address of Judge Cradlebaugh," *New York Times*, 21 March 1860.

7. TO 1862

1. Ball, "Liberty, Empire, and Civil War," 68.
2. U.S. House of Representatives, "Territory of Nevada."
3. Humphreys to Dole, 30 September 1861, in U.S. Department of the Interior, *Report of the Commissioner of Indian Affairs, 1861*, 140.

4. Humphreys to Mix, 12 November 1860, in U.S. Department of the Interior, *Report of the Commissioner of Indian Affairs, 1860*, 170.
5. Humphreys to Mix, 12 November 1860.
6. Humphreys to Dole, 30 September 1861, U.S. Department of the Interior, in *Report of the Commissioner of Indian Affairs, 1861*, 140.
7. Humphreys to Dole, 30 September 1861; Dole, in U.S. Department of the Interior, *Report of the Commissioner of Indian Affairs, 1861*, 21; Jackson, Rieske, and Christy, "Indian Farms and Reservations," 105.
8. Dole, in U.S. Department of the Interior, *Report of the Commissioner of Indian Affairs, 1861*, 21.
9. Ball, "Liberty, Empire, and Civil War," 68.
10. Dole, in U.S. Department of the Interior, *Report of the Commissioner of Indian Affairs, 1861*, 21.
11. Burton, *History of Uintah County*, 24; Conetah, *History of Northern Ute*, 78–79.
12. Doty to Dole, 12 September 1862, in U.S. Department of the Interior, *Report of the Commissioner of Indian Affairs, 1862*, 198–99, 202.
13. Dole, in U.S. Department of the Interior, *Report of the Commissioner of Indian Affairs, 1862*, 32.
14. Humphreys, Report, 1 October 1861, in U.S. Department of the Interior, *Report of the Commissioner of Indian Affairs, 1861*, 135–36; Burton, *History of Uintah County*, 24–25; Treaty with the Utah, Yampah Ute, Pah-Vant, Sanpete Ute, Tm-p-nogs, and Cum-nm-Bah Bands of the Utah Indians, 8 June 1865.
15. Peterson, *Utah's Black Hawk War*, 2–5.
16. In a series of treaties with the Shoshone, Bannock, and Goshute in 1863 and with the Ute and Southern Paiute in 1865, the federal government moved to extinguish Indian land claims in Utah and to confine all Indians on reservations, particularly on the Uintah Reservation. Burton, *History of Uintah County*, 84; U.S. Department of the Interior, *Report of the Commissioner of Indian Affairs, 1865*, 149–52, 168–90.
17. Doty to Dole, 12 September 1862, in U.S. Department of the Interior, *Report of the Commissioner of Indian Affairs, 1862*, 198–99.
18. Buchanan, "Fourth Annual Message," 3 December 1860.
19. Moorman, *Camp Floyd and the Mormons*, 271.
20. Carruth, Autobiography and Journal, CHL.
21. Bagley, "Terror to Evil-Doers," 314–33.
22. This became abundantly clear following the withdrawal of the soldiers from Camp Floyd and was reiterated again when federal officials discussed removing Connor's troops from Utah during the Civil War. See Governor Stephen S. Harding to General George Wright, 16 February 1863, in Lamont, Davis, Perry, and Kirkley, *War of Rebellion*, 314–15.

23. Patrick Connor to Richard C. Drum, 20 December 1862, in Lamont, Davis, Perry, and Kirkley, *War of Rebellion*, 256–57; James Duane Doty to General Wright, 9 August 1863, Lamont, Davis, Perry, and Kirkley, *War of Rebellion*, 583–84.
24. James Duane Doty to General Wright, 9 August 1863, in Lamont, Davis, Perry, and Kirkley, *War of Rebellion*, 583–84; Bagley, "Terror to Evil-Doers," 325; Long, *Saints and the Union*, 26, 36, 168, and 271.
25. Richard Drum to Patrick Connor, 16 July 1864, in Lamont, Davis, Perry, and Kirkley, *War of Rebellion*, 909–10.
26. Childers, *Failure of Popular Sovereignty*, 274.
27. Douglas, "Dividing Line," 519.
28. Childers, *Failure of Popular Sovereignty*, 263–65; Etcheson, *Bleeding Kansas*, 160–74.
29. Douglas, "Dividing Line," 526.
30. Douglas, "Dividing Line," 528.
31. Curtis, *Just Supremacy of Congress*, 3 and 5.
32. Black, *Observations on Senator Douglas's Views*, 10, 11, and 14–15.
33. Bullough, "Polygamy," 119–23.
34. Stephen Douglas, Proposed Law in Regards to Marriage in the Territories, undated, in SDP, box 44; see also Hartog, *Man and Wife in America*, 17.
35. Morrill, "Utah Territory and Its Laws—Polygamy and Its License," 285.
36. MacKinnon, *At Sword's Point*, 86. See the following contemporary newspaper articles: "The Mormon Problem Must Be Solved," *San Francisco Daily Evening Bulletin*, 18 June 1857; "The Mormon Question," *New York Herald*, 3 May 1857; "Douglas on Utah: The Two Faces of the Little Giant," *Chicago Daily Tribune*, 25 June 1857; "Utah and Popular Sovereignty," *National Era*, 30 April 1857; "The Mormons," *Harper's Weekly*, 25 April 1857; "The Question of the Mormons," *Harper's Weekly*, 4 July 1857.
37. Kerstetter, *God's Country, Uncle Sam's Land*, 74–75.
38. U.S. House of Representatives, "Polygamy."
39. U.S. House of Representatives, "Polygamy."
40. App. to Cong. Globe, 36th Cong., 1st Sess. 197 (1860).
41. Cong. Globe, 36th Cong., 1st Sess. 1410 (1860).
42. S. Foster, "Republican Land Policy," 5.
43. S. Foster, "Republican Land Policy," 5.
44. An Act to Secure Freedom to All Persons with the Territories of the United States, 19 June 1862, in *Statutes at Large, Treaties, and Proclamations of the United States of America*, vol. 12 (Boston, 1863), 432.
45. Kerstetter, *God's Country, Uncle Sam's Land*, 75.
46. Gordon, *Mormon Question*, 130.
47. "Admission of Utah as a State," *Deseret News*, 21 December 1859.

48. Acts, Resolutions and Memorials Passed by the Utah Legislative Assembly at the Eighth Annual Session, Chapter 38, "Memorial to Congress, for the Election of Governor, Judges, Secretary and other Territorial Officers, by the People," M12.
49. U.S. House of Representatives, Constitution of the State of Deseret, 1862, 1.
50. U.S. House of Representatives, Constitution of the State of Deseret, 1862, 2.
51. U.S. House of Representatives, Constitution of the State of Deseret, 1862, 3.
52. Flake, *Politics of American Religious Identity*, 19–20.
53. Daynes, *More Wives than One*, 47.
54. Daynes, *More Wives than One*, 47–48.
55. Quoted in Daynes, *More Wives than One*, 48.
56. An Act to Amend Section Fifty-three Hundred and Fifty-two of the Revised Statutes of the United States, in Reference to Bigamy, and for Other Purposes, *U.S. Statutes at Large*, 12, sec. 1–5, 30–31.
57. Flake, *Politics of American Religious Identity*, 28.
58. See Gordon, *Mormon Question*, 204–20.

CONCLUSION

1. Wooster, *American Military Frontiers*, xii–xv.
2. Cumming, Governor's Message to the Legislative Assembly of the Territory of Utah, 13 December 1858, Alfred Cumming Papers.

BIBLIOGRAPHY

ARCHIVES AND MANUSCRIPT MATERIALS
Brigham Young University, L. Tom Perry Special Collections, Provo UT (BYU)
    John Bagley, Record Book
    Lewis Barney, Journal
    Seth Millington Blair, Diary and Autobiography
    Matilda Dudley, Relief Society Minutes
    Luke William Gallup, Diary
    Thomas L. Kane Papers
    Andrew Love, Diary
California State Library, Sacramento CA (CSL)
    Henry Sterling Bloom Gold Rush Letters, MS 2315
    Mason Family, Letters, MS 1878
    Henry Atkinson Stine, Letters and Journal, BS 85
    John B. Weller, Governor's Inaugural Address
Church History Library, The Church of Jesus Christ of Latter-day Saints, Salt Lake City UT (CHL)
    George W. Bean, Journal, MS 7805
    William Carruth, Autobiography and Journal, MS 8139
    Margaret Gay Judd Clawson, Reminiscence, MS 3712
    Deseret (State) Papers, MS 2918
    Jonathan Oldham Duke, Reminiscences and Diary, MS 136
    East Bountiful Ward, Davis Stake, Relief Society Minutes, LR 2399 / 14
    Jacob Hamblin Papers, MS 1951
    Dimick B. Huntington, Journal, MS 1419
    ———. *Vocabulary of the Utah and Sho-Sho-Ne or Snake Dialects*, 1st. ed. (1853)
    Journal History of the Church of Jesus Christ of Latter-day Saints, CR 100 137
    Albert Sidney Johnston, Letters, MS 22667

William Lee Papers, MS 21162
Sylvester Mowry Letters, MS 23526
Nauvoo Legion Records, MS 3430 (NLR)
Nauvoo Relief Society, Minute Book
William W. Phelps Collection of Missouri Documents, MS 657 (WWP)
Parley P. Pratt, "The Angel of the Prairies, or, A Dream of the Future," MS 7506
Sixteenth Ward Relief Society, Journal, MS 12481
George A. Smith, Journal, MS 17190
Joseph Smith Collection, MS 155 (JSC)
Joseph Smith, "General Smith's Views on the Powers and Policy of the Government of the United States." Nauvoo IL: John Taylor, 1844, M243.3 S653g 1844
State of Deseret, Constitution, 1850
Cynthia Jane Park Stowell, Biographical Sketch, MS 4054
Pleasant Green Taylor, Family Record, MS 13357
Twelfth Ward Relief Society, Minutes, in Amanda Barnes Smith, Notebook, MS 2005
Brigham Young Collection, CR 1234 / 1 (BYC)
Brigham Young letter to George Q. Cannon, 3 November 1859, MS 7261
Duke University, Rare Book, Manuscript, and Special Collections Library, Durham NC
  Alfred Cumming Papers
Florida Department of State, Division of Library and Information Services, Tallahassee FL
  Secretary of State, Territorial and Early Statehood Records, 1821–1878, Series 2153, box 4.
Historical Society of Pennsylvania, Philadelphia
  James Buchanan Papers (JBP)
Huntington Library, San Marino CA
  Rachel Woolsey Lee, Diary, in John Doyle Lee Collection
Kansas Historical Society, Topeka KS (KSHS)
  William Clark Papers and Records of the United States Superintendency of Indian Affairs
  James W. Denver Collection
  Halderman Collection
  Lambert Bowman Wolf, Diary
Library of Congress, Washington DC
  Lee-Palfrey Family Papers, MMC 3329
  Justin S. Morrill Papers, MSS 33555
  Fitz-John Porter Papers, MSS 36590

The Congressional Globe: Containing the Debates and Proceedings of Congress
U.S. Army, Corps of Engineers Report, 1858–61, MMC-2261
Massachusetts Historical Society, Boston
   Theodore Parker Papers, reel 2 (TPP)
National Archives and Records Administration, College Park, MD
   United States, Department of State, Territorial Papers, Utah Series National Archives, Washington DC, M12, State Department Territorial Papers, Vol. 1, April 30, 1853–December 24, 1859 (M12)
   United States, Department of the Interior, Records of the Pacific Wagon Road Office, RG 48
   United States, General Records of the Department of State, Appointment Records, Resignations and Declinations, Letters of Resignation and Declination of Federal Office, RG 59 (RG59), M12
   United States, Office of Attorney General, Department of Justice, Records Relating to the Appointment of Federal Judges, Attorneys, and Marshals for the Territory and State of Utah, 1853–1901, RG 60, M680
   United States, Records of the Office of the Secretary of War Letters Sent, Letters Sent to the President, 1800–1863, Vol. 6, December 26, 1855–July 1, 1861, M127, reel 6
   United States, War Department, Office of the Chief of Engineers, Fortifications Map Files, RG 77
National Archives and Records Administration, Washington DC
   Letters Received, Utah Superintendency, roll 898, m234, RG 75
   United States, Department of the Interior, Records of the Office of Indian Affairs, Letters Sent, RG 75, m21, reel 58 (M21)
   United States, Department of the Interior, Records of the Utah Superintendency of Indian Affairs, 1853–1870, M834
   United States House of Representatives, Territorial Papers and Committee Records, RG 233 (TRG 233)
   United States Senate, Committee on Public Lands Records, RG 46 (CPL)
   United States Senate, Committee Records, RG 46 (USSC)
   United States War Department, Department of Utah, Letters sent July 16, 1857–July 15, 1861 and 5035 General and Special Orders and Circulars issued, RG 393
   United States, War Department, Topographical Bureau, Letters Issued, 13 October 1848–14 September 1849
Nebraska State Historical Society, Lincoln (NSHS)
   Augustus Hall and John Fitch Kinney Collection, MS 619
   John Comly Past, Papers and Journal, MS 487
Stanford University Library, Department of Special Collections, Stanford CA (SUL)
   Thomas L. Kane Papers, M0058

BIBLIOGRAPHY   345

University of Chicago, Special Collections Research Center
    Stephen A. Douglas Papers (SDP)
University of Michigan, William L. Clements Library, Ann Arbor
    Lewis Cass Papers
    Native American Collection
University of Utah, J. Willard Marriott Library Special Collections, Salt Lake City (MLSC)
    Camp Floyd Letters, MS 191
    Richard D. Poll Papers, MS 0674
    Oliver Lee Robinson, Journal, MS 0024
Utah State Historical Society, Salt Lake City (USHS)
    Richard Thomas Ackley, "A Trip across the Plains in 1858," MSS A 11
    A. J. Allen, Diary, MSS A 33
    Lieutenant E. G. Beckwith, *Report of Exploration of a Route for the Pacific Railroad, Near the 38th and 39th Parallels of Latitude, from the Mouth of the Kansas to Sevier River, in the Great Basin*, 917.8 B38r
    Biography of Charles Ramsden Bailey from his journal, MSS A 82
    Camp Floyd at Fairfield, Utah, July 8, 1858–July 27, 1861, PAM 3093
    Pricilla Merriman Evans, Autobiography, MSS A 2362
    Jacob Forney Letters, MSS A 420
    John Ginn, Diary
    G. E. Gould, Letters from Camp Floyd, MSS A 579
    Charles Emerson Griffin, Autobiography, MSS A 1565
    Nicholas Harmon Groesbeck, Autobiography, MSS A 556
    William Wallace Hammond, Autobiographical Sketch, MSS A 574
    Daniel W. Jones, Autobiography, MSS A 675
    Journal of William Luck, 1824–1868, MSS A 721
    Letter from the Secretary of War, Transmitting a Report Relative to Captain Gunnison's Survey, &c., 33d Cong., 1st Sess., House of Representatives, Exec. Doc. No. 18, PAM 22272
    Lafayette McLaws, Letter Excerpts, MSS A 711
    John Wolcott Phelps, Papers, MSS B 120
    Records of the War Department, Office of the Adjutant General, Misc. Collection, Mowry, MSS A 15 (MMCU)
    Squire Thornton, Diary, MSS A 1260
    United States Indian Affairs Department, Correspondence, 1855–1859, MSS A 458
    Utah Territorial Executive Papers, 1850–1896, Series 241
    Brigham Young Papers, MSS B 93
Yale University, Beinecke Library, New Haven CT
    LaRhett L. Livingston, Letters

PUBLISHED WORKS

Acts, Resolutions and Memorials, Passed at the Several Annual Sessions of the Legislative Assembly of the Territory of Utah. Salt Lake City: Joseph Cain, Public Printer, 1855.

Alexander, Thomas G. "Carpetbaggers, Reprobates, and Liars: Federal Judges and the Utah War (1857–1858)." *The Historian* (May 2008): 215–19.

———. *Utah, The Right Place: The Official Centennial History.* Salt Lake City: Gibbs Smith, 1995.

Allen, James B. "Joseph Smith vs. John C. Calhoun: The States' Rights Dilemma and Early Mormon History." In *Joseph Smith Jr.: Reappraisals after Two Centuries*, edited by Reid L. Neilson and Terryl L. Givens, 73–90. New York: Oxford University Press, 2009.

Alley, John R., Jr. "Prelude to Dispossession: The Fur Trade's Significance for the Northern Utes and Southern Paiutes." *Utah Historical Quarterly* 50, no. 2 (Spring 1982): 104–23.

American State Papers, Indian Affairs. Washington DC: Gales and Seaton, 1834.

An Act to Provide for the Organization of a Regiment of Mounted Volunteers for the Defence of the Frontier of Texas, and to Authorize the President to Call into the Service of the United States Two Additional Regiments of Volunteers, chap. 13, 35th Cong., 1st Sess., 7 April 1858. In *Statutes at Large*, edited by George P. Sanger, 262–63. Boston: Little, Brown, 1858.

Anderson, Benedict. *Imagined Communities: Reflections on the Origin and Spread of Nationalism.* London: Verso, 1983.

Arrington, Leonard J. *Brigham Young: American Moses.* Urbana: University of Illinois Press, 1986.

———. *Great Basin Kingdom: An Economic History of the Latter-Day Saints, 1830–1900.* Repr., Salt Lake City: University of Utah, 1993.

Arrington, Leonard J., and Davis Bitton. *The Mormon Experience: A History of the Latter-day Saints.* New York: Alfred A. Knopf, 1979.

Ashurst-McGee, Mark. "Zion Rising: Joseph Smith's Early Social and Political Thought." PhD diss., Arizona State University, 2008.

Auchampaugh, Philip Gerald. *James Buchanan and His Cabinet on the Eve of Secession.* Boston: J. S. Canner, 1965.

———. *Robert Tyler: Southern Rights Champion, 1847–1866: A Documentary Study Chiefly of Antebellum Politics.* Duluth MN: Himan Stein, Printer, 1934.

Bagley, Will. *Blood of the Prophets: Brigham Young and the Massacre at Mountain Meadows.* Norman: University of Oklahoma Press, 2002.

———. "A Terror to Evil-Doers: Camp Douglas, Abraham Lincoln, and Utah's Civil War." *Utah Historical Quarterly* 80, no. 4 (Fall 2012): 314–33.

Bain, David Haward. *Empire Express: Building the First Transcontinental Railroad.* New York: Viking, 1999.

Ball, Durwood. *Army Regulars on the Western Frontier, 1848–1861.* Norman: University of Oklahoma Press, 2001.

———. "Liberty, Empire, and Civil War in the American West." In *Empire and Liberty: The Civil War and the West,* edited by Virginia Scharff, 66–86. Oakland: University of California Press, 2015.

Bataille, Gretchen M., ed. *Native American Representations: First Encounters, Distorted Images, and Literary Appropriations.* Lincoln: University of Nebraska Press, 2001.

Bauer, K. Jack. *The Mexican War, 1846–1848.* Introduction to the Bison Book Edition by Robert W. Johannsen. Lincoln: University of Nebraska Press, 1992.

Baugh, Alexander L. "A Call to Arms: The 1838 Mormon Defense of Northern Missouri." PhD diss., Brigham Young University, 2000.

Beecher, Maureen Ursenbach, and Lavina Fielding Anderson, eds. *Sisters in Spirit: Mormon Women in Historical and Cultural Perspective.* Urbana: University of Illinois Press, 1987.

Bennett, Richard E. *Mormons at the Missouri: Winter Quarters, 1846–1852.* Norman: University of Oklahoma Press, 2004.

Bennion, Lowell C. "Plural Marriage, 1841–1904." In *Mapping Mormonism: An Atlas of Latter-day Saint History,* edited by Brandon S. Plewe, 122–25. Provo UT: Brigham Young University Press, 2013.

Berkhofer, Robert F., Jr. "The Northwest Ordinance and the Principle of Territorial Evolution." In *The American Territorial System,* edited by John Porter Bloom, 45–55. Athens: Ohio University Press, 1973.

———. *The White Man's Indian: Images of the American Indian from Columbus to the Present.* New York: Alfred A. Knopf, 1978.

Berman, Jacob Rama. *American Arabesque: Arabs, Islam, and the 19th-Century Imaginary.* New York: New York University Press, 2012.

Bhabha, Homi K. *The Location of Culture.* London: Routledge, Classics Edition, 2004.

Biber, Eric. "The Price of Admission: Causes, Effects, and Patterns of Conditions Imposed on States Entering the Union." *American Journal of Legal History* 46, no. 2 (April 2004): 119–208.

Bigler, David L. "The Aiken Party Executions and the Utah War, 1857–1858." *Western Historical Quarterly* 38, no. 4 (Winter 2007): 457–76.

———. *Forgotten Kingdom: The Mormon Theocracy in the American West, 1847–1896.* Logan: Utah State University Press, 1998.

———. *Fort Limhi: The Mormon Adventure in Oregon Territory, 1855–1858.* Spokane WA: Arthur H. Clark, 2003.

———. "Garland Hurt, the American Friend of the Utahs." *Utah Historical Quarterly* 62, no. 2 (Spring 1994): 149–70.

———. "A Lion in the Path: Genesis of the Utah War, 1857–1858." *Utah Historical Quarterly* 76, no. 1 (Winter 2008): 4–21.
Bigler, David L., and Will Bagley, eds. *Innocent Blood: Essential Narratives of the Mountain Meadows Massacre*. Norman: University of Oklahoma Press / Arthur H. Clark, 2008.
———. *The Mormon Rebellion: America's First Civil War*. Norman: University of Oklahoma Press, 2011.
Binder, Frederick M. *James Buchanan and the American Empire*. Selinsgrove PA: Susquehanna University Press, 1995.
Birkner, Michael J., ed. *James Buchanan and the Political Crisis of the 1850s*. Selinsgrove PA: Susquehanna University Press, 1996.
Bitton, Davis, and Gary L. Bunker. "Double Jeopardy: Visual Images of Mormon Women to 1914." *Utah Historical Quarterly* 46, no. 2 (Spring 1978): 184–202.
Black, Jeremiah S. *Observations on Senator Douglas's Views of Popular Sovereignty, as Expressed in Harper's Magazine, for September, 1859*. Washington DC: Thomas McGill, Printer, 1859.
Blackhawk, Ned. *Violence over the Land: Indians and Empires in the Early American West*. Cambridge MA: Harvard University Press, 2006.
Bowers, Michael W. *The Sagebrush State: Nevada's History, Government, and Politics*, 3rd ed. Reno: University of Nevada Press, 2006.
Boyd, Julian P., Charles T. Cullen, John Catanzariti, Barbara B. Oberg, et al., eds. *The Papers of Thomas Jefferson*. Vol. 4. Princeton NJ: Princeton University Press, 1950.
Bringhurst, Newell G. *Brigham Young and the Expanding American Frontier*. Boston: Little, Brown, 1986.
Brocchus, Perry E. *Letter of Judge Brocchus, of Alabama, to the Public, upon the Difficulties in the Territory of Utah*. Washington DC: Henry Polkinhorn, 1859.
Brooks, Juanita. "Indian Relations on the Mormon Frontier." *Utah Historical Quarterly* 12, nos. 1–2 (January–April 1944): 1–48.
———. *Journal of the Southern Indian Mission: Diary of Thomas D. Brown*. Logan: Utah State University Press, Western Text Society Number 4, 1972.
———. *The Mountain Meadows Massacre*. Norman: University of Oklahoma Press, 1950.
———, ed. *On the Mormon Frontier: The Diary of Hosea Stout*. Vol. 2, 1848–1861. Salt Lake City: University of Utah Press, 1964.
Brown, Kathleen M. *Good Wives, Nasty Wenches, and Anxious Patriarchs*. Chapel Hill: University of North Carolina Press, 1996.
Buchanan, James. "First Annual Message from the President of the United States to the Two Houses of Congress at the Commencement of the First Session of the Thirty-Fifth Congress." Washington DC: Cornelius Wendell, 1857.

---. "Fourth Annual Message to Congress on the State of the Union." December 3, 1860. Online by Gerhard Peters and John T. Woolley, *The American Presidency Project*. http://www.presidency.ucsb.edu/ws/?pid=29501.

---. *Mr. Buchanan's Administration on the Eve of the Rebellion*. New York: D. Appleton, 1866.

---. "Second Annual Message to Congress on the State of the Union." December 6, 1858. Online by Gerhard Peters and John T. Woolley, *The American Presidency Project*. http://www.presidency.ucsb.edu/ws/?pid=29499.

Buckley, Jay H. *William Clark: Indian Diplomat*. Norman: University of Oklahoma Press, 2008.

Bullough, Vern L. "Polygamy: An Issue in the Election of 1860?" *Utah Historical Quarterly* 29, no. 3 (April 1961): 119–26.

Bunker, Gary L., and Davis Bitton. "Illustrated Periodical Images of Mormons, 1850–1860." *Dialogue* 10, no. 3 (Spring 1977): 82–94.

---. *The Mormon Graphic Image, 1834–1914: Cartoons Caricatures, and Illustrations*. Salt Lake City: University of Utah Press, 1983.

Burton, Doris Karren. *A History of Uintah County: Scratching the Surface*. Salt Lake City: Utah State Historical Society and Uintah County Commission, 1996.

Burton, Sir Richard. *The Look of the West, 1860: Across the Plains to California*. Foreword by Robert G. Athearn. Lincoln: University of Nebraska Press / Bison Books, 1963.

Bushman, Richard L. *Believing History: Latter-day Saint Essays*, Reid L. Neilson and Jed Woodworth, eds. New York: Columbia University Press, 2004.

---. "The Book of Mormon and the American Revolution." *BYU Studies* 17 (Autumn 1976): 3–20.

---. *Joseph Smith: Rough Stone Rolling*. New York: Vintage Books Edition, 2007.

Campbell, Eugene E. *Establishing Zion: The Mormon Church in the American West, 1847–1869*. Salt Lake City: Signature Books, 1988.

Cannon, M. Hamlin. "Winfield Scott and the Utah Expedition." *Military Affairs* 5, no. 3 (Autumn 1941): 208–11.

Carter, Sarah. *The Importance of Being Monogamous: Marriage and Nation Building in Western Canada to 1915*. Edmonton: University of Alberta Press, 2008.

Carvalho, Solomon Nunes. *Incidents of Travel and Adventure in the Far West with Colonel Fremont's Last Expedition: Across the Rocky Mountains: Including Three Months' Residence in Utah, and a Perilous Trip across the Great American Desert to the Pacific*. Introduction by Ava F. Kahn. Lincoln: University of Nebraska Press, 2004.

Casey, Michael W., and Douglas A. Foster, eds. *The Stone-Campbell Movement: An International Religious Tradition*. Knoxville: University of Tennessee Press, 2002.

Césaire, Aimé. *Discourse on Colonialism*. New York: Monthly Review Press, 2000.

Childers, Christopher. *The Failure of Popular Sovereignty: Slavery, Manifest Destiny, and the Radicalization of Southern Politics*. Lawrence: University Press of Kansas, 2012.

———. "Interpreting Popular Sovereignty: A Historiographical Essay." *Civil War History* 57, no. 1 (March 2011): 48–70.

Christy, Howard A. "Open Hand and Mailed Fist: Mormon-Indian Relations in Utah, 1847–1852." *Utah Historical Quarterly* 46, no. 3 (Summer 1978): 215–35.

———. "The Walker War: Defense and Conciliation as Strategy." *Utah Historical Quarterly* 47, no. 4 (Fall 1979): 395–420.

Clayton, John M. "Speech of John M. Clayton, of Delaware, on the Bill to Organize the Territorial Governments of Nebraska and Kansas, 1–2 March 1854." Washington DC: Congressional Globe Office, 1854.

Coates, Lawrence G. "Brigham Young and Mormon Indian Policies: The Formative Period 1836–1851." *BYU Studies* 18, no. 3 (1978): 428–52.

Compton, Todd M. *A Frontier Life: Jacob Hamblin, Explorer and Indian Missionary*. Salt Lake City: University of Utah Press, 2013.

Conetah, Fred A. *A History of the Northern Ute People*. Edited by Kathryn L. MacKay and Floyd A. O'Neil. Salt Lake City UT: Uintah-Ouray Ute Tribe, Printed by the University of Utah Printing Service, 1982.

Conkin, Paul K. *Self-Evident Truths: Being a Discourse on the Origins and Development of the First Principles of American Government—Popular Sovereignty, Natural Rights, and Balance & Separation of Powers*. Bloomington: Indiana University Press, 1974.

Cooley, Everett L., ed. *Diary of Brigham Young, 1857*. Salt Lake City: University of Utah and Tanner Trust Fund, 1980.

Cornwall, Marie, Camela Courtright, and Laga Van Beek. "How Common the Principle? Women as Plural Wives in 1860." *Dialogue: A Journal of Mormon Thought* 26, no. 2 (Summer 1993): 139–53.

Cott, Nancy F. *Public Vows: A History of Marriage and the Nation*. Cambridge MA: Harvard University Press, 2000.

Coward, John M. *The Newspaper Indian: Native American Identity in the Press, 1820–90*. Urbana: University of Illinois Press, 1999.

Crawley, Peter L. "The Constitution of the State of Deseret." *BYU Studies* 29, no. 4 (Fall 1989): 7–22.

Cuch, Forrest S., ed. *A History of Utah's American Indians*. Salt Lake City: Utah Division of Indian Affairs and the Utah Division of State History, 2000.

Curtis, George Ticknor. *The Just Supremacy of Congress over the Territories: Intended as an Answer to the Hon. Stephen A. Douglas, on Popular Sovereignty*. Boston: A. Williams, 1859.

Davidson, Karen Lynn, Richard L. Jensen, and David J. Whittaker, eds. *The Joseph Smith Papers: Histories.* Vol. 2, *Assigned Histories, 1831–1847.* Salt Lake City: Church Historian's Press, 2012.

Daynes, Kathryn M. *More Wives than One: Transformation of the Mormon Marriage System, 1840–1910.* Urbana: University of Illinois Press, 2001.

———. "Mormon Polygamy: Belief and Practice in Nauvoo." In *Kingdom on the Mississippi Revisited: Nauvoo in Mormon History,* edited by Roger D. Launius and John E. Hallwas, 130–46. Urbana: University of Illinois Press, 1996.

DeLay, Brian. *War of a Thousand Deserts: Indian Raids and the U.S.-Mexican War.* New Haven CT: Yale University Press, 2008.

Derr, Jill Mulvay, Janath Russell Cannon, and Maureen Ursenbach Beecher. *Women of Covenant: The Story of Relief Society.* Salt Lake City UT: Deseret Book Company / Brigham Young University Press, 1992.

Derr, Jill Mulvay, and Karen Lynn Davidson, eds. *Eliza R. Snow: The Complete Poetry.* Provo: Brigham Young University Press / University of Utah Press, 2009.

Deverell, William, ed. *A Companion to the American West.* Malden MA: Blackwell, 2004.

DeVoto, Bernard. *The Course of Empire.* Boston: Houghton Mifflin, 1952.

———. *The Year of Decision: 1846.* Boston: Houghton Mifflin, 1942.

Dinger, John S. "Joseph Smith and the Development of Habeas Corpus in Nauvoo, 1841–1844." *Journal of Mormon History* 36, no. 3 (Summer 2010): 135–71.

Dirkmaat, Gerrit J. "Enemies Foreign and Domestic: U.S. Relations with the Mormons in the U.S. Empire in North America, 1844–1854." PhD diss., University of Colorado, 2010.

Dirkmaat, Gerrit J., Brent M. Rogers, Grant Underwood, Robert J. Woodford, and William G. Hartley, eds. *The Joseph Smith Papers: Documents.* Vol. 3, *February 1833–March 1834.* Salt Lake City: Church Historian's Press, 2014.

The Doctrine and Covenants of the Church of Jesus Christ of Latter-Day Saints, Containing Revelations Given to Joseph Smith, the Prophet, with Some Additions by His Successors in the Presidency of the Church. Salt Lake City: Church of Jesus Christ of Latter-Day Saints, 1990.

Douglas, Stephen A. "The Dividing Line between Federal and Local Authority: Popular Sovereignty in the Territories." *Harper's New Monthly Magazine* (September 1859): 519–37.

Drinnon, Richard. *Facing West: The Metaphysics of Indian-Hating and Empire-Building.* Minneapolis: University of Minnesota Press, 1980.

Durham, Michael S. "The Utah War." *MHQ: The Quarterly Journal of Military History* 10, no. 3 (1998): 28–37.

Dwyer, Robert Joseph. "The Gentile Comes to Utah: A Study in Religious and Social Conflict (1862–1890)." Washington DC: Catholic University of America Press, 1941. A dissertation at the Catholic University of America.

Eckman, Wayne Miles. "Brigham Young's Indian Superintendency (1851–58): A Significant Microcosm of the American Indian Experience." Master's thesis, Brigham Young University, 1989.

Eicher, John H., and David J. Eicher. *Civil War High Commands*. Stanford CA: Stanford University Press, 2001.

Embry, Jessie L. "Effects of Polygamy on Mormon Women." *Frontiers: A Journal of Women Studies* 7, no. 3 (1984): 56–61.

English, Thomas Dunn. *The Mormons, or, Life at Salt Lake City: A Drama in Three Acts*. New York: Samuel French, 1858.

Esplin, Ronald K. "The Emergence of Brigham Young and the Twelve to Mormon Leadership." PhD diss., Brigham Young University, 1981.

———. "'A Place Prepared': Joseph, Brigham, and the Quest for Promised Refuge in the West." In *Window of Faith: Latter-day Saint Perspectives on World History*, edited by Roy A. Prete, 71–97. Provo UT: Religious Studies Center, Brigham Young University, 2005.

Etcheson, Nicole. *Bleeding Kansas: Contested Liberty in the Civil War Era*. Lawrence: University Press of Kansas, 2004.

———. "The Goose Question: The Proslavery Party in Territorial Kansas and the 'Crisis in Law and Order.'" In *Bleeding Kansas, Bleeding Missouri: The Long Civil War on the Border*, edited by Jonathan Earle and Diane Mutti Burke, 47–64. Lawrence: University Press of Kansas, 2013.

———. "The Great Principle of Self-Government: Popular Sovereignty and Bleeding Kansas." *Kansas History: A Journal of the Central Plains* (Spring–Summer 2004): 14–29.

Etulain, Richard W. *Beyond the Missouri: The Story of the American West*. Albuquerque: University of New Mexico Press, 2006.

Fanon, Frantz. *The Wretched of the Earth*. New York: Grove Press, 2004.

Faragher, John Mack. *A Great and Noble Scheme: The Tragic Story of the Expulsion of the French Acadians from their American Homeland*. New York: W. W. Norton, 2005.

Farmer, Jared. *On Zion's Mount: Mormons, Indians, and the American Landscape*. Cambridge MA: Harvard University Press, 2008.

Faulkner, Charles J. "Speech of the Hon. C. J. Faulkner, of Virginia, in Favor of an Increase of the Army and in Opposition to the Employment of Volunteers in Utah, Delivered in the House of Representatives," 9 March 1858. Washington DC, 1858.

Ferris, Benjamin G. *Utah and the Mormons: The History, Government, Doctrines, Customs, and Prospects of the Latter-day Saints, from Personal Observations during a Six Months' Residence at Great Salt Lake City*. New York, 1854.

Fielding, Robert Kent. *The Unsolicited Chronicler: An Account of the Gunnison Massacre, Its Causes and Consequences*. Brookline MA: Paradigm Publications, 1993.

Flake, Kathleen. *The Politics of American Religious Identity: The Seating of Senator Reed Smoot, Mormon Apostle.* Chapel Hill: University of North Carolina Press, 2004.

Flanders, Robert Bruce. *Nauvoo: Kingdom on the Mississippi.* Urbana: University of Illinois Press, 1965.

Fliegelman, Jay. *Prodigals and Pilgrims: The American Revolution against Patriarchal Authority, 1750–1800.* New York: Cambridge University Press, 1982.

Fluhman, J. Spencer. *"A Peculiar People": Anti-Mormonism and the Making of Religion in Nineteenth-Century America.* Chapel Hill: University of North Carolina Press, 2012.

Ford, Thomas. *A History of Illinois from Its Commencement as a State in 1818 to 1847.* Chicago: S. C. Griggs, 1854.

Foster, Lawrence. *Women, Family, and Utopia: Communal Experiments of the Shakers, the Oneida Community, and the Mormons.* Syracuse NY: Syracuse University Press, 1991.

Foster, Stephen C. "Republican Land Policy—Homes for the Million." Washington DC: Buell & Blanchard, Printers, 1860.

Frazer, Robert W. *Forts of the West: Military Forts and Presidios and Posts Commonly Called Forts West of the Mississippi River to 1898.* Norman: University of Oklahoma Press, 1965.

Freeman, Joanne B. *Affairs of Honor: National Politics in the New Republic.* New Haven CT: Yale University Press, 2001.

Fremont, John C. *Report of an Exploring Expedition to the Rocky Mountains in the Year 1842 and to Oregon & North California in the Years 1843–44.* Washington DC: Gales and Seaton, 1845.

Friedman, Lawrence M. *Crime and Punishment in American History.* New York: Basic Books, 1993.

Fritz, Christian G. *American Sovereigns: The People and America's Constitutional Tradition Before the Civil War.* New York: Cambridge University Press, 2009.

Furniss, Norman F. *The Mormon Conflict, 1850–1859.* New Haven CT: Yale University Press, 1960.

Garrison, Tim Alan. *The Legal Ideology of Removal: The Southern Judiciary and the Sovereignty of Native American Nations.* Athens: University of Georgia Press, 2009.

Gates, Susa Young. *John Stevens' Courtship. A Story of the Echo Canyon War.* Salt Lake City: Deseret News, 1909.

———. "Relief Society Beginnings in Utah." *The Relief Society Magazine* (April 1922): 185.

Gibbons, Francis M. *John Taylor: Mormon Philosopher, Prophet of God.* Salt Lake City: Deseret Book, 1985.

Gienapp, William E. "The Crisis of American Democracy: The Political System and the Coming of the Civil War." In *Why the Civil War Came*, edited by Gabor S. Boritt, 79–124. New York: Oxford University Press, 1996.

———. "'No Bed of Roses': James Buchanan, Abraham Lincoln, and Presidential Leadership in the Civil War Era." In *James Buchanan and the Political Crisis of the 1850s*, edited by Michael J. Birkner. Selinsgrove PA: Susquehanna University Press, 1996.

Gilje, Paul A. *Rioting in America*. Bloomington: Indiana University Press, 1996.

Givens, Terryl L. *The Viper on the Hearth: Mormons, Myths, and the Construction of Heresy*. New York: Oxford University Press, 1997.

Givens, Terryl L., and Matthew J. Grow. *Parley P. Pratt: The Apostle Paul of Mormonism*. New York: Oxford University Press, 2011.

Godfrey, Audrey M. "Housewives, Hussies, and Heroines, or the Women of Johnston's Army." *Utah Historical Quarterly* 54, no. 2 (Spring 1986): 157–78.

Godfrey, Matthew C. "'Seeking after Monarchal Power and Authority': Joseph Smith and Leadership in the Church of Christ, 1831–1832." *Mormon Historical Studies* 13, nos. 1–2 (Spring–Fall 2012): 15–37.

Godfrey, Matthew C., Brenden W. Rensink, et al., eds. *The Joseph Smith Papers: Documents*. Vol. 4, *April 1834–September 1835*. Salt Lake City: Church Historian's Press, 2016.

Goetzmann, William H. *Army Exploration in the American West, 1803–1863*. Lincoln: University of Nebraska Press, 1979.

———. *Exploration and Empire: The Explorer and the Scientist in the Winning of the American West*. New York: Alfred A. Knopf, 1967.

Gordon, Sarah Barringer. *The Mormon Question: Polygamy and Constitutional Conflict in Nineteenth-Century America*. Chapel Hill: University of North Carolina Press, 2002.

Gould, Eliga H. *Among the Powers of the Earth: The American Revolution and the Making of a New World Empire*. Cambridge MA: Harvard University Press, 2012.

Gove, Jesse A. *The Utah Expedition, 1857–1858; Letters of Capt. Jesse A. Gove, 10th Inf., U. S. A . . . . to Mrs. Gove, and Special Correspondence of the New York Herald*. Concord: New Hampshire Historical Society, 1928.

Graebner, Norman A. *Empire on the Pacific: A Study in American Continental Expansion*. Santa Barbara CA: ABC-Clio, 1983.

Grandin, Greg. "The Liberal Traditions in the Americas: Rights, Sovereignty, and the Origins of Liberal Multilateralism." *American Historical Review* 117, no. 1 (February 2012): 68–91.

Greeley, Horace, with an introduction by Jo Ann Manfra. *An Overland Journey from New York to San Francisco in the Summer of 1859*. Lincoln: University of Nebraska Press, 1999.

Green, Harvey. *Fit for America: Health, Fitness, Sport and American Society.* New York: Pantheon Books, 1986.

Greenberg, Amy S. *Manifest Manhood and the Antebellum American Empire.* New York: Cambridge University Press, 2005.

Grimsted, David. *American Mobbing, 1828–1861: Toward Civil War.* New York: Oxford University Press, 1998.

———. "Rioting in Its Jacksonian Setting." *American Historical Review* 77, no. 2 (April 1972): 361–97.

Grow, Matthew J. *"Liberty to the Downtrodden": Thomas L. Kane, Romantic Reformer.* New Haven CT: Yale University Press, 2009.

———. "The Whore of Babylon and the Abomination of Abominations: Nineteenth-Century Catholic and Mormon Mutual Perceptions and Religious Identity." *Church History* 73, no. 1 (March 2004): 139–67.

Grow, Matthew J., Ronald K. Esplin, Mark Ashurst-McGee, Gerrit J. Dirkmaat, and Jeffrey D. Mahas, eds. *The Joseph Smith Papers: Administrative Records.* Vol. 1, *Council of Fifty Minutes, March 1844–January 1846.* Salt Lake City: Church Historian's Press, 2016.

Grua, David W. "Memoirs of the Persecuted: Persecution, Memory, and the West as a Mormon Refuge." Master's thesis, Brigham Young University, 2008.

Gunnison, John W. *The Mormons, or Latter-Day Saints, in the Valley of the Great Salt Lake: A History of Their Rise and Progress, Peculiar Doctrines, Present Condition, and Prospects, Derived from Personal Observation, during a Residence among Them.* Philadelphia: Lippincott & Grambo, 1852. reprint ed. Robert Kent Fielding. Brookline MA: Paradigm Publications, 1993.

Hafen, Leroy R., and Ann W. Hafen. *Mormon Resistance: A Documentary Account of the Utah Expedition, 1857–1858.* Lincoln: University of Nebraska Press, 2005, new printing.

Hagan, Albert. *Reports of Cases Determined in the Supreme Court of the Territory of Utah, from the Organization of the Territory Up to and Including the June Term, 1876.* Vol. 1. San Francisco: A. L. Bancroft, 1877.

Hansen, Klaus J. *Quest for Empire: The Political Kingdom of God and the Council of Fifty in Mormon History.* East Lansing: Michigan State University Press, 1967.

Hardy, B. Carmon. *Doing the Works of Abraham: Mormon Polygamy, Its Origin, Practice, and Demise.* Norman: University of Oklahoma Press / Arthur H. Clark, 2007.

———. *Solemn Covenant: The Mormon Polygamous Passage.* Urbana: University of Illinois Press, 1992.

Hardy, B. Carmon, and Dan Erickson. "'Regeneration—Now and Evermore!': Mormon Polygamy and the Physical Rehabilitation of Humankind." *Journal of the History of Sexuality* 10 (January 2001): 40–61.

Hartog, Hendrik. *Man and Wife in America: A History.* Cambridge MA: Harvard University Press, 2000.

Haslam, Larry. "Utah's Delegates to Congress, 1851–1896." Master's thesis, Utah State University, 1962.

Hatch, Nathan O. *The Democratization of American Christianity.* New Haven CT: Yale University Press, 1989.

Hawthornthwaite, Samuel. *Mr. Hawthornthwaite's Adventures among the Mormons.* Manchester UK: Samuel Hawthornthwaite, 1857.

Haynes, Sam W., and Christopher Morris, eds. *Manifest Destiny and Empire: American Antebellum Expansionism.* College Station: Texas A&M University Press, 1997.

Heaton, John W. "'No Place to Pitch Their Teepees': Shoshone Adaptation to Mormon Settlers in Cache Valley, 1855–70." In *Being Different: Stories of Utah's Minorities*, edited by Stanford J. Layton. Salt Lake City: Signature Books, 2001.

Hedges, Andrew H., Alex D. Smith, and Richard Lloyd Anderson, eds. *The Joseph Smith Papers: Journals.* Vol. 2, *December 1841–April 1843.* Salt Lake City: Church Historian's Press, 2011.

Hedges, Andrew H., Alex D. Smith, and Brent M. Rogers, eds. *The Joseph Smith Papers: Journals.* Vol. 3, *May 1843–June 1844.* Salt Lake City: Church Historian's Press, 2015.

Heiss, Mary Ann. "The Evolution of the Imperial Idea and U.S. National Identity." *Diplomatic History* 26, no. 4 (Fall 2002): 511–40.

Hickman, Martin B. "The Political Legacy of Joseph Smith." *Dialogue: A Journal of Mormon Thought* 3, no. 3 (Fall 1968): 17–36.

Hicks, L. Edward. "Republican Religion and Republican Institutions: Alexander Campbell and the Anti-Catholic Movement." In *The Stone-Campbell Movement: An International Religious Tradition*, edited by Michael W. Casey and Douglas A. Foster, 204–18. Knoxville: University of Tennessee Press, 2002.

Hill, Roscoe R., ed. *Journals of the Continental Congress, 1774–1789.* Vol. 32, *January 17–July 20, 1787.* Washington DC: United States Government Printing Office, 1936.

Holt, Michael F. *The Fate of Their Country: Politicians, Slavery Extension, and the Coming of the Civil War.* New York: Hill and Wang, 2004.

———. *The Political Crisis of the 1850s.* New York: W. W. Norton, 1983.

Homer, Michael W. "The Federal Bench and Priesthood Authority: The Rise and Fall of John Fitch Kinney's Early Relationship with the Mormons." *Journal of Mormon History* 13 (1986–87): 89–110.

———. "The Judiciary and the Common Law in Utah Territory, 1850–61." *Dialogue: A Journal of Mormon Thought* 21, no. 1 (Winter 1988): 97–108.

Horowitz, Helen Lefkowitz. *Attitudes toward Sex in Antebellum America: A Brief History with Documents*. New York: Palgrave Macmillan, 2006.

Howe, Daniel Walker. *What Hath God Wrought: The Transformation of America, 1815–1848*. New York: Oxford University Press, 2007.

Hoyt, Amy, and Sara M. Patterson. "Mormon Masculinity: Changing Gender Expectations in the Era of Transition from Polygamy to Monogamy, 1890–1920." *Gender & History* 23, no. 1 (April 2011): 72–91.

Huston, James L. "Democracy by Scripture versus Democracy by Process: A Reflection on Stephen Douglas and Popular Sovereignty." *Civil War History* 43, no. 3 (1997): 189–200.

Hyde, Anne F. *Empires, Nations, and Families: A History of the North American West, 1800–1860*. Lincoln: University of Nebraska Press, 2011.

Indian Appropriations Act. An Act Making Appropriations for the Current and Contingent Expenses of the Indian Department, and for Fulfilling Treaty Stipulations with Various Indian Tribes, for the Year Ending June thirtieth, Eighteen Hundred and Fifty-Eight, also Known as the Indian Appropriations Act, *Laws of the United States*, in Appendix to the *Congressional Globe*, 34th Cong., 3rd Sess., 3 March 1857.

Isenberg, Nancy. *Sex and Citizenship in Antebellum America*. Chapel Hill: University of North Carolina Press, 1998.

Jackson, Richard H., ed. *The Mormon Role in the Settlement of the West*. Provo UT: Brigham Young University Press, 1978.

Jackson, Richard H., William Rieske, and Howard A. Christy. "Indian Farms and Reservations." In *Atlas of Utah*, edited by Wayne L. Wahlquist, 106–7. Provo UT: Weber State College and Brigham Young University Press, 1981.

Jacobson, Matthew Frye. *Whiteness of a Different Color: European Immigrants and the Alchemy of Race*. Cambridge MA: Harvard University Press, 1998.

Jaffa, Harry V. *Crisis of the House Divided: An Interpretation of the Issues in the Lincoln-Douglas Debates*. Seattle: University of Washington Press, 1959.

Jennings, Warren. "Zion Is Fled: The Expulsion of the Mormons from Jackson County, Missouri." PhD diss., University of Florida, 1962.

Jensen, Joan M. *Army Surveillance in America, 1775–1980*. New Haven CT: Yale University Press, 1991.

Jensen, Richard E., ed. *The Pawnee Mission Letters, 1834–1851*. Lincoln: University of Nebraska Press, 2010.

Jensen, Richard L. "Forgotten Relief Societies, 1844–67." *Dialogue: A Journal of Mormon Thought* 16, no. 1 (Spring 1983): 105–25.

Jensen, Robin Scott, Robert J. Woodford, and Steven C. Harper, eds. *The Joseph Smith Papers: Revelations and Translations*. Vol. 1, *Manuscript Revelation Books*. Salt Lake City: Church Historian's Press, 2011.

Johannsen, Robert W. *The Frontier, the Union, and Stephen A. Douglas.* Urbana: University of Illinois Press, 1989.

———. *The Lincoln-Douglas Debates of 1858.* New York: Oxford University Press, 1965.

Johnson, Clark V., ed. *Mormon Redress Petitions: Documents of the 1833–1838 Missouri Conflict.* Provo UT: Religious Studies Center, Brigham Young University, 1992.

Jones, Megan Sanborn. *Performing American Identity in Anti-Mormon Melodrama.* New York: Routledge, 2009.

Jones, Sondra. "'Redeeming' the Indian: The Enslavement of Indian Children in New Mexico and Utah." *Utah Historical Quarterly* 67, no. 3 (Summer 1999): 220–41.

———. "Saints or Sinners? The Evolving Perceptions of Mormon-Indian Relations in Utah Historiography." *Utah Historical Quarterly* 72, no. 1 (Winter 2004): 19–46.

———. "The Trial of Don Pedro León: Politics, Prejudice, and Pragmatism." *Utah Historical Quarterly* 65, no. 2 (Spring 1997):165–86.

Journal of Discourses. Vol. 2. Reported by G. D. Watt. Liverpool: F. D. Richards, 1855.

———. Vol. 6. Reported by G. D. Watt, J. V. Long, and Others. Liverpool: Asa Calkin, 1859.

———. Vol. 7. Reported by G. D. Watt, J. V. Long, and Others. Liverpool: Amasa Lyman, 1860.

Kagan, Robert. *Dangerous Nation.* New York: Alfred A. Knopf, 2006.

Kammer, Sean M. "Public Opinion Is More than Law: Popular Sovereignty and Vigilantism in the Nebraska Territory." *Great Plains Quarterly* (Fall 2011): 309–24.

Kaplan, Amy. "Manifest Domesticity." *American Literature* 70, no. 3 (September 1998): 581–606.

Kaplan, Amy, and Donald E. Pease, eds. *Cultures of United States Imperialism.* Durham NC: Duke University Press, 1993.

Kenney, Scott G. *Wilford Woodruff's Journal.* Vol. 5, 1 January 1857 to 31 December 1861. Midvale UT: Signature Books, 1984.

Kerber, Linda K. *Women of the Republic: Intellect and Ideology in Revolutionary America.* Chapel Hill: University of North Carolina Press, 1980.

Kern, Louis J. *An Ordered Love: Sex Roles and Sexuality in Victorian Utopias— the Shakers, the Mormons, and the Oneida Community.* Chapel Hill: University of North Carolina Press, 1981.

Kerstetter, Todd M. *God's Country, Uncle Sam's Land: Faith and Conflict in the American West.* Urbana: University of Illinois Press, 2006.

Kimball, James L., Jr. "The Nauvoo Charter: A Reinterpretation." *Journal of the Illinois State Historical Society* 64 (Spring 1971): 66–78.

———. "A Wall to Defend Zion: The Nauvoo Charter." *BYU Studies* 15, no. 4 (1975): 491–97.

Kimmel, Michael. *Manhood in America: A Cultural History.* New York: The Free Press, 1996.

Kitchen, Richard Darrell. "Mormon-Indian Relations in Deseret: Intermarriage and Indenture, 1847 to 1877." PhD diss., Arizona State University, August 2002.

Kvasnicka, Robert M., and Herman J. Viola, eds. *The Commissioners of Indian Affairs, 1824–1977.* Lincoln: University of Nebraska Press, 1979.

Lamar, Howard R. *The Far Southwest, 1846–1912: A Territorial History*, rev. ed. Albuquerque: University of New Mexico Press, 2000.

Lamont, Daniel S., George W. Davis, Leslie J. Perry, and Joseph W. Kirkley. *The War of Rebellion: A Compilation of the Official Records of the Union and Confederate Armies.* Ser. I, vol. L, pt. 2. Washington DC: Government Printing Office, 1897.

Langley, Harold D., ed. *To Utah with the Dragoons and Glimpses of Life in Arizona and California 1858–1859.* Salt Lake City: University of Utah Press, 1974.

Larson, Gustive O. *The Americanization of Utah for Statehood.* San Marino CA: Huntington Library, 1971.

Larson, Robert. *New Mexico's Quest for Statehood, 1846–1912.* Albuquerque: University of New Mexico Press, 1968.

Lawson, Gary, and Guy Seidman. *The Constitution of Empire: Territorial Expansion and American Legal History.* New Haven CT: Yale University Press, 2004.

Layton, Stanford J., ed. *Being Different: Stories of Utah's Minorities.* Salt Lake City: Signature Books, 2001.

Lea, Luke. *Annual Report of the Commissioner of Indian Affairs.* Washington DC: Office of the Commissioner of Indian Affairs, 1850.

Leonard, Glen M. *Nauvoo: A Place of Peace, a People of Promise.* Salt Lake City: Deseret Book Company; Provo: Brigham Young University Press, 2002.

LeSueur, Stephen C. *The 1838 Mormon War in Missouri.* Columbia: University of Missouri Press, 1987.

Levin, Daniel Lessard. *Representing Popular Sovereignty: The Constitution in American Political Culture.* Albany: State University of New York Press, 1999.

Limerick, Patricia Nelson. *Something in the Soil: Legacies and Reckonings in the New West.* New York: W. W. Norton, 2001.

Lindell, Jennifer. "Mormons and Native Americans in the Antebellum West." Master's thesis, San Diego State University, Spring 2011.

Long, E. B. *The Saints and the Union: Utah Territory during the Civil War.* Urbana: University of Illinois Press, 1981.

Loughran, Trish. *The Republic in Print: Print Culture in the Age of U.S. Nation Building, 1770–1870.* New York: Columbia University Press, 2007.

Lund, Matthew B. "A Society of Like-Minded Men: American Localism and the Mormon Expulsion from Jackson County." *Journal of Mormon History* 40, no. 3 (Summer 2014): 169–200.

Lutz, Donald S. *Popular Consent and Popular Control: Whig Political Theory in the Early State Constitutions*. Baton Rouge: Louisiana State University Press, 1980.

Lyman, Edward Leo. *The Overland Journey from Utah to California: Wagon Travel from the City of Saints to the City of Angels*. Reno: University of Nevada Press, 2004.

———. *Political Deliverance: The Mormon Quest for Utah Statehood*. Urbana: University of Illinois Press, 1986.

Lyon, Caleb. "No Government Bounty to Polygamy: Speech of Hon. Caleb Lyon, of Lyonsdale, New York, in the House of Representatives, 4 May 1854." Washington DC: Congressional Globe Office, 1854.

MacKay, Michael Hubbard, Gerrit J. Dirkmaat, et al., eds. *The Joseph Smith Papers: Documents*. Vol. 1, *July 1828–June 1831*. Salt Lake City: Church Historian's Press, 2013.

MacKinnon, William P. "And the War Came: James Buchanan, the Utah Expedition, and the Decision to Intervene." *Utah Historical Quarterly* 76, no. 1 (Winter 2008): 22–37.

———. *At Sword's Point*, pt. 1: *A Documentary History of the Utah War to 1858*. Norman: University of Oklahoma Press / Arthur H. Clark Company, 2008.

———. "Epilogue to the Utah War: Impact and Legacy." *Journal of Mormon History* 29, no. 2 (2003): 186–248.

———. "Hammering Utah, Squeezing Mexico, and Coveting Cuba: James Buchanan's White House Intriques." *Utah Historical Quarterly* 80, no. 2 (Spring 2012): 132–51.

———. "'Like Splitting a Man Up His Backbone': The Territorial Dismemberment of Utah, 1850–1896." *Utah Historical Quarterly* 71, no. 2 (Spring 2003): 100–124.

———. "125 Years of Conspiracy Theories: Origins of the Utah Expedition of 1857–1858." *Utah Historical Quarterly* 52, no. 3 (Summer 1984): 212–30.

———. "Sex, Subalterns, and Steptoe: Army Behavior, Mormon Rage, and Utah War Anxieties." *Utah Historical Quarterly* 76, no. 3 (Summer 2008): 227–46.

———. "The Utah War and Its Mountain Meadows Massacre: Lessons Learned, Surprises Encountered." *FARMS Review* 20, no. 2 (2008): 237–51.

Madsen, Brigham D., ed. *Exploring the Great Salt Lake: The Stansbury Expedition of 1849–50*. Salt Lake City: University of Utah Press, 1989.

Madsen, Carol Cornwall. "'At Their Peril': Utah Law and the Case of Plural Wives, 1850–1900." *Western Historical Quarterly* 21, no. 4 (November 1990): 425–43.

Mann, John W. W. *Sacajawea's People: The Lemhi Shoshones and the Salmon River Country*. Lincoln: University of Nebraska Press, 2004.

Marr, Timothy. *The Cultural Roots of American Islamicism*. Cambridge: Cambridge University Press, 2006.

Mason, Patrick Q. "God and the People: Theodemocracy in Nineteenth-Century Mormonism." *Journal of Church and State* 53, no. 3 (Summer 2011): 349–75.

McDonald, Forrest. *States' Rights and the Union: Imperium in Imperio, 1776–1876*. Lawrence: University Press of Kansas, 2000.

McPherson, James M. *This Mighty Scourge: Perspectives on the Civil War*. New York: Oxford University Press, 2007.

Meinig, Donald W. "The Mormon Nation and the American Empire." *Journal of Mormon History* 22, no. 1 (Spring 1996): 33–51.

———. *The Shaping of America: A Geographical Perspective on 500 Years of History*. Vol. 3, *Transcontinental America, 1850–1915*. New Haven CT: Yale University Press, 1998.

Memmi, Albert. *The Colonizer and the Colonized*. Boston: Beacon Press, 1991.

Merk, Frederick. *Manifest Destiny and Mission in American History: A Reinterpretation*. New York: Vintage Books, 1966.

Moorman, Donald R., with Gene A. Sessions. *Camp Floyd and the Mormons: The Utah War*. Salt Lake City: University of Utah Press, 1992.

Morgan, Dale L. "The Administration of Indian Affairs in Utah, 1851–1858." *Pacific Historical Quarterly* 17, no. 4 (November 1948): 383–409.

———. *The State of Deseret*. Logan: Utah State University Press, 1987.

Morgan, Edmund S. *Inventing the People: The Rise of Popular Sovereignty in England and America*. New York: W. W. Norton, 1989.

Morrill, Justin S. "Utah Territory and Its Laws—Polygamy and Its License." Appendix to the *Congressional Globe*, 34th Cong., 3rd Sess., 23 February 1857, 284–90.

Morris, Jr., Roy. *The Long Pursuit: Abraham Lincoln's Thirty-Year Struggle with Stephen Douglas for the Heart and Soul of America*. Lincoln: University of Nebraska Press, 2010.

Morrison, Michael A. *Slavery and the American West: The Eclipse of Manifest Destiny and the Coming of the Civil War*. Chapel Hill: University of North Carolina Press, 1997.

Mullis, Tony R. *Peacekeeping on the Plains: Army Operations in Bleeding Kansas*. Columbia: University of Missouri Press, 2004.

Neil, William M. "The Territorial Governor as Indian Superintendent in the Trans-Mississippi West." *Mississippi Valley Historical Review* 43, no. 2 (September 1956): 213–37.

Nichols, Jeffrey D. "Polygamy and Prostitution: Comparative Morality in Salt Lake City, 1847–1911." *Journal of Mormon History* 27, no. 2 (Fall 2001): 1–39.

Nichols, Roy Franklin. *The Disruption of American Democracy.* New York: The Free Press, 1948.

———. "The Territories: Seedbeds of Democracy." *Nebraska History* 35 (September 1954): 159–72.

Norgren, Jill. *The Cherokee Cases: Two Landmark Federal Decisions in the Fight for Sovereignty.* Norman: University of Oklahoma Press, 2003.

Nugent, Walter. *Habits of Empire: A History of American Expansion.* New York: Vintage Books, 2009.

———. "The Mormons and America's Empires." *Journal of Mormon History* 36, no. 2 (Spring 2010): 1–27.

Oaks, Dallin H., and Marvin S. Hill. *Carthage Conspiracy: The Trial of the Accused Assassins of Joseph Smith.* Urbana: University of Illinois Press, 1979.

Okin, Susan Moller. *Women in Western Political Thought.* Princeton NJ: Princeton University Press, 1979.

O'Neil, Floyd A., and Stanford J. Layton, "Of Pride and Politics: Brigham Young as Indian Superintendent." *Utah Historical Quarterly* 46, no. 3 (1978): 236–50.

Onuf, Peter S. *Jefferson's Empire: The Language of American Nationhood.* Charlottesville: University of Virginia Press, 2000.

———. *Statehood and Union: A History of the Northwest Ordinance.* Bloomington: Indiana University Press, 1987.

Ostler, Jeffrey. "Empire and Liberty: Contradictions and Conflicts in Nineteenth-Century Western Political History." In *A Companion to the American West,* edited by William Deverell, 200–218. Malden MA: Blackwell, 2004.

Paludan, Phillip Shaw. *A People's Contest: The Union and Civil War, 1861–1865.* New York: Harper & Row, 1988.

Papanikolas, Helen Z., ed. *The Peoples of Utah.* Salt Lake City: Utah State Historical Society, 1976.

Paul, Rodman W. *The Far West and the Great Plains in Transition, 1859–1900.* Norman: University of Oklahoma Press, 1998, repr. ed.

Peterson, John Alton. *Utah's Black Hawk War.* Salt Lake City: University of Utah Press, 1998.

Peterson, Paul H. "The Mormon Reformation of 1856–1857: The Rhetoric and the Reality." *Journal of Mormon History* 15 (1989): 59–88.

Poll, Richard D. "Joseph Smith and the Presidency, 1844." *Dialogue: A Journal of Mormon Thought* 3, no. 3 (Fall 1968): 17–36.

———. "The Mormon Question Enters National Politics, 1850–1856." *Utah Historical Quarterly* 25, no. 2 (1957): 117–32.

———. "The Move South." *BYU Studies* 29, no. 4 (Fall 1989): 65–88.

———. *Quixotic Mediator: Thomas L. Kane and the Utah War.* Ogden UT: Weber State College Press, 1985.

———. "Thomas L. Kane and the Utah War." *Utah Historical Quarterly* 61, no. 2 (Spring 1993): 112–35.

Poll, Richard D., and Ralph W. Hansen. "'Buchanan's Blunder': The Utah War, 1857–1858." *Military Affairs* 25, no. 3 (Autumn 1961): 121–31.

Pomeroy, Earl S. *The Territories and the United States, 1861–1890: Studies in Colonial Administration*. Seattle: University of Washington Press, 1969.

Porter, Kirk H., and Donald Bruce Johnson, eds. *National Party Platforms*. Urbana: University of Illinois Press, 1966.

Potts, James B. "Nebraska Territory, 1854–1867: A Study of Frontier Politics." PhD diss., University of Nebraska–Lincoln, 1973.

———. "North of 'Bleeding Kansas': The 1850s Political Crisis in Nebraska Territory." *Nebraska History* 73, no. 3 (Fall 1992): 110–18.

Prete, Roy A., ed. *Window of Faith: Latter-day Saint Perspectives on World History*. Provo UT: Religious Studies Center, Brigham Young University, 2005.

Prince, Carl E. "The Great 'Riot Year': Jacksonian Democracy and Patterns of Violence in 1834." *Journal of the Early Republic* 5, no. 2 (Spring 1985): 1–19.

Prior, David. "Civilization, Republic, Nation: Contested Keywords, Northern Republicans, and the Forgotten Reconstruction of Mormon Utah." *Civil War History* 56, no. 3 (September 2010): 283–310.

Prucha, Francis Paul, ed. *Documents of United States Indian Policy*, 3rd ed. Lincoln: University of Nebraska Press, 2000.

———. *Indian Policy in the United States: Historical Essays*. Lincoln: University of Nebraska Press, 1981.

Quaife, Milo Milton, ed. *The Diary of James K. Polk, During his Presidency, 1845 to 1849*. Vol. 1. Chicago: A. C. McClurg, 1910.

Quale, G. Robina. *A History of Marriage Systems*. New York: Greenwood, 1988.

Reeder, Andrew Horatio. "Speech of Governor Reeder at New Haven." In *The Election and the Candidates: Governor Reeder in favor of Fremont; Reasons for Electing Fremont and Dayton; "The Poor Whites of the South."* New York, 1856.

Reeve, W. Paul. *Religion of a Different Color: Race and the Mormon Struggle for Whiteness*. New York: Oxford University Press, 2015.

Reid, John B., and Ronald M. James, eds. *Uncovering Nevada's Past: A Primary Source History of the Silver State*. Reno: University of Nevada Press, 2004.

Remy, Jules, and Julius Brenchley. *A Journey to Great Salt Lake City, with a sketch of the History, Religion, and Customs of the Mormons* Vol. 1. London: W. Jeffs, 1861.

Richardson, James D., ed. *Messages and Papers of the President, 1789–1897*. Washington DC, 1897.

Ricks, Nathaniel R. "A Peculiar Place for the Peculiar Institution: Slavery and Sovereignty in Early Territorial Utah." Master's thesis, Brigham Young University, August 2007.

Robbins, Sarah. "'The Future Good and Great of Our Land': Republican Mothers, Female Authors, and Domesticated Literacy in Antebellum New England." *New England Quarterly* 75, no. 4 (Winter 2002): 562–91.

Rockwell, Stephen J. *Indian Affairs and the Administrative State in the Nineteenth Century.* New York: Cambridge University Press, 2010.

Rogers, Brent M. "To the 'Honest and Patriotic Sons of Liberty': Mormon Appeals for Redress and Social Justice, 1843–44." *Journal of Mormon History* 39, no. 1 (Winter 2013): 36–68.

Rogin, Michael Paul. *Fathers and Children: Andrew Jackson and the Subjugation of the American Indian.* New York: Alfred A. Knopf, 1975.

Roland, Charles P. *Albert Sidney Johnston: Soldier of Three Republics.* Austin: University of Texas Press, 1990. 2nd ed.

Romig, Ronald E., and Michael S. Riggs. "Reassessing Joseph Smith's 'Appointed Time for the Redemption of Zion.'" In *The Missouri Mormon Experience*, edited by Thomas M. Spencer, 27–49. Columbia: University of Missouri Press, 2010.

Rotundo, E. Anthony. *American Manhood: Transformations in Masculinity from the Revolution to the Modern Era.* New York: Basic Books, 1993.

Ryan, Mary P. *Civic Wars: Democracy and Public Life in the American City during the Nineteenth Century.* Berkeley: University of California Press, 1997.

Said, Edward W. *Culture and Imperialism.* New York: Vintage Books, 1994.

———. *Orientalism.* New York: Vintage Books, 1979.

Satz, Ronald N. *American Indian Policy in the Jacksonian Era.* Lincoln: University of Nebraska Press, 1975.

Scott, James C. *Seeing Like a State: How Certain Schemes to Improve the Human Condition Have Failed.* New Haven CT: Yale University Press, 1998.

Seefeldt, Douglas. "Horrible Massacre of Emigrants!!: The Mountain Meadows Massacre in Public Discourse." http://mountainmeadows.unl.edu.

Seifrit, William C. "Charles Henry Wilcken, an Undervalued Saint." *Utah Historical Quarterly* 55, no. 4 (Fall 1987): 308–21.

Sessions, Gene A. *Mormon Thunder: A Documentary History of Jedediah Morgan Grant.* Urbana: University of Illinois Press, 1982.

Shipps, Jan. *Mormonism: The Story of a New Religious Tradition.* Urbana: University of Illinois Press, 1985.

Silver, Peter. *Our Savage Neighbors: How Indian War Transformed Early America.* New York: W. W. Norton, 2008.

Simmons, Virginia McConnell. *The Ute Indians of Utah, Colorado, and New Mexico.* Boulder: University Press of Colorado, 2000.

Slater, A. M. *Fruits of Mormonism, A Fair and Candid Statement of Facts Illustrative of Mormon Principles, Mormon Policy, and Mormon Character, by More than Forty Eye Witnesses.* Coloma CA: Harmon & Springer, 1851.

Smart, Donna Toland, ed. *Mormon Midwife: The 1846–1888 Diaries of Patty Bartlett Sessions*. Logan: Utah State University Press, 1997.

Smith, Elbert B. *The Presidency of James Buchanan*. Lawrence: University Press of Kansas, 1975.

Smith, Joseph, Jr., Oliver Cowdery, Sidney Rigdon, and Frederick G. Williams. *Doctrine and Covenants of the Church of the Latter Day Saints: Carefully Selected from the Revelations of God*. Kirtland OH: F. G. Williams, 1835.

Smith, Kimberly K. *The Dominion of Voice: Riot, Reason, and Romance in Antebellum Politics*. Lawrence: University Press of Kansas, 1999.

Smithers, Gregory D. "The 'Pursuits of the Civilized Man': Race and the Meaning of Civilization in the United States and Australia, 1790s–1850s." *Journal of World History* 20 (June 2009): 245–49.

The Southern Utes: A Tribal History. Ignacio CO: Southern Ute Tribe, 1972.

Stampp, Kenneth M. *America in 1857: A Nation on the Brink*. New York: Oxford University Press, 1990.

Stephanson, Anders. *Manifest Destiny: American Expansionism and the Empire of Right*. New York: Hill and Wang, 1995.

Stoler, Ann Laura. *Carnal Knowledge and Imperial Power: Race and the Intimate in Colonial Rule*. Berkeley: University of California Press, 2002.

Talbot, Christine. *A Foreign Kingdom: Mormons and Polygamy in American Political Culture, 1852–1890*. Urbana: University of Illinois Press, 2013.

Tate, Michael L. *The Frontier Army in the Settlement of the West*. Norman: University of Oklahoma Press, 1999.

Thomas, William G. *The Iron Way: Railroads, the Civil War, and the Making of Modern America*. New Haven CT: Yale University Press, 2011.

Thompson, John. "Mormonism—Increase of the Army." Washington DC: Buell & Blanchard, Printers, 1858.

Todorov, Tzvetan. *The Conquest of America*. New York: Harper & Row, 1984.

Tucker, Robert W., and David C. Hendrickson. *Empire of Liberty: The Statecraft of Thomas Jefferson*. New York: Oxford University Press, 1990.

Turley, Richard E., Jr., and Brent M. Rogers. "Found: Rare First Edition of the Earliest Ute and Shoshone Vocabulary." *Utah Historical Quarterly* 83, no. 3 (Summer 2015): 234–37.

Turner, John G. *Brigham Young: Pioneer Prophet*. Cambridge MA: The Belknap Press of Harvard University Press, 2012.

Tyler, Ron, ed. *Prints of the American West: Papers Presented at the Ninth Annual North American Print Conference*. Fort Worth TX: Amon Carter Museum, 1983.

Ulrich, Laurel Thatcher. "An American Album, 1857." *American Historical Review* 115, no. 1 (February 2010): 1–25.

——. "Runaway Wives, 1830–1860." *Journal of Mormon History* 42, no. 2 (April 2016): 1–26.

United States, Utah Commission. *Report of the Utah Commission to the Secretary of the Interior, 1886*. Washington DC: Government Printing Office, 1886.

Unruh, John D., Jr. *The Plains Across: The Overland Emigrants and the Trans Mississippi West, 1840–1860*. Urbana: University of Illinois Press, 1979.

U.S. Congress. House of Representatives. B. D. Harris to Millard Fillmore, January 12, 1852 in Message of the President. 32nd Cong., 1st Sess., 20 January 1852. Exec. Doc. No. 33, Utah.

——. Carson's Valley. 35th Cong., 1st Sess., 13 April 1858. Exec. Doc. No. 102.

——. Cessation of Difficulties in Utah. Message from the President, Washington City. 35th Cong., 1st Sess., 10 June 1858. Exec. Doc. No. 138.

——. Constitution of the State of Deseret, 1850. 31st Cong., 1st Sess., 1850. H.R. Misc. Doc. No. 18.

——. Constitution of the State of Deseret, 1862. Memorials of the Legislature and Constitutional Convention of Utah Territory, Praying the Admission of Said Territory into the Union as the State of Deseret. 37th Cong., 2d Sess., 1862. H.R. Misc. Doc. No. 78.

——. Letter from the Secretary of the Treasury, Transmitting Communications in Regard to the Necessity of Further Appropriations for Public Buildings in Utah. 33rd Cong., 1st Sess., 5 April 1854. Misc. Doc. No. 58.

——. Message of the President of the United States, Transmitting Information in Reference to the Condition of Affairs in the Territory of Utah. 32nd Cong., 1st Sess., 9 January 1852. Exec. Doc. No. 25.

——. "Polygamy in the Territories of the United States." Report from the Committee on the Judiciary. 36th Cong., 1st Sess., 14 March 1860. H.R. Rep. No. 83.

——. Report of the Secretary of War in Message from the President of the United States. 35th Cong., 1st Sess., 1857. Exec. Doc. No. 2. Washington DC: Cornelius Wendell, Printer, 1857.

——. Report of the Secretary of War in Message from the President of the United States. 35th Cong., 2nd Sess., 1858. Exec. Doc. No. 2. Washington DC: James B. Steedman, Printer, 1858.

——. "Territory of Nevada, [to Accompany Bill H.R. No. 567]." 35th Cong., 1st Sess., 12 May 1858. H.R. Rep. No. 375.

——. Utah. Memorial of the Members and Officers of the Legislative Assembly of the Territory of Utah, Setting forth Their Grievances, and Praying Congress to Give Them a Voice in the Selection of Their Rulers." 35th Cong., 1st Sess., 17 March 1858. Misc. Doc. No. 100.

——. "The Utah Expedition." 35th Cong., 1st Sess., February 1858. Exec. Doc. No. 71.

U.S. Congress. Senate. *Exploration and Survey of the Valley of the Great Salt Lake of Utah*, by Captain Howard Stansbury. 32nd Cong., Special Sess., March 1851. S. Exec. Doc. No. 3. Serial No. 608.

U.S. Congress. Senate. "Federal Aid in Domestic Disturbances, 1787–1903." 57th Cong., 2d Sess., 1903. S. Doc. No. 209. Washington DC: Government Printing Office, 1903.

———. Message of the President of the United States Communicating a Dispatch from Governor Cumming, Relative to the Termination of the Difficulties with the Territory of Utah. 35th Cong., 1st Sess., 10 June 1858. S. Exec. Doc. No. 67.

———. Report of the Secretary of War, Communicating, in Compliance with a Resolution of the Senate, Captain Simpson's Report and Map of Wagon Road Routes in Utah Territory. 35th Cong., 2nd Sess., 2 March 1859. S. Exec. Doc. No. 40.

U.S. Department of the Interior. *Annual Report Transmitted with the Message of the President, at the Opening of the Second Session of the Thirty-Third Congress, 1854.* Washington DC: A. O. P. Nicholson, 1855.

———. *Annual Report Transmitted with the Message of the President, at the Opening of the First Session of the Thirty-Fourth Congress, 1855.* Washington DC: A. O. P. Nicholson, 1856.

———. *Report of the Commissioner of Indian Affairs, Accompanying the Annual Report of the Secretary of the Interior, for the Year 1856.* Washington DC: A. O. P. Nicholson, Printer, 1857.

———. *Report of the Commissioner of Indian Affairs, Accompanying the Annual Report of the Secretary of the Interior, for the Year 1860.* Washington DC: George W. Bowman, Printer, 1860.

———. *Report of the Commissioner of Indian Affairs, Accompanying the Annual Report of the Secretary of the Interior, for the Year 1861.* Washington DC: Government Printing Office, 1861.

———. *Report of the Commissioner of Indian Affairs, Accompanying the Annual Report of the Secretary of the Interior, for the Year 1862.* Washington DC: Government Printing Office, 1862.

———. *Report of the Commissioner of Indian Affairs, Accompanying the Annual Report of the Secretary of the Interior, for the Year 1865.* Washington DC: Government Printing Office, 1865.

U.S. Department of the Interior. Commissioner of Indian Affairs. *Annual Report, Accompanying the Annual Report of the Secretary of the Interior, for the Year 1857.* Washington DC: William A. Harris, Printer, 1858.

Utley, Robert M. *The Indian Frontier of the American West, 1846–1890.* Albuquerque: University of New Mexico Press, 1984.

Van Alstyne, Richard W. *The Rising American Empire.* Oxford: Basil Blackwell, 1960.

Van Develder, Paul. *Savages and Scoundrels: The Untold Story of America's Road to Empire through Indian Territory.* New Haven CT: Yale University Press, 2009.

Van Hoak, Stephen P. "Waccara's Utes: Native American Equestrian Adaptations in the Eastern Great Basin, 1776–1886." *Utah Historical Quarterly* 67, no. 4 (1999): 309–30.

Van Orden, Bruce A. "Stephen A. Douglas and the Mormons." In *Regional Studies in Latter-day Saint Church History: Illinois,* edited by H. Dean Garrett, 359–78. Provo UT: Department of Church History and Doctrine, Brigham Young University, 1995.

Van Wagenen, Michael Scott. "Sam Houston and the Utah War." *Utah Historical Quarterly* 76, no. 1 (Winter 2008): 66–78.

———. *The Texas Republic and the Mormon Kingdom of God.* College Station: Texas A&M University Press, 2002.

Varon, Elizabeth R. *Disunion!: The Coming of the American Civil War, 1789–1859.* Chapel Hill: University of North Carolina Press, 2008.

Veracini, Lorenzo. *Settler Colonialism: A Theoretical Overview.* New York: Palgrave Macmillan, 2010.

Vitale, Gary. "Abraham Lincoln and the Mormons: Another Legacy of Limited Freedom." *Journal of the Illinois State Historical Society* 101, nos. 3–4 (Fall-Winter, 2008): 260–71.

Vogel, Dan. *Indian Origins and the Book of Mormon.* Salt Lake City: Signature Books, 1986.

Walker, Ronald W. "The Affairs of the 'Runaways': Utah's First Encounter with the Federal Officers, Part 1." *Journal of Mormon History* 39, no. 4 (Fall 2013): 1–43.

———. "Buchanan, Popular Sovereignty, and the Mormons: The Election of 1856." *Utah Historical Quarterly* 81, no. 2 (Spring 2013): 108–32.

———. "President Young Writes Jefferson Davis about the Gunnison Massacre Affair." *BYU Studies* 35, no. 1 (1995): 147–70.

———. "Seeking the 'Remnant': The Native American during the Joseph Smith Period." *Journal of Mormon History* 19, no. 1 (Spring 1993): 1–33.

———. "Thomas L. Kane and Utah's Quest for Self-Government, 1846–51." *Utah Historical Quarterly* 69, no. 2 (Spring 2001): 100–119.

———. "Toward a Reconstruction of Mormon and Indian Relations, 1847–1877." *BYU Studies* 29, no. 4 (Fall 1989): 23–42.

———. "Wakara Meets the Mormons, 1848–52: A Case Study in Native American Accommodation." *Utah Historical Quarterly* 70, no. 3 (Summer 2002): 215–37.

Walker, Ronald W., and Matthew J. Grow, "The People Are 'Hogaffed or Humbugged': The 1851–52 National Reaction to Utah's 'Runaway' Officers, Part 2." *Journal of Mormon History* 40, no. 1 (Winter 2014): 1–52.

Walker, Ronald W., Richard E. Turley Jr., and Glen M. Leonard. *Massacre at Mountain Meadows*. New York: Oxford University Press, 2008.

Wallace, Anthony F. C. *Jefferson and the Indians: The Tragic Fate of the First Americans*. Cambridge MA: Harvard University Press, 1999.

———. *The Long, Bitter Trail: Andrew Jackson and the Indians*. New York: Hill and Wang, 1993.

Watson, Harry L. *Liberty and Power: The Politics of Jacksonian America*. New York: Hill and Wang, 1990.

Weeks, William Earl. *Building the Continental Empire: American Expansion from the Revolution to the Civil War*. Chicago: Ivan R. Dee, 1996.

West, Elliott. "Reconstructing Race." *Western Historical Quarterly* 34, no. 1 (Spring 2003): 7–26.

White, Richard. *"It's Your Misfortune and None of My Own": A New History of the American West*. Norman: University of Oklahoma Press, 1991.

Whittaker, David J. "Mormons and Native Americans: A Historical and Bibliographical Introduction." *Dialogue: A Journal of Mormon Thought* 18, no. 4 (Winter 1985): 33–64.

Wicks, Robert S., and Fred R. Foister. *Junius and Joseph: Presidential Politics and the Assassination of the First Mormon Prophet*. Logan: Utah State University Press, 2005.

Wiebe, Robert H. *Self-Rule: A Cultural History of American Democracy*. Chicago: University of Chicago Press, 1995.

Wilentz, Sean. *The Rise of American Democracy: Jefferson to Lincoln*. New York: W. W. Norton, 2005.

Williams, William Appleman. *Empire as a Way of Life: An Essay on the Causes and Character of America's Present Predicament Along with a Few Thoughts about an Alternative*. New York: Oxford University Press, 1980.

Winders, Richard Bruce. *Mr. Polk's Army: The American Military Experience in the Mexican War*. College Station: Texas A&M University Press, 1997.

Wolfe, Patrick. "After the Frontier: Separation and Absorption in U.S. Indian Policy." *Settler Colonial Studies* 1 (2011): 13–50.

———. "Settler Colonialism and the Elimination of the Native." *Journal of Genocide Research* 8, no. 4 (December 2006): 387–409.

Wood, Gordon S. "Evangelical America and Early Mormonism." *New York History* (October 1980): 358–86.

———. *The Radicalism of the American Revolution*. New York: Vintage, 1993.

Wooster, Robert. *The American Military Frontiers: The United States Army in the West, 1783–1900*. Albuquerque: University of New Mexico Press, 2009.

———. *The Military and United States Indian Policy, 1865–1903*. Lincoln: University of Nebraska Press, 1995.

———. "Military Strategy in the Southwest, 1848–1860." *Military History of Texas and the Southwest* 15, no. 2 (1979): 5–15.

Wunder, John R., and Joann M. Ross, eds. *The Nebraska-Kansas Act of 1854*. Lincoln: University of Nebraska Press, 2008.

Young, John R. *Memoirs of John R. Young: Utah Pioneers, 1847*. Salt Lake City: Deseret News, 1920.

INDEX

Ackley, Richard Thomas, 247
adultery, 73, 78, 82, 86
Alexander, Edmund, 193, 196
Allen, A. J., 254
American flag, 243–45, 276
Anderson, Kirk, 242
Andrews, T. P., 168–69
Anterro, 198
Arabs, 88
Arapeen, 125, 127, 206
Arthur, Timothy, 86

Bailey, Charles, 247–48
Bangor Daily Whig and Courier (Bangor ME), 148–49
Bannocks, 203, 205, 256
Barney, Lewis, 195, 237–38
Bean, George W., 113
Beckwith, Edward G., 68–69, 119, 260
Bell, John, 66–67
Benson, Ezra T., 42
Benton, Thomas Hart, 3
Bernhisel, John M., 46, 136
Bicknall, Edward J. "Ned," 76, 78, 82
Bigler, William, 153
Black, Jeremiah, 156, 157, 279–80
Black Hawk War, 274
"Bleeding Kansas," 3–4
Bloom, Henry Sterling, 53–54

Boggs, Lilburn W., 26
Book of Mormon, 23–24, 100–101
Branch, Lawrence D., 284
Brandebury, Lemuel, 46, 50, 71
Bridger, James, 197
British colonies, 20
Brocchus, Perry, 46, 47–48, 50, 71, 234
Brown, Albert G., 221–22
Brown, Isaac, 106
Brown, Thomas D., 112
Buchanan, James: in 1856 election, 139–43; main goal of, 156; Mormons' praise of, 186; on peace in Utah Territory, 275; in post-1856 crusade against Utah Territory, 150, 153, 154–56, 161–64, 181–83; post–Utah War actions of, 236–38, 240, 241, 250–51, 258–59, 267, 292; in Utah War, 17–18, 199, 207–8, 213–22, 226, 228
Burr, David H., 168
Bushman, Richard Lyman, 101
Butterfield, Nancy, 81

Calhoun, John C., 29
California, 66–70, 80, 93, 209, 236, 262
Camp Crittendon, 275
Camp Douglas, 276
Camp Floyd, 238–44, 246–48, 258, 275

373

Camp Scott, 196–97
Cannon, George Q., 191, 223, 246
Carrington, Albert, 177–78
Carruth, William, 185, 275
Carson County, 92
Carson Valley, 92–96, 145–46, 232, 234
Cass, Lewis, 1–2, 25–26, 29, 156, 157, 267–68
Catholics, 12, 56
Cayuses, 203
Cedar Valley, 238, 242, 259
Cheyenne people, 202
Chicago Daily Tribune, 173
Christian Advocate and Journal, 89
Church of Jesus Christ of Latter-day Saints (LDS). *See* Mormons
Cincinnati Platform, 140, 180
Civil War, 245–46, 275, 277, 290–91, 296
Clark, William, 101–2, 129
Clarke, Newman S., 203, 204
Clawson, Margaret, 195–96
Clay County, Missouri, settlement, 25
Clayton, John, 60
Clements, Gilbert, 231–32
Collins, James, 201–2
Colorado Territory, 271
Comanches, 202
common law, 116–17
Compromise of 1850, 55, 58
Connor, Patrick, 276–77
corruption, 247–48
Council of Fifty, 11, 31
Cradlebaugh, John, 264–68
Craig, Columbus L., 127
Cumming, Alfred, 163, 182, 197, 224–28, 231, 236, 255, 263–68, 295
Cumming, Elizabeth, 197, 223, 263
Cummins, Richard W., 101–2
Curtis, George Ticknor, 278–79

Daily National Intelligencer (Washington DC), 93, 130, 150–51
Daily News (Nashville TN), 205
Davis, Jefferson, 65, 67, 69–70, 217–18, 224
Day, Henry R., 100
Daynes, Kathryn, 72
Democratic Party: belief in states' rights by, 27; Compromise of 1850 and, 58; in 1856 election, 135, 140–43; growth of slavery and, 1–2; influence of Utah War on, 18–19; Kansas-Nebraska Act and, 59–60, 63, 64; in post-1856 crusade against Utah Territory, 147, 153–54, 164–65, 169–71; during Utah War, 214
Denver, James W., 199–202, 231
Department of Utah, 239, 266
Deseret: application for statehood of, 41–43, 287; church governance of, 9–12; council-house construction for, 49–50; founding of, 40–41; maps of, 2; provisional government of, 41–45; U.S. surveyor's opinion of, 52–53
Deseret News (Salt Lake City UT), 110, 177–80, 185, 190, 213, 247, 254–56
Dole, William P., 273
Douglas, Stephen A., 1–2, 36–37; in Carson Valley disputes, 95; in creation of Utah Territory, 44; 1856 election speech of, 135; in extradition cases of Joseph Smith, 166; fort named after, 276; growth of railroad and, 67; Kansas-Nebraska Act and, 58–60, 62; in post-1856 crusade against Utah Territory, 147, 164–80; post–Utah War changes and, 233; in presidential campaign of 1860, 277–80; in Utah War, 213–14

Dowdell, James F., 213
Dred Scott decision, 165, 170
Drum, Richard C., 277
Drummond, William W., 117, 120, 156–57
dual sovereignty, 6, 22

Edmunds, George F., 289
Edmunds Act (1882), 289–90
Edmunds-Tucker Act (1887), 290
Egan, Howard, 261
Eldredge, Horace, 180, 256
elections, in Utah, 286–87
Elliott, John M., 128
Enquirer (Richmond VA), 152
Evans, Priscilla Merriman, 195
Examiner (Richmond VA), 176

Fairfield, 242
Farnsworth, Elon John, 249–50
Faulkner, Charles J., 168, 218–20
federal government: appointees of, in Utah Territory, 70–71; authority of, over Indian policies, 99; concerns of, regarding Brigham Young's power, 48; in early history of Utah Territory, 45–64; funding of Utah Territory by, 49–50; Kansas-Nebraska Act and, 61–64; lack of response to Illinois persecutions, 33–34; lack of response to Missouri persecutions, 27–29; Mormons' views of, 26–27, 45–48, 186–87; in preparation for state's self-governance, 21; presence of, in western territories, 7–8; protection of territories by, 30, 35–36, 41; role of, in dual sovereignty, 6, 22; suspicion of theocracy by, 11–12; varied treatment of western territories by, 4

Ferris, Benjamin G., 168
Ficklin, Benjamin Franklin, 255, 256
Fillmore, Millard, 9–50, 46–47, 99, 100, 141
Flag of Our Union (Boston MA), 233–34
Flatheads, 203, 205
Floyd, John B., 7–8, 151–52, 157–58, 202, 239–41, 266
Ford, Thomas, 28, 32–33, 34
Forney, Jacob, 182, 198, 236, 255–56
Fort Bridger, 194, 196, 206, 224, 240–43, 258, 260
Fort Duchesne, 275
Fort Limhi, 203, 205, 255
Fort Uintah, 275
Foster, Stephen C., 284
Frémont, John C., 37, 139, 141
Frogtown, 242–43

gender roles, political, 140
Getty, Thomas M., 241
Gibbs, George, 203–4
Goshutes, 198
Gould, G. E., 241–42
governors, territorial: appointment of, in Utah Territory, 46; election of, 287; Kansas-Nebraska Act and, 64; in Northwest Ordinance's regulations, 22; as superintendent of Indian affairs, 158–61; Young's replacement as, 182
Great Britain, 20, 179
Great Salt Lake, 9, 50–52
Greene, John P., 32
Gunnison, John W., 50–53, 65, 67–70, 108
Gunnison trial, 115–20
Gwin, William, 66, 221

Haight, Isaac, 186
Hall, Augustus, 61

INDEX 375

Harney, William, 183
Harper's Weekly, 152, 174–75, 193, 221, 248
Harris, Broughton D., 46, 49
Herald of Freedom (Lawrence KS), 153
Higbee, Francis, 32
Hispanic people, 55–56
Holeman, Jacob H., 49–50, 99–100, 208
Homestead Act (1862), 285
House Committee on the Territories, 233
House Judiciary Committee, 282–83
Huntington, Dimick, 198, 257
Hurt, Garland, 13, 121, 122–24, 126, 128–29
Hyde, Orson, 35–37, 92–94

Illinois settlements, 26–34
imperialism, 83, 179
imperium in imperio, 54–58, 63, 95, 139, 143
Indian Appropriations Act (1857), 160–62, 163
Indian policies: Brigham Young and, 48, 99–100, 104–8, 110–15, 132, 159–60, 179; federal government's authority over, 99; Gunnison trial and, 118–20; Mormon influence over, 97–134; Mormon–Native American conflicts and, 106–8; Mormon's violation of, 12–13; in post-1856 crusade against Utah Territory, 158–62; in 1860s Utah, 270–71, 272–75; territorial governors' power over, 158–61; Trade and Intercourse Act and, 123–24, 131–34. *See also* Native Americans
Indian Relief Society, 113–14
infrastructure: after Utah War, 257–63, 269; in election of 1856, 142–43; post-1856 military occupation of Utah and, 185
Ingalls, Rufus, 81
intermarriage, 120–21, 126
Iron County Mission, 105, 106
Islam, 216
Iverson, Alfred, 219

Jackson, Andrew, 25–26
Jackson County, Missouri, settlement, 24–25, 103
Jefferson, Thomas, 6
Jensen, Joan M., 163
Johnson, Andrew, 220–21, 222–23, 224
Johnston, Albert Sidney, 183, 192, 197, 206, 226, 235, 238–39, 255, 259, 265
Jones, Nathaniel V., 113
Jones, Thomas Catesby, 245
judicial affairs: after passage of Morrill Act, 289, 290; post–Utah War changes in, 264–68; in Utah Territory, 115–20
Judiciary Act (1789), 163

Kane, John K., 225
Kane, Thomas L., 44, 46, 225–28, 254
Kanosh, 115, 125, 199
Kansas: competing governments in, 136; in rhetorical comparison with Utah Territory, 153, 164, 165, 175–77
Kansas-Nebraska Act (1854): as applied to Utah Territory, 60–64; congressional debates on, 63; election of 1856 and, 140; federal government's authority in, 61–64; Mormons' interpretation of, 167; Native Americans and, 62; overview of, 3–4, 58–59; purpose of, 166; slavery and, 3–4, 59–60, 166–67, 174, 212; territorial governors and, 64; Utah War and, 211–13

Keitt, Laurence M., 211, 283–84
Kimball, Heber C., 81, 82
Kimmel, Michael, 140
Kinney, John F., 116–19, 156, 157, 208
Kirkham, Ralph, 203

Lamanites. *See* Native Americans
language studies, 108–9
LDS. *See* Mormons
Lea, Luke, 13, 99
Lecompton Constitution, 164, 213–14, 215
Lee, Rachel Woolsey, 113, 186, 253, 268
Lieber, Francis, 90–91
Lincoln, Abraham: election of, 270, 280; laws signed into effect by, 271, 285; on Mormon rebellion, 277; Native American reservations created by, 270–71, 273; in post-1856 crusade against Utah Territory, 147, 170–71; Utah War and, 19
literacy, of Americans, 16
Livingston, LaRhett, 78, 81–82
Love, Andrew, 118, 253–54, 265
Luján, Don Pedro León, 123
Lyon, Caleb, 88

Madison, James, 6
Magraw, W. M. F., 197
Manypenny, George W., 130–31, 160, 179
maps, 2, 7, 184
marriage laws, 281–86, 288–91
masculinity, 84–87, 140, 248
mass media: coverage of Utah War by, 193, 196, 204–5, 212–13; depiction of Mormon–Native American relations in, 120–21; depiction of polygamy in, 88–91, 223–24; on post-1856 crusade against Utah Territory, 147–54, 172–80; post-1856

military occupation of Utah in, 185–86; role of, in Americans' perception of Mormons, 16–17, 56–57
McClelland, Robert, 124, 131
McConnel, M., 172
McCoy, Isaac, 102–3, 123
McCulloch, Benjamin, 228, 234–35
McDowell, Irvin, 259
McLaws, Lafayette, 244–45
medical care, 241
Mexican lands, 1, 9, 37–38
Mexico, U.S. war with, 38, 40–41, 58, 245
Miles, Samuel, 191
military forces: early calls for occupation in Utah Territory, 57; Joseph Smith's view of, 32; Mormon's appeal to Jackson for, 25; post-1856 occupation of Utah Territory by, 154–64, 167, 181–88; role of, in national security, 292–93; Trade and Intercourse Act and, 133; in Utah War, 17–18. *See also* U.S. Army troops
Millennial Star, 190
missionaries, Mormon: federal agents' opinions of, 123; versus non-Mormon missionaries, 129; polygamy and, 78; public's view of, 130; of Southern Indian Mission, 108–11; Trade and Intercourse Act and, 134; in Utah War, 191, 203
missionaries, non-Mormon, 129
Missouri Compromise, 59, 140
Missouri settlements, 24–26, 28–29, 103
Mix, Charles E., 124, 207–8
mob activities, 32–33
monarchy, 24
Monks, Martha, 80

INDEX   377

monogamy, 223–24, 288
Mormons: after U.S. conquer of Mexican lands, 9; Americans' suspicion of, 11–12, 15–17, 28, 56; early history of, 24–41; origin of faith of, 23–24; relationship with federal government, 45–46; self-view of, 15; views of federal government by, after 1856, 186–87, 286
The Mormons (Gunnison), 51–53
Morrill, Justin: boundary changes in Utah Territory and, 233; marriage laws of, 281–82; on non-Mormons' grievances, 145–47; in post-1856 crusade against Utah Territory, 171
Morrill Anti-Bigamy Act (1862): creation of, 281–85; early years of, 288–89; Mormon polygamy and, 15, 269, 271; overview of, 285–86; signing of, 285, 288; Supreme Court's ruling on, 286, 289–90
Moshoquop, 68
Mountain Meadows Massacre, 188, 267
Mowry, Sylvester, 13, 71, 76–81, 121, 124–27
"Mr. Buck" (Nebraskan), 168
Muslims, 88

National Era (Washington DC), 118–19, 149–50, 173–74
Native Americans: in Book of Mormon, 24, 100–101; in death of Gunnison party, 68; invasion of, 97–98, 114–15; Justin Morrill's report of, 146; Kansas-Nebraska Act and, 62; media's portrayal of Mormon relationships with, 120–21; military campaigns against, 257; Mormon conflicts with, 106–8; Mormon enterprise and, 105–6; Mormon expansion and, 10, 98, 112; Mormon proselytizing to, 101–2, 107–15, 122–30; Mormons' post–Utah War relations with, 231, 232, 234, 238–40, 250–57, 272–74; in post-1856 crusade against Utah Territory, 146–47, 157, 158–63, 178–79; public's suspicion of Mormons' relationship with, 103–4, 120–30; removal of, 129; reservations for, 270–71, 272–75; tribes of, in Utah Territory, 52; U.S. survey of, 50–51, 52; in Utah War, 188, 197–209, 220, 226. *See also* Indian policies; *specific tribes*
Nauvoo, Illinois, settlement, 26–34
Nauvoo Expositor (Nauvoo IL), 32, 33
Nauvoo Legion, 107, 190, 192
Nauvoo Neighbor (Nauvoo IL), 35
Nebraska Territory, 193
Nelson, Thomas, 94–95
Nevada Territory, 233–34, 271
New Mexico Territory, 44, 55–56
New York Herald, 149, 204–5, 212–13
New York Times, 88, 120, 268
Nez Percé, 203, 205, 256
North American and United States Gazette (Philadelphia PA), 56–57, 148, 177
Northwest Ordinance (1787), 20, 21–22, 158–59
Nowell, Rachel, 81

Observer (Salem MA), 149
Office of Indian Affairs, 130–31
Oregon settlement, 35, 37
Oregon Territory, 39, 42–43, 61, 70, 131, 160, 203
Ormsby, William M., 95, 232

Pacific Railroad Act (1862), 271, 285
Pahvant Utes, 68, 108, 115, 117–19, 199
Paiutes, 98, 106, 112–13
Past, John Comly, 196
Peck, George, 86
People v. Moroni Green, 116–17
Peteetneet, 105, 106
Phelps, John Wolcott, 192, 195
Piutes, 205
plural marriage. *See* polygamy
Poland Act (1874), 289
Polk, James K., 38–39, 141, 143
polygamy: adoption of, in Mormon faith, 73; versus adultery, 73; Americans' view of, 14, 85–92; of Brigham Young, 77; in Carson Valley disputes, 94–95; as depicted in mass media, 223–24; in Edmunds Act, 289–90; in Edmunds-Tucker Act, 290; history of, in Mormon Utah, 14; influence of, in Utah statehood, 91, 288; Justin Morrill's report of, 146; media's depiction of, 88–91; Mormon missionaries and, 78; Mormon priesthood and, 74–75; Mormons' defense of, 14, 72–74, 81–82, 86–87; Mormon women's opinions of, 77–78, 87, 223; Morrill Anti-Bigamy Act and, 15, 269, 271, 281–86, 285, 288; overland travelers' opinions of, 53–54; in post-1856 crusade against Utah Territory, 150, 152, 171, 180–81; Republican Party's response to, 13–14; in Republican platform of 1856, 137–39; role of, in Mormon patriarchy, 72; as unique popular sovereignty issue, 3; U.S. Constitution and, 73, 282; U.S. survey findings about, 51, 76–81; Utah War and, 216, 222–24
Pony Express, 263

popular sovereignty: definition of, 59; intent of, 59–60; introduction of and popularity of, 58–60; Mormons' interpretation of, 214; overview of, 1–9; requirements for, 280–81; shortcomings of, 4–5; slavery and, 2–4, 14–15
Porter, Fitz-John, 193–94, 251–52, 259–60
posse comitatus model, 163–64, 183
Powell, Lazarus W., 228, 231, 234–35
Pratt, Orson, 54, 180
Pratt, Parley P., 80, 109
priesthood, 74–75
prophet-kings, 24
proselytizing, 101–2, 107–15, 122–30, 203
prostitution, 224
Protestantism, 23
provisional government, 41–45
Provo, 227, 238, 265
Putnam's Monthly, 9091

railroads, 65–67, 258–59, 285
Raleigh Register (Raleigh NC), 57
Reeder, Andrew H., 139–40
Register (Norristown PA), 202–3
Relief Society, 75, 195
republican governance: Americans' view of Mormons as threat to, 11–12, 90–92; Brigham Young's interpretation of, 10–11, 45–46; during 1856 election, 137; establishment of, in western territories, 8, 20–21; federal crusade against, in Utah Territory, 147–56, 172; Northwest Ordinance's regulations on, 21–22; overview of, 20–21; preparation for, 21; religious groups' use of, 56; U.S. surveyor's call for, in Utah Territory, 52–53

Republican Party: bolstering of, 271; creation of, 3–4; 1856 platform of, 135, 136–40, 280, 284, 294; in election of 1860, 278, 280; in post-1856 crusade against Utah Territory, 169–71; response to polygamy by, 13–14; Utah War and, 18–19, 214
Reynolds, George, 289
Reynolds v. United States, 289
Rose, Stephen B., 99

Salmon River Fort, 255–56
Salt Lake City: army posts near, 238; Indian Relief Society in, 114; post-1856 military occupation of, 183; railroads and, 69–70; in Utah War, 192
San Francisco Daily Evening Bulletin, 202
Scott, Winfield, 157–58, 202, 262
Second Great Awakening, 23
self-government: process of achieving, 21, 23; purpose of, 2–3; of states versus territories, 6, 43–44; in U.S. Constitution, 20–21
Sessions, Patty Bartlett, 114
Sevier Lake, 68
Seward, William, 138–39, 143, 215
sexual relations: masculinity and, 85–87; Mormons' view of, 74, 223; of Mormon women and U.S. Army troops and, 65, 76–84
Shoshones, 109, 111, 203, 205–6, 256
Simpson, James H., 259–62
slavery: Compromise of 1850 and, 58; *Dred Scott* ruling and, 165; in election of 1856, 137–39, 142; growth of, 2–4; influence of Utah War on, 18–19; and intent of popular sovereignty, 59–60; Kansas-Nebraska Act and, 3–4, 59–60, 166–67, 174, 212; legislation outlawing, 285; Mormon–Native American conflict regarding, 107; popular sovereignty and, 2–4, 14–15; in post-1856 crusade against Utah Territory, 148–50, 154, 165, 170–71, 174

Smith, Caleb B., 273
Smith, George A., 105, 106, 136, 186, 253
Smith, Hyrum, 33
Smith, Joseph: accusations against, 24, 28; belief in federal protection of territories, 30; death of, 33; division of governmental power as viewed by, 29–30; extradition cases of, 166; interpretation of Constitution by, 31–32; military forces, view of, 32; Missouri persecution and, 27, 28–29; mob activity in opposition to, 32–33; in origin of Mormon faith, 23–24; plans for Oregon settlement by, 35; polygamy and, 73; presidential campaign of, 31–32, 35; Stephen Douglas's relationship with, 36–37
Smith, Martin, 232
Snow, Eliza R., 47–48
Southern Indian Mission, 108–11
squatter sovereignty, 170
Stansbury, Howard, 50–51, 76
statehood, 21, 91, 287–88
states' rights, 27, 59, 218
Stephens, Alexander, 3
Steptoe, Edward J., 13; Gunnison trial and, 118; on Mormon–Native American relations, 118, 121–22; murder of U.S. surveyors and, 70, 71; sexual relations of Mormon women and Army troops, 80–81
Stiles, George P., 92–93

Stine, Henry Atkinson, 54
Stokely, Samuel, 70–71
Stout, Hosea, 117
Stowell, Cynthia Jane Park, 227
Stowell, Saphronia, 227
Stowell, William, 227
Sumner, Charles, 60

Tanner, Amanda Matilda, 80
Tauguant, 106
Taylor, John: post–Utah War views of, 232; purpose of Mormon settlement, 9–10; request for statehood by, 287; Utah state constitution and, 136; views of federal government by, 186–87
Taylor, Pleasant Green, 254
Territorial Organic Act, 117, 131, 287
territorial self-government. *See* provisional government; Self-government
territories. *See specific territories*
Texas Republic, 35
theocracy: according to Book of Mormon, 24; Brigham Young's belief in, 11; federal government's suspicion of, 11–12; marriage laws and, 283; of Mormons in Utah Territory, 9–12; in post-1856 crusade against Utah Territory, 151–52; public's fear of, 54–55
Thompson, Jacob, 157, 158
Thompson, John, 215–17
Timpanogos Canyon, 259, 261
Tintic War, 136
Toombs, Robert, 214–15
Trade and Intercourse Act (1834), 102, 123–24, 131–34, 161–62, 163, 208
Treaty of Guadalupe Hildago, 41
Tyler, John, 33, 35
Tyler, Robert, 153

Uintah Indian Reservation, 273, 275
U.S. Army Corps of Topographical Engineers: after Utah War, 259–62; before Utah War, 50–53, 65, 67–70, 76–81
U.S. Army troops: departure from Utah by, 275; Mormons' post–Utah War reaction to, 231–32, 292; Mormons' reaction to, 71–72; post–Utah War role of, 230–31, 235–70; presence of, in Utah Territory, 65, 70–72; sexual relations of Mormon women and, 65, 76–84, 192–93, 248–50. *See also* Military forces
U.S. Constitution: dual sovereignty in, 6, 22–22; Joseph Smith's interpretation of, 31–32; management of territories according to, 8; in Mormon's defense of polygamy, 14; Mormon's view of, 24, 26–27; Mormon theocracy within, 10; polygamy and, 73, 282; in post-1856 crusade against Utah Territory, 147, 163, 172; republican governance in, 20–21; territorial provisional governments and, 43
U.S.-Mexico War, 38, 40–41, 245
Utah and the Mormons (Ferris), 168
Utah Legislative Assembly, 286–87
Utah Organic Act, 45; in post-1856 crusade against Utah Territory, 154, 165, 167, 172–75; schools of thought of, during Utah War, 210–11
Utah Territorial Legislature, 289
Utah Territory: administration of, during Utah War, 196–97; creation of, 44–45, 98–99; cutting away of, 271–72; early history of, 45–64; 1856 constitutional convention in,

Utah Territory (*cont.*)
135–36; federal appointees to, 70–71; federal funding of, 49–50; government appointments in, 46–49; Justin Morrill's report of, 145–47; Kansas-Nebraska Act and, 60–64; maps of, 2; Mormon's settlement in, 9–10, 38–41, 98; Mormon theocracy in, 9–12; non-Mormons in, 92–96, 240, 242–43, 246–47, 284–85; petition of 1857 from, 143–45; popular sovereignty's unique issues in, 3–5; post-1856 crusade against, 147–81; post–Utah War changes in, 230–51, 292; requests for elections in, 286–87

Utah War: discussion of Organic Act repeal during, 210–11; early fighting in, 194–95; events leading to, 182–94; Kansas-Nebraska Act and, 211–13; media coverage of, 193, 196, 204–5, 212–13; missionaries in, 191, 203; Mormon petition during, 209–10; Mormon women in, 195–96; Native Americans in, 188, 197–209, 220, 226; overview of, 17–19; pardons granted in, 228, 230, 234–36; peace negotiations during, 224–28, 237–38, 263; political parties during, 214; polygamy and, 216, 222–24; president's use of force in, 214–24, 292–93; timing of, 182; U.S. territorial administration during, 196–97; in winter of 1858, 196–97, 209

Utes, 68, 98, 105–20, 198–99, 206

Valley Tan (Salt Lake City UT), 235–36, 242
Van Buren, Martin, 27
Van Vliet, Stewart, 183–85, 186, 193

Waite, Morrison R., 289
Wákara, 105, 106, 108
Walker War, 107
Walla-Wallas, 203
War Department, 262
Washaki, 205–6, 256
Washington Union, 264
Weller, John, 209
Wells, Daniel, 287
Western Standard (San Francisco CA), 223–24
western territories: federal government's protection of, 30, 35–36, 41; federal government's varied treatment of, 4; growth of, 6–7; lack of federal presence in, 7–8; presidential call for expansion in, 34–35; republican government in, 8, 20–21
White Clay Creek, 260, 261
white settlers, in western territories, 8
Whitney, Asa, 66
Wick, William, 169
Wilmot Proviso, 58, 154, 175
Wirtz, Horace R., 81
women, Mormon: desire of, to leave Utah Territory, 80, 82, 83–84; in Indian Relief Society, 113–14; Mormon men's cautions regarding, 53–54; opinions of, regarding polygamy, 77–78, 87, 223; in post-1856 crusade against Utah Territory, 158; priesthood authority and, 74–75; role of, in Mormon patriarchy, 72, 74–75; sexual assault of, 54; sexual relations of U.S. Army troops and, 65, 76–84, 192–93, 248–50; in Utah War, 195–96
Woodruff, Wilford, 178, 290

Yellow Creek, 260

Young, Brigham: appointment as governor of Utah, 46; appropriations of federal funding by, 49–50; belief in theocracy by, 11; calls for territorial self-governance by, 38–39, 45–46; colonization efforts of, 10; in discussions regarding western settlement, 38–39; in events leading to Utah War, 185, 186–94; federal government's concerns about, 48–50; general Indian affairs and, 1 59–160, 48, 99–100, 104–8, 110–15, 119, 128, 132, 179; Indian alliances of, during Utah War, 198–201, 203, 205–8; interpretation of republican government by, 10–11, 45–46; Kansas-Nebraska Act and, 62, 63, 167; Mormon military and, 38; non-Mormons of Carson County and, 92–93; peace negotiations of, during Utah War, 225–27, 238; photo of, 40; polygamous marriage of, 77; in post-1856 crusade against Utah Territory, 146, 153, 159–62, 177–80; post–Utah War changes and, 243, 246–47, 256–57; as proponent of railroad, 67; provisional government of Desert and, 42, 44; replacement of, as governor, 182; Republican Party's view of, 139; sexual relations of Mormon women and Army troops, 79–80, 82–83, 84

Young, Joseph A., 77

Young, Mary J. Ayers, 77–79

CPSIA information can be obtained
at www.ICGtesting.com
Printed in the USA
LVOW11s1820241117
557337LV00005B/814/P